After Postmodernism

Studies in Austrian Literature, Culture and Thought

After Postmodernism
Austrian Literature and Film in Transition

Edited and with a Preface by

Willy Riemer

Ariadne Press
Riverside, California

Ariadne Press would like to express its appreciation to the Austrian Cultural Institute, New York for assistance in publishing this book.

Library of Congress Cataloging-in-Publication Data

After Postmodernism : Austrian literature and film in transition / edited and with a preface by Willy Riemer.
      p.   cm. -- (Studies in Austrian literature, culture and thought)
Includes bibliographical references and index.
ISBN 1-57241-091-4
    1. Austrian literature--20th century--History and criticism. 2. Motion pictures and literature--Austria. 3. Postmodernism--Austria. I. Riemer, Willy. II. Series.

PT3818.A33 2000
830.9'09045--dc21
                                      00-029275

Cover Design:
Art Director, Designer: George McGinnis

Copyright ©2000
by Ariadne Press
270 Goins Court
Riverside, CA 92507

All rights reserved.
No part of this publication may be reproduced or transmitted in any form or by any means without formal permission.
Printed in the United States of America.
ISBN 1-57241-091-4 (paperback original)

Contents

Preface   9

1 Orbits of Cultural Complexity

Postmodernism on Both Sides of the Atlantic   17
Ernestine Schlant (Montclair State University)

Hybridity as Aesthetic Discourse in Austrian Art,   34
Film, and Literature
Ingeborg Hoesterey (Indiana University)

Commuting to Klagenfurt   44
Peter Demetz (Yale University)

2 Austrian Film: Interviews with Producers and Directors

Austrian Film between Festival Success   55
and Market Constraints
Martin Schweighofer (Austrian Film Commission)

Producer's Challenge: Art and Commerce   62
Veit Heiduschka (Wega-Film)

Tolerance for a Complex World   68
Dieter Pochlatko (Epo-Film)

Comedy and Cultural Identity   73
Niki List (Cult-Film)

Parables for Our Time   80
Werner Swossil (Austrian Broadcasting Corporation)

3 The New Austrian Cinema

Films for Entertainment and Reflection 89
An Interview with Houchang Allahyari

Lovable Foreigners: Gestures of Cross-Cultural 94
Embracing in Austrian Film
Jutta Landa (University of California, Los Angeles)

Wohin und zurück: Perspectives on Axel Corti's Jewish Trilogy 106
Christopher J. Wickham (University of Texas at San Antonio)

Michael Glawogger's Film *Die Ameisenstraße*: 127
Representing the Modern Malaise
Robert Acker (University of Montana)

Abschied von Sidonie, A Farewell Twice-Visited: 138
Erich Hackl's Novella and Karin Brandauer's Film
Robert C. Reimer (University of North Carolina, Charlotte)

4 The Films of Michael Haneke

Beyond Mainstream Film 159
An Interview with Michael Haneke

71 Fragments of a Chronology of Chance: Notes to the Film 171
Michael Haneke

Fragmentation and the Real: Michael Haneke's Family Trilogy 176
Brigitte Peucker (Yale University)

Iterative Texts: Haneke/Rosei, *Wer war Edgar Allan?* 189
Willy Riemer (University of Delaware)

The Question of Cultural Identity: The Figure of the Outsider in   199
Michael Haneke's Adaptation of Joseph Roth's *Die Rebellion*
Thomas R. Nadar (Auburn University)

5 Discourse of Aesthetics: Text and Intertext

Passion. Devoir. Contingency. And No Time.   211
Marlene Streeruwitz

The (Non)Position of Woman in Marlene Streeruwitz' Work   217
Sigrid Berka (Massachusetts Institute of Technology)

The *Abjectum*: Peter Waterhouse's Reappropriation of   235
Hölderlin and the Poem-in-Progess
Erk Grimm (Barnard College)

6 Gender and (Post)Gender

Imaging (Post)Gender under Transnational Capital: 267
Valie Export's *Perfect Pair*
Nora M. Alter (University of Florida)

The War Between the Sexes: Gender Relations in the   283
Works of Elisabeth Reichart
Linda C. DeMeritt (Allegheny College)

The Female Poet as Persecuted Jew: Gender (Mis)representation   298
in the Works of Ingeborg Bachmann and Sylvia Plath
Kirsten A. Krick-Aigner (Wofford College)

7 Borders and Boundaries

Transcultural Profiles in Contemporary Austrian Jewish   315
Literature
Matthias Konzett (Yale University)

Modeling a Dialectic: Peter Handke's *A Journey to the Rivers or*   340
Justice for Serbia
Scott Abbott (Brigham Young University)

Theorizing the Internet: Scholarly Collaboration, Authorial   353
Identity, and the Bounds of Listserver Culture
Angelica Fenner (University of Minnesota)

Index   367

Preface

The surge of globalization and the digital revolution are bringing momentous changes to literature and film. Film festivals are thriving as never before, but their films more often than not find a place in niche markets rather than in the multiplex facilities designed for hi-tech mainstream movies. Increasingly, commercial ventures use the new information technologies to attach market constraints to cultural activities. Though postmodernism does not adequately take into account the commercial aspects of culture, it serves as a suitable point of departure for introducing the contributions of this volume, each of which offers a distinct view of the mosaic of contemporary Austrian literature and film.

Postmodernism has stood for many things. For Charles Jencks, one of its principal proponents, and for Hal Foster it was so vague a term as to mean almost anything. Indeed, the many articles and books on postmodernism tend to avoid definition and resort to descriptive approaches instead. Central to the various interpretations of postmodernism, however, is the sense that the time for universalist theories, comprehensive explanations and privileged formations has come to an end. The grandly orchestrated polyphony of discourses has given way to smaller ensembles engaged in loosely coupled performances.

In the introductory essay of this volume Ernestine Schlant considers the cybernetic basis of postmodernism and surveys its variants and prospects. Though the vehement debates about postmodernism have ranged over a great deal of intellectual terrain, the differences mostly come down to the interpretation of pluralism. As Schlant points out, in America postmodernism takes a cultural slant centered on a politics of inclusion. In contrast, the European approach tends to focus on aesthetic and philosophical matters, on the fragmentizing rather than the inclusive aspects of postmodernism. With exhilarating freedom all forms and traditions of creative experience become available; citation and hence hybrid forms add an intriguing luster to works of art. With great insight Ingeborg Hoesterey discusses hybridity as stylistic marker in contemporary Austrian architecture, literature and film. She shows, for example, that the very different projects of Valie Export and Michael Schottenberg both have intertextual filiations that span the arts.

The products of pluralistic environments, however, need not themselves be postmodern. Peter Demetz' observations on the media pageant for the Ingeborg-Bachmann-Prize in Klagenfurt are most revealing in this regard. Although during his tenure as "Speaker of the Jury" the event by no means pursued an agenda of postmodernism, the arrangement for dealing with GDR writers can be taken as postmodernism in action. The openness to diverse voices had consequences, "...in Klagenfurt the wall came tumbling down long before it happened in Berlin" (50).

Postmodernism and the deconstruction of the grand narratives that were propping up long-established discourses seemed to promise ready access to the adventure of exploring less essentialist modes of thought. But as with the twist of a kaleidoscope, the pluralistic optic in turn has led to discourses relating to identity, to multiculturalism, ethnicity and gender, concepts that gained prominence especially in the analysis of literary texts. All along, the prodigious innovations in the information technologies and the practices of the free market economy were preparing the ground for the industrialization of culture. The grand narratives were being replaced by the operating principles of the commercial machine—profitability became the lodestar to steer by and commodification its vehicle. Of all cultural production, film is most susceptible to the pressures of commerce.

In the short term, economics of scale and the historical concentration of film distribution distinctly favor the big-budget productions made to be consumed in multiplex facilities. Such films are designed and merchandised with an international box office in mind. In the long run the convergence of digital technologies will undoubtedly revolutionize all aspects of the film industry, from production to distribution. For Austria and small countries in general, the commodification of film and the competition from the juggernaut of American majors turn out to threaten the very survival of their film industry. Quite apart from the difficulty of sustaining the infrastructure for a viable film culture, questions of cultural identity and creative diversity arise. Three sections of this volume engage these issues and also provide a discussion of a sampling of recent Austrian films.

Apart from aesthetic considerations, the way a film looks has a lot to do with how much it cost to make. In the fragmented market of the European Union even low-budget feature films cannot recoup their production costs. Indeed, without substantial subsidies there would be no Austrian film industry today. A series of interviews provides some insights into the challenge of making films under such conditions.

Most of the feature films screened in Austria and shown on TV are of American provenance. It is well understood that in their global circulation they blur national boundaries and erode local film cultures. As Martin Schweighofer explains, success at film festivals therefore not only gives recognition to Austrian filmmakers, performers and production teams, but also contributes to a kind of corporate identity for Austrian film. The appeal to cultural identity then makes it somewhat easier to justify subsidies, to subsidize form rather than contents. The contributors to this volume have no simple answer to the question, what is Austrian about Austrian film? Nonetheless, in the words of Veit Heiduschka, "for a small country, a sense of identity is important" (65).

ORF (Austrian Broadcasting Corporation) has played an important role in subsidizing film production and in programming feature films. According to Werner Swossil, regional authenticity is prerequisite for successful films on TV. However, the concern for ratings and revenue from commercials increasingly determines programming. Indeed, Dieter Pochlatko suggests that with the popularization in programming, TV and film are beginning to go separate ways—one concentrating on entertainment, the other on film art.

Some Austrian filmmakers have successfully bridged the gap between art and entertainment, Niki List among them. His *Müllers Büro* (Müller, Private Detective, 1986)—a parody of the detective genre—combined clever intertextuality with riotously funny situations to produce one of the top-grossing films of the past decades. With his most recent film, *Helden in Tirol* (1998), he uses pop music and ethnic references to deconstruct the tradition of the *Heimatfilm* genre.

Postmodernism stresses difference rather than uniformity of view. With this pluralistic approach, critical attention has shifted from the analysis of metasystems to the study of discourse and individuals in social contexts. In overlapping spheres theorizing now concerns the body, with related questions of gender and race, and the constructions of history. The prevailing notion of identity, whether asserted or endured, has provided an instrument for taking issue with realities past and present.

The films of Houchang Allahyari are full of gentle warmth and subtle humor, but they also unsparingly expose the prejudice and abuse facing migrants, prisoners, and the disenfranchised of society. With her analysis of Allahyari's *I Love Vienna* (1991) and films by Anton Peschke and Paul Harather, Jutta Landa reveals the difficulty of representing alterity and ethnicity in feature films. To various degrees, binary oppositions based on stereotypes and exoticisms undermine the multicultural project of the filmmakers. Robert Acker discusses the multitiered aggregate of characters in Michael Glawogger's *Die Ameisenstraße* (1995) and suggests that the construction of identity involves history. The most difficult aspect of recent Austrian history has to do with the racist practices of the Third Reich. Numerous Austrian literary works and films have confronted this Nazi past. In his essay Christopher J. Wickham examines the narratology of Axel Corti's film trilogy on Austrian Jews in the Third Reich and considers the representation of the experience of exile. The atrocities committed by the Nazis on the Romany people are less well known, but no less appalling. After providing historical background on Gypsy persecution, Robert C. Reimer discusses Erich Hackl's narrative *Abschied von Sidonie* (*Farewell Sidonia*, 1991) and its film adaptation by Karin Brandauer. He regards both works as cautionary tales.

Michael Haneke is the most accomplished filmmaker in Austria today. In his interview he makes illuminating observations about his aesthetics and style of directing. From his programmatic notes to *71 Fragments of a Chronology of Chance* (1994) it is evident that Haneke strives to expose the debilitating effects of commodification in the media; he challenges the viewing habits of the mainstream spectators by alluding to their complicity in media violence and by fragmenting the packaged reality that they have come to expect. In her trenchant analysis Brigitte Peucker considers this fragmented social reality, but also the transition between reality and its representation, between image and sound. Peucker suggests that for all the prominence of fragmentation, Haneke's films nonetheless retain a complex notion of organicism. Willy Riemer considers some iterative aspects of a film adaptation by Haneke, while Thomas R. Nadar explores Haneke's use of sound track and cinematography in his adaptation of Joseph Roth's *Die Rebellion*.

Marlene Streeruwitz' crisp and fresh remarks on theater practice strike at commodification in the bastion of high culture. As a prominent playwright she points to the persistence of nineteenth-century aesthetics and to the related patriarchal structures. Women as professionals are constrained with an identity that is put in place mostly by men. In her carefully argued essay Sigrid Berka suggests that in Streeruwitz' plays women have no voice of their own; they are trapped in the insidious dominance patterns of language itself. To breach such constraints Streeruwitz employs extreme parataxis and fragmentation at all levels. In a very detailed analysis of poetry by Peter Waterhouse, Erk Grimm finds a similar turn to the fragmentary, to a preoccupation with "semantic openness in the textual space of a poem-in-progress" (254).

To break the multiple constraints of imposed identity, writers have especially examined two variants related to the gendered body and to the histories about the Third Reich. In her narratives Elisabeth Reichart engages both. Linda C. DeMeritt discusses the "everyday fascism founded in patriarchy" (294) that Reichart's works expose and also notes at least the possibility for change. In a comparative study Kirsten A. Krick-Aigner shows that Ingeborg Bachmann and Sylvia Plath go further and tend to identify their female characters with the Jewish victims of the Holocaust.

Cultural boundaries and identities do not exist of themselves but are constructed. Matthias Konzett examines the complex issues facing contemporary Austrian-Jewish writers and concludes that identity is achieved not by reference to ready categories and historical affiliations, but by accepting the multicontextual world that is becoming the reality of modern life. But as Scott Abbott shows with his comments on an essay by Peter Handke, taking ideological positions, however motivated, is risky even in such context of tolerance.

While grand narratives continue to have a now palliated presence, fractal projects, hybrid formations and irreverent transgressions of discursive boundaries are at the fore. In no small measure technology is transforming society and dramatically changing the way realities are constructed and perceived. In her analysis of Valie Export's contribution to *Seven Women Seven Sins* (1986/87) Nora M. Alter suggests that technoculture both affirms and goes beyond postmodernism. In a very personal account Angelica Fenner explores the notion of listserver identity, that is, an identity in a realm beyond the issues associated with postmodernism.

Many people have collaborated with me in producing this volume. I would especially like to thank the contributors for their essays, for unwavering enthusiasm and collegial patience. Particularly for the film sections of this volume I have greatly benefitted from conversations with Martin Schweighofer, Veit Heiduschka, Dieter Pochlatko, Niki List, Milan Dor, Birgit Reichert, Werner Swossil, Kurt J. Mrkwicka, Gerhard Schedl, Peter Marboe, Wolfgang Ainberger, Andreas Lindenberg, Michael Haneke, C.D. Yazi, Barbara Albert and Houchang Allahyari. My wholehearted thanks to them all. I would like to acknowledge the generous support of Wega-Film, Dor-Film, Epo-Film, Cult-Film, ORF, Austrian Film Commission, Austrian Film Archive, Austrian Cultural Institute (NY), Literar-Mechana, and the University of Delaware. My thanks also to Ursula Weidschacher, Joe Remick, Elisabeth Streit, Günter Krenn and Peter Mikl, who in different ways facilitated my research. The interviews were conducted in German and then translated by me. I would like to thank Maria Luise Caputo-Mayr for permission to reprint the interview with Michael Haneke; it first appeared in the Journal of the Kafka Society of America. A good many of the essays had their beginning as papers at a symposium on "Crossing Cultural Bounds in Contemporary Austrian Literature and Film" at the University of Delaware (1996). I am very grateful to Jorun Johns and the anonymous readers at Ariadne Press for their very helpful suggestions.

1
Orbits of Cultural Complexity

Postmodernism on Both Sides of the Atlantic

Ernestine Schlant
Montclair State University

Over the past two decades, intellectual discourse in America and in Europe has centered on attempts to answer the question "What is postmodernism?" The question first arose in relation to architecture and has since then engaged scholars in the fields of philosophy, particularly aesthetics and epistemology, and those concerned with periodization and the history of cultural, social, and intellectual movements. On this side of the Atlantic, the critique of postmodernism has tended to include practically all social, economic, and cultural phenomena associated with the post-industrial, hi-tech, cybernetic society. The salient features of postmodernism are so pervasive on this side of the Atlantic, that one can in fact speak of a postmodern *Zeitgeist*. I would like to present the positions on both sides of the Atlantic, show how these definitions play out in sample disciplines, and then conclude with an overview on problems and prospects.

Postmodernism is seen in response and in opposition to modernism which dominated various fields of art with varying emphasis during the first half of our century and, by general consensus, expired in the 1960s, one of the casualties of the Vietnam war.[1] Even before the word "postmodernism" or "postmodern" gained currency, early discussions centered on what was to become of the chief criteria for it on this side of the Atlantic, namely its relation to mass culture and marginalized aspects of cultural and social life.[2] Here, postmodernism traces its roots to "camp," institutionalized in Susan Sontag's essay of 1964, "Notes on 'Camp,'" in which she defines camp as "a good taste of bad taste," elevates artifice, stylization, and exaggeration to the core elements of this new aesthetics, and proclaims a love of "things-being-what-they-are-not"; to be camp, things have to be in quotation marks (275-92). Of equal importance is Leslie Fiedler's iconoclastic essay of 1970, "Cross the Border—Close the Gap," where the border and the gap that exist are those between high art, that is, the art of modernism, and mass culture (461-85). What characterizes this thrust of American postmodernism is an aesthetics and politics of inclusion that draws its vitality from a continuous infusion of new energy through the constant absorption of new fields. Based on the assumption that all pieces of this gigantic puzzle are of equal importance, this inclusiveness tends to abolish dominant values or canonized hierarchies. Critics insist that this inclusiveness results in eclecticism or even randomness and ultimately produces indifference.

In Germany and Austria the debates concerning postmodernism were reactive rather than original and drew for their theorizing on art created decades earlier or on the other side of the Atlantic. Peter Bürger, author of the seminal study *Theorie der Avantgarde* (1974), traced the problematics of postmodernism back to the avantgarde movements of the interwar years, namely the Dada, futurism, and surrealism. Here he is particularly interested in the political thrust of these avantgarde aesthetics, in their attempts to break the confines of established canons. His essay of 1987 "Der Alltag, die Allegorie und die Avantgarde" continues the lines of argument offered in his earlier work, as he now appraises contemporary artistic practices in the context of postmodernism. In contrast to an aesthetics of inclusion, however, he shifts his attention to the consequences of such inclusiveness, namely a leveling of opposites:

> Universalizing of the citation, allegory without referent, emancipation of the signifier, art merging with a wholly aestheticized everyday experience—all these attempts at defining postmodernism have one thing in common: they assert the leveling of opposites. (196)

This "leveling of opposites" can be considered a clear, if less enthusiastic, or socially and politically alert restatement of Fiedler's battle cry to "cross the borders—close the gap."

In France, Germany, and Austria postmodernism took a different road, ironically the "high road" of intellectual discourse, of philosophical language analysis and semiotics; it largely bypassed the cultural and social phenomena of the United States to arrive nevertheless at similar postmodern conclusions. Discussion focussed less on the inclusiveness of "cross the border—close the gap," perhaps because, as fairly homogeneous societies, these countries could ignore the social and political implications of these demands. Instead, intellectual discourse followed a path that was first suggested by Ferdinand de Saussure: the severance of signifier and signified invited a reevaluation of practically all of Western culture and civilization.[3] French philosophers were the first to rigorously explore the implications of such a severance in post-structuralism and deconstruction, both of which can be considered the philosophical province of postmodernism. They legitimized their positions by going back to Nietzsche and Heidegger, attracted by Nietzsche's dictum that "facts are fictions," and by Heidegger's radical historicism (Calinescu, 271-72). In his polemic study *The Postmodern Condition: A Report on Knowledge* (1979) Jean-François Lyotard then repudiated the legacy of the Enlightenment, as he expressed his profound skepticism toward metanarratives. He speaks of "that severe reexamination which postmodernity imposes on the thought of the Enlightenment, on the idea of a unitary end of history and of a subject" (73) and in this call for a "severe reexamination" he subverts the metanarrative of the absolute autonomy of reason. Consequently, if there are no criteria of judgment intrinsic to reason as such, then extrinsic, historically contingent interests and circumstances must be considered. Hierarchical distinctions (between different cultures, for example between First and Third worlds; or between different fields of inquiry, for example between pure as opposed to applied science) no longer make sense and must be abolished. The French cultural sociologist Jean Baudrillard then drew on the radical severance of signifier and signified (which he saw already operating in Plato) to substantiate his theory of simulacra and simulations, which for him are the dominant phenomena in a cybernetic society without metanarratives: "... simulation is no longer that of a territory, a referential being or a substance. It is the generation by models of a real without origin or reality: a hyperreal" (166-84).[4] While this simulation echoes and seems to develop Susan Sontag's definition of "camp," the cult of "things-being-what-they-are-not," it radicalizes Sontag's definition under the impact of cybernetics, as Baudrillard continues: "It is no longer a question of imitation, nor of reduplication, nor even of parody. It is rather a question of substituting signs of the real for the real itself ..." (167).

One of the great philosophical controversies on these very aspects of postmodernism took place in the late 1970s and early 1980s between Lyotard and Jürgen Habermas, with American philosophers arbitrating and proposing their own alternatives. In this controversy, Habermas presents himself essentially as a "modernist," evident in the title of his polemic "Die Moderne—ein unvollendetes Projekt."[5] He argues that abandoning metanarratives will deprive us of a grounding in theoretical approaches which alone allow "rational criticism" and, he insists, ultimately distinctions and values. Richard Rorty, whose American pragmatism agrees with Lyotard's abolition of metanarratives, nevertheless sympathizes with Habermas' "philosophy of consensus" when he opts for a "communicative consensus" as the vital force "which drives ... culture" (41-42). In explicating the controversies between Lyotard and Habermas and the philosophical traditions that contextualize their stands, Rorty offers his own postmodern position—a position that can dispense with Habermas' demands for universalistic criteria without abandoning the need for socially guiding values. But instead of deriving these values from the idealistic tradition that is traced back to Descartes, he suggests a recovery of Baconian, non-Cartesian attitudes (39) that would play out in social practice as "untheoretical sorts of narrative discourse which make up the political speech of the Western democracies" and draws the conclusion that "[it] would be better to be frankly ethnocentric" (35).

After this rather cursory glance around the arena of postmodernism, let us sample two specific fields. In the United States the term postmodernism first gained wide recognition in relation to the most conspicuous and "impure" of artistic endeavors, architecture. Here, the blatant turn away from the modernist austerity of functionalist purity provided the impetus for debate, and the vocabulary in which it was conducted. The gestures of inclusion

Postmodernism 21

implied ample borrowings from the past under the name of "citations," "quotations," and "allusions," executed in a spirit of playfulness. One might as well have spoken of neobaroque, neorococo, neorenaissance, as indeed we have a neogothic, had not the simultaneous presence of all these styles invited an umbrella term. Fredric Jameson speaks in his foreword to Lyotard's *The Postmodern Condition* of

> ... a mannerist postmodernism (Michael Graves), a baroque postmodernism (the Japanese), a rococo postmodernism (Charles Moore), a neoclassicist postmodernism (the French, particularly Christian de Portzamparc), and probably even a "high modernist" postmodernism in which modernism is itself the object of the postmodernist pastiche. (xviii)

Jameson's valuation is all the more surprising since he does not always approve of the multifaceted offers of a postmodern society driven by consumerism; he takes issue with the austere impositions of modernism in favor of postmodernism when he says:

> This is a rich and creative movement, of the greatest aesthetic play and delight, that can perhaps be most rapidly characterized as a whole by two important features: first, the falling away of the protopolitical vocation and the terrorist stance of the older modernism and, second, the eclipse of all of the affect (depth, anxiety, terror, the emotions of the monumental) that marked high modernism and its replacement by what Coleridge would have called fancy or Schiller aesthetic play, a commitment to surface and to the superficial in all senses of the word. (xviii)

Other options in postmodernist architecture renounce playful citations and make pastiche the structure and core of their work. A building in the shape of a duck, sculptures of dolphins and Mickey Mouse cast in concrete and situated in positions reserved by earlier ages for saints, or of the Seven Dwarfs as caryatides appear yet more radical and more political in their unrelenting abolition of distinctions between mass, popular, and high culture.[6] Sensitivities trained under the precepts of modernism may dismiss these enterprises as *kitsch*. But that is too easy a position, and one increasingly peripheral.[7]

In literature, the use of citation, montage, "borrowings," and collage of other texts had long been an element of high modernism. What distinguishes the postmodern use of citations from that of modernism is their political stance: borrowings from previously established and clearly identifiable authors or styles no longer thematize, as they did for example for Thomas Mann, the problem of artistic exhaustion or sterility; nor do they impose structure and reference points, even if they are ironically refracted, as in James Joyce's *Ulysses*. In postmodern literature citation and montage express the deliberate, political intent of deconstructing high modernism with its austere insistence on the autonomy of the work of art, its hermetic status and self-sufficiency. Here, as in postmodern architecture, discovering the quotations may be a playful activity, a detective game within a detective novel.[8] In fact, playfulness and openness, based on the exhilaration of inclusion, are some of the more salient characteristics of postmodernism on this side of the Atlantic, as opposed to the Continental version, where similarly observed phenomena often lead to apocalyptic presentiments.[9]

Citation and collages open up a two-track reception/response where one track could conceivably contradict the very inclusiveness on which postmodernism prides itself. Citation and quotation in architecture, literature, film, or painting are playful and invite the viewer or reader to play the detective game of identifying the various quotations; but this very playfulness presupposes a sensitivity and a body of knowledge that can recognize and therefore delight in these citations—an elitist assumption that suits modernism better than postmodernism. On the other hand, the enjoyment may not come from a literary or art historical game, but from the "naive" reading or viewing of decorative surfaces, from a delight in "fancy" or "aesthetic play," from a "commitment to the superficial in all the senses of the word" of which Jameson speaks. This would place the contemporary viewer or reader in the same position as when he/she enters a Gothic cathedral and cannot "read" the stories of the stained glass windows. At the same time, "delight" without the realization of historical depth-dimensions flattens the historicity of the object and its inherent self-reflective play with historicity, as much as the consumer (viewer/reader)-object relation into an ongoing simultaneity. In the process, history as a consciously acknowledged passing of sequential time is abolished.

Citation and allusion, and the uses to which they are put are not the only literary strategies to break down established canons. Leslie Fiedler's "cross the border—close the gap" has borne fruit in a vast literature of inclusiveness and anti-elitism that reflects the pluralism and ethnic diversity of society. The proliferation of minority literatures (ethnic minority literatures as well as the literatures of other marginalized groups, such as feminist or gay literature, children's literature) and the upgrading of minor canons, such as science fiction, the detective novel, *Trivialliteratur*, harlequin novels, are indicative of a postmodern society that struggles to give voice to its cultural and social diversity. These novels may, individually examined, not necessarily be postmodern in their structure, vision, or techniques. The inclusiveness of minority literatures, of ethnic literatures, particularly the literature of ethnic displacement, with their battle cry to bring down the canon as well as resist canonization does not in itself produce literature that embodies postmodern perspectives. For example, Louise Erdrich's narratives about native Americans, John Wideman's on being black in American society, or Bharati Mukherjee's on cultural displacement are products of a postmodern era, but do not necessarily use the techniques that Robert Alter, unsympathetic to postmodern fiction, has characterized like this:

> ... in this vehemently contemporary fiction, there is a cultivated quality of rapid improvisation, often a looseness of form; love of pastiche, parody, slapdash invention; a willful neglect of psychological depth and subtlety or consecutiveness of characterization; a cavalier attitude toward consistency of incident, plot unity, details of milieu, and underlying all these a kind of despairing skepticism, often tinged with the exhilaration of hysteria, about the validity of language and the very enterprise of fiction.[10]

Equipped with these critical tools, Alter misses the fun.

Ihab Hassan has for more than two decades made the most important efforts to arrive at clear-cut distinctions between modernism and postmodernism. He proposes and opposes:

> ... closed and conjunctive form—open, disjunctive antiform; purpose—play; design—chance; hierarchy—anarchy; art object/the finished work—process/performance/happening; distance—participation; centering—dispersal; genre/boundary—text/intertext; symptom—desire; metaphysics—irony; determinacy—indeterminacy; transcendence—immanence; genital/phallic—polymorphous/androgynous; a thinking in origins/causes—difference-differance/trace. (34)

One could add further to this list homogeneity vs. heterogeneity; or the functional vs. the decorative. Clearly, some of these terms are at home in social culture, some in literary criticism or in philosophy, in the natural sciences and the social sciences. Hassan emphasizes this inclusiveness when he states:

> As an artistic and philosophical, erotic and social phenomenon, postmodernism veers toward open, playful, optative, disjunctive, displaced, or indeterminate forms, a discourse of fragments, and ideology of fracture, a will to unmaking, an invocation of silence—veers toward all these and yet implies their very opposites, their antithetical realities. It is as if *Waiting for Godot* found an echo, if not an answer in *Superman*. (35-36)

It is of course quite legitimate to view the ample use of "quotations" and the anti-canonical inclusiveness as eclecticism on a major scale that leads inevitably to an inquiry into aesthetic judgment and values. Does postmodernism in its radical leveling and in its insistence on cultural/historical inclusiveness as equivalence programmatically abandon value judgments? And if it does, what instruments of navigation (no longer "principles") will guide in this choppy sea of mutually inclusive equivalent values? Efforts to recongregate around new definitions of value are under way, although these values may appear to have little in common with those of earlier times and may on first sight offer little consolation to those yearning for the fantasized stability of yesterday.[11] This brave new world with its "open-ended, polymorphous future" (Fekete, xv) may be unlike anything we are accustomed to, but in contrast to the apocalyptic sentiments on the other side of the Atlantic, there is here a vision of continuity.

> What appears to be decisive to the emergent postmodern configuration is the committal to do without foundational, asituational, representational, and hypostatizing-stabilizing closures, objectivist or subjectivist. It is possible to put a skeptical or nihilistic construction on this, but ... I think we can identify as postmodern *a certain value-rational opening to the human world ... as home*, though a home whose plan we do not have and which we have never quite (and will never quite) finish building and fitting to ourselves, just as we who build it and for whom it is to be fit change with every alteration of it, with every bit and construction and deconstruction. I put it this way to acknowledge that the postmodern ethos has a certain continuity with the projects and horizons of secularising and historicising modernity, but also to suggest its difference from the ethos of modernity. (Fekete, x-xi)

I would now like to turn to some more general implications of postmodernism, to the "problems and prospects" suggested in my outline. The *éminence grise* behind the culture of postmodernism and postmodern society is without doubt cybernetics and its technologies. We have shaped and live in a society of instant communications that have created not only new forms of businesses and the manner in which all business is conducted, but that have impinged on our personal relations, on our work and leisure time, on all the activities in which we engage. These systems determine how we hear or see, and they constantly pioneer new ways of "simplifying" communication, in the process restructuring our sensual repertoire and the manner in which it functions; these systems have a profound influence on how we learn, how we decide what to learn, and what constitutes knowledge. Again, Lyotard has raised these questions most poignantly:

> ... it is common knowledge that the miniaturization and commercialization of machines is already changing the way in which learning is acquired, classified, made available, and exploited. It is reasonable to suppose that the proliferation of information-processing machines is having, and will continue to have, as much of an effect on the circulation of learning as did advancements in human circulation (transportation systems), and later, in the circulation of sounds and visual images (the media) ... (4)

He concludes that "... along with the hegemony of computers comes a certain logic, and therefore a certain set of prescriptions determining which statements are accepted as 'knowledge' statements" and he sees the consequences of this "proliferation of information-processing machines" in these terms:

> We may thus expect a thorough exteriorization of knowledge with respect to the "knower," at whatever point he or she may occupy in the knowledge process. The old principle that the acquisition of knowledge is indissociable from the training (*Bildung*) of minds, or even of individuals, is becoming obsolete and will become ever more so. (4)

The consequences of this exteriorization of knowledge are that knowledge becomes a product separable from the knower rather than understood as an inherent, if acquired quality that characterizes personal achievement. The implications of this realization will inexorably determine our future as Lyotard sees it:

> The relationship of the suppliers and users of knowledge to the knowledge they supply and use is now tending, and will increasingly tend, to assume the form already taken in the relationship of commodity producers and consumers to the commodities they produce and consume—that is, the form of

value. Knowledge is and will be produced in order to be sold, it is and will be consumed in order to be valorized in a new production. ... Knowledge in the form of an informational commodity indispensable to productive power is already, and will continue to be, a major—perhaps *the* major—stake in the worldwide competition for power. (4-5)

Lyotard's discussion of postmodern knowledge as exteriorization shows how far the reaches of postmodernism extend and remind us of Jameson's aesthetic "commitment to surface and to the superficial in all the senses of the word."

I would now like to speculate on the impact of the cybernetic revolution as it impinges on our sensitivities, on our sense orientations, and on how these impingements manifest themselves. Ultimately, this raises the question whether postmodernism is a cultural and aesthetic phenomenon that will eventually lose its current position of prominence, or whether it is "a social phenomenon, perhaps even a mutation in Western humanism" (Calinescu, 280), "a mutation and the dawning of a wholly new social structure" (xiii).

The inclusiveness characteristic of postmodernism, the breaking down of social hierarchies and aesthetic canons, the skepticism toward metanarratives, the intrusiveness of computer technology with the creation and transfer of new knowledge as much as new kinds of knowledge, and the abolition of the inner/outer boundaries through the "media machines" have consequences that extend beyond the current debates over definitions of the terms and into a future that may not exist—sublated into a continuous now. These very aspects of postmodernism are expressed in the destruction of time and history through simultaneity, the destruction of place and local identity through instant ubiquity, the destruction of a sensually accessible reality through image and simulacrum, and a resultant de-realization of our world (in the broadest sense), including ourselves.

Postmodernism is taking possession of the "global village" heralded in the 1960s by Marshall McLuhan. We can get around in this village quite easily and speedily; a flick of our wrist can send us to any part of the world, in the present, in the distant past, or anywhere in between. The only cost for transportation is derealization and a denaturing of the times and places we visit. As all places of history and events around the globe become equidistant, we lose/they lose their sense of specificity and dissolve into a now that can be stored, retrieved, and changed.

At the same time, the inclusiveness of a pluralistic society corroborates the effects of this cybernetic revolution: the simultaneous availability in our artificial environments of cultures, religions, fashions, and foods (on and off the TV screen) has abolished any sense of local identity. This, even though we may romantically believe that we experience the "real thing" when, for example, we have an Italian espresso in a shopping mall. On the side of high culture, we are at most *Bildungstouristen*, rushing through overcrowded museums, sold on being entertained through the consuming of artefacts, more profoundly affected by the conditions of the restrooms than the works of art on display; on the popular end, we may pick and choose among restaurants or neighborhoods, always guided by the search for the "authentic" local flavor, only rarely realizing that we are moving in the world of Baudrillard's hyperreal. Whether the products offered for consumption are artefacts of millennia displayed in museums, living- or boardrooms; animals from around the globe displayed in zoos or "nature parks" (a contradiction in terms); exotic plants displayed in botanical gardens or private greenhouses; thoughtful arrangements for photo safaris made in domesticated habitats; hiking in national parks, touring Antarctica—we are always consuming, but always consuming simulacra, the images of something that does not exist (because at the least, our very presence and intrusiveness destroys what we want to experience). On the most simplistic level, we can agree with Lyotard, when he says: "... one listens to reggae, watches a western, eats McDonald's food for lunch and local cuisine for dinner, wears Paris perfume in Tokyo and (retro)clothes in Hong Kong," while "knowledge is a matter for TV games" (76).

The inclusiveness of postmodern society, the instant accessibilities and simultaneous availabilities at the price of derealization are, in my opinion, the qualities that will remain with us, indeed catapult us forward; and as the speed increases, we will find ourselves in a continuous now.[12] For some of us, this may appear to be a pessimistic outlook, conjuring up the apocalypse, the end of the world as we know it. I would prefer to say, as we have known it. But nostalgia and conservatism, and the desire to find familiar footing in a world that seems increasingly unfamiliar to us, cannot sustain themselves indefinitely, although they can cause great social and political upheaval while they are struggling to hold on.

It is clear that postmodernism will not continue in its present form; it is equally clear that the United States has spearheaded culturally—and continues to implement socially in often agonizing and shamefully circuitous manners—the society of the future: a society of inclusiveness and instantaneity, composed of fragments that reconstitute in fluid, constantly shifting patterns, with individual members arranged in eclectic assemblages of bits and bytes of multipurpose functions, operating under the impact of derealization, even as derealization absorbs all domains. It will be, and in fact is even now, a society of advocacy groups, seemingly without metanarratives, trying to get along by consensual arrangements and democratic processes in perennial ad hoc configurations. This may well be the model for future societies that want to succeed (and not vanish like species that become extinct because they cannot adapt, or that are preserved in some kind of artificially arranged "natural" habitats, fossilized, musealized). The global village does not grant escape routes.

When I think of contemporary Europe, I also think of the migration it is trying to contain: of North Africans to France, Indians and Hong Kong Chinese to England, of East Europeans and the former Yugoslavs to Germany and Austria: these major tectonic shifts in population flows will cause anxiety, but they can also make enormous contributions and enrich staid, homogeneous societies with vitality, perhaps even exuberance.

To suggest that these prospects can be invigorating, not traumatizing, I would like to conclude by quoting Richard Rorty, who insists that there is no need for metanarratives; instead: "What is needed is a sort of intellectual analogue to civic virtue—tolerance, irony, and a willingness to let spheres of culture flourish..." (38).

Notes

1. On periodization, see for example Huyssen, 160 ff.

2. On the philosophical implications of the word "postmodernism" and its historical foundations, see Behler.

3. On this side of the Atlantic, some critics object to this radical view of postmodernism. See Graff; I quote from the reprint in Putz and Freese, esp. 37.

4. See also Pefanis.

5. English translation "Modernity versus Postmodernity" in *new german critique* 22 (Winter 1981) 3-14. This entire issue focuses on postmodernism and contains replies to Habermas.

6. Among the many publications on postmodern architecture should be cited the pathbreaking study of Venturi et al, as well as the volumes by Jencks, and, on dolphins, Mickey Mouse, and related matters, by Brown.

7. Aesthetics as defined through modernism, including the excised field of *kitsch*, or of the ugly and the outrageous, no longer seems a serviceable field of inquiry. These definitions and categories only work against a background of commonly accepted standards. The "leveling of opposites" radically annihilates distinctions. Debates over the possibilities—and the formulation—of a new aesthetics are, for example, carried on in Bürger.

8. See de Lauretis' article on Eco's novel *The Name of the Rose*, 251-69; similarly Ryan on Suskind's novel *Perfume* in *The German Quarterly* 63 (1990), 396-403.

9. Compare in this respect Hoesterey's review essay (507).

10. Alter quoted in Newman, 31-32.

11. Compare *Life after Postmodernism*, ed. and introd. Fekete, where articles have titles such as "Value without Truth Value," "Vampire Value, Infinitive Art, and Literary Theory," or "Panic Value: Bacon, Colville, Baudrillard and the Aesthetics of Deprivation."

12. For a radical statement on this science fiction present, compare: "No longer the Cartesian thinking subject, however, but *fractal subjectivity* in an ultramodern culture where panic science is

the language of power: no longer ratiocination to excess, but *parallel processing* as the epistemological form of postmodern consciousness (where Mind is exteriorized in the structural paradigm of telematic society); ... no longer univocal (grounded) perspective, but the fatal implosion of perspective into the *cyberspace of virtual technology*. And this is as it should be when we are already living beyond gravity (in hyperreal bodies) and beyond representational space (in the mathematical reality of fuzzy sets where individual particles have no meaning apart from the patterning of the larger totality). For the Cartesian self no longer exists—except perhaps as an optical afterimage of the present condition of the post-Cartesian body as the dangling subjectivity in a quantum reality." Kroker in Fekete, 181-82.

Works Cited

Baudrillard, Jean. "Simulacra and Simulations." *Selected Writings*. Ed. and intro. Mark Poster. Stanford, CA.: Stanford UP, 1988.

Behler, Ernst. "Modernism and Postmodernism in Contemporary Thought." *Irony and the Discourse of Modernity*. Seattle: University of Washington Press, 1990.

Benhabib, Seyla. "Kritik des 'postmodernen Wissens'—eine Auseinandersetzung mit Jean-Francois Lyotard." *Postmoderne: Zeichen eines kulturellen Wandels*. Ed. Andreas Huyssen und Klaus R. Scherpe. Reinbek bei Hamburg: Rowohlt, 1986. 103-127.

Brown, Patricia Leigh. "Disney Deco." *The New York Times Magazine* 8 April 1990.

Bürger, Christa. "Moderne als Postmoderne." *Postmoderne: Alltag, Allegorie und Avantgarde*. Ed. Christa Bürger and Peter Bürger. Frankfurt/Main: Suhrkamp, 1987.

Bürger, Peter. "Der Alltag, die Allegorie und die Avantgarde." *Postmoderne: Alltag, Allegorie und Avantgarde*. Ed. Christa Bürger and Peter Bürger. Frankfurt/Main: Suhrkamp, 1987.

---. *Theorie der Avantgarde*. Frankfurt/Main: Suhrkamp, 1974.
Calinescu, Matei. *Five Faces of Modernity: Modernism, Avant-Garde, Decadence, Kitsch, Postmodernism*. Durham, NC: Duke UP, 1987.
Fekete, John, ed. and intro. *Life after Postmodernism*. New York: St. Martin's Press, 1987.
Fiedler, Leslie. "Cross the Border—Close the Gap." *The Collected Essays of Leslie Fiedler*, Vol.II. New York: Stein and Day, 1971.
Graff, Gerald. "The Myth of the Postmodernist Breakthrough." *TriQuarterly* 26 (1973): 383-417. Rpt. in *Postmodernism in American Literature: A Critical Anthology*. Ed. Manfred Putz and Peter Freese. Darmstadt: Thesen Verlag, 1984.
Habermas, Jürgen. "Die Moderne—ein unvollendetes Projekt." *Die Zeit* 26 September 1980. Trans. "Modernity versus Postmodernity." *new german critique* 22 (1981): 3-14.
Hassan, Ihab. "The Question of Postmodernism." *Performing Arts Journal* 16 (1981): 30-37.
Hoesterey, Ingeborg. "Literatur zur Postmoderne." *The German Quarterly* 62 (1989): 501-09.
Huyssen, Andreas. "The Search for Tradition: Avantgarde and Postmodernism in the 1970's." *After the Great Divide: Modernism, Mass Culture, Postmodernism*. Bloomington, IN: Indiana UP 1986.
Huyssen, Andreas and Klaus R. Scherpe, eds. *Postmoderne: Zeichen eines kulturellen Wandels*. Reinbek bei Hamburg: Rowohlt, 1986.
Jencks, Charles. *What is Post-Modernism?* New York: St. Martin's Press, 1986.
Lauretis, Teresa de. "Das Rätsel der Lösung—Umberto Ecos *Der Name der Rose* als postmoderner Roman." *Postmoderne: Zeichen eines kulturellen Wandels*. Ed. Andreas Huyssen und Klaus R. Scherpe. Reinbek bei Hamburg: Rowohlt, 1986. 251-269.
Lyotard, Jean-Francois. *The Postmodern Condition: A Report on Knowledge*. Foreword by Fredric Jameson. Minneapolis, MN: University of Minnesota Press, 1984.

Newman, Charles. *The Post-Modern Aura: The Act of Fiction in an Age of Inflation*. Evanston, IL: Northwestern UP, 1985.

Pefanis, Julian. *Heterology and the Postmodern: Bataille, Baudrillard, and Lyotard*. Durham, NC: Duke UP, 1991.

Rorty, Richard. "Habermas and Lyotard on Postmodernity." *Praxis International* 4,i (1984) 41-42. Rpt. in *Habermas and Modernity*. Ed. and introd. Richard J. Bernstein. Cambridge, MA: MIT Press, 1985.

Ryan, Judith. "The Problem of Pastiche: Patrick Süskind's *Das Parfum*." *The German Quarterly* 63 (Summer/Fall 1990), 396-403.

Sontag, Susan. "Notes on 'Camp.'" *Against Interpretation*. New York: Dell, 1964.

Venturi, Robert, Denise Scott Brown, and Steven Izenour. *Learning from Las Vegas*. Cambridge, MA: MIT Press, 1989.

Hybridity as Aesthetic Discourse
in Austrian Art, Film, and Literature

Ingeborg Hoesterey
Indiana University

For many contemporaries in this country and in Europe the term "postmodernism" continues to connote conceptual fuzziness, irrationality, an "anything goes" attitude, a grab bag of diverse desires. The seemingly unlimited semiosis of the concept of the postmodern is reflected in the more than 1500 titles in the MLA electronic bibliography devoted to the term that is now a buzzword in sociology, ethnography, political science, history and some natural sciences. In this essay I shall not show how these different communities construct their notion of the postmodern; rather I shall focus on *aesthetic* postmodernism and its stylistic features as they have evolved in the now historical discourse formations in the arts: literature, architecture, and visual art.

My archive on these developments, now more than twenty years old, has over the years allowed me to observe those structural and stylistic similarities in the contemporary arts that are hailed both transnationally and transculturally as features of a postmodern aesthetic. One of these stylistic markers of the postmodern is hybridity. Hybridity, the juncture of two or more heterogeneous substances, was anathema to the modernist program that posited the internally unified work of art and the quasi-autonomy of its aesthetic status vis-a-vis the *Lebenswelt*. Postmodern works quote from past artistic production, mix different genres in conspicuous ways, and with a vengeance opt for the equation of art and life. Naturally, any anti-high art attitude also produces style, and we find plenty of it in Austrian culture today.

The discourse in architecture shaped postmodern style as did no other art; in both theory and practice Austria participated in the new "language" of architecture earlier and more prominently than did its European neighbors. Hans Hollein is the most eminent of the Austrian architects who joined the international postmodern movement, and it is his highly unusual façade for the first Schullin boutique, built in 1974 on the Graben, that made him famous—via an infamous shape. The broken-up black polished granite accommodating air-conditioning elements shocked the bourgeois public by suggesting decay and a messy incompleteness. For Charles Jencks the "fissures and skin-like bronze layers" of the ragged cave-like shape took on a psychoanalytic contents; he saw a "warped uterus violated by the polished air-conditioning pipes" (54). This reading would not have occurred to my female eyes which tend to go for form and artistic tradition. In my view they connoted first and foremost a harking back to the pittoresque tradition in art and, in particular, to the topos of the ruin that appears in painting and architecture from the sixteenth century onward.

Hollein's reinstatement of the ruin topos—the American architectural group SITE parallels his efforts—was used in many variations by other postmodern architects in their effort to activate cultural memory by reintegrating past architectural motifs into contemporary building technology.[1] Together with the much quoted classical column, the motif of the pittoresque ruin became part of the strategy of architectural postmodernism to narrativize and semantically enrich a building.

The second Schullin shop, built on the Kohlmarkt in the eighties, blends playfully displaced classical elements and primitive ax-like shapes into the neo-art deco typical of 1980s postmodernism. The Haashaus (1990), provocatively situated opposite the St. Stephen's Cathedral, is also highly referential in that it quotes, in one section, the greenish stone of the Loos house on the Michaelerplatz. Its interior is a pastiche of numerous styles and formal effects—an art deco sculpture of a dancing girl draws the heterogeneous elements together. For those who enjoy visual surprises, the interior is a haven of delights in beautiful stone, painted surfaces, and playful architectural elements. The exterior of the Haashaus shows the architect in transition from postmodernism to what is called, in a daring intermedial leap, "deconstruction" in architecture. Like many other avant-garde architects, Hollein has moved on, and this change of paradigm in architectural discourse enables us now to historicize aesthetic postmodernism, that is, to treat it as a period style rather than to problematize it as the advent—or false proclamation—of a new epoch.

The architectural firm Coop Himmelblau, which a few years ago had a substantial exhibition in the Centre Beaubourg in Paris and earlier in Chicago, practices a deconstructionist style that avoids the decorative idiom of the postmodern but retains its tendency toward hybrid form. Wolf D. Prix and Helmut Swiczinsky achieve a hybrid effect by juxtaposing neo-constructivist formations with historicist structures. Their design for a law office in Vienna has been called an "energy field in a lightning storm" (Giovannini, 262). Their controversial, dramatically asymmetric structures should be seen in the context of a worldwide practice of this style prominently practiced by the architects Frank Gehry and Daniel Libeskind.

The last example of this *tour d'horizon* of Austrian contemporary architecture and design is a structure that provokes the equation of hybrid with eclectic. The painter Ernst Fuchs, a member of the Vienna School of Phantastic Realism and professor of art, designed the interior of a church near Graz, St. Jakob in Thal. Phantastic Realism turned postmodern; in the interior the artist stirred together an extravagant variety of decorative effects combined with religious scenes that are pastiches of older pictorial traditions. The ensuing effect is a gaudy splendor that is to symbolize "heavenly Jerusalem." As in Lessing's drama *Nathan der Weise* (*Nathan the Wise*), the Jerusalem of St. Jakob in Thal functions as a sign for a multi-religious space where weddings are celebrated in the Christian and Jewish religion, less visibly in the Islamic tradition. The hybrid glamour harbors, alas, a multicultural aesthetic. In its ambiguous, albeit intentional embrace of *kitsch* the church interior by Ernst Fuchs is well within a certain direction in visual postmodernism that celebrates "low" art as a populist version of the untraditional.

Valie Export's hybrid artistic persona evolved during the late sixties while Ernst Fuchs continued to experiment with phantastic motifs in one major medium, painting. The young Waltraud Höllinger, née Lehner—Export's official identity—is shaped first by the "Wiener Aktionismus" (Viennese actionism) of the sixties that made the body of an artist part of his/her work of art. Export transports the sensualist "Orgien-Mysterien-Theater" (Orgy-Mysteries Theatre) of Otto Mühl and Hermann Nitsch into a feminist discourse: she makes her debut in the art scene with a three-minute work in 8 mm, *Menstruationsfilm* (1967). From the beginning, Valie Export conceived of the cinematic medium as part of a spectrum of diverse formal modes that could facilitate an *art engagé* of a new kind which she called "expanded cinema." In 1968 she created a stir with her "Touch Cinema," a contraption mounted on her upper torso to simulate the dark screening room of a cinema. The performance, during which Export invited male bystanders to feel her bare breasts protruding into the dark of the box, was to heighten the awareness of moviegoers of the space of cinematic reception.[2] Formally this performance echoes Carol Schneeman's cello act with tiny TV monitors fastened to her bare breasts, a New York avant-garde staple of the sixties. Like the group of artists banding together under the banner of *Fluxus* (Nam June Paik, Joseph Beuys et al.), Valie Export opts for a radically extended notion of art. Multimedia installations—multiple video objects and recitation—as well as mixed media performances blending sculpture, nude body, and text are Export's major modes of expression in the art scene of the seventies.

Valie Export works in the space defined by artistic practices current at different points in time. Thus the Korean composer and conceptual installation artist Nam June Paik can be detected as an influence in many of the video installations that Export, frequently together with Peter Weibel, creates in the seventies. Whenever Valie Export avails herself of new modes, however, she does so to serve her feminist project.

All of the directions discernible in Export's work— conceptual photography, video art, installation and performance— revive with a twist earlier tendencies in Dada. Marcel Duchamp's anti-art manifestations like his famous Mona Lisa travesty inform a piece such as "Knitting Madonna" of 1976. Export quotes not Leonardo, but Michelangelo, namely his *Pietà*. Her travesty serves to correct the history of all those Dadaist quotations from high art which were almost exclusively produced by males. With a montage entitled *Rogier van der Weyden* (1974) Valie Export concretizes visually the confrontation of the contemporary spectator, the female spectator in particular, with a famous work from the old-masterly (male) tradition. The photomontage suggests that the experience of alterity is made explicit precisely by the attempt of a female viewer (perhaps Export) to mimic the gesture of a marginal female figure in the Netherlandic painting. In these and many other works the textual code is dominant: "Ontological Leap," "Genital Panic" (1969), "Judith within the Structure of Looking" (*The Practice of Love* 1984), "Eros/ion." In fact, the theoretical commentary Export bestows on her art is, in my eyes, her *forte*, and it is not surprising that the well-known Italian-American feminist Teresa de Lauretis borrows Export's film title *The Practice of Love* for her book.[3] Export's visualization of her ideas, that is, their physical shape, tends to be somewhat derivative; something that would necessarily escape the author of a recent important monograph on the artist, Roswitha Mueller, who comes from the side of literature and feminist theory, not art history or art criticism.[4]

The textual bent of visual postmodernism does not, as is often surmised, spare the artist a confrontation with the ever present demands of visual form. *Geburtenbett* (Birth Bed, 1980) is a blunt feminist text that asserts the presence of the message over sculpture as form although this type of narrative installation is well within the extended parameters of current aesthetics.

Valie Export's artistic potential clearly emerges in her handling of the filmic medium and in her experimental photography. Her films made for ORF (Austrian Broadcasting Corporation), such as the early *Menschenfrauen* (Female Humans, 1976, with Peter Weibel) and in particular the non-narrative work *Syntagma* attest to her considerable talent for both narrative and structural film. *Syntagma*, a visually compelling work of 1983, harks back to the abstract film of the early Walter Ruttmann, a cinematic tradition that since the 1930s has fallen in disfavor under the dominance of narrative film. The contemporary feminist artist replaces Ruttmann's geometric vocabulary and reinscribes his abstract shapes with organic form—female limbs that simultaneously connote beauty and fragmentation in their move away from the cool geometric abstraction of Ruttmann's *Opus* films of 1921-24. Valie Export's hybrid artistic production deserves closer attention than can be

Hybridity as Aesthetic Discourse 39

alotted in the present context; my argument must move on to search for structures of hybridity in literary production and their transposition into the visuality and physicality of performance, on screen or stage.

The transposition of a literary text into the cinematic medium always provokes reflection upon the structural and formal differences of the verbal art of literature and the verbo-visual art of film.[5] Michael Schottenberg's two-part film entitled *Landläufiger Tod* (Ordinary Death, 1992), made for ORF, was adapted from Gerhard Roth's prose texts *Landläufiger Tod* (1984) and *Am Abgrund* (Abyss, 1986). As so often with cinematic adaptations, the filmic image tends to reduce the wealth of references generated by the literary text to a certain one-dimensionality. Gerhard Roth, like Günter Grass, is an author who thinks in images, yet who also insists, as did Grass on the occasion of the filming of *The Tin Drum*, on cinematic identity as being essentially separate and different (Hoesterey, 25). Lessing's *Laocoon* paradigm is now applied to a new intermedial constellation.

As a director, Michael Schottenberg is clearly sensitive to the pitfalls of adaptation when he announces that his visual counteroffer merely addresses "themes" of Roth's texts. The latter are indeed most complex works with multiple narrative perspectives, unreliable narration galore, featuring arrangements of seemingly unconnected textual items as well as pastiche. *Am Abgrund* updates Dostoevsky's Raskolnikov in *Crime and Punishment* and the notion of *acte gratuit*, the murder without motive—nihilism.

Roth's prose texts can indeed make a narratological heart beat faster; with regard to the thematic mandate of this volume, however, it seems more prudent to briefly explore one particular stylistic juncture between filmic text and literary text—the use of Surrealism. Surrealist imagery structures the text in *Landläufiger Tod* throughout; it is the only language available to the mute son of a beekeeper who writes as his imagination dictates. Dream logic: "when the horse's head began to talk, rain fell in the shape of harebells" or "the men in the village use talking corn cobs to make burial music" (136). Such bizarre textuality rejects being transposed into the cinematic medium. Obviously aware of the specificity of the literary work, Schottenberg has chosen to visualize Franz Lindner's notions, poetic and abstruse, as surrealist image.

The American master photographer Richard Avedon made a stunning portrait of a Californian beekeeper whose naked torso is covered with bees, an image reminiscent of Dali's crawling ants in Buñuel's *Un chien andalou* (An Andalusian Dog). A variant of the image appears at the end of the first part of Schottenberg's film: Franz is totally engulfed by bees. A dramatization of the quoted photograph has taken place that connotes angst, paranoia, and the destruction of the self. Avedon referred back to Buñuel's and Dali's famous surrealist film of 1928; Schottenberg and his scriptwriter Roth carry the intertextual play further by having Alois Jenner, the modern-day Raskolnikov, ask: "Do you know the Andalusian dog?" There are other instances of verbal-visual intertextuality that contribute to the provocative character of this remarkable cooperative effort between writer and filmmaker.

Handke's play *Die Stunde da wir nichts von einander wußten* (The Hour When We Knew Nothing of Each Other, 1996) eliminates a crucial, perhaps the most important structural feature of the dramatic genre, spoken language. The performance is not generated from a dramatic text; the only textual matter in print are stylized stage directions that move this normally marginal genre to centerstage.[6] Handke's uncompromising "Theater der Blicke" (theatre as gaze) was first performed during the Vienna Festival in May 1992 at the Burgtheater; some of its motifs were introduced earlier, especially in the prose text of *Die Abwesenheit* of 1987 (*The Absence*, 1990). The *nunc stans* of the "Sturzplatz," a dream place, oddly prefigures the "Sturzplatz" of hurried figures and figural constellations of the play, of eyes fleetingly meeting in that perpetual, subtle drama of seeing and being seen.

Handke's fictional and nonfictional texts abound with instances of purely visual dialogue. There is, for example, the "Antwortblick" (glance as response) that the children in *Kindergeschichte* (Story about Children) search for, and there are texts such as *Der Chinese des Schmerzes* (The Chinaman of Pain) that can be read as a phenomenology of the gaze as an existential mode.[7] In public places, cafés, airports or on train platforms the author is unable to muster respect for people, only to be shocked when he perceives, at a glance, his own isolation in theirs. It is this sudden perception of the self in the other that stops the writer from categorizing the other person.

In *Die Stunde da wir nichts von einander wußten* the interplay of non-verbal signs celebrates the many minute and momentary utopias that come about on the "Platz" which incidentally looks much like the "Platz des Volkes" (people's square) that the trapeze artist Marion envisages at the end of the Wenders/Handke film *Himmel über Berlin* (*Wings of Desire*, 1987). In the play, the moment of seeing the other means becoming the other, if only for an instant, as when the somber wanderer is suddenly greeted by a runner and, to his own surprise, lifts his hand in a countergreeting (32). Looks are exchanged in varying configurations, now as signs of collegial acknowledgment as between two mailmen on bicycles, then in the peculiarly clandestine manner of flirtatious dialogue between a man and a woman in a brief moment of "knowing."

A beauty crosses the "Platz" several times, an allegory of the desire to be seen, and of the spectator's desire to see and desire. One is reminded of the author's Lacan quotation, "das Begehren begehren" (to desire the desire) in *Die Lehre der Sainte-Victoire* (The Lesson of St. Victoire). His/her eyes are the necessity that generates the future of all on the "Platz." "Do not betray what you have seen. Stay inside the picture." Handke chose these words from the enigmatic lead tablets extant from the Greek oracle of Dodona to preface his play without words but with sounds that speak, such as the rustling sound that sweeps over the "Platz," as it allegedly did at Dodona.[8] It is the communality of glancing subjects as an everyday myth, a utopian space in which the most mundane activity may figure as the most life-enhancing.

Die Stunde da wir nichts von einander wußten borrows from the visual theatre of Robert Wilson, from Performance Art, and the dance theater for its hybrid aesthetics. Nonverbal sound events, gestures, bodies in movement create a revue of humanity that emphatically calls upon the associative powers of the viewer's imagination. As performance, in Vienna and elsewhere, Handke's play joins the other hybrid artistic endeavors discussed here. They exhibit the Austrian art scene as experimental and unconventional as one has come to expect from this exemplary locus of innovation.

Notes

1. Thus Stirling incorporates crumbling stones denoting a ventilation opening in the garage of his addition to the Stuttgart Staatsgalerie, and Graves has a pittoresque hole in the marble entrance hall of the Humana Building in Louisville, Kentucky.

2. For this and other works by Valie Export mentioned below see Mueller.

3. In her acknowledgments de Lauretis writes: "to Valie Export for her title, which has haunted me since I saw her film *Die Praxis der Liebe*."

4. Mueller's monograph on Valie Export came about in close cooperation with the artist.

5. I am grateful to Willy Riemer for referring me to the Schottenberg-Roth intermedial project.

6. The first publication of the play in the *Programmbuch No. 94* of the 1991/1992 Burgtheater season graphically represented the text as stage directions. This effect is lost in both the Suhrkamp edition of 1992 and Honegger's sensitive translation (New Haven and London: Yale UP, 1996).

7. Alice Kuzniar offers a subtle and highly sensitive discussion of the motif of "looking" in Handke's texts in "Suture in/Suturing Litera-ture and Film: Handke and Wenders," in Hoesterey and Weisstein, 201 ff. The next two sentences also draw on her reading of Handke.

8. The oracle of Dodona, a structure 22 km south of Jannina, was named by Homer in the *Iliad*; it consisted of an open area surrounded by a wall containing a number of small temples.

Works Cited

Avedon, Richard. "Ronald Fischer, Beekeeper, Davis, California, 5/9/81." New York: Fotofolio.

Giovannini, Joseph. "Gone Ballistic!" *Harper's Bazaar* (March 1993).

Hoesterey, Ingeborg. "Das Literarische und das Filmische. Zur dialogischen Medialität der *Blechtrommel*." Ed. Hans Adler and Jost Hermand. *Günter Grass. Ästhetik des Engagements*. Bern and Frankfurt/Main: Peter Lang, 1996.

Hoesterey, Ingeborg and Ulrich Weisstein, eds. *Intertextuality: German Literature and Visual Art*. Columbia, SC: Camden House, 1993.

Jencks, Charles. *Architecture Today*. New York: Harry N. Abrams, 1988.

Lauretis, Teresa de. *The Practice of Love: Lesbian Sexuality and Perverse Desire*. Bloomington and Indianapolis: Indiana UP, 1994.

Mueller, Roswitha. *Valie Export: Fragments of the Imagination*. Bloomington and Indianapolis: Indiana UP, 1994.

Roth, Gerhard. *Landläufiger Tod*. Frankfurt/Main: Fischer, 1984.

---. *Am Abgrund*. Frankfurt/Main: Fischer, 1986.

Commuting to Klagenfurt

Peter Demetz
Yale University

Each summer for ten years I traveled to Klagenfurt where I was a member and the speaker of the literary jury awarding the Ingeborg-Bachmann-Prize and three other awards. On the way to and from Klagenfurt I stayed, often for months, in Vienna. Since Klagenfurt does not have any real cinemas, I let myself go in Vienna, taking in among the *chic* crowds and the avantgarde what the *Stadtkino* and the *Votivkino* had to offer. Eager to know more about the history of the Austrian film industry of the thirties, forties and fifties, I also went to the incomparable *Bellaria-Kino* to see the ancient repertory of the Hans Moser/Theo Lingen *Verwechslungskomödien* (comedies of mistaken identity) as well as the *Alpenschnulzen* (Alpine hits) of the fifties. My Austrian impressions were perhaps sharpened rather than blunted by the rhythm of coming and going to the same places, and I trust that I have learned more by arriving and leaving again and again than by staying on for years, without changing my perspective in between.

We were usually told by the media, that for some twenty years now Klagenfurt was the metropolis of German writing, but only for the last week each June. It certainly was an illustrious gathering of writers, publishers, editors, students and regular hangers-on, the real *Adabeis*, who came to read or to watch the ritual, declaring that Austrian, German (East or West), or Swiss writing was now definitely dead. We also rushed to have dinner at the famous *Loreto* restaurant on the shore of the lake, and to attend the yearly party of the Lord Mayor who was as amiable as Kaiser Franz Josef and always gave the same speech, rain or shine. Yet discipline was strict. Every day from nine to one and from three to five, seven authors read, twenty-two in all. The jury discussed each manuscript for thirty minutes after it had been read, and in the end publicly voted and awarded the splendid Ingeborg-Bachmann-Prize, the Carinthian-Prize, the Ernst-Willner-Prize, the woefully undersubscribed Prize of the Publishers and, more recently and not to be outdone by anybody, the Bertelsmann-Stipend, causing a certain anxiety that Bertelsmann ultimately would take over, lock, stock, and barrel. Of course, it was not only a matter of the award itself but the pleasant consequences. Each writer who received an award was immediately offered a good contract by a leading publisher (they tried to outbid each other in the corridors), and prime-time-interviews of the winners, by all the networks, helped a good deal to increase the market value of the fortunate ones and, it must also be said, deepened the despair of those who went home with empty hands and less.

It is deplorable that the mythology of the Klagenfurt meetings has not yet been written down. It would be a collection of stories from the oral tradition as they are circulated at the parties and over *Tafelspitz*. Though the grand Klagenfurt epic would lack the classical *edle Einfalt*, it would certainly compensate with its wild and wooly episodes and sound like an ancient Sanskrit poem of vital and divine disorder. There would be the *canto* about the young writer who came to the lectern bleeding profusely from a self-inflicted wound (even before the jury had started its job), or the adventure of another author who arrived in Klagenfurt by train but *minus* his manuscript because (he claimed) it was torn from his hand by the wind and scattered, through the open window, along the rails, *gone with the wind*. Wind and water. There was also the promising writer from the GDR who was not particularly successful, wanted more media attention, and suddenly jumped from the deck of the lake steamer, where the Mayor's party was in full swing. Fully clothed he plunged into the water. Since I had nominated him, I also knew that he was a lifeguard by profession, and I feared more for his Sunday pants than for his life—it all goes to show that literary parties should not be held on lake steamers gliding through the waters because it is so difficult to go home. Yet there are more productive ways to transform Klagenfurt disappointments than to jump into the Wörthersee; just recently I nominated a young Munich writer (let's call her Sonja Röder) who in her prose piece tried to rewrite Ingeborg Bachmann's *Undine geht* in a more contemporary and *tough cookie* way. She was told by an almost unanimous jury that the text was awful. I say "almost," because I defended her prose, admittedly close to being a wonderful Bachmann parody, because I thought it demonstrated the vitality of Ingeborg Bachmann's story more than mute admiration, and I was happy to read in the *Süddeutsche Zeitung* that somebody shared my opinion. Only a few weeks ago, I received a thick envelope from Munich with a new piece of prose by Sonja Röder, attacking Klagenfurt and perhaps the world, in a language truly impassioned, frank and powerful. It is the beginning of a new book, and I hope that Sonja Röder will finish it soon.

The Klagenfurt mythology says that the first ten years of competition were the time of a merciless jury and its thumbs-down chairman Marcel Reich-Ranicki, but I am hesitant to believe every word of the ancient reports. It is true that the Klagenfurt competition, instituted about ten years after the demise of the Group 47 (when radical students and a few of their allies within the group demonstrated against the "fathers"), was possibly burdened by an awareness of its renowned antecedents—but in Klagenfurt discussions were public, broadcast by the media, at least selectively, and the attendant journalists had an opportunity to report about the proceedings in their papers, day by day. It is also true, however, that the selection of the authors was done in the manner of a constitutional monarchy; individual jurors submitted names of talented writers to the chairman but the final decision was his, though he was ably assisted by Humbert Fink, an Austrian writer of note.

I am not going to indulge in Marcel Reich-Ranicki bashing, the favorite sport of all younger *littérateurs* in the mid-eighties, because I have known Marcel for too long; and if it is said that he was, for a considerable time, the "Pope" of German literary criticism I have to add that I have known him when he was a hard-working chaplain. He has a few lodestars, among them Goethe, Thomas Mann, Richard Wagner and, critically, Anna Seghers, but I know few people who have taken literature as seriously as he does, and in spite of his lust for playing out his many egos and his inclination to vote for traditional writing rather than for experiments, the names of the award winners during his tenure speak for themselves—Gerd Jonke,

Hans J. Froehlich, Ulrich Plenzdorf, Sten Nadolny, Friedericke Roth, Erica Pedretti, Ginka Steinwachs, or Hermann Burger, to mention just a few.

The great Klagenfurt epic also says that in the subsequent ten years procedures miraculously changed, brutality ceased, and the members of the jury changed into a band of helpful angels whose first idea it was to protect the writers, nursing and nourishing their uncertainties and praising their virtues. There *were* a few changes, and not the least of them was purely technological; instead of selective local or national coverage, the entire proceedings, from morning till night, were continuously transmitted by the *3 Sat* network, and writers and jurors were confronted, for seven hours every day, with the glare of the Klieg lights, the rolling TV cameras and with the necessity to formulate critical judgments to an invisible audience of millions, all over Europe, as the network people proudly declared. More importantly perhaps, the constitutional monarchy changed into a *republic* in which every juror had the privilege to nominate his or her own writer, as did the speaker of the jury, and slowly, the jury itself began to change, and instead of practicing writers and professional critics writing for the newspapers, the number of professors, myself included, sub-stantially increased; and if, initially, Peter Härtling, Joachim Kaiser, Klara Obermüller, Hilde Spiel, Friedrich Torberg, or Ulrich Weinzierl outnumbered the academics, proportions began to change in the eighties. Unfortunately, Helmut Karasek left the jury after a few years. The professors Jörg Drews, Klaus Amann, Konstanze Fliedl took their seats behind the jury tables. There was more technical analysis and close reading of the text, the shadows of the German seminar loomed larger than before, and the media people began to complain that the professors did not really contribute to the entertainment of the TV audiences—surely with the exception of the witty Swiss, Peter von Matt and Iso Camartin, who now runs his own talk show at home.

For a number of years my colleagues of the press, trying to trip me, asked me about my definition of literature and I usually answered that literature was, to my mind, a sequence of words and sentences that I should like to hear or read twice or three times, not excluding whodunits by Ross MacDonald. I revealed myself to be a culinary philologist who is not satisfied alone by plot, character, or story unless they are presented in a language of at least some surprises, traps, barbs, reverberations, in short, a kind of verbal pastry, even if it should taste poisonous. I am not content with the timely or the political correct alone if it does not consciously operate with all the available phonetic, syntactical and semantic means (Roman Jakobson would have said that the writer should *mobilize* these means but I am satisfied with literature in a field of games and maneuvers rather than marching to a front) and, inevitably, I had little difficulty with voting for Franzobel, the most gifted of the present Vienna experimentalists, or for Fritz Krenn whose texts belong to the tradition of Austrian *Arbeiterliteratur*, even though in his own original way.

In my experience, the question of literature was usually followed, in Klagenfurt, by another one, often articulated in a more irritated way—namely, how I or others could judge a literary text which I had just heard for twenty or thirty minutes while the authors had worked on it for twenty or thirty weeks. It is a purely metaphysical question; I *cannot* but I try, a critic being somebody who has been reading books for twenty or thirty years and ultimately responds, at the drop of a hat, from his or her amassed intertextual experience. As for the stiff authority of the critic concerned, I can only confess that I have always suffered, in Klagenfurt or elsewhere, from virulent attacks of *Lampen-* or rather *Scheinwerferfieber* (stage fright). I always came to town too early and restlessly walked up and down the peaceful *Lendkanal* to assuage my self-doubts, and I suspect that my colleague Helmut Karasek, formerly of the *Spiegel*, suffered at times from similar afflictions, but preferred, as his personal therapy, an early walk before breakfast, to the nearby market, where he bought, for everybody, the choicest *Walderdbeeren* (forest strawberries).

There are many Klagenfurt observers who complain that literary quality has come down in recent years, and many of these complaints have a grain of truth, a good deal of mythology, and a definite unwillingness to see the surprise and the new. Ten years after the demise of the Group 47, the organizers of the Klagenfurt competition had an excellent chance to make their choices from a marvelous reservoir of talent. But it would be foolish and unfair to say that in recent years first-rate talents were missing among those receiving awards. I just have to list a few names to argue to the contrary: Norbert Gstrein, Thomas Hettche, Ingeborg Harms, Alois Hotschnig or Stefanie Menzinger. Yet there was another task that the Klagenfurt competition took upon itself, perhaps without intending to do so, and that was to provide encouragement for younger writers of the GDR in the last years of its existence and at the time when the dogmatists and the more vital minds confronted each other in the East Berlin Writers' Union and elsewhere. I am tempted to speak of a difficult and paradoxical *charade* that was played out by the Klagenfurt jury and the GDR Writers' Union, and the young authors concerned, and it would be difficult to describe the charade in less than a combination of ironic and serious terms. I first ran into the GDR group, or rather delegation, some nine years ago on the night flight from Vienna to Klagenfurt, a thirty minute flight enlivened with a lot of champagne thanks to the Austrian Airlines. It was hard to ignore that the GDR group was organized along the lines of an Olympic sports team, including the leaders of the group, the official *Betreuer*, and the hapless individual writers, moving in depressing unison. The difference was, of course, that these writers were selected by the GDR authorities, unlike the writers from the West who were nominated by individual jury members. The GDR authorities had declared that we should either accept their selection or the group would not be able to come at all; and eager to hear from the GDR people, the jury accepted the condition and hoped for the best. What went on was somewhat complicated; originally their texts were mostly traditional, with only a few revealing both talent and innovative intention. The jury was more inclined to praise the innovators than the traditionalists. The GDR Writers' Union understood the message well enough. It could send traditionalists, but these would return home empty-handed and with little international attention. It therefore began to delegate the most interesting younger people. They were serious, tremendously concerned with *new* writing, and trying to speak of their GDR experience in a frank language appropriate to their particular situation. They came, male and female, literally smashing the competition and returning home (where they were not particularly favored) with the most distinguished awards. In 1987 the Bachmann Prize went to Uwe Saeger, the Publishers Prize to Irene Liebmann, born in Moscow, a stipend to Anna Langhoff, and in the immediately following years Bachmann Prizes went to Angela Kraus, Wolfgang Hilbig and Kurt Drawert. It is perhaps not entirely an overstatement to say that in Klagenfurt the wall came tumbling down long before it happened in Berlin.

Another change that occurred in the Klagenfurt competition was a turn to multicultural texts, although I would plead to modify the sense of the overused term. German writing always came close, constitutionally, to being multicultural in many respects. The more geographical and idiomatic regions in our age take precedence over the republics at large as authentic scenes of experience and articulation, the more difficult it is to speak of German or Austrian literature instead of Tyrolean or Westphalian literary fields, not to mention the Swiss Cantons. Often the questions to which culture a German writer belonged were difficult to answer, as e.g., in the case of the distinguished author Franz Hodjak (Carinthia Award of 1990) who came from Romania where he had lived for a long time in miserable conditions and worked as a gravedigger, continuing to write in German all the time. It is almost easier to say that the Klagenfurt competition has come to appreciate fully the German prose written by the children, sons and daughters, of immigrants and foreign workers—that is, writers who have learned their German in schools rather than at home with their families. They are increasingly rewarded for their excellence, a process of social and historical import that has just begun. In 1991, Emine Sevgi Özdamar was awarded the Bachmann Prize for her prose *Das Leben ist eine Karawanserei* (Life Is a Caravan Stop) and, just in 1995, Ilja Trojanow received the new Bertelsmann Literary Prize for a story about a Bulgarian family crossing a dangerous border. In these cases, Turkish and Bulgarian writing has lost gifted authors, but writing in German has been enriched by ways of storytelling going back to Anatolian ballads and the Bulgarian folk epic. It is not, however, a process entirely new in recent world literature; a similar transformation has enriched, in our time, American writing (to offer one example) by the novels of Henry Roth, lost to Yiddish but bringing to the American narrative a particular, perhaps ceremonious and melodramatic quality.

These developments do not mean that Klagenfurt has become a hotbed of political enthusiasm, unless we are ready to define political elements in a way different from that of the age of Heinrich Böll. Younger writers, even those coming to Klagenfurt from Berlin, are not necessarily concerned with events described in the *first* pages of the newspapers, and even if they do, they prefer to speak about them from their unmade beds. Klagenfurt is geographically closer to Bosnia than any other German-speaking town, but political prose in the older sense has become rare—it was eight years ago that Angela Kraus received an award for telling the story of a Stasi-Officer who commits suicide because he does not understand anymore what is happening in his homeland; the most political story, in the old sense, to receive an award was written by an author of Bulgarian descent. I confess, I am surprised; the most demanding and inflexible Utopia of our age, with its universal demands, decayed from the inside only a few years ago; younger writers do not look at the grand scenes of the public world anymore or the gory trouble that is called Srebrenica. During the most recent Klagenfurt competition it quickly became clear that a monological *attitude*, of many forms, competed with another minority stance still believing in sociability and dialogue, and after two days observers began to speak about a new literature of *Rumpf-Existenzen*, of patients paralyzed in their hospital beds or flaneurs wending their urban ways, totally uninterested in anybody but the frozen self.

Narrative analyses of difficult family situations fully satisfy, and if, some years ago, it was said that politics was alive in the private situation, we are now living with the consequences of these ideas. I am not obsessed at all with expecting an unmediated reflection of political issues in writing (it is not that easy); and I think I know that in writing, and elsewhere in artistic production including the movies, the aesthetic use of the sign combines with a diminished referential function, the sign is not the thing, and yet the sign and its handling is in the hands of vulnerable human beings.

It was not surprising that a remarkable story written by Lydia

Mischkulnig, from Vienna, particularly challenged the jury, not by its characters, including a musician faultlessly clad in Armani suits, at least not primarily, but because she shifted the characters, especially an Austrian fashion journalist, equally at home at the Café Bräunerhof and at the Plaza oyster bar, to smart Manhattan. Many jurors breathed a sigh of relief to be able to move out of the Tyrolean and Bernese villages to the Manhattan scene of the Upper East Side, with a journey to a Thai island for erotic relief. I confess that I was less impressed than many of my colleagues because I felt that Ms. Mischkulnig's Manhattan was too *chic* to be true, but I liked the implicit narrative argument, that is the significant choice of location, to use a term from the movies. Attention has long shifted from the big town to the green valleys again, and the recent discussion of Austria's participation in the European Union and the question of Austrian neutrality has intensified, as Walter Klier has shown in an illuminating book. An Austrian provincialism of Paradeiser (tomatoes) and Karfiol (cauliflower) that was once the privilege of the right has now become the reserve of the intellectual left, much concerned with German, not American capital investments and the European threat to Austrian *Eigenständigkeit* (cultural autonomy). Times are changing; the ancient voting habits, ingrained in Austrian families for generations, *rouge et noir*, fade away; the grand old parties have difficulties to keep their electorate together, and the intellectuals, often relying on a system of subsidies dispensed by the parties have, in the age of the austerity budgets, ample reason to ask questions about the future of publishers, books, and films that so often depend on support from the benevolent state. Here I stop and conclude by suggesting that Klagenfurt, in my memory a lively place, never ceased to respond to the pressures and issues of the moment, and whatever happened and happens there was of relevance to literature and the media far beyond the Carinthian frontiers.

Presented on 27 September 1996 at the Symposium on *Crossing Cultural Bounds in Contemporary Austrian Literature and Film*, at the University of Delaware.

2

Austrian Film:
Interviews with Producers and Directors

Austrian Film between Festival Success and Market Constraints

Interview with Martin Schweighofer

As Managing Director of the Austrian Film Commission (AFC) Martin Schweighofer has been instrumental in developing and promoting the Austrian representation at international film festivals. Apart from serving as the gateway to film festivals, the AFC functions as a clearinghouse for information on the Austrian film industry, publishing, for example, the journal *Austrian Film News* and an annual catalog on Austrian film productions. Schweighofer has directed the *Diagonale* in Salzburg, an annual film festival showcasing Austrian productions.

In recent years Austrian films have been well received at international film festivals. Could you explain this successs and locate Austrian film in the larger European context?

I'm well aware that Austrian films have a very good reputation in cinéastic circles; we always do seem to come up with film directors who make very exciting films. Not the kind of mainstream films that break box office records, mind you, simply because our film industry is not really in a position to produce big budget films. Within the production means, our films target a discerning audience, a niche in the global film market. A major handicap is that of language. In America, for example, dubbed films have not found acceptance. But subtitled versions meet a certain resistance from the audience as well. Such films might be screened in New York or Los Angeles, or on the art theater circuit and in universities, but they do not find much favor with the general public. In Europe dubbing is common, but here we encounter another problem: fragmentation of the market at all levels. In general, Austrian production companies have very little experience in promoting their films on international markets; to some degree the AFC plays a mediating role by providing information, advice and promotional support. It functions as an umbrella organization. The lack of expertise is aggravated by the fact that the distribution system for European films is not very well developed, even though the European market is one of the biggest by now, bigger than the American market. It is very difficult, for example, to release an Austrian film in one of the Scandinavian countries or for that matter to show a Norwegian film in Austria. Larger countries, such as Germany or France, have a big enough domestic market so that this deficiency is not quite so serious. But for the smaller European countries the problem of distribution is really crucial. I have devoted much time and effort to cooperative projects with other countries that would improve this situation in the long run. Returning to your question, for all of these reasons successful participation in film festivals is very important to us.

As a showcase for Austrian film, supplementing the distribution activities?

Yes, in the present situation film festivals provide an instrument for getting our films out to an audience, films that are worth seeing, that critics then write about and hopefully that attract distributors. This past year we had something like 250 screenings of Austrian films at international film festivals. Surely that enhances market awareness for all Austrian films.

In commercial terms, success at a prestigious film festival contributes to the name recognition of Austrian film and gives it a kind of corporate identity. These films then are important beyond their own box office performance?

Absolutely, yes. These films, after all, are produced in Austria and therefore serve as show pieces that stimulate further interest in other Austrian films as well. For example, *Tierische Liebe* (*Animal Love*, 1995), a documentary directed by Ulrich Seidl, was shown at thirty-five film festivals and we declined another twenty invitations. We were thrilled that we got Egon Humer's intense documentary *Emigration, NY* into the New York Film Festival, especially since it was then the first film to sell out at the festival. Such films and, to mention another example, the feature films directed by Michael Haneke, are a major force, because they establish a solid reputation for themselves and by association also for Austrian film. I should like to mention that the Austrian system of subsidizing the arts is quite excellent in comparison to some other countries. However, at present there is an on-going discussion regarding the relative merits of funding art films and mainstream popular films. But there can be no doubt that without these subsidies there would be no Austrian film industry and therefore no Austrian film of any kind.

That then is the market reality in Europe. Do you foresee a change as the European Union begins to make its influence felt, are there initiatives that will improve matters?

Austria is a participant in a variety of collaborative projects established by the EU. The European Film Distribution Office or EFDO, for example, was set up to promote European films. But as a condition of support it requires the collaboration of distributors in three countries at least, a condition that is not easily met. The release of Haneke's *71 Fragments of a Chronology of Chance* in Norway, Holland, France and Germany was subsidized in this way. The Council of Europe established a program called "Eurimage," which is intended to encourage co-productions between countries. Considering that these subsidy programs are for all of Europe, the amounts involved are not really all that significant. And particularly in the early phase it was plagued by a misconception: the programs were to compensate for the market dominance of the American majors. A similar approach was therefore used, stars from different countries were engaged, directors, an international setup and so forth. The outcome was less than a success. In fact, it produced a series of flops. At this time the most effective approach surely can't be a head-to-head competition with the American majors with their efficient distribution systems and their market dominance. I'm therefore somewhat pessimistic when it comes to the prospects of European cooperation. There is too much concern about national interests. In the short term at least we should target our films to segments of the market, to audiences that wish to see films which challenge their imagination and their mind.

For example, the kind of films that Haneke has made?

Michael Haneke is probably the premier film director in Austria today. He is radical, he opens new perspectives, his artistic horizon is a very broad one, from the fine arts to music. The way he uses Bach's music, for example, or take his film adaptation of Kafka's *The Castle*. The challenge of finding a form that will do justice to this legacy and yet leave room for the interpretation of each spectator. Since film is such an iconic medium suggesting an immediate realism, it is difficult to convey the kafkaesque flavor. As I see it, Haneke's solution is ingenious in the way it retains the integrity of Kafka's text. As he works with it in the film, he keeps the smallest possible distance to it, without touching and therefore changing it. The film works mostly with tracking shots, thus keeping a respectful distance to the story. He accompanies the actors, he accompanies everything that happens, and that has a very theatrical effect. And in similar fashion the dialog has the background of a narrator, sometimes overlapping the voices of the actors. In its dispassionate tone the film leaves the viewers to produce their own interpretation, it retains the experience that one has in reading Kafka's fragment.

The work of Kafka and Haneke seems to follow a cultural vein that is often associated with the Austrian mind. More generally, how would you characterize films that are Austrian, what is Austrian about Austrian films?

It is a most difficult question to answer, quite frankly, because if you would ask anybody to name the most famous Austrian film, they would probably say *The Sound of Music*. It was shot in Austria, to be sure, but it has very little to do with Austria. And it's definitely not an Austrian film. Austria had a strong film culture until the hiatus from the thirties to the early fifties. Filmmakers then either tried to suppress the past with light entertainment or they tried to come to terms with it in more serious films. What was lacking was a continuing tradition. During this time film adaptation came into vogue, some absolutely fabulous Ödön von Horváth films were made, or Joseph Roth and others. And then a younger generation came to the fore and rebelled against the film establishment. These examples illustrate that Austrian film is a rich tapestry. But there are perhaps some common threads in this complex weave, one of them has to do with a somewhat skeptical, even pessimistic attitude to or lack of enthusiasm for the progress of civilization. Here again the work of Haneke can be taken as example. In his trilogy especially the notion of "emotional glaciation" recurs, the increased alienation and violence in today's world. But Haneke's films never provide a ready answer to the problems, they simply pose the questions in their ruthless truth. If Haneke is the more radically skeptical, pessimistic representative of the New Austrian Film, then somebody like Axel Corti would represent a more romantic pessimism. His last film, *Der Radetzkymarsch* (*Radetzky March*, 1994), can be considered his legacy, a baroque legacy. While Haneke is an artist of reduction—at every turn he reduces and minimizes—Corti is somebody who blows things up and makes them grand. I couldn't name anybody else in Europe at the moment who did films like Corti, films with a kind of grandeur that nonetheless had something to say. Perhaps Fritz Lehner comes closest to this approach. But to return to your question: yes, location is important, we have a pretty mountainous country, but there are also some themes and genres that seem prevalent. The new kind of *Heimatfilm*, for example.

Perhaps another approach to the question of what makes an Austrian film would be to consider comedies and to compare them with German comedies. Since in these past few seasons the comedies have so remarkably increased the market share for domestic productions.

The pressure to succeed with commercial films and to appeal to a large audience has resulted in the so-called cabaret films. The idea behind this strategy is quite simple. In Vienna and in other cities we have a very active comedy scene. Films based on these stage productions would thus have a ready cabaret audience. It all started with *Indien* (*India*), a popular cabaret program. Paul Harather, its director, made a film out of this play; in the cast he included the two lead actors. *Indien* was very successful, and of course the minute you have something successful, you consider possible spin-offs. A good number of films which cast cabaret stars were then made. A fashion that will pass. Now coming back to how exportable these films are and how well humor translates. Viennese humor seems to be quite different from what you'd hear, for example, in Vorarlberg, which is the other end of Austria. The cabaret films are much stronger in the east than they are in the west of Austria. So, I think, humor doesn't translate so well, there are limits to all these things that are humorous. How do our comedies do in a market like Germany? I'd say that they are probably easier to understand in Bavaria, which is the south of Germany, and they're quite difficult to understand when they are screened in Hamburg. There is a bonus though: the further we get away from home, the more exotic we seem. *Indien*, for example, did have quite good attendance in Germany, but you couldn't say that it was a hit comparable to its run in Vienna. In general one could say that if humor depends too much on play of words, then it doesn't translate very well. And how does Austrian humor compare with German? I'm not too fond of German humor and I cannot very much relate to it. I think Austrian humor, if it's good, is that much more elegant, it's playful and a bit more tongue in cheek.

Comedies seem to draw large audiences and large audiences like to see popular film actors and actresses. Have comedies produced film stars?

One could argue that the cabaret film was invented because of the lack of stars. With the possible exception of France, Europe does not really have a star system. Attempts have been made to create such a system. The "Felix," for example, was conceived as the European answer to the "Oscar." But the "Felix" never generated much interest. The award ceremony was produced with much glamor, but the novelty soon wore off when the television audience realized that it was watching actors and actresses that they had never before seen in their life. One can't really say that Europe has international stars. In Austria an additional factor impedes the formation of a star system: the film industry is just too small to allow actors and actresses to embark on careers in film as their sole employment. As a consequence there are many excellent stage professionals who also work in film and television. Even though the acting style is quite different for stage and camera, their training no doubt has contributed to the high quality of their work and to the success of some of the films.

Producer's Challenge: Art and Commerce

Interview with Veit Heiduschka

Veit Heiduschka is a key player in the Austrian film scene. With Wega-Film, which he founded in 1980, he produced hits, as well as feature films whose high artistic merit resulted in numerous awards at prestigious film festivals. For example, *Müllers Büro* (Müller, Private Detective; 1986, directed by Niki List) was one of the greatest Austrian box office successes of the past decades and has become a cult film since. More recently, Michael Haneke's *Funny Games* (1997) was the first Austrian feature film in thirty-five years to be invited to the competition category at the Cannes Film Festival. Heiduschka has effectively served the Austrian film industry on various committees and trade associations, including positions as President of the Austrian Film Commission and as Vice-President of the Association of Austrian Film and Video Producers. He has taught at the Film Academy in Vienna and he represented Austria in the negotiations leading to the MEDIA agency of the European Union.

You once said that making a feature film is the last great adventure in this world. What is the nature of this adventure for a film producer in Austria today?

Producing a feature film involves a considerable on-going risk, particularly in Austria. For such a small market the producer needs to be more than an agent who issues checks and looks after the funding. He needs to be creatively versatile and also flexible in the business aspect of film making. The producer reads scripts, maintains contact with directors, assembles production teams, on occasion he resembles a co-director for the sake of the project, and when necessary he participates in the editing phase. And then, when the film is finished, he almost becomes a distributor as he promotes and places the film in the market. Even for an experienced producer every film is different and every stage of the production, from script to distribution, may harbor challenges that one has never before confronted. That then is the adventure. And unlike films commissioned for television, feature films bring no return on investment until they are in fact sold. An important factor in this risk is the director. I have never met a director who from the start set out to make a bad film, yet such films happen. In Austria subsidies are generally awarded to a film project with its production team, of which the director is an important member. Since every director has an individual style or signature, a replacement is not feasible.

You then collaborate with directors on their own terms, their filmic signature?

An example. When Michael Haneke came to me with the screenplay for *Der siebente Kontinent* (*The Seventh Continent*), I considered the text and then told him that if indeed the ideas in the screenplay could be done right, then it would be a true art film. But how does one sell art? After some discussion, I suggested that the material, together with other ideas that he had presented, would make an effective trilogy with a common theme concerning the alienation and indifference in modern life, or "emotional glaciation," to use his words. It is easier to sell three related art films, since at least one of them is likely to be of high quality and in any case, each film may appeal to different audiences. And so it was. When it comes to the making of the film, I try to provide an impartial view, the view of the first spectator. And I insist on a consistent style. Thus for Haneke's films I had all shots removed that seemed to dilute his precision and pander to the audience through setup or lighting; each shot consistently needs to have the right tone. Especially films with claims to artistic value need the quality that will result in good international reviews.

Apart from the stylistic signature of each director, is there not also a cultural signature, are there characteristics that reflect the culture in which a film is made?

Some years ago the Council of Europe set up "Eurimage," a foundation for subsidizing European filmmaking. Most European countries belong to it. At one of the meetings we considered how screenplays should be evaluated. I represented the opinion that Austrians could not, for example, reasonably judge a Portuguese or Scandinavian screenplay, simply because they are unfamiliar with these specific cultures. In other words, what may well be of great interest in one country and may indeed draw a large audience there, may not work at all in the rest of Europe. I for one would be reluctant to say, this is not a good screenplay, no, let's not fund this project. Instead we should take care to be tolerant, to accept cultural multiplicity. That is the strength of the European film, but also its dilemma in the world market. To put it simply: in no small measure the success of American film is due to its international orientation.

What then could one say is Austrian about a film made in Austria?

That is not so easy to specify. I would say, a certain imagination or way of looking at things. The language itself, of course. Some of the films that we export to Germany need to be subtitled or dubbed for that reason. But perhaps a more significant factor has to do with history. Austria is and has been a multicultural state, it has a long tradition of accommodating different cultures. This has contributed to the richness of its cultural production. As producer, I try to make films that reflect their Austrian origins. Not necessarily *Sissi*-films, nor films about the Habsburg Empire, but rather something that is characteristic of Austria today. These qualities may then arouse interest in other countries. We are not in a position to produce *Ben-Hur*; our films necessarily are smaller in budget: we make films that reflect life in Austria today.

Comedies appear to enjoy great popularity just now, yet in terms of language and sense of humor they are closely bound to each culture. Does this present a problem for the distributor?

Comedies produced in Austria don't necessarily work elsewhere. In principle it is possible to make comedies that on some level are as much appreciated in Hong Kong as in Los Angeles or in Johannesburg, slapstick, for example. But that involves a loss of cultural identity. And for a small country, a sense of identity is important.

You produced Müllers Büro, *one of the most successful films made in Austria in the past decades. How well did this film do in other countries?*

Müllers Büro was a great box office success in Austria, though not in the television showing of it years later. Perhaps for two reasons. Films need to be seen in a movie theater. Many things that are evident on a large screen just are not visible on the small image of a television set. It is not the same experience. Film and television are two very different media. We now have the inverse problem with Michael Haneke's film adaptation of Kafka's *The Castle*. Haneke had intended that the title include the words *A Film for Television*. But that was refused by the subsidy agency, with the explanation that the funding had been intended for a feature film for the cinema, not for a television production. Haneke is not pleased that this film will be shown in movie houses, since the kinds of images used in film are different from television. For example, long shots are ineffective in television, since the detail cannot be recognized; television, on the other hand, uses close-ups, which are used less frequently in film. Returning to *Müllers Büro*, yes, in Austria it did very well indeed as film, but not on television. As for its reception abroad. The film went very well in Scandinavia, and in Germany, of course, but not so well in Switzerland, where there seems to be a different sense of humor. Judging by the reviews, the film was not at all understood. In the DDR the film was enormously successful, since it was perceived as a political film. But here one should differentiate. Women critics strongly criticized the film for being misogynous. But in general the film conveys an irrepressible optimism for life, a zest for life. The spectators with whom we spoke saw this as a political message. To our surprise, *Müllers Büro* also was a success in Japan. At the Tokyo Film Festival it received the award for most popular film, in Japan the film obviously was understood. Something that I can't say of France. Yes, the reception of comedy very much depends both on the country of origin and on the host country. In Germany people were given to saying, oh yes, *Müllers Büro* is a typical Austrian film, without being able to explain the criteria for such a characterization.

Comedies and humor. It seems to me that humor very frequently borders on the tabu, and that tabus are specific to each culture.

I'm inclined to say, for a film to be successful, it has to break a tabu. That too constitutes a risk. But perhaps it is a necessary strategy. In the USA and Europe alone, some thousand feature films are produced every year. Three new films every day, no critic or spectator can absorb so much. American film producers solve the problem by always making sure of having at least two great stars in the cast, that in itself will attract a good audience to the movies. We don't have a star system in Austria. Consequently we have to use other means. I always say, we have to break a tabu. Not necessarily as a moral provocation, but as something that had never been done before. In Haneke's *The Seventh Continent*, for example, the outrage, the broken tabu is the destruction of money. Money flushed down a toilet. Haneke came to me and asked, do you think we can show that for three and a half minutes? Yes, I said, absolutely. Ten seconds would convey the information, nothing more. It would be registered as data. We want to confront the audience with the image for a long enough time so that they will physically respond to it, they will be revulsed in their gut. We did the same thing in *71 Fragments*. The shot with the protagonist practicing his table tennis skills against a machine shows how this person has himself become a machine, and it shows it in a way that we all can feel. In this connection I should say that at its premiere in Cannes, some five people walked out in protest to this scene; the remaining spectators, however, an audience of perhaps a thousand, spontaneously burst into applause. They understood what the film was trying to do. And a year later they still remember this almost visceral impression. Breaking a tabu, that's it; only, in today's society we don't have that many tabus left to break! But tabus are culturally based, so that new difficulties may arise as well. In 1986 *Müllers Büro* had been invited to the Austrian Film Week in Moscow. But because it had some nudity, the film could not be shown. The matter of tabus poses a problem even within the European market. In a sense, film is merchandise subject to the usual economic principles. A film that has been accepted in one country should therefore be readily exportable throughout the European Union. But that is not how it works. For example, the kind of eroticism that is taken for granted in films produced in France may still be prohibited in England. According to regulations of the EU, it should be possible to show these films in all other member states and without further censorship. Thus the cultural barriers, the tabu thresholds play an important role in the European film market. And contribute to the adventure of producing films in Austria.

Tolerance for a Complex World

Interview with Dieter Pochlatko

Dieter Pochlatko is President of the Association of Austrian Film and Video Producers and a Member of the Board of the Austrian Film Institute. His production company, Epo-Film, has developed a diversified program, with a distinguished record. Epo-Film has been honored with numerous festival invitations and awards for its feature films and with recognitions for films produced for television. For *I Love Vienna* Pochlatko received the "Golden Ticket" for the most successful Austrian feature film of the year 1992; the film was selected as the Austrian entry to the Academy Awards. In 1997 Dieter Pochlatko was awarded the *Romy* for "best producer of the year."

Feature film production in Austria is subsidized, in part because such films are thought to contribute to the cultural identity of Austria. What makes a film Austrian, and more specifically, in what way does it differ from a German film?

I would say that Austrian and German films differ particularly in their subject matter and choice of themes. Austrian writers and directors are concerned with fundamental questions about the fabric of society, about the forces that shape community and the place of the individual in it. Perhaps one could say, the work of Austrian film artists has to do with who we are and what role we have in our society, while in Germany the focus tends to be on external secular questions. Somewhat oversimplified, of course.

In the larger international context, what significance does the development of the European Union have for the Austrian film industry?

Austria joining the European Union was a most important development for us. It immediately gave an international dimension to our productions. It raised questions of style, to be sure, but also the matter of financing, that is, the possibility of co-production. And I can say so out of my own experience with Epo-Film. For example, at present we have a project that would just not have been possible without EU support. But in addition to that, of course, it has broadened our horizons, it has opened our cultural borders too; we have become more cosmopolitan, as is appropriate for film. In the opinion of some, this affiliation leads to a loss of cultural identity. I, however, do not count myself among them.

The question of cultural identity. Perhaps more than for other genres, local context and tradition contribute to the appeal and domestic success of comedies. But perhaps it is precisely this quality that makes such films difficult to export, even to other countries in which German is spoken.

I certainly agree with you. A successful run here in Austria is no guarantee that a comedy will also do well in Germany, which after all is our main market. Again an example from our own production. *Der Bockerer II* was the most successful Austrian film of this past year. Yet I've not been able to place the film with a distributor in Germany. Its idiom is too strongly Viennese, its tone of language, and even the story itself. Another example is *Indien*, a domestically successful film produced by a colleague at Dor-Film. This film did make it to the movie houses in Germany, it was heavily promoted and raised high expectations. But it also did not turn out. Yet another example would be *Freispiel* directed by Harald Sicheritz. Our experience suggests that Austrian humor is not the same as German or Swiss humor. Of course, we could simply accept this and say with relief, thank God, we don't really want German humor in our films. But then we have a problem marketing our films. Making films is an expensive enterprise and somehow one has to recover the cost of the productions. And then, of course, there remains the question, why Austrian comedies of the fifties, films with Paul Hörbiger or Hans Moser, did just as well in Germany as here in

Austria. This may be too simple an answer, but I'm inclined to say that they were successful because they transported emotions that could be understood anywhere. Stories with emotion, with a Viennese flavor, to be sure, but not too much of it. That is my tentative explanation. It is notable and perhaps symptomatic that among the films that have a humorous aspect and that were successful internationally are the films by Houchang Allahyari, a film director of Iranian descent. Perhaps he has a more cosmopolitan access to humor and wit, a broader cultural sensibility.

Reaching a larger audience with films has been possible by showing them on television, but film and television have had an uneasy relationship.

Well, it is essential to recognize that specifically as a medium for the arts, television has run its course. As I see it, television is primarily an information medium, and only to a much lesser degree a medium that demands of us any artistic quality in our productions. Once you understand this, you no longer take issue with the shift in programming. One simply has to adapt to this new reality, programming has become popularized in the same way that daily newspapers set standards that are different from those of a quality weekly journal. In order to survive in the multiplicity of program offerings becoming available, ORF (Austrian Broadcasting Corporation) must accept a degree of popularization. For this reason I personally have no objection to the new areas of activity. Fewer film adaptations, fewer quality plays made for television, but instead crime series that people want to watch, political satires, sitcoms, light entertainment, which is just as much of a challenge to produce. I'm certainly prepared to go along with this, I have no problem with it. If the cultural vacuum brought about by this new orientation were to be filled in with subsidized films, then there is really no loss to Austria. We can't after all regard ORF as a kind of vehicle for adult education; it did have that role once, but those times are now gone. Television no longer serves this purpose, it is not the right medium for it. For that reason it is important to say, yes, there is film, and that is where we set high artistic standards, that is where art is produced. I would not be in favor of using public funds to subsidize light entertainment, as is the case in Germany. That would seem to be a subsidy on economic grounds, rather than a subsidy of culture. It is important to see that, and for that reason the discussion regarding television is no longer relevant for me. I don't regret this development, there is no demand for the kind of programming that worked in the past, we have to go with the market, we have to go with the times. There was a time when quality plays made for television were most important and inspired and stimulated the entire cultural scene, it had a place for writers, first-rate actors and actresses. It was a particular art form which now has become popularized.

You seem to suggest that film should not only be regarded as a commodity for entertainment, but that it also serves an important function in defining cultural identity, a role that should be subsidized. This special status is persuasively argued in stand:bild. drei, *published by the Association of Austrian Film and Video Producers. What should this position paper achieve?*

I was instrumental in starting this initiative, and I will therefore gladly comment on its goals. The Austrian film industry is working to establish a lobby to represent its interests in government and relevant ministries. For this purpose we produced documentation that includes analyses, proposals and strategies for strengthening the Austrian film industry so that it will remain competitive in the international context. That is what we set out to do. *stand:bild. drei* in particular takes a position on Austria as a center for film production. *stand:bild. zwei* has to do with legal matters. We also consider how tax incentives can be used to open up new financing resources. Thereby easing the subsidies by the state. Our initiative has been very well received, it is an effective instrument for putting our case before relevant agencies and indeed the public. I should like to add that we are very proud of our system of subsidies, it works well, and with periodic adjustments it has been effective and has truly sustained the film industry in Austria with its reality of a small market for films. By comparison to some other European countries, we are doing very well. It has enabled us to hold on to a very impressive pool of truly talented film artists, not only for Austria, but for the cultural enrichment of Europe and beyond.

A final word?

Yes, it seems to me that quite apart from commercial considerations, films should convey a sense of humanity, democratic principles, and tolerance for the complex world we all live in.

Comedy and Cultural Identity

Interview with Niki List

Recognition and public acceptance of the New Austrian Cinema was greatly enhanced by the exceptional box office success of *Müllers Büro* (Müller, Private Detective; 1986), a musical parody of the detective genre directed by Niki List. List has directed feature films, documentaries and television dramas that have received numerous awards at film festivals. In his most recent feature film, *Der Schatten des Schreibers* (*The Poet's Princess*, 1995), he elegantly takes up the Pygmalion theme; currently he is completing *Helden in Tirol*, a musical parody of the *Heimatfilm* genre. List is producer and managing director of Cult-Film. He has played an important role in representing the interests of the film industry with the Austrian Film Institute and the Austrian Film Commission; he has served as vice-president of the Association of Austrian Feature Film Directors.

Müllers Büro *set a benchmark for attendance, it was an enormous success. How do you account for its popularity and how well was your film received in other countries?*

First I should mention the matter of language. Films that are not done in English have a large handicap on the international market. In the European Union there are initiatives to compensate for this disadvantage, attempts to counteract the dominance of the American film distribution network. As for *Müllers Büro*, it was a hit in Austria and it had a very good run internationally as well; interestingly enough it had excellent success in Japan. Why was it popular? Perhaps because it works on several levels. It is a film for the cinéaste. There are something like a hundred quotations and allusions embedded in the film, references to the gangster movies of the thirties and others as well. An audience that is not familiar with this film tradition is denied the pleasure of recognition, of recognizing the parody. For example, at screenings in art theaters the audience frequently bursts into laughter at places where the general audience would show no response. But the film can be enjoyed on its own merits as well, as its popularity shows. That then may be the reason; the film can be enjoyed on a variety of levels. I do not use this approach with *Der Schatten des Schreibers*, only one obvious allusion occurs, a reference to the asylum scene in *One Flew Over The Cuckoo's Nest*. With *Der Schatten des Schreibers* I tried to make a film in the French tradition, touched with the charm of a French film, its subtle humor.

Müllers Büro *is full of exuberance and fun. To what extent does this reflect the production atmosphere, how much of this was planned in detail?*

In principle *Müllers Büro* was carefully planned and it adhered to the screenplay quite closely. But, you know, we were young then, gags and witty lines occurred to us on the set, some of which we included. *Der Schatten des Schreibers* was more tightly controlled. I should mention that for all of my films I either write the screenplay or contribute to its ultimate shape. And as I work on the text, I do not see images and pictures, but rather a direction in which they are headed. That is I don't try to imagine what a particular picture might look like, but instead follow a sense what the picture should express. Since I generally don't know the locations and other details of the film in advance, the actual pictures take shape during the production itself.

Is it reasonable to say that your sense of humor has an Austrian quality, and what could that possibly mean?

A comparison to German humor might be a good way to start. People say that Austrian humor has more charm than German humor, that it has a lightness, that it makes its point with tongue in cheek, that it is self-reflexive. In the seventies and eighties filmmakers tended to search for suitable social problems on which they could then base their films. They made serious films addressing weighty issues, films that soon alienated the audience. I was one of the first to turn to comedy. It turned out that audiences liked to see comedies. More comedies were made. In the past few years we've had a string of comedies that were remarkably successful, and in fact, of late the trend has become somewhat inflationary, almost nothing but comedies are being produced nowadays. But the comedies served an important purpose, they opened up the market, so that now other genres may be well received. *Jenseits der Stille* is a magnificent German film that has to do with a deaf and dumb couple and their daughter who becomes a musician. This may be a first step in the direction of serious drama. But it is difficult to make generalizations about humor, since it seems so specific to each individual. I have had many offers from Germany to direct and frequently to direct comedies. But I can't warm up to these screenplays; even though they are being promoted as comedies, I don't find them in the least funny. I do understand what is intended to be funny, but it seems just too flat to me. I rather think that Austrian humor is closer to French humor than it is to German humor. At the Habsburg court French was cultivated, and there is the influence of the Jewish humor and the long tradition of the multicultural state; perhaps for that reason Austrian humor tends to be multifacetted.

With the prominence of ratings, television has an interest in films that attract a large audience, yet in Austria it is also supposed to have a kind of cultural mission. How do you see the relationship of television to film?

There is a distinct development in the programming of ORF that I consider to be misguided. It appears that the television drama, which in its artistic dimensions is closest to a feature film, is losing in support, every year its numbers are reduced. ORF tries to secure market share by offering the same categories and by the same means as do the private channels. But that is not likely to work, since private television has attained too powerful a position. That is, ORF should concentrate on what it does best, namely produce programs that are of high quality and that are culturally worthwhile. Once the soaps and series are adequately provided by the private stations and cable companies, then ORF may well come back to its strength. Some German television companies who used to rely on American entertainment products have in the meantime recognized that it costs little more to do their own productions, with the added benefit that such programming establishes an identity, a kind of corporate identity. They are beginning to include quality programs in their generally light entertainment. In fact, it can be maintained that the current boom in the German film industry in no small measure is due to these private television companies. When subsidies are used in this way, a multiplication effect occurs. North Rhine-Westphalia, for example, has invested a great deal of money in the media, with the result that private television stations like RTL have now located in Cologne. It used to be that Munich, Hamburg and Berlin were the centers of media production, but now the center of activity has shifted to Cologne. By contrast, in Austria there is talk of reducing the subsidies, while at the same time ORF is reducing its production. The Austrian film industry is thus threatened from two directions; these are difficult times for filmmakers. Since Austrian resources no longer suffice for the financing of feature films, co-productions have become almost unavoidable. My current project, for example, is a co-production with financing from three countries. The European Union has established an agency, MEDIA II, with the intention of supporting just such collaboration. However, there seems to be a trend towards the globalization of the film industry; that is, there are more American-European co-productions than ever before, where the European producer is now coming to be regarded as an equal partner rather than as a provider of services in a colonial context.

In the co-productions, when you work together with producers from different countries, does this not dilute what is specifically Austrian in the project? Does MEDIA II require a variety of locations, actors and actresses from different countries?

Not in our experience. Regional films, films that retain the flavor of

Comedy and Cultural Identity 77

a particular area tend to be the most successful. They retain their cultural identity. It would, of course, be a mistake to take a French actor for one role, an English actress for another, an Austrian for yet another and so on, just for the sake of parity, it would be a confusing mess. In general one can say that European co-productions retain a cultural frame for a film. Co-production then mostly concerns financing, with a reciprocal understanding for subsequent projects.

Well-known actors and actresses, celebrities, improve the marketability of a film. How does this work in Europe, where you have so many regional markets?

Yes, certainly in America the star system is a crucial factor for the film industry. This also existed in Germany until the thirties, and to a certain extent it still exists in the France of today, given its strong film industry and general high regard for this art form. In Germany a number of film personalities have emerged that are well known, Til Schweiger, for example, or Katja Riemann. But we have nothing comparable to that Austria. In addition to that, we have the language barrier between countries, which constitutes yet another obstacle.

To return to the matter of comedies. Your films draw on reality, but do not attempt to represent it directly. There are situations that we all recognize, but then you filter these scenes and recombine them in interesting new ways.

I believe that every film needs to create a world of its own. Realism in film is not possible, since film necessarily takes a position, whether by choice of location or camera perspective, and thereby creates a world that is different from that of its constituent components. Films have a perspective or point of view; there can be no objective representation of reality. And in creating the film world I use all means accessible to me.

By presenting the spectators with such a singular world, you challenge them and invite their participation as they enter this world. It is not simply a matter of sitting in the comfortable chair of a theater and for two hours enjoying the fun and wit on the screen in front of you. To be sure, there are many details that one has come to expect from the genre, but then there is also another level of surprises.

Certainly the element of surprise is an important ingredient in comedies and perhaps in all films, that the audience may develop a sense of familiarity as the film unwinds, but also is confronted with the unexpected, which then requires an active engagement. This element of surprise operates on all levels, including the flow of the screenplay, the shot selection, the choice of location, and especially in the editing phase it comes into play.

But that is not so, of course, for all comedies, not for The Sound of Music, *for example.*

A good example. *The Sound of Music* was originally a German-Austrian production called *Die Trapp-Familie*; this famous American film was a remake. Something that is done frequently, a remake of a successful European film is done, taking into account American taste. *The Sound of Music* is a *Heimatfilm*, a genre that is for German film what the Western is for the American cinema. The most popular genre in the fifties, with location in the Alps, the most common location for the *Heimatfilm*. My current project, *Helden in Tirol*, is a parody of the *Heimatfilm*, as *Müllers Büro* was a parody of the detective film. As the Western has certain stereotypes, the sheriff, the good guys and the bad guys and such, so the *Heimatfilm* has recurring characters and plot ingredients. The priest, the poacher, the beautiful virgin, the village fool, a group of stereotypes. In my film I retain the setting, but these figures assume a different role, they behave in an unexpected way. The poacher is the good guy, rather than the villain, for example. And the story is one that has often been told in the *Heimatfilm*, namely the intrusion of tourism into an idyllic Alpine community. The story takes place in a village that had been totally forgotten, in a little forsaken valley in

Tirol. The evil mayor tries to make a tourist center out of it. But by doing so, he sells out all traditional values. That is, I use familiar archetypes, but they play an unexpected role.

And I suppose there is a good deal of music?

Yes, almost half of the film is sung, this is another tradition in the *Heimatfilm*. In other words, here is yet another aspect with which I can work. In the past five or six years pop music discovered folk music. And just as pop music is now absorbing all kinds of ethnic traditions, there are musicians across Europe who are trying to remember their roots and who ask themselves, how much of this material they can use in their music so that it will still be understood internationally. What is there in my region that can be used. This has led to a resurgence of various ethnic instruments and traditional styles, and new combinations of these elements. The music in my film can be seen in this development.

Parables for Our Time

Interview with Werner Swossil

In the context of the film-television agreement of 1981 ORF (Austrian Broadcasting Corporation) plays an important role in the subsidy of Austrian film productions. As Artistic Director for ORF, Werner Swossil holds a pivotal position in the film industry. While he represents the interests of this large organization, he also has the reputation of being responsive to the artistic ambitions of writers and film directors. Over the years he has worked with many directors and writers, Axel Corti and Gerhard Roth among them. His delicate balancing act between program ratings for ORF and the individual creativeness of film artists has been most successful, as the many awards for his productions attest.

Feature films are an important ingredient in the programming of any television station. As contributor to the film subsidies, ORF has the television rights to many Austrian productions and thus benefits from this collaboration. How does this arrangement look from within ORF, particularly now that cable and satellite providers are beginning to penetrate the market?

I would like to begin with the premise that films for the movie theater as well as for television are forms of audiovisual communication, of dramatic audiovisual messages. Although they may deviate in detail, they amount much to the same thing. A dramatic narrative recorded on film stock can be projected in a movie theater or it can be converted and then transmitted in the form of television signals. Since the product is so similar, collaboration makes good sense, it is surely to the benefit of both media. As it is, a large part of programming consists of feature films; the expectation of this level of quality then necessarily also applies to in-house productions. As for the countless channels that are now beginning to bombard us from the skies, I rather see them as a challenge. Stations will need to develop a certain flair to entice people to tune in to them, they must seem like a home base to the viewer. When I switch to ORF, I do so because its programming, from news reporting to cultural presentations, is from an Austrian perspective. Only then can a small enterprise like ORF survive. It must have its own unmistakable image, an image that is attractive in its presentation.

Programming that projects an Austrian quality: how could one describe such Austrian quality in feature films or productions intended for the larger international market?

Given the dominance of American distributors in the European market, the international potential for Austrian films is rather limited. And what is Austrian about Austrian films? Perhaps only Austrians themselves would know! Apart from its geographical location, I would say that Austria has a history of accommodating different peoples and therefore a variety of cultures. This has shaped our life style and, of course, our arts. In the operettas, for examples, Hungarians, Czech or Slovenes tended to be stereotypes that represented the relationships with neighbors living within our borders. But more generally, I would say this conglomerate of cultures also produces an attitude that is more skeptical and tentative, and less imperious in its claims than you see, for example, in German literature. I would see Schopenhauer as the mentor of the Austrian mind, his mentality is most evident in the works of Nestroy. Nestroy's plays are less popular in Germany not only because of their language, but also because their characters are just not German. The skeptical disposition of his characters derives from Schopenhauer, a kind of disinterested perception, that is Nestroy. German literature always seems to have an agenda, such as in classicism or in the political dramas about German rulers. The goal was always to convey something concerning the people or the state. Austrian dramas did not really tend to do this.

Perhaps humor and comedy can be said to be specific to each culture. What then is Austrian humor? Now that comedies in film enjoy such popularity, it is of interest to know how well Austrian comedies do abroad.

Yes, there is Austrian humor, it is more relaxed in the way it deals with vanities and consequently it is also more dangerous. There is, of course, the plain Alpine humor, as country humor is anywhere. But in its developed form in the city it can be bitter and malicious, inflicting injury more on oneself than on others, and it is succinctly formulated. Karl Kraus' *Die letzten Tage der Menschheit*, for all its tragic elements, is Austrian humor. The tragic dimension is to be found in all good humor, only bad humor does not have it. That is the difference between Charlie Chaplin and Jerry Lewis: one makes faces and jumps around, while the other is a person threatened in his very existence. And if you take the tragic as ultimate basis of the self, and as basis for humor and wit, then that would seem to be specifically Austrian. With a certain suicidal flavor.

Films based on cabaret acts and featuring cabaret performers are much in vogue just now.

The current crop of cabaret films seems to foreground characters that are losers. And as these films illustrate, Austrian humor is not pure in genre. *Indien*, one of the most popular films of the past few years, begins as slapstick comedy and ends as tragedy. It involves the tragic loss of a newly won friend. And even from the deeply tragic end a humorous element is then extracted.

Popularity on the domestic market is an important step to a film's success elsewhere. If humor is specific to each culture, how then does this affect co-productions, particularly given the various initiatives of the European Union?

The attempts to find a common film language for all of Europe have failed in television. Seven European television companies using four different languages had set up a European production company.

This attempt has not brought any convincing results. With regard to co-productions in Europe, I would say that it is difficult enough for two partners to come to terms. Precisely because humor is regional, because the Swiss and the Austrians, for example, laugh about different things; it is a large obstacle to overcome. What may be utterly funny for one viewer, may be an affront for another. Basic episodes drawn from fundamental emotions and constellations familiar since the commedia dell'arte can, of course, be understood everywhere. But even here, humor only arouses interest if it has local color or authenticity, if it is regionally characterized. A well-made French film about a love triangle will be different from one made in Hungary. But one can accept it and get to know something about one's neighbors. But to have a common emotional basis or sensitivity for the formal aspects of art, that I cannot imagine. Still, regional authenticity seems to be a prerequisite for successful film productions and should be retained in the European context.

Crossing cultural bounds can, of course, also take place between different forms of cultural expression. Television in particular seems to have supported film adaptations, the crossing from literature to film. Why are they made, how are the texts chosen?

Film adaptations can be considered successful only if they transfer the spirit of the literary work into the other medium. In principle, they are to be welcomed, because even passable film adaptations can convey the idea of literary works and may promote the desire to read. Certainly a film adaptation cannot be a substitute for reading the work itself. In the eighteenth or nineteenth century there was an English writer who converted Shakespeare's plays into large novels. That is, he trivialized in order to bring the reader to the original text. At that time the novel was the popular medium of its time, as television is today. That is how I see film adaptations. They expose viewers to the subject matter, introduce them to literature, with the hope that they will then read the texts themselves.

Because of its concrete visual representation, film or television then projects one possible interpretation of the work.

Just as *Romeo and Julia* is produced differently at every theater, so the interpretations of film directors, of course, are their private conceptions. One has learned to accept thousands of *Hamlet* stage interpretations, but for a film adaptation there is usually only one. This brings us back to the matter of Austrian qualities in a creative work. Austrian literature tends towards prose, to epic forms rather than to drama. This prose tends to be self-reflexive, even in its humorous elements. An adaptation of such a work requires a specific film language, a language which does not correspond with the language of the dominant cinema, with the conventions of films produced in Hollywood. Now a great many American films are based on novels. That does not appear to be problematic, because American literature seems to be more given to realism and has a stronger dramatic flow. This is a significant difference from Austrian works.

By what criteria does ORF choose texts for adaptation, are there general policies or guidelines?

Every case is considered on its own merits. I should say, however, that given the size of Austria, there is very good communication between writers and directors. And in this on-going discussion the interests and phenomena of our time are shaped into stories that are readily understood and that serve as parables for our contemporary world. These stories then form the basis for the films. Whenever I'm asked about such matters, I quote the famous passage from Hamlet's address to the players, in which he tells them that they are the abstract and brief chronicle of the time. That is, where he tells the players, how and what they are to represent, namely to bring history to the stage with the eyes of the present and as example of the present. That in general is also our guideline, writers and filmmakers know that and everybody then brings us their version of such a project.

A facility that at one time was part of ORF, the Rosenhügel *studios, are now being developed with the intention of making Vienna once again an attractive center for film production in Europe.*

Yes, the enterprise was founded for this reason—*Filmstadt Wien*—and its promoters are firmly convinced of its potential. The old studios were renovated and brought up to the standards of today. There are not only studios, but as in an industrial park, there are provider companies on location, whose services can be booked for film production. And since the beginning of 1996 this facility has been in operation. I understand that the studios and workshops have had excellent bookings. Of course, Vienna as a city has a great deal to offer for filmmaking, and this initiative therefore would seem to make good sense.

What project are you currently working on, what project have you recently completed?

To stay with the film adaptations, we have now produced or are nearing completion two interesting film adaptations, Gerhard Roth's *Der See* (The Lake), directed by Thomas Roth, and Kafka's *The Castle*, directed by Michael Haneke. Those were two large productions of the past year. At present we are preparing a film of the young Austrian writer Thomas Baum. And also a film that has to do with the Austrian ski girls. By ski girls I mean those young women who are born and who grow up in some small village in the mountains. And who have an exceptional aptitude for skiing. In time they are chosen for the Austrian national ski team. Suddenly they make a transition from a village of perhaps one hundred souls into the large world. They go wherever the races take place, from Austria and Switzerland to Canada and South America. That constitutes considerable psychological stress for these young people. They are uprooted, suddenly tossed into the high life, for which, of course, they were not prepared. The careers of such ski stars is very short, there looms the ever-present question of where it will lead, what the future will bring at a certain age. And out of this complex of questions we are once again producing a film about conditions in our time, about the condition of our time in Austria.

3

The New Austrian Cinema

Films for Entertainment and Reflection

An Interview with Houchang Allahyari

Houchang Allahyari was born in Teheran. To further develop his early interest in film and theater, but also to study medicine, he went to Austria. He now has a medical practice in Vienna and also works as a psychiatrist for the prison system. To the public he is best known as an accomplished filmmaker. Following early experimental and avantgarde films, he collaborated with Epo-Film on highly successful feature films that have been screened at international film festivals: *Pasolini inszeniert seinen Tod* (*Pasolini Directs His Death*), 1985; *Borderline*, 1989; *Fleischwolf* (*Meat Grinder*), 1990; *Höhenangst* (*Fear of Heights*), 1994. *I Love Vienna*, 1991, was the Austrian entry in the Academy Awards. In 1997 Allahyari completed *Black Flamingos*; his current project is called *Geboren in Absurdistan* (*Born in Absurdistan*). Allahyari has also directed films commissioned by ORF, the Austrian national television network: *Und morgen der Opernball* (*And Tomorrow the Ball at the Opera*) 1992; *Der Tag, an dem sie Jack Unterweger fingen* (*The Day They Caught Jack Unterweger*) 1992; *Eine tödliche Liebe* (*Deadly Love*), 1995.

Your film I Love Vienna *was awarded the "Golden Ticket" as the most successful Austrian feature film of 1992; it was the Austrian entry to the Academy Awards for the "Best Foreign-Language Film." In this film you explore the multicultural dimension of Austrian life, and you do so with humor and satirical aplomb. If you were to make this film today, would you need to make changes, would there be a different undertone?*

I'm afraid so, yes. Particularly with the events in Bosnia, Austrians have become apprehensive about foreigners, about the part that foreigners play in Austrian life. It seems to me that with the changed attitude to questions of migration and asylum, xenophobia has become far more prevalent. Foreigners are treated differently now, they meet with less compassion. In this circumstance I can't very well make a film that is all fun and joy, even if I give it the cloak of a comedy. For some time now my son and I have been working on a screenplay that resembles that of *I Love Vienna*. But it was conceived in a rather different mood, I just can't imagine it as a comedy. The film is called *Geboren in Absurdistan*, but of course, it concerns Austria. It is a story of mistaken identity. In a maternity ward two babies, one Austrian, the other Turkish, are inadvertently switched. In accordance with current law, one of the babies is extradited to Turkey, but of course, it is the wrong baby, the Austrian baby. This then allows me to explore the regulations that determine the status of foreigners in Austria and in other European countries too. Most of all, the children of foreigners are of concern to me, the so-called "Second Generation." They are born in Austria, but are not considered Austrian citizens, they are treated as foreigners. These young people have no voice in the direction that their life may take. To return to your question: yes, today *I Love Vienna* would have to be a different film.

In your films you seem to open a view from the margin, you reveal the workings of Austrian society by showing the everyday problems encountered by foreigners, by prisoners, by the disenfranchised. Is this at the heart of your work, your principal concern?

First of all I should say that I derive the themes of my films from an environment that I know well, from the experiences that every day brings anew, from the problems which confront people I've come to know. This detailed and intimate knowledge gives me the courage to make these films and to know that they are right. For some years now I have been working as a psychiatrist in a prison, helping inmates deal with an institution whose harsh realities are not generally known to the public. I know of their hopes and fears, and

I know of the conditions that inmates must endure. *Fleischwolf* has to do with prison life, and *Höhenangst* tells the story of a young man released from prison, now stigmatized, now an outsider, someone who needs reassurance and a caring hand, who needs love. And who finds it not in Vienna but in a small village in the mountains. And so through the prison experiences and the subsequent release he too becomes alienated, a stranger in his own land. Such a confrontation of cultures is also central to my film *I Love Vienna*. In this case I wanted to bring two cultures together, to show up their beliefs and values, yet avoid the antagonism and aggression that so easily springs up. At heart I'm an optimist, and I try to instill this optimism and hope in my films as well, even if that may seem utopian. Better that than to show hate and aggression, which surely can't lead to anything worthwhile. Hope, compassion, love, yes, and the touch of humanity in the small details between people. The film that I've just completed, *Black Flamingos*, is such a satire, a black comedy really.

Your films address serious issues, but without heavy-handed lessons and without overly simple solutions; made with a light touch, your images linger and provoke.

I intend for my films to be seen: people should go to the cinema, they should enjoy the film that is screened, and they should take something away with them, something to think about. It seems to me that films that treat serious matters predominantly in a grave manner will only attract an audience that already supports a cause; they preach to believers. With my films I would like to bring a broader audience to the movies. To accomplish this, the films need to be enjoyable to begin with, but with impressions and insights that are not forgotten once the showing ends. They are films that entertain and that have something to say. *Höhenangst*, for example, is about a decidedly serious matter, but the film is also full of humor and human warmth. You can laugh along with the characters, feel their happiness and their sadness. And then you can have your own thoughts on the matter. I don't make festival films. I can well imagine that with my training in psychiatry I could make films that would be strong contenders at festivals. But I don't think of festivals when I set out to make a film.

The Austrian film market is rather small, therefore the financial success of its films depends to some extent on the larger markets abroad. How well do Austrian comedies and films in general cross borders?

Yes, I believe that it is possible to make films that are understood and appreciated in other countries. Austrian films will have success and will be accepted when they have a signature, when it is evident that the subject matter and style come from Austria. It would surely be misguided to try to imitate fashions and trends from abroad.

You said earlier that you derive your themes from the environment in which you live. Are you equally receptive to your team, to the cast on location? Is this approach reflected in your style of directing?

Making a film involves several stages. Once the project has been approved, I make plans, of course. But you could say that the storyboarding mostly takes place in my head, I have a very clear idea of the sequences and selection of shots. Then we search for a suitable location. But alas, locations were not made with my film in mind, and I therefore have to change the story to fit the location; new possibilities arise and a new set of images. At this stage I discuss the details of the film with my cinematographer and we work out the shooting script. And finally, once we are set to begin, it may happen that all the thoughts and plans of the preceding months no longer seem right; as it all comes together, the set and the cast, out of conversations, I may then make substantial changes. And so it is with the dialogues, instead of insisting on the text, I frequently ask the actors and actresses to improvise. That is exactly what happened in *I Love Vienna*. Yes, if I feel that it is appropriate, I give the actors and actresses a great deal of leeway; in this collaboration they then think along with me, contribute ideas for shaping shots, and then perform their part. Take *Höhenangst*, for example. Leon Askin, whom I had met at a film festival and who had decided to return to live in Vienna, was amazed by this approach. And thrilled. In all his acting career he had never encountered anything like it, he said. That I'm told what to do and what my role is, but not what I'm supposed to say. That I'm supposed to produce my part out of a sense for the emotional tone of the role. Forget the dialogue you read last night, and say what you feel now. He adapted quickly and happily and, as it turned out, he did an excellent job in the role.

Directing as a dynamic process.

Yes, making a film is team work, I try to tap into the creative potential of all participants. This kind of team work can be compared to group therapy in which the leader also cannot intercede, for then it would all fall apart, nothing would be accomplished. The result is more emotional depth and more authenticity. Improvisation and spontaneity, of course, has its downside as well. To the dismay of the editor, the shots don't always correspond to the script; this makes the editing job so much more complex. But when creativity has a certain momentum, then you can't very well break off to follow the script, that can't be good for the film. I'm not a director with script and shooting schedule in hand.

Lovable Foreigners: Gestures of Cross-Cultural Embracing in
Austrian Film

Jutta Landa
University of California, Los Angeles

"You (Du) speaking German good," the sleazy owner of the *Hotel am Praterstern* in Houchang Allahyari's *I Love Vienna* compliments his guest Ali Mohamed. "But you (Sie) don't!" is the Persian immigrant's terse repartee. Mohamed's retort cleverly exposes the hotel keeper's underhanded compliment as a gesture of condescension. Pidgin German and especially the familiar form of address ("Du") are ubiquitous devices for belittling and marginalizing foreigners in a country that esteems propriety and well understands the insidious edge of language. By using correct German and the courteous form of address ("Sie") Mohamed turns the tables on the hotel owner and teaches him a lesson in good manners, thereby evading the intended degradation.

Houchang Allahyari's *I Love Vienna* (1991), Anton Peschke's *Zeit der Rache* (Time of Vengeance, 1990), and somewhat unexpectedly Paul Harather's *Indien* (India, 1993) all deal with migrants who are disadvantaged by their foreignness and ethnicity, yet struggle to gain footing and respect in a hegemonic Austrian culture. While Allahyari's and Peschke's films overtly deal with the topic of culture clashes, *Indien* on the surface appears as a mere cabaret film, showcasing two popular Austrian cabaret artists, Josef Hader and Alfred Dorfer, who deliver gags and exchange pointed dialogue. A closer look, however, reveals that the film is in fact preoccupied with Austrian prejudice towards other cultures. Each of the three films presents a different ethnicity, Persian, Turkish, and Indian. All three films make use of standard entertainment patterns, with *I Love Vienna* and *Zeit der Rache* relying heavily on love and crime themes, while *Indien* adheres to an odd couple formula. The films were quite popular, had good attendance figures and were all nominated as Austria's official entries for the Academy Awards for Best Foreign Film. However, box office success is not synonymous with the accomplishment of such humanitarian goals as the unbiased presentation of alterity and ethnicity. The cinematographic apparatus, collaborative techniques and genre-orientation all move film towards reduction and bipolar narration. Especially comedies about culture clashes thrive on binary oppositions between guests and host cultures. They posit a dominant majority against which the minority culture is defined (Peck, 203-04). Thus a film narrative that portrays foreigners as lovable does not necessarily escape the pitfalls of stereotyping or exoticising. Both strategies ultimately amount to exclusion.[1] With this problematic in mind, the films under discussion will be analyzed as humanistic projects that aim to replace the discourse of exclusion with gestures of cross-cultural embracing. Cross-cultural embracing, however, goes beyond the acceptance of the foreigner, in that it extends an invitation to stay in the host country. Through their symbolic texts of welcome or expulsion Allahyari's *I Love Vienna*, Peschke's *Zeit der Rache*, and Harather's *Indien* participate in the recent public debate on immigration.

In the nineties *Fremdenhaβ* and *Ausländerfeindlichkeit* (hostility towards foreigners) were on the rise in Austria, particularly in Vienna.[2] With the opening of Communist Europe, Austria became a host country for asylum seekers from Eastern European countries. Other migrants from African countries such as Nigeria stayed after their development aid contracts had expired. Meanwhile the existing *Gastarbeiterproblem* (migrant workers problem) had not disappeared. The second generation of Italian, Yugoslavian, and Turkish immigrant workers was now entering an already tight job market. In addition, the war in Yugoslavia dramatically increased the number of refugees seeking shelter in Austria. These developments, paralleled by economic setbacks, resulted in a widespread fear of foreign influx. Jörg Haider's Freedom Party capitalized on this fear. In November 1990 at the elections in Vienna, Haider's motto "Österreich ist kein Einwanderungsland" (Austria is not an immigration country) contributed to his victory. Haider's landslide jolted the other parties into introducing new laws against foreigners. Applicants now had to document residency, employment, and appropriate accom-modation. Furthermore, applicants had to prove that they were politically persecuted in their homeland. These laws, adopted and enforced under the Secretary of the Interior Franz Löschnak, led to widely reported instances of hardship or even harassment of applicants. It is in this climate that the films under review were made, obviously in an attempt to counterbalance what was perceived as Austrian xenophobia.

The widespread appeal of Houchang Allahyari's *I Love Vienna* is mirrored by its official recognition. Awarded the "Preis der Österreichischen Filmtage 1992" the film was praised as "a successful contribution to the current discourse on increasing xenophobia"[3] that characterized modern man's migratory existence.[4] On the other hand the director also received the Nestroy Ring for the valorization of specifically Viennese qualities. The awards are descriptive of the film's polarized attempt to paint a positive picture of the Viennese—the host culture— while giving voice to a foreign culture that professes its love for Vienna (as Ali does, when asked to justify his application for legal immigrant status). The foreign culture is represented by the film's protagonist, the Iranian Ali Mohamed, a German teacher, who emigrates to Austria with his sister Mariam and his 15-year old son Kurus because he does not want his son to be drafted. This rather weak premise allows Allahyari to avoid the denunciation of his own country. While vaguely hinting at the Islamic Revolution by merely alluding to possible warfare, Allahyari avoids implicating Iranian fundamentalism in any wrongdoing.[5] Ali does commit some verbal blunders. But by making Ali a German teacher, Allahyari empowers his protagonist, avoiding the crass, self-insulting clichés of language incompetence, a danger in any film about immigrants. Ali's ideal image, nourished by a diet of *Sissi* films, of a resplendent monarchical Austria, is soon shattered, as he finds himself harassed by ticket-writing police, a greedy hotel owner, an arrogant lawyer, money-oriented doctors, and last but not least, a sexually promiscuous environment that threatens to corrupt his sister and his son. Taking rooms in a cheap hotel for foreigners in Vienna's 2nd District, it does not take him long to realize that he is in a red-light district where whores cavort with asylum applicants and illegal immigrants.

Things go awry as he tries to impose his strict orthodox beliefs on this liberal, secularized world. The ensuing culture clash leads to the film's many incongruous and thus comic situations, aptly described in one review as "islamic chicken topped with whipped cream" (Franz 26). For example, Ali's Islamic religion forbids him to have sex with a woman unless he is married to her. He therefore performs a three-day Islamic marriage ceremony, only to be thoroughly scandalized when he finds out that the love-hungry Marianne has lied to him and has not yet gotten her divorce from Swoboda. Similarly, his scruples forbid him to pretend he suffered religious persecution in his home country, when such a ruse, on the advice of his Viennese lawyer, would greatly facilitate his visa application. It is within these intercultural relations that Allahyari steps around in a minefield. His goal is fairness: "I hope that it is one of the stengths of the film that I critically deal not only with the Viennese, but also with my protagonist, who is made to do some learning" (Wagner, *Salzburger Nachrichten* 11). In spite of the director's assurances, the film's purported equilibrium leaves the foreign culture vulnerable. Thus the rare Islamic mock marriage (originally intended to provide legitimate status to a possible offspring, an explanation that is not given in the film, but in an interview with Heinrich) appears as a routine hypocritical maneuver which solely serves Persian men's sexual appetite. Ali's verbal abuse of Marianne, repeatedly calling her a whore, makes him hopelessly misogynous in our eyes. No wonder reviewers like Ruth Rybarski read the film as a corroboration of their own wholesale rejection of Islamic traditions, "whose character now clearly reveals itself here in the occident. They are pigheaded, medieval and stubborn—and also a bit romantic" (104).

In contrast to Iranian inflexibility, Viennese behavior towards the refugees, while disrespectful and exploitative at times, is always tinged with good naturedness and proverbial Viennese charm. Even the miserly Swoboda offers to make a phone call on behalf of the rebellious Polish psychologist in need of a job. Allahyari however refutes the accusation that his film is too mild: "I don't accept this allegation. I show bureaucrats who can be bribed, dim-witted policemen, I describe the appalling conditions in the hospitals. And when Hanno Pöschl as owner of the refugee hostel keeps on smiling, then that is the characteristic behavior of people who cynically exploit helpless fellow human beings, just as he does" (Wagner, *Wiener Zeitung*). Allahyari's other defense is his own biography. When asked why he made the film, he professed his love for Vienna:"[I] love...Vienna, truly. In contrast to some other foreigners, that may well be. But I have never had difficulties here. I feel utterly content. I say this quite openly" (Heinrich). Part of Allahyari's positive experience might have to do with the fact that he is happily married to an Austrian and has three children (two of whom act in the film). Thus it comes as no great surprise that the great equalizer in the film is love. Love makes Marianne prepare the chicken Iranian style, love overlooks cultural boundaries and embraces difference. Unfortunately, the film's emphasis on love leaves the question open as to what happens to those refugees that are not lovable.

Not only in its insistence on equal representation of the "faults of the Austrians and of the Iranians alike" (Heinrich), but also in its presentation of "oriental" sexuality, as embodied in the belly dance, the film teeters on the edge of stereotyping. The representation and indeed appropriation of the belly dance epitomizes our "enlightened" Western sexualized reading of oriental culture. Such a reading professes abhorrence of the harem and the veil as tokens of barbarism, while it succumbs to their erotic allure. A perfect example of the commodification of the exotic in the interest of profit, the belly dance has become a staple in dingy bars and strip clubs around the world. Thus a film that stoops to use the belly dance as the focus of erotic excitement betrays its ultimate exploitative intent. It is to Allahyari's credit that in spite of using the spectacle of the gyrating dance three times, he avoids fetishizing it, by choosing rather less than perfect performers. In fact, he counterbalances the belly dance, performed by an overweight Marisa Mell, with the more graceful, less sexualized, and much more difficult Persian dance that in Marianne's performance becomes an attempt to bridge the two cultures. He also stays away from eroticizing the veil as an invitation to explore forbidden sexual secrets in his presentation of Mariam, Ali's sister, probably because the actress is his own daughter. Nevertheless, the veil is still imbued with erotic magnetism, as the Polish refugee promptly falls in love with the veiled and silent Mariam. In fact, a close-up shot of what appear to be the mysterious dark eyes of a veiled Persian beauty serves as the catching opening scene of the film, an erotic promise whose mystique is quickly dispelled when the eyes turn out to belong to Mohamed's adolescent son. In spite of thwarting the audience's voyeuristic desires for exotic (here synonymous with erotic) gratification, the film remains exclusionary in its narrow focus on a transient Viennese subculture. Transition and migration are indicated by images of trains and cars (the car repair shop underneath the hotel) but also by the underworld milieu in which the story is set and in which the hotel is the only place that offers at least temporary stability. It is an underground composed of uprooted, dubious existences like Selina, the aging Rose of the Orient of Italian descent, or the crazed woman who envisions herself as the famous singer and belly dancer she might have once been. In this extended family of transients, acceptance and even embracing of the foreigner seems to follow naturally, but does this embracing reach beyond the subculture and if so, how far into the mainstream? Or is Austria just another *Hotel Praterstern*, where refugees are temporarily accepted, but then spit out again by a ruthless Swoboda? Thus Allahyari's film is a well-intended effort, not without moments of cultural insight, but overall it resembles the neon heart across the hotel: it flashes the message of love, but remains a mere advertisement for Vienna's dubious charm towards migrants.

Peschke's *Zeit der Rache* is set in the same underground milieu as Allahyari's film, possibly lower down. The film's title summarizes the main plotline: the boy Orhan (played by the twelve year old Cumhur Vural) travels from Anatolia to Vienna to take blood revenge on the driver who killed his father in a car accident. In the course of his voyage he realizes that the culprit is not a murderer, and abandons the idea of revenge. The end of the film finds him back home in Anatolia. Superimposed on this culture conflict is a love triangle story between the belly dancer Silvie, Werner, the unscrupulous owner of a nightclub, and the honest but down and out violinist Roberto (Otto Sander). Orhan becomes the outside force in their conflict, as especially the belly dancer and the violinist (who turns out to be the driver of the car that killed his father) take him in. By contrasting Orhan's innocence with a milieu of sleaze and porn, Peschke elicits the audience's sympathy for the lovable little foreigner in his Turkish trousers. Nevertheless the film does not rise above stereotypes.

Peschke visually posits a binary cultural opposition by taking us on location to Anatolia to observe the harsh conditions of Orhan's sheep-herding clan, where blood revenge apparently still rules. In spite of the film's several superimpositions that facilely fuse the two cultural landscapes, the cultures can never communicate as is indicated by Orhan's muteness throughout most of the film. While the gesture of the outsider who merely looks in on the host culture is meant to increase our sympathy for Orhan, he remains excluded and eventually returns home. Somewhat disturbingly, the love triangle story conflates the problems of foreigners with those of underachieving artists like himself, for whom Peschke professes the same undivided concern.[6] Even though Peschke claims in the press book that he never intended to make a film solely about blood revenge, the cheap thrills provided by the blood revenge motif (misunderstanding, misrecognition, misfired shots) take precedence over his plea for cultural understanding. This becomes especially noticeable in the belly dance scenes of the film. Although the connection between belly dancing and prostitution is unveiled when Werner asks his "Fatima of 1001 Nights" to be "friendly" to the influential guests, the camera happily coopts the seduction. Shot with the conventional techniques of fetishization and fragmentation, the belly dance, in Hollywood movie fashion, makes the diegesis pause to allow the voyeuristic gaze of the real film audience to fuse with the leering night club audience (including a mesmerized Orhan) in the film. Why Fatima *alias* Silvie emancipates herself from Werner by tearing off her black wig and performing an even more voluptuous belly dance is also not sufficiently explained. One suspects that the fact that a blonde is equally adept at wiggling her hips is less a cross-cultural embrace than an added allure. Here the film fails miserably to point to the Western exploitation of the foreign culture.

Similarly to *I Love Vienna* the culture clash in *Zeit der Rache* serves up funny moments, as when Orhan assumes from a postcard that his uncle owns the Ambassador hotel, when in fact he works there as a janitor in the basement. Cultural misunderstanding is also signified in the various displays of the *Riesenrad*, the ferris wheel in the Viennese Prater, the amusement park in Vienna's 2nd District, increasingly the haunt of illegal immigrants. A picture of the splendid *Riesenrad* guides Orhan to his destiny. But, signifying Orhan's disillusionment, its empty "houses" do not contain cakes for the dead, as his Turkish grandfather made him believe. The *Riesenrad* miraculously turns up again in the shape of a tacky music box in Silvie's apartment. In the final image of the film the broken toy, displaced onto the barren plains of Anatolia, magically lights up one more time under the smile of the grandfather. The image underlines the irritating irresolution of the film: is Turkish culture, embodied in the patriarch, in possession of deeper truths, or has it digested a Western lesson about the barbarity of blood revenge? The same ambiguity is spelled out in Orhan's mix of clothes. He wears traditional Turkish garb, over which he puts a man's coat with a European cut. The coat becomes a visual symbol of the child weighed down by the adult task of blood revenge, but it also spells out the film's uncomfortable culture mix, where a European overcoat imperfectly covers up ethnicity. Although the film through its strong identification with Orhan tries to drum up support for the Turkish culture, any gesture of cross-cultural embracing again remains confined to an underground milieu. The erotic promise a half-naked Silvie's embrace offers to the boy is nothing less than disturbing. Only the disarray and lack of stability in their own lives—Robert lives in a wrecked bus, Silvie, after a fight with Werner during which he throws her out, hitches a truck ride to Turkey for Orhan and herself only to leave en route—allows them to briefly sympathize with the foreigners and their migratory existence.

The third film under review, the highly popular *Indien* seems to be quite different from the first two in that the protagonists are true-blooded Austrians. The press book summarizes the plot as follows: "Heinzi Bösel, a small town red neck and Kurt Fellner, a new age, eager beaver yuppie, travel together as restaurant and hotel health and food inspectors throughout the Austrian provinces. What starts as a trying and hostile relationships turns into a strong and loving friendship that remains true to the end ..."[7] Upon closer inspection it becomes clear that the odd couple formula is acted out against the backdrop of Austrian prejudice against foreign cultures. The first giveaway is the title of the film, *Indien*; it is in no way warranted by the film's bleak settings of Austria's Eastern provinces. Next, the occupation of the protagonists, hotel and restaurant inspectors, not only make for an itinerant life-style on the road, but brings them in close vicinity to tourism, another source of cultural confrontation. But it is the apparently senseless prattle of the dialogue that turns the entire film into a discourse on stereotypes. Most of the conversation between Bösel and Fellner revolves around foreign food, with occasional forays into other cultures' sexual habits, thus building a dense web of stereotypes and exotic trivia. The sharing of such gastronomic curiosities as "in India they eat nothing but rice, and laugh all the while, some of them starve to death," "the Japanese, for example, eat the soup at the end," "in the Philippines they are the worst, they eat warm monkey brains" lay the groundwork for the rapprochement of the two seemingly incompatible characters. Their bonding is celebrated in the climactic sequence of the film, when both men dance an Indian dance, a masculinized version of a belly dance of sorts, to Fellner's favorite Indian song. At the nadir of their relationship Fellner suffers the insidious and somewhat mysterious onset of what will turn out to be cancer of the testicles. After Fellner has died, the grieving Bösel has an experience that converts him to his dead friend's belief in reincarnation. An Indian *Kurierverkäufer* (newspaper hawker), his hair wound in a turban, sits down on a park bench next to him, playing Fellner's favorite song on a cassette recorder and offering him Fellner's favorite fruit, a banana. Bösel reads the message: give up your bias against foreigners, he could be your own countryman reincarnated. In spite of this erasure of cultural prejudice, the pantomime scene fails to make a prominent statement. Bösel's epiphany is not followed up by a gesture of embracing as he passively watches the stranger leave the transient space of the park bench. One also wonders whether the average Austrian can come to terms with its lovable foreigners only *in extremis*, as when confronted with death. In addition, the film can be faulted with crass misogyny: the bonding process of the men really does not come under way until Fellner is betrayed by his girlfriend, thus joining the ranks of jilted men. Their common hatred against women—Bösel, for instance, confides that he forces sex on his wife out of pure spite—does not qualify either one of them as messengers of cultural tolerance. Once more, the crossing of cultural bounds remains a half-hearted gesture confined to a fringe milieu.

In conclusion, one has to applaud the filmmmakers for actually addressing, on its home turf and with government funds, a topic as controversial as Austrian xenophobia. It is also to the filmmakers'credit that they give visual space to fully fleshed foreigners in their films and allow for their point of view. Yet, in spite of the good intentions, none of the films go to great length to contribute towards a hermeneutics of the foreign. Mixing ethnicity and alterity into popular plot formulae of crime and love and spicing them up with comical collisions makes the cultural content of the films palatable, yet less stringent. Also, by adopting a binary model the films involuntarily assert the elite culture's dominance over the immigrant culture. Furthermore, by focusing on the exotic the films ultimately exclude rather than embrace their foreign protagonists. This happens even in Allahyari's film which portrays its hero as a religiously overzealous man, who has to retrain in order to become acculturated. The film's end withholds information as to Ali's decision to emigrate to the United States, keeping him and the Austrian audience in limbo. Exclusion happens overtly in *Zeit der Rache* where the Turkish boy is sent home. *Indien*, which actually ridicules the overbearing attitude that lurks behind the accumulation and dissemination of cultural trivia, gives us only a speechless *Kurierverkäufer* with a very short screen life. Thus the films' respective endings provide no symbolic welcome, rather they offer mostly a return to the status quo, aptly visualized by the circular motion of the recurrent *Riesenrad* in two of the films. Most importantly, the very gestures of cross-cultural embracing that the films extend are belittled by the fact that they originate among the marginalized, almost as if contact with the foreigners contributed to their hosts being further ostracized. The temporary niche the foreigners can carve in such a milieu seems humble enough. One possible reason for the failure of the films to rise above cultural hegemony is that Vienna is a hopelessly mythologized social space (Palm), too burdened by its self-declared "Golden Heart" to function as a neutral backdrop. In the last analysis, with the emphasis of all three films on spaces of transition such as container trucks, hotels, cars, park benches, hospital beds, and the ubiquitous *Riesenrad*, Vienna appears as a large transit area, where foreigners are shuffled through in order to be conveniently sent on to new destinations.

Notes

1. This problematic is, of course, not limited to film, but applies to other modes of representation and even pervades the criticial discourse on cultural diversity. Thus Gökberg speaks of the "dangers of the neocolonialist mentality, in which the non-Western is either absorbed once again in the hegemonic structures of the Western or excluded as the remote exotic" (144).

2. That especially Allahyari's *I Love Vienna* was seen as a response to the xenophobic climate of the nineties is apparent in Wagenhofer's review.

3. Excerpt from the jury's rationale, mentioned in Steiner.

4. Cf."Wir leben in einem Jahrhundert der räumlichen und seelischen Verpflanzung." Excerpt from the jury's rationale, mentioned under the heading "Preis der österreichischen Film Tage 1992," in *Falter* 29 April 1992: 29.

5. In hindsight, such caution seems pardonable. Tragically, the film's popular Iranian actor, Fery Farokhzad, who was quite critical of the Khomeiny regime, was found murdered in his Munich apartment in 1992. Although no evidence has been found, the *ORF Programm* for 29 May - 4 June 1993, in advertising for its May 31, 1993 television screening of the film, claims that the actor was the victim of Islamic fundamentalists.

6. "Apart from the Turks, *Time of Vengeance* has a second marginal group—the artists and dreamers." Peschke in the press

release for the film, distributed by Dor Film Produktion.
7. Plot synopsis in "Indien der Film," pressbook, distr. by Dor Film.

Works Cited

Allahyari, Houchang, dir. *I Love Vienna*. Perf. Fery Farokhzad and Dolores Schmidinger. Epo-Film, 1991.
Franz, Veronika. "Huhn mit Schlag." *Kurier* 19 September 1991.
Gökberg, Ülker. "Understanding Alterity: *Ausländerliteratur* between Relativism and Universalism." *Theoretical Issues in Literary History*. Ed. David Perkins. Cambridge, MA: Harvard UP, 1991.
Harather, Paul, dir. *Indien*. Perf. Josef Hader and Alfred Dorfer. Dor-Film, 1993.
Heinrich, Ludwig. "Kultur-Aufprall am Praterstern." *Oberösterreichische Nachrichten* 14 February 1991.
Marischka, Ernst, dir. *Sissi* (1955), *Sissi—die junge Kaiserin* (1956), *Sissi—Schicksalsjahre einer Kaiserin* (1957).
Palm, Michael. "Die Gnadenlosigkeit des Schmähs." *Der Standard* 20 September 1991.
Peck, Jeffrey M. "Methodological Postscript: What's the Difference? Minority Discourse in German Studies." *New German Critique: Special Issue on Minorities in German Culture* 46 (1989).
Peschke, Anton, dir. *Zeit der Rache*. Perf. Cumhur Viral and Otto Sander. Dor Film, 1990.
Rybarski, Ruth. "Wien ist anders." *Profil* 23 September 1991.
Steiner, Ulrike. "Der Ball wird weitergespielt." *Oberösterreichische Nachrichten* 27 April 1992.
Wagenhofer, Philipp. "Ohne Penetranz für Toleranz." *Neues Volksblatt* 20 September 1991.
Wagner, Renate. "'Ich kann nichts machen, was ich nicht selbst erlebt habe.'" *Salzburger Nachrichten* 5 October 1991.
---. "Er liebt Vienna tatsächlich." *Wiener Zeitung* 22 Sept 1991.

Wohin und zurück (*Somewhere and Back*):
Perspectives on Axel Corti's Jewish Trilogy

Christopher J. Wickham
University of Texas at San Antonio

In the two decades preceding his death in 1993 at age 60, Axel Corti established himself as one of Austria's preeminent filmmakers. Specializing in television productions for ORF, Corti garnered numerous national and international prizes for his work.[1] In many respects Corti was as European as one could imagine. He was born in Paris in May 1933 to an Austrian-Italian father and a mother from Berlin with Polish grandparentage, and educated in France, Switzerland, Italy (South Tirol 1945), England, Germany, and Austria. Yet it is Austria and a dedication to Austrian cultural life which informs his life's work. Corti came to national prominence in the late 1960s with the weekly radio show *Der Schalldämpfer* (*The Silencer*), in which he appeared as what Egon Netenjakob calls a "literary lay-preacher of an indeterminate sort" (3). An enthusiastic defender of writers such as Thomas Bernhard and equally impassioned critic of the questionable attitudes of entrenched cultural potentates and their lackeys, Corti became on *Der Schalldämpfer* an important and engaging voice in the cultural forum of the late 1960s. By this time Corti had already made his first film *Kaiser Joseph und die Bahnwärterstochter* (*Emperor Joseph and the Railwayman's Daughter*, 1963), based on a text by Fritz von Herzmanovsky-Orlando.

Corti's fascination with things Austrian is reflected in this title and continues through his œuvre, whether his subject matter is Austrian history—*Der Bauer und der Millionär* (*The Peasant and the Millionaire*, 1977), *Wie der Mond über Feuer und Blut* (*Like the Moon over Fire and Blood*, 1981), *Radetzkymarsch* (*Radetzky March*, 1994)—, Austrian figures—*Der Fall Jägerstätter* (*The Jaegerstaetter Case*, 1971), *Der junge Mann aus dem Innviertel* (*The Young Man from the Innviertel*, 1973), *Der junge Freud* (*Young Freud*, 1976)—, or the work of Austrian writers—Peter

Rosegger's *Jakob der Letzte* (*Jacob the Last*, 1976), Gernot Wolfgruber's *Herrenjahre* (*Life at the Top*, 1984), Franz Werfel's *Eine blaßblaue Frauenschrift* (*A Woman's Pale Blue Handwriting*, 1985), Joseph Roth's *Radetzkymarsch* (1994). The centrality of Austria in Corti's work is evident also in his treatment of one of the most important stories of the mid-twentieth century: the fate of the European Jews under National Socialism.

This paper examines Corti's trilogy, *Wohin und zurück*, the story of the experience of Austrian Jews between 1938 and 1945. It asks three questions: what drives the narrative of the trilogy? what does the trilogy have to say about the experience of exile? and how does the trilogy relate to the ongoing debate on appropriate representation of Jews during the Third Reich? By means of this tripartite optic we can explore diverse points of entry into Corti's cinematic construct.

Wohin und zurück is the product of a ten-year collaboration between Corti and Georg Stefan Troller. The three films are based loosely on Troller's experience and follow the fates of Austrian Jews from the morning after the *Kristallnacht* (Night of Broken Glass) 9/10 November 1938, through the perilous flight across Europe to Marseilles, emigration to New York, the aimlessness of exile in an indifferent foreign city, to the return as liberator with the victorious US armed forces and the identity crisis of the stranger in his own land.

Part I, *An uns glaubt Gott nicht mehr* (*God Doesn't Believe in Us Any More*, made for TV in 1982), follows Ferry Tobler (Johannes Silberschneider), the seventeen-year-old son of a clothier, who witnesses the events in which his father is murdered and the aryanization of the family business. Accepting the offer of the local policeman, who for a price provides information on how to escape to Czechoslovakia, Ferry makes his way from Vienna to Prague and thence to Paris in the company of Gandhi (Armin Mueller-Stahl). This German nobleman, whose real name is Fritz von Gandersheim, escaped from Dachau where he had been imprisoned for anti-Nazi activities. Ferry and Gandhi are assisted by the half-Jewish Czech woman, Alena (Barbara Petritsch), who makes it as far as Marseilles with Ferry. Gandhi is captured due to a turn of bad luck in the

French countryside on the way south and dies in a German cell. At the end of *An uns glaubt Gott nicht mehr* Alena and Ferry are trying to board a ship bound for America when a French police raid scatters the would-be émigrés. Alena is caught, while Ferry is ambiguously held by the freeze-frame which closes the film, as he runs through the streets with a German officer's Mercedes bearing down on him.

As the second film, *Santa Fé* (1985) opens, Ferry Tobler has reached America but has no papers and cannot be admitted to the country. He drowns trying to save a desperate woman who, likewise without documents, has leapt into the sea. Ferry is replaced as Troller's surrogate by Freddy Wolff (Gabriel Barylli), whose fortunes we follow through the second and third parts of *Wohin und zurück*. Freddy's dream is to make his way to Santa Fe, where, he believes, people know no fear. Santa Fe remains a dream and serves as a metonymic signifier of the various dreams of the Jews in New York into whose circle this film takes us. In this group the photographer, Popper (Gideon Singer), from Prague waits for a letter containing a job offer from *Life* magazine; the actor, Feldheim (Ernst Stankowsky), waits for the call from Hollywood but has to content himself with performing as a barking dog on radio—until the chance comes to play—irony of ironies—a Nazi officer; the surgeon, Dr. Bauer (Heinz J. Klein), without knowledge of English can find no hospital that will employ him; the poet, Dr. Treumann (Peter Lühr), is forced to run a delicatessen but dreams of having his work recognized by Stefan Zweig. The frustrations and illusions of this group form the substance of *Santa Fé*.

Welcome in Vienna, the third film in the trilogy, was the only part made for cinematic release. Like parts one and two, it was a coproduction of ORF, ZDF, and SRG. Freddy Wolff has now joined the US army and at the beginning of *Welcome in Vienna* is part of the force overrunning the *Wehrmacht* in Alsatia in 1944. He meets Treschensky (Karlheinz Hackl), an Austrian fighting for the Germans, whom he recognizes as the custodian of his school in Vienna. Their paths cross repeatedly during the narrative as Treschensky establishes himself as the unscrupulous blackmarketeer and wheeler-dealer whose instinct for survival carries him seamlessly from *Wehrmacht* soldier to dynamo of the Lucky Strike economy and presumably to prosperity in postwar Austria. Freddy, meanwhile, can comprehend neither the willingness of the US army to tolerate, even sponsor, the Treschenskys, nor the Austria which shows him (Freddy) respect while he wears the uniform of the liberator but rejects him the moment he sheds it. His anti-Nazi idealism makes it impossible for him to exist in the real world of postwar Austria. But at the same time, he never unpacked his suitcase in New York and never became American in anything more than citizenship. At the close of the trilogy he is as homeless as was Ferry Tobler at its beginning.

The preoccupations of the trilogy shift from the focus in *An uns glaubt Gott nicht mehr* on the Jewish individual, Ferry Tobler, and his response to his circumstances, to the fate of the group in exile in New York of *Santa Fé* which has individual dreams but a shared predicament and lack of prospects, finally to the idealist individual, Freddy Wolff, in part three, *Welcome in Vienna*, who is defined less by his Jewishness than by his homelessness as an Austrian, an American, and a Jew with no place to call his own. In all three films the protagonists are marked by an aimlessness and passivity. Their fate is determined by the circumstances of their existence and, secondarily, by their response to those circumstances. Because they are, in general, weak willed and can never determine their own lot, they are in all cases more victims than agents of their destiny.

It is precisely this reactive quality of his characters which so intrigues Corti. "What really interests me," Corti said in an interview with *Der Standard*, is "[w]hat happens between people? What do they experience in extreme situations?" (Rebhandl). Netenjakob has referred to this preoccupation as Corti's "cineastic phenomenology" (11). Corti is interested less in extraordinary people than in the response of ordinary people to extraordinary circumstances. The theme pervades Corti's work, whether it is the undistinguished Trotta of *Radetzkymarsch*, the invertebrate Leonidas of *Eine blaßblaue Frauenschrift*, the self-serving Melzer of *Herrenjahre*, or the victim-turned-victimizer, Link, of *Die beiden Freundinnen* (*The Two Friends*); it is the attitude (*Haltung*) of these characters and their behavior (*Verhalten*) in given circumstances

(*Verhältnisse*) which is foregrounded in Corti's work. So it is also in the trilogy *Wohin und zurück*. "(We) intended to highlight facts and situations of a historic period of time and to display how everybody responds or, maybe, must respond to them, in his or her own special way" (Courtade).

The reactions of Corti's characters manifest themselves as much inwardly as they do in behavior. For this reason Corti's is a cinema of words with pictures rather than a cinema of plot and action. Inner states are revealed in dialogue, what happens between people emerges in the language they exchange. Judy Bloch traces this aspect of Corti's style to his theater background. Corti expresses the big picture by means of attention to relevant detail, "the doubts that change by the hour" and "the furtive exchanges and small treacheries that make life possible but not liveable in 'an age of ideologies.'"[2]

In all three parts of *Wohin und zurück* the dominant reactive response is fear. It becomes explicit in *An uns glaubt Gott nicht mehr* where Ferry Tobler and Alena on their way to Marseilles hide in a cowshed from a German patrol. Gandhi, Ferry's friend and Alena's lover, is dead. Ferry confesses, "I don't think I've ever not been afraid." Alena reacts violently to what she reads as an expression of self-pity and counters with "For yourself!" She proceeds to berate Ferry for his attitude of observer and resents his coldly taking notes while others suffer and die. But for Ferry this is a way of sublimating his fear and, as we know, without the note-takers—like Troller, like Peter Glinz in Theresienstadt, like Anna Frank—the legacy of this period of history would be greatly impoverished.

In the second film, *Santa Fé*, Freddy Wolff in exile in New York, has had enough of being afraid and yearns to reach Santa Fe, a place he has decided is free from fear because of its romantic image as a courageous outpost of the Wild West. Santa Fe remains a mere projection of Freddy's fantasy. In fact, he returns to Austria where his fears and his pain intensify to the point where he is incapable of decision and action. Severed from family and any place of belonging, and released from the army, he is as unable to commit to the new Austria as he was to America.

Corti liked to quote Franz Werfel: "Whatever happens in this life is a result of being afraid of pain" (Courtade). He builds this line into his film version of Werfel's short novel *Eine blaßblaue Frauenschrift,* whose protagonist Leonidas marries well and makes a successful career as a bureaucrat more by evading confrontation and conflict than by asserting ambition. So it is with Ferry Tobler and Freddy Wolff and almost all the other characters of the trilogy: the actor Kron (Georg Corten) carries cyanide capsules with him in case his pain becomes too great, Mrs. Shapiro (Monica Bleibtreu) in *Santa Fé* invents a son in Kansas City with whom she deceives her fellow exiles and herself and tries to alleviate the pain of her isolation by this deception, Sgt. Adler (Nicolas Brieger) in *Welcome in Vienna* takes the line of least resistance and renounces his communist idealism when he feels the pain of rejection from a Soviet officer: "Listen, I want to live now. Nobody ever wanted my hopes. So I'm looking for new ones."

The absence of triumphant idealism in Corti's films is striking. His figures are undistinguished, anti-heroic personages who have to deal with their circumstances as best they can, given their lack of fortitude. It is a losing battle; even the idealistic Dr. Treumann, who struggles valiantly to write good poetry and to complete a novel in exile in New York feels his language slipping away from him in spite of his best efforts to prevent it. But Treumann's idealism is entirely retrospective and his refusal to compromise absolute. For Treumann there can be no question of willful assimilation. Exile and New York are for him equated with the demise of true, noble feeling: "My book takes place in a time where people still had feelings. Not like here in this proletarian country" (*Santa Fé*). The line is reminiscent of Maria Braun's observation in Fassbinder's film about postwar conditions in Germany, "I think these are bad times for feelings." Interestingly, Maria speaks these lines in an American GI bar.

It is the Adlers, the Treschenskys, and the Feldheims, who survive in Corti's reality, those who adapt to the circumstances, show flexibility of attitude and modify their behavior. Morally impeachable they may be, but they are the survivors. In Adler's words, "One can live well enough without believing in anything"

(*Welcome in Vienna*).

The good German, Gandhi, one of the few principled, if powerless, characters in the trilogy, stands in defiance of Adler's position. In *An uns glaubt Gott nicht mehr* he had warned the detached and weak Ferry Tobler, "Watch out!... If you don't believe in anything anymore, you believe in the end that things don't concern you. That fate will make an exception for you." This is perhaps the strongest positive ethical statement of principle in a trilogy which otherwise paints a gray picture of the human condition. But it remains an exhortation and is never the determining force behind behavior. Indeed, Gandhi, who according to poetic justice, ought to survive—in spirit if not in body—does not triumph. Far from it. He is dispatched by the most arbitrary of circumstances. In a masterful scene of cinematic irony on a beautiful spring day in the countryside during his flight to Marseilles he is discovered by a French child. He jokes with her that he is a spy; her brothers take him to the *gendarmerie* which has just been taken over by the German troops. The idyll of the sunny French landscape contrasts with the life-and-death desperation of the wounded man who is betrayed by his own good humor. The innocence of the child becomes the tool of the Nazi thugs. The arbitrariness of fortune knows no good or bad. Idyll and catastrophe are separated by a whim of fate.

The interplay of *Haltung, Verhalten,* and *Verhältnisse* is illustrated in one of the final scenes of the third film in the trilogy, *Welcome in Vienna*. The scene, set at a skating rink in Vienna, encapsulates the dominant dynamics of the film: Freddy Wolff has shed his American uniform and thus his identity as a soldier; he is pair-skating with his actress girlfriend, Claudia (Claudia Messner), and is struggling with whether or not he can become an Austrian. Claudia, who is determined to make a success of her career in Austria, rejects him. As he takes off his skates, Claudia offers a pair to Adler, who as Cultural Superintendent in the US sector of Vienna will now be her sponsor—and presumably her lover. The indomitable Treschensky is busy doing black-market business and has reached an accommodation with Adler and the Americans. He is summoned off the ice by Austrian law enforcement officials who demand that he account for himself. The conversation soon turns to doing business as the inspector offers Treschensky confiscated saccharin. The skating party continues with the partners changed. A new power structure is in place where principles are a hindrance to survival. The visual metaphors of "skating on thin ice" and "sich aufs Glatteis begeben" suggest themselves, for such are the *Verhältnisse* at this point in Austrian history; such are the real conditions for these figures.

My second perspective on Corti's trilogy is related to the first. At issue here, however, is not so much the psychological, attitudinal, and behavioral response to circumstance, but rather the nature of the exile experience, of *Heimatlosigkeit* (being without a homeland) and its cinematic emplotment. At this point the question of the Jewish situation moves to the foreground. What does it mean to be forced from one's home into exile?

The individuals whose fate as a group Corti plots in *An uns glaubt Gott nicht mehr* and *Santa Fé* are characterized less by their Jewishness than they are by their status as expellees, exiles, and emigrants. We hear no Yiddish spoken, we witness part of only one religious ceremony (for Yom Kippur) in the French internment camp, and this is purely instrumental to show to what extent Gandhi and Ferry Tobler are prepared to demonstrate belonging to a group; we are party to no Jewish family life; at one point a Hebrew word is used as a shibboleth to establish identity, but there is no distinctive clothing or icons of Jewish cultural identity. Jewish resentments toward Gandhi, the German, surface in Prague at the emigration center, but otherwise, the signals are unobtrusive that this group is Jewish. And yet the spectator is never in doubt as to this fact. Corti and Troller succeed in identifying the group by its predicament and not by inherent characteristics or repeated visual or acoustic cues as to its identity. They are defined cinematically from without rather than within. And this indeed reflects the historical reality that Nazi policy decided who belonged to the group labeled as Jews and not the affected individuals themselves.

The cinematic aesthetic, especially of *An uns glaubt Gott nicht mehr*, accomplishes this definition from without with several consistent devices: The passage of time is marked by relentless clocking of the dates for each scene of the film. In many cases, these are the significant dates of the Nazi campaign: *Kristallnacht*, the dates of the advances into Czechoslovakia, Belgium, and France, the signing of the Ribbentrop-Molotov Pact, etc. At many of these points Nazi *Wochenschau* (Weekly Newsreel) footage is cut into the film, sometimes diegetically motivated when characters visit a movie theater and view newsreels, and sometimes inserted to punctuate the transition to a new scene. The original Nazi commentary is retained and its arrogant tone informs the atmosphere of the film. Radio news broadcasts of significant events serve the same purpose.

A more subtle device to identify the group of Jews from without is their reference to Hitler. Hitler is always referred to as "he," never by name. Perhaps no one wants to "speak of the devil," perhaps there is an unconscious resistance to dignifying him with a name, perhaps it is a gesture of pure defiance against the man who insisted on being lauded even in everyday greetings ("Heil Hitler"). But whatever the reason, this appellation serves to bond the group together.

The Jews of *Wohin und zurück* are defined as a group above all by their predicament, and Corti's primary interest lies in their response to this predicament. The predicament is loss of home, forceful deprivation of the means to live in the accustomed fashion. It has been said that the trilogy constitutes a counterpart to Edgar Reitz's TV series *Heimat* (1984), in fact Gernot Roll, the director of photography for Corti's trilogy, was also behind the camera for Reitz's project (S[auvaget]). Insofar as *Wohin und zurück* is about homelessness, what does the trilogy have to say about it?

The answer to this question with all its nuances comes in the dialogue of the trilogy rather than in its plot. The screenplay harbors numerous philosophical nuggets on the subject. In essence, they align with Alfred Polgar's statement: "Still a stranger in foreign lands, and now in time a stranger at home as well"(quoted by Groth). The observer, Ferry Tobler, asks early on in *An uns glaubt Gott nicht mehr*, when being questioned about his religion so that emigration assistance workers can assign him to an aid agency: "Do I have to belong somewhere?" The trilogy explores the effects of not belonging and not being able to belong. That fixed point of orientation and identity has been erased for these characters. Ferry is surprised when Gandhi says they may have to head to Uruguay. Ferry responds, "Uruguay? That's a long way," and Gandhi says, "A long way from where?" There is no geographical reference point any more. All that remains is life (in a biological sense) and the will to live; Marshall Fine commented in a review of the trilogy, "These people have their lives, but everything which made those lives meaningful has been taken from them." The meaningfulness of existence suddenly has to be defined differently or sought elsewhere. If "Heimat" has to do with place of security, activity, and identity, then it is indeed lost to these exiles.[3] Even the identity acknowledged by anti-Semitism is an identity, and it offers a measure of perverse security and group affirmation in its predictability and familiarity. But as Lissa Treumann (Doris Buchrucker) observes in exile in New York, even this is lost, "Over there we were all OK. In spite of anti-Semitism and all that. We had our proper face. And here we're all lost, all the way."

Georg Stefan Troller invokes Kafka in his attempt in an article in the *Frankfurter Allgemeine Zeitung* to characterize the experience of exile. "But the essence of it, this secret shame, which Kafka anticipated, [is] that from now on you will only act out your life, because you have become detached from your dwelling place on this earth." The sense of enforced isolation from reality is articulated at various points in the trilogy, as for instance in Freddy Wolff's line in *Welcome in Vienna* when he complains to his Austrian girlfriend, Claudia, that no one in bombed out Vienna understands what it means to be in exile. "It's as if you were cut off not just from your home, but from your own feelings. As if there were a big hole there." Typically, ties to "Heimat" are predominantly irrational, emotional bonds, and that one's trust in feelings should be shattered on losing "Heimat" should come as no surprise. Needless to say, Freddy, now an American soldier, does not win much sympathy from Claudia, whose city is in ruins and who is herself struggling to gain a foothold in a new life.

Troller's reference to "acting out living" and Kafka's insight into the hollowness of existence under such circumstances finds resonance in *Santa Fé*. One of the few exiles to find acceptable work in America is, in fact, the actor Feldheim, the man for whom "acting out living" is indeed "living." When Feldheim announces his success in finally landing a Hollywood role as a Nazi to fellow Austrian exiles assembled at the Cafe Eclair, he acts out his part and induces a screaming fit in Frau Marmorek (Dagmar Schwarz), whose experiences at the hands of the Nazis robbed her of her speech. In this scene the collision between "acting out living" and "living" is skillfully realized by Corti. In the same film illusion is held up to be the essence of America. The unreality of "if...then" defines American life for Mrs. Shapiro, who maintains an imaginary son in Kansas City. Feldheim calls her bluff and she must confess the deception, but adds, "If I had a son in Kansas then I would go there. And that is the true America" (*Santa Fé*). The mood of America is the subjunctive.

The idea of "acting out living" or "having to act out living" is implicit in the issue of language, which resurfaces at intervals in the trilogy: portentiously in Kron's rehearsal of Hamlet's life-and-death speech with poor English pronunciation *(An uns glaubt Gott nicht mehr)*, desperately in the poet Treumann's admission in *Santa Fé*, "I have lost the words"—as his old language and "Heimat" desert him and he is unwilling to play life in a new one, indecisively as Adler and Freddy Wolff switch between English and German in the late scene in *Welcome in Vienna* at a point where Freddy's crisis of belonging is at its peak.

The figure of Claudia in *Welcome in Vienna* provides two interesting links to the "home/being away from home/homelessness" complex, which I will refer to only in passing. On the one hand, she represents Mother Austria and serves metonymically as the homeland to which Freddy Wolff is drawn.[4] He is deeply attracted to her but the differences between them are too great. She is willing to work with old Nazis and to reach an accommodation with the Treschenskys and Adlers, where Freddy Wolff cannot forget so easily. In her emblematic embodiment of the Austria of 1945 she resembles Maria Simon in Edgar Reitz's *Heimat*, the essence of the nurturing, rural world from whom all the main characters spring and to whom they are all drawn back. We might, therefore, see Corti's trilogy, as Judy Bloch does, as a "Heimatfilm" for the homeless.

On the other hand, Claudia is an actress and thus belongs to the group which is adept at "acting out living" and is equipped to survive. More than that, however, her role as a performer integrates her intertextually into a running debate on how the predicament of Jews in the Third Reich and in the shadow of the holocaust can adequately be portrayed. Though Claudia is not Jewish, her involvement as an actress or performer in a Jewish story in the wake of the Third Reich places her in the wider context established by such films as *Mephisto, Lili Marleen, Cabaret,* and even *The Producers*—all of which utilize the theme of performance as a component in the representation of the Third Reich. I shall pursue this line of inquiry under the rubric of my third optic, the question of how Corti and Troller approach the issue of the aesthetics of portraying the Jewish experience in this historical context.

In his article titled "subject positions, speaking positions. from *holocaust, our hitler,* and *heimat* to *shoah* and *schindler's list*" Thomas Elsaesser broaches numerous issues relevant to the debate surrounding the cinematic orthodoxy of representation of the Jewish story in the Third Reich. Many of these issues offer access points to Corti's trilogy. Elsaesser's article frames the problem in essence as a contention between the aesthetics of melodramatic versus documentary approaches, Hollywood dramaturgy versus European ideologies, life-affirming versus tragic emphases. The NBC *Holocaust* series represents clearly one pole in the debate, while Claude Lanzmann's *Shoah* represents the other. In between lie the many other films on the subject. How is Corti's trilogy to be placed in the context of holocaust cinema?

Underlying much of the debate is the question of narrative emplotment. How does one tell the story? To what extent is it legitimate to encode the Jewish experience in a narrative? Does dramatization necessarily and inherently trivialize the experience? Can the telling of one story or a few stories satisfactorily "stand for" all the other stories? Elsaesser argues that Spielberg's use of the "list" in *Schindler's List*, which is repeatedly read, name by name, preserves the dignity of the individual victims at the same time as it stands for the collective (163).[5] Corti has no such device, but does bring groups to the screen in *An uns glaubt Gott nicht mehr* and *Santa Fé*. He avoids the melodramatic, (e)motion picture style of the TV series *Holocaust*, which reduces the entire complex to two families; instead he presents rounded characters with their everyday flaws who provide vehicles for partial identification. Similarly, it is the day-to-day existence of these people, often mundane, though always charged with tension, which intrigues Corti. There are certainly dramatic moments, but the quotidian struggle is at the center of attention. His characters are not the dry statistics of soulless documentary presentation which appeals exclusively to a cerebral response; nor do they demand our total emotional commitment. Rather, they are unexceptional people in exceptional circumstances. Elsaesser writes that "in order to have any kind of credibility, [fiction films] must not create sympathy for the victims of the holocaust, since that very sympathy trivializes and betrays them" (175). Corti succeeds in keeping emotional distance between his spectators and his characters. The shades of gray occupied by Ferry Tobler, Freddy Wolff, and the others permit reception both through rational and emotional channels.

Nor are Corti's characters merely types—it is true, different specific trades and professions are represented among the refugees and exiles but they are all "mixed characters" in Lessing's sense. And while the individual stories of Ferry Tobler and Freddy Wolff are foregrounded in the first two films, the fates of Kron, Mehlig, Dolba, and Dr. Fein (in *An uns glaubt Gott nicht mehr*) and Dr. Treumann, Lissa, Popper, and Dr. Bauer (in *Santa Fé*)) provide the index that problems stretch outward infinitely into a community.

Are we justified in regarding Corti's trilogy in the context of holocaust films like *Shoah, Schindler's List, Night and Fog*, and NBC's *Holocaust*? *Wohin und zurück* is, after all, about the experience of exile, not about deportation and the camps. In so far as it complements the cinema of the concentration-camp experience and is unthinkable without an audience awareness of the historical and/or cinematic holocaust, the trilogy is inseparable from holocaust cinema. I would further argue that the decision to portray the exile experience paradigmatically implies the existence of the alternative, namely to portray the camp experience, and that the latter is therefore categorically implied in the former. The decisions to be made in depicting an exile narrative are in many cases identical with those applicable in making a holocaust film: what to show, what not to show? How to make clear the magnitude of the threat? How strongly to identify the victims as Jews represented by Jewish cultural signifiers? To what extent should they be presented as victims? Is simple good versus evil an adequate paradigm for a cinematic narrative? How are the Germans to be portrayed? To what extent should familiar Nazi icons be deployed?

Corti's answers to these questions allow us to place his trilogy at a unique site on the campus of cinematic treatments of the Jewish experience in the Third Reich. He tells the story largely against the grain of cinematic orthodoxy for this theme. His use of black and white film stock, though, is certainly not original. *Schindler's List* is also shot in monochrome, except for the final scene at the graveside—an important "except," to be sure. Corti opted to shoot the trilogy in black and white in order to identify with the "look" of the period.[6] He occasionally makes good use of this congruency by using the match-cut to identify his characters with the refugees shown in the documentary shots, as when Alena is seen pushing a bicycle following a *Wochenschau* shot of refugees with bicycles. The quality of Corti's black and white images through Gernot Roll's camera work is constitutive for the impact of the films, however. The striking beauty or originality of an image occasionally reminds us that the filmmaker and his cameraman are suppressing an urge to make beautiful pictures. In general, they resist the temptation to "specular seduction" (Elsaesser 157). This is not a beautiful reality, after all.[7] For Corti black and white represents the period, and here he is acknowledging what Anton Kaes has so effectively analyzed, that our memory of history is determined—even superseded—by cinematic images. There is a level at which this period *belongs* in black and white because authentic images from that period are monochrome.

Further, of course, like Spielberg, Corti integrates historical documentary footage into his narrative. And though for the most part such insertions identify themselves for what they are, for instance as newsreel footage, at other times a seamless transition is used for an effect, as when Freddy Wolff rides the train in New York and archival footage of 1940s New York and its trains is intercut with shots of Freddy in a train car. Or when archival footage of street scenes is used as an establishing shot. Netenjakob and others have pointed out that Corti's mise-en-scène is defined by its detail.[8] Fidelity to period, precise chronology—even to the point of blatantly placing calendars conspicuously in the frame to plot time, and precision of historical detail in costume, props, and soundtrack are hallmarks of Corti's work. By this means, he is able to manage a compelling sense of period authenticity.

Corti's solution to the problem how to represent the Germans is innovative. The only German individual with a significant role is the good German, Gandhi, in *An uns glaubt Gott nicht mehr*. For the rest, just as the fate of the Jews is determined by the capriciousness of the Germans, so the German presence in the film is determined by the Jews; Germans are essentially absent except as we are aware of them through observing the reactions of the Jewish characters to their circumstances. With very few exceptions, there are no Nazi icons (banners, swastikas, boots, marching columns, military parades, bands, songs, or speeches). Instead, the situation of their victims and the response of these people to the Germans provides the necessary information. Hitler is simply "he." Corti thus avoids tapping into our personal archive of pre-programmed responses to the familiar Nazi signals. His aesthetic strategy is to open up a revised response to this period based on his own narrative and its images. Corti's avoidance of Nazi iconography also discourages his audience from readily identifying the Nazis with Germans as it is predisposed by media exposure to do. The trilogy portrays an Austrian condition, where Austrian Jews are forced into exile by Austrian complicity and Austrian anti-Semitism. To the extent that Nazi symbols are identified in an audience's mind with Germany, their avoidance here is appropriate. By the same token, Corti avoids Jewish cultural icons also. A star of David from a concentration camp uniform appears briefly in *Santa Fé*, but this is an exception. Instead, Corti creates his own symbol for the Jew in exile: the unpacked suitcase.

The conspicuous exception to the strategy of absenting the

Germans is the use of Nazi *Wochenschau* footage in *An uns glaubt Gott nicht mehr*. The newsreels serve a threefold function: the precise events portrayed and the dates given help map out the chronology and indicate who is controlling the wider historical narrative; the original voice-over commentary allows the Nazis to present themselves and reveal their hubris and mendacity in their own terms without mediation; and the juxtaposition of Corti's images with those of the newsreels emphasizes not only that propaganda specializes in concealing much of the story, but that point-of-view is everything. Corti's pictures present the other reality, which is absent from the *Wochenschau* footage. The clash between what Elsaesser calls the "speaking positions" of these intercut texts challenges the spectator to reflect on both of them.

The attentive observer of cinematic portrayals of Nazi Germany cannot fail to notice the extensive use made of show business as a signifier in films about this period. The actor or performer assumes a metaphorical quality in this context. Frequently, the performer is the archetypal *Mitläufer* (fellow traveler) in denial: Henrik Höfgen in Szabo's *Mephisto*, the singer in Fassbinder's *Lili Marleen*, even Sally Bowles in Bob Fosse's *Cabaret* are all coopted by a system which wants to exploit their vanity and professional ambition for its own ends.[9] Performance acquires an aura of suspect hollowness at the same time as it exerts a specular fascination, much like the visual fascination of fascism itself. Denying political responsibility as a performer is portrayed as a flaw. Corti picks up this traditional trope. Claudia, who in many ways represents the new Austria, is an actress and the spectator is invited to use her attribute of "performance" in evaluating her character. As an aspiring cabaret performer she rehearses "As Time Goes By," the signature song from *Casablanca*, whose central figure, Rick, spends most of the film denying any political responsibility. Further, she is identified with the new post-1945 Austria by her leading role in a production of Thornton Wilder's *By the Skin of Our Teeth* and its American ideals, although this production is directed by an apparently unreconstructed Nazi. Corti implicitly carries over the questionable valuation of performers from the stock cinematic representations of Nazi Germany and applies it to the new Austria.

Corti's acknowledgment of cinematic tradition in his trilogy emerges at other points too, and helps in determining the appropriate site of his three films. Though Corti and Troller are not interested in questions of culpability and distance themselves from cinema which places guilt at the center of attention, intertextuality links *Wohin und zurück* with earlier films. Several commentators point to locational and thematic allusions to *The Third Man*. The setting of *Welcome in Vienna* in the Austrian capital of the immediate postwar years is congruent with that of Carol Reed's film and at points shares some of the same "feel" with its dramatic backlighting of some of the night scenes. Like Harry Lime, Treschensky is engaged in peddling stolen medical supplies. Harry Lime's girlfriend too, was an actress. Whereas *The Third Man* opens and closes in a cemetery, *Welcome in Vienna* places a central dialogue between Claudia and Freddy on the nature of belonging and "Heimat" in a cemetery. Tellingly, Freddy shows more interest in the dead artists buried there, while Claudia focuses on living.

One might also see allusions to *The Third Man* in Corti's use of music. Where Reed used the solo zither of Anton Karas as a conveyor of Viennese atmosphere and as dramatic commentator, Corti uses one piece of music for the entire trilogy. It is the melancholy Adagio from the string quartet in c-major (Opus 163) by Franz Schubert (performed by the Alban Berg Quintet). It introduces and closes each film of the trilogy and is used very sparingly to punctuate the narrative. No other extra-diegetic music is heard; music is not employed as a ubiquitous manipulator of the emotional response. The mood of the Schubert piece, however, is decisive as the filmmaker's statement about his work. This musical selection provides a clue as to where Corti belongs in Elsaesser's distinction between European and Hollywood representations of the holocaust. Schubert's melancholy underscores the predominantly tragic European speaking position and denies the life-affirming stance more typical of Hollywood.

The response of Corti and Troller to the aesthetic questions faced by a filmmaker working with the topic of Jews in the Third Reich is determined ultimately by the audience. Troller describes the difficulty in these words: "Again and again your enemy close on your heels...who has now become the consumer of television programs (or his sons or grandsons) and appeal to him? His identification? His soul searching?" How can one effectively present the story of victims to their oppressors and their philosophical heirs? This may account for Corti's choice to represent the Jewish plight as a human plight which is not marked by repeated cultural signals of Jewish and Nazi culture.

It is certainly true that the trilogy is designed to direct audience response beyond consideration of the topic portrayed. Corti wrote a letter to the team working on *Wohin und zurück* in which he stressed the importance of seeing: "It is no use if we look but we don't see." This sentiment is also central to the principles behind the programming of ORF's artistic director in the 1980s, Gerald Szyszkowitz, who evaluates the importance of historical representation based on its relevance for the present: "the examination of the past with a view to the future" (quoted by Thieringer).

The three films, *An uns glaubt Gott nicht mehr, Santa Fé,* and *Welcome in Vienna,* articulate a challenge to their audience, whether that audience consists of the perpetrators, their ideological heirs, or anyone else in the late twentieth century. The films offer multiple "points of entry" (Elsaesser) for different audiences by declining to establish over-simplified, black and white moral parameters, and they resist simple categorization in terms of their cinematic aesthetic. *Wohin und zurück* holds up a mirror to an Austria which long regarded itself solely as a victim of Nazi ambitions and examines the experience of Austrian Jews forced from their home by their countrymen. It is a short step to transfer the historical specificity of 1938-45 to other historical specificities. Dr. Treumann in *Santa Fé* characterizes the seemingly irreconcilable positions of Austrians and Jews in his sentence: "They will never forgive us for what they have done to us." Corti's challenge to his audience is to banish from history the conditions which make possible this aporia.

Notes

1. Among other awards, Corti received the Adolph Grimme Prize for *Herrenjahre*, a Golden Nymph and the International Press Award at the 1985 TV Festival in Monte Carlo for *Eine blaßblaue Frauenschrift*, and the Prix Italia for the same film. In February 1986 Corti received another Golden Nymph, the International Press Award, and the Prize endowed by the Monaco Red Cross at the Monte Carlo TV Festival for *Santa Fé*. At the 1987 Chicago International Film Festival *Welcome in Vienna* received the Golden Hugo for Best Film; the same film also received the Prix de la Mise-en-Scène at the San Sebastián Film Festival.

2. *The North California Jewish Bulletin* (March 20, 1987). Corti directed theater in Vienna, Berlin, and Brussels, and specialized for a time in the staging of opera for television.

3. These are the three criteria used by Greverus to define "Heimat." She adopts them from Ardrey's analysis of territory. Cf. Greverus, *Der territoriale Mensch: Ein literaturanthropologischer Versuch zum Heimatphänomen* 51 passim, and Greverus, *Auf der Suche nach Heimat* 24.

4. In Troller's words Claudia stands for Freddy's "erträumte Heimkehr" to Austria.

5. S(auvaget) writes of *An uns glaubt Gott nicht mehr* that it is "une de ces chroniques qui brassent plusieurs destins pour mieux approfondir l'Histoire sans expulser toute sensibilité." "Vienne pour mémoire. Aller-retour Vienne/New York," *La revue du cinéma,* No. 426 (April 1987) 92.

6. "Pour moi le noir et blanc était une nécessité. Et une logique. Les photos de l'époque, tous les documents, tout est noir et blanc, c'est notre mémoire, c'est l'Histoire. On fait beaucoup de films sur le passé en couleurs—souvent s'ils manquent d'authenticité, c'est à cause de la couleur. La couleur pour moi, c'est plus de fiction et moins d'authenticité," Axel Corti in an interview with Sauvaget from January 1987 published in *La revue du cinéma*, No. 426 (April 1987) 93.

7. Such images occur as Ferry Tobler and Gandhi taste a tentative freedom on their escape route to Prague, and in the ironic

counterpoint of beauty and death when Gandhi is apprehended by the French youths; in *Santa Fé*, when a tender love scene is illuminated by a refrigerator light and when a backlit profile appears in a shop doorway.

8. Rebhandl calls his style "kritischer Realismus."

9. The montage of *Cabaret* suggests strongly, though it is not stated explicitly, that the demonic Master of Ceremonies (spirit of the Nazi times) has impregnated Sally.

Works Cited

Bloch, Judy. "Jews flee Austria in haunting S.F. film fest trilogy." *The Northern California Jewish Bulletin* 20 March 1987.

Corti, Axel. "Nicht nur hinschauen, sondern auch wahrnehmen." *Süddeutsche Zeitung* 1 March 1986.

Courtade, Francis. Interview with Corti. *Welcome in Vienna* press packet.

Elsaesser, Thomas. "subject positions, speaking positions. from *holocaust, our hitler*, and *heimat* to *shoah* and *schindler's list*." *The Persistence of History: Cinema, Television, and the Modern Event*. Ed. Vivian Sobchack. London: Routledge, 1996. 145-83.

Fine, Marshall. "Film Trilogy Tracks Jews into WWII." *Marin Independent Journal* 26 March 1987.

Greverus, Ina-Maria. *Der territoriale Mensch: Ein literaturanthropologischer Versuch zum Heimatphänomen*. Königstein/Ts: Athenäum, 1972.

---. *Auf der Suche nach Heimat*. München: Beck, 1979.

Groth, Michael. "Heimat Fremde Heimat." *Frankfurter Allgemeine Zeitung* 1 March 1986.

Kaes, Anton . *Deutschlandbilder: Die Wiederkehr der Geschichte als Film*. München: edition text + kritik, 1987); English version: *From "Hitler" to "Heimat": The Return of History as Film*. Cambridge: Harvard UP, 1989.

Netenjakob, Egon. *Der neugierige Existentialist: Eine Zeitreise mit 17 Filmen von Axel Corti*. Köln: Katholisches Institut für Medieninformation e.V., 1995.

Rebhandl, Bert. "Sensible Protokolle menschlichen Fühlens." *Der Standard* 31 Dec. 1993 / 1,2 Jan. 1994.

Sauvaget, Daniel. *La revue du cinéma* April 1987.

Thieringer, Thomas. "Die Vergangenheit der Gegenwart." *Süddeutsche Zeitung* 7 March 1986.

Troller, Georg S. "Wohin und zurück." *Frankfurter Allgemeine Zeitung* 7 March 1986.

Michael Glawogger's Film *Die Ameisenstraße*:
Representing the Modern Malaise

Robert Acker
University of Montana

Michael Glawogger is not a name well known to most filmgoers, but he promises to be one of the rising stars on the Austrian film scene. Born in 1959 in Graz, Glawogger first became interested in films by showing them in a film club while still in school. In 1981-82 he studied film at the San Francisco Art Institute, and then returned to Austria to continue his film studies at the Vienna Film Academy between 1983 and 1989. He started making shorts in 1980, and these early works were extremely avant-garde and experimental in nature. Glawogger has also worked as a scriptwriter and cameraman. For the past several years he has collaborated extensively with the documentarist Ulrich Seidl (Seibel 22-23). *Die Ameisenstraße* (*Street of Ants*) is his first feature film as a director. It was awarded the Viennese Film Prize in 1995, was submitted as the Austrian entry for nomination for an Oscar for Best Foreign Language Film and at the Saarland Film Festival received the Film Prize for the best German-language debut film.

Glawogger's film centers around a Kafkaesque and almost surrealistic plot: the lives of the strange inhabitants of a contemporary Viennese apartment house take bizarre turns and twists as the result of the new owner's attempt to evict them. One could perhaps find parallels between this story and Terry Gilliam's *Brazil*, or find connections with David Cronenberg, Peter Greenaway, David Lynch or even Luis Buñuel (Seibel, Horvath), but it is probably best to look for sources and influences within the Austrian cultural tradition. The most obvious in this regard is the film's indebtedness to documentary techniques, which Glawogger no doubt acquired from his mentor Seidl, who was also the casting director for *Die Ameisenstraße*. First, the film uses an authoritative voice-over narrator, who is somewhat paradoxically one of the protagonists, Alfred Navratil. This narrator is privy to a wide range of information and also provides an orientation and interpretation of events, twisted though it might be, for the viewers. Second, the takes are usually very short, and changing scenes follow each other in rapid succession. Third, there is great use of mise-en-scène: each shot is crammed full of authentic artifacts to create the illusion of documentary accuracy. Fourth, the film is interrupted three times with intermediate titles to give the birth and death dates of deceased apartment dwellers. And finally, there are frequent repetitions of motifs and several intra-filmic references (Rothschild, Horvath). Even the heavy emphasis on animals can be traced to Seidl's 1995 documentary film, *Tierische Liebe (Animal Love)*, where the real heroes are dogs, rabbits and hamsters (Angerer).

The script also falls within the tradition of the Viennese *Volksstück* (folk play). The most obvious reference is to Nestroy's play *Zu ebner Erde und erster Stock (On the Ground Floor and the First Floor)*. While not many parallels can be established, we find that, like in the play, the bourgeois or proletarian existence of the apartment renters is contrasted with the life of the rich owner, the younger Wanecek, who tries to manipulate the lives of the individuals in the apartment he inherited in order to increase his wealth. As in the play, the tables are also turned somewhat and Wanecek's Döblinger residence burns to the ground (torched, or so it is implied, by Navratil), and he loses everything as the result of his wild speculations. He is forced at the very end of the film to turn the apartment over to the "next asshole." The Nestroy reference is here complete with the final song played over the credits: "...an angel you become slowly, but you're an asshole real fast."

Other references to the *Volksstück* abound. While there is still disagreement and debate about the exact nature of this genre, we can probably agree on the following components—the preponderance of dialect, a plot ranging between the comedic and the tragic, the use of music and dance, characters who represent certain types or who somehow fall outside of the norm, and a critical stance towards the actions and views of the characters, who most often belong to the lower social class.[1] Most of the dialogue in the film is in varying degrees of Viennese dialect and the changes between humor and drama are easily discernible, but it would be well to consider in greater detail how the other components are reflected in the film.

We encounter the musical component at the very beginning of the movie. A soothingly pleasant and even *gemütlich* zither melody, reminiscent of *The Third Man*, accompanies the opening credits and would seem to portend a happy and lighthearted story to follow. But just as in *The Third Man*, the music proves to be ironic, and the viewer is immediately confronted with a disturbing situation, where the surface tranquility is broken and confusion and pandemonium soon prevail. Dance, too, plays a central role. Young Ignaz, dressed up in an ant costume, struts and bobs on the pavement in front of the house in an overhead shot accompanied by a cacophonous melody. Shortly thereafter, all chaos breaks out, again to the accompaniment of this dance tune—strings of ants and other insects run through the various apartments and terrorize the elderly women, the Poles run back and forth on the scaffolding to steal items from Frau Gerhartl's apartment, accompanied by the disenfranchised Herr Weinberger, and then hastily return them after the younger Wanecek unexpectedly shows up to reclaim his deceased uncle's apartment. Another tune, slapstick in nature, accompanies the younger Wanecek as he flips out after a threatening note wrapped around a stone is thrown into his apartment: he runs across the scaffolding and into Fräulein Dorli's apartment in search of the perpetrator. He then slides down the scaffolding to the sidewalk, whereupon he is kidnapped by the apartment house manager, who tries to extort promises from him by locking him in her bathroom. The song at the end of the film serves as a summary of the whole absurd situation.

Particularly interesting is Glawogger's use of "Volksstück" typology, for his standard set of characters is not just a handy tool to provide for viewer identification, but is at the same time a means to proffer a critical stance. Alfred Navratil, played by the Burgtheater actor Robert Meyer, is the ultimate pedant and demands precision, exactitude and regularity in all aspects of his life, from counting the number of steps between his office and the traffic signal, to sitting at attention while his microwave dinner cooks, to painstakingly constructing model ships and homes out of matches.

He thinks he can find an explanation for everything. When his daily routine is broken, he immediately suspects a subversive plot. His paranoia increases until he can bear it no more; he then actively engages in countermeasures, from destroying the Waneceks' residence to calling a renters' meeting. He wishes to maintain the status quo at all costs and is constantly fearful that someone is out to get him. Yet he is not too far wrong. Wanecek does want to drive out all the old renters through the usual tricks in order to make a huge profit by converting the apartments to condos. Glawogger seems to be saying that modern paranoia is not without its foundation in reality.

Other characters provide similar insights into the modern malaise. The kleptomaniac Frau Gerhartl accumulates masses of consumer goods which she cannot possibly use; her activity is a direct critique of the contemporary consumer society, where one's happiness seems to be equated with the possession of a glut of objects. Ernstl Freitag is the epitome of the proletarian—a second Mundl if you will (from the TV series "A True Viennese Doesn't Go Under." He runs about in his Arbeitskittel (white work coat) sans trousers complaining and criticizing, both of which seem to give his life meaning. He has no obvious means of support or outside activity—he seems just about ready to go to work, but not quite. When his world is turned topsy-turvy he resorts to alcohol to calm his nerves, while at the same time neglecting everything around him, as is evidenced by the fish tank in his apartment, which grows more putrid and slimy in each shot. Frau Haslinger is in a loveless marriage and seeks consolation by having an affair with the hairdresser. The obese Herr Haslinger only wants to make love to his wife after working on a crossword puzzle where the Greek island of Lesbos is one answer—he probably wants to prove to everyone that he is not gay. Near the end of the film he is left staring, in almost total isolation, at an empty table after his wife finally runs off for good with her lover. Herr Halbgebauer's sole interest is his clocks, and he neglects everything else, which forces his wife to devote her entire existence to her dog Willi. The Viennese preoccupation with dogs is well known and is here carried to the extreme. The loss of her pet is so severe that Frau

Halbgebauer has Willi stuffed to preserve him forever. The Weinbergers depart at the beginning of the film for the typical Austrian vacation on the Maldives, only to return to find they have been evicted. (Just this summer a regulation was passed in Austria forbidding such evictions when tenants are absent.) Upon grasping the situation Herr Weinberger resorts to violence with a pistol to reclaim what is his. When this attempt proves hopeless he succumbs to complete intoxication at the end of the film.

No typology of contemporary Vienna would be complete without the foreign component. On the one hand we find the Sliskovitz family, who tries to live within the system as a "caretaker family." These ex-Yugoslavians live in cramped quarters and try their best to communicate in broken German. On the other hand, the new arrivals, the Poles, who live in the Wanecek apartment for a paltry 1500 Schillings per month (the younger Wanecek hopes they will help destabilize the whole apartment complex and thus further his aims), take the opposite approach. They work against the system: they engage in illegal activities and also break into Frau Gerhartl's apartment to steal her stolen goods so that they can sell them on the black market. They are even able to purchase a car from their ill gotten gains. Their influence is pervasive—Frau Gerhartl eventually joins forces in their activities.

It is notable that there are only three children in the apartment house. Two are absent on vacation for most of the film and the third, Ignaz, is described by one critic as an "emotional cripple."[2] And indeed it is well known that Vienna has a largely aged population that is anything but "catering to the needs of children." Thus, the large number of elderly in the apartment house is a reflection not only of the current situation, but also of the typical Austrian/Viennese preoccupation with death, disease and dying. The elderly are everywhere, and Glawogger attaches special emphasis and importance to their frequent deaths.

The apocalypse in the film is precipitated by the death of the older Wanecek, a death hastened, no doubt, by his nephew's birthday gifts of cigars and whiskey. According to the narrator, the older Wanecek was a charming and compassionate "Viennese of the old school," one of a dying breed, whose presence kept everything in its established harmony and order. He lives in well appointed surroundings and could even be seen as a monarchist, a left-over from the Habsburg empire, where everyone had a well established role and function. He gives everyone in the apartment house, particularly the elderly, a sense of tradition, history and thus identity. With his death this identity was to disappear for good, and all hell was to break loose, quite literally.

The next to go is the extremely deaf Antal Zwokic. Antal spends his days in front of the TV, with the sound running full blast, watching pans of the "Central Municipal Cemetery" to the accompaniment of a jive "folk music." When he channel surfs to other stations he is so disgusted with the American influence that he quickly returns to the original program. It is no accident that he dies in front of the T.V., his only contact to the outside world. The final death is that of Frau Erika Vymlatil, who is barricaded by accident inside of her apartment by the construction workers. She dies (in homage to Hitchcock's *Psycho*) seated on a chair waiting for the barricades to be removed. These two characters, Antal Zwokic and Erika Vymlatil, seem all-consumed by their loneliness and isolation, and death comes, perhaps, as a blessing in disguise. Death even enters the Yugoslavian family—at the very beginning of the film they receive a letter that states that one of their relatives has passed away.

Even the elderly who do not die suffer immensely. Antal's wife, Frau Zwokic, is forced out of her apartment by the younger Wanecek since the apartment was rented in her husband's name only. When Alfred Navratil moves her into an empty apartment, which formerly belonged to his mother on the other side of the building, she is so confused and disoriented by this change of locale that she cannot even find her way to the stores where she has shopped for years. All the stuffed animals from the taxidermist's overturned car appear to her as if they have come to life and she hastily retreats back into her apartment. In another case study, an elderly gentleman, not further named, is so disturbed by the recent events that he is unable to eat his soup—his hand trembles terribly at each attempt. He soothes his nerves by consuming large quantities of schnapps and by employing a certain gallows humor. One time he tries to get some water from the faucet but is unsuccessful since the water has been turned off. When he sits down disgustedly the water suddenly spurts out in a tremendous geyser. This he finds extremely amusing, and he continues to laugh throughout the entire film, even until his final scene when he is consumed in his apartment by a fire that erupted from his leaky heating oil container. Another character, Frau Morgenwind, is barely able to walk, and bemoans the fact that she is no longer physically capable of visiting her husband's grave. She lives in the past—she constantly complains about an illicit affair she witnessed a long time ago in an apartment across the courtyard. She writes a letter, with the help of the shy and introverted Fräulein Dorli, in which references to death abound. After all, she is only waiting for her own death.

Even many of the characters who are not at death's door seem to be consumed by the past or are so alienated from their surroundings that they are unable to live their lives in the present to any significant degree. Ernstl Freitag is affected by nothing and cares about nothing, be it the deceased apartment dwellers or his outward appearance—he never even bothers to change his clothes. In fact, he wants his peace and quiet at all costs with as little change as possible. He confronts life with empty and hollow phrases. Ignaz behaves more like an adult than a child; youth seems to pass him by. His one major preoccupation is his collection of dead insects. Other characters, such as Ignaz' father or Herr Halbgebauer, seem to have shut any feelings or sensitivity for the present out of their lives. For most of these characters death would no doubt come as a welcome relief from the tedium of their everyday existence. This attitude is demonstrated strongly in the scene where the renters gather to discuss their plight. Twelve of them are seated at a long table reminiscent of the Last Supper. In the very middle of the group is seated a seemingly minor character, a bearded homeless man, whom the elderly gentleman who burns to death invites to share his apartment, and who bears a striking resemblance to the typical representations of Christ. This Christ-figure is silently presiding over the imminent death of the old order. Will a new order, purged of the past, ascend from the grave?

The theme of death is intimately connected with another theme in the film, namely a preoccupation with time. After each death of a character the camera tilts down the stairwell while the coffin is carried metaphorically down the steps into Hades.³ There immediately follows a cut to the raucous clanking and ticking of the clocks in Herr Halbgebauer's shop. Herr Halbgebauer's prime goal in life is to get all of his several hundred clocks to strike the hour at exactly the same time. When he finally succeeds in this bizarre undertaking his ecstasy is greeted by a dead and stuffed mountain-cock which comes flying through his plate glass window when the taxidermist's truck careens out of control on its way to deliver his wife's dead and stuffed dog, Willi. He stares at the bird in amazement and is, as the narrator informs us, "lost in time." There are many other references to this senseless preoccupation with time. Herr Navratil works at the Office of Statistics. As mentioned, he counts the steps it takes him to get home, and he knows how many hours it took him to complete his model of the apartment house. Ignaz purchases a stop watch with a double time function to measure all sorts of things, including how long it takes his mother to prepare the meal. Later his mother complains to Herr Halbgebauer that her egg timer doesn't function correctly and that as a result her husband's breakfast eggs are always "runny."

This Baroque-like obsession with time and death remains internal, almost abstract and theoretical. It causes the individuals to turn in upon themselves and to create their own little worlds almost devoid of human contact. Instead of having time for each other, they seem to primarily have time for themselves and for maintaining their set order. The scaffolding surrounding the apartment house is a good metaphor for the walls they have built around themselves.⁴ When their established world is disrupted by the younger Wanecek's machinations, they scurry about like little ants whose hill has been destroyed, desperately trying to rebuild and restore their sacred little domains. They feel themselves "betrayed and sold out" as Alfred says in his famous final scene, where he is dressed in ant-design pajamas and is lying on matching ant-design sheets. Yet in the end they can barely function, literally and figuratively—there are large gaping holes in the floors, doors and entrances are barricaded, the toilets do not function, and insects of all kinds are swarming about. Workers trace and mark strange symbols everywhere and carry building materials in every direction, thus impeding movement. Near the conclusion of the film the would-be owners of the new condominiums run wildly about after they discover that the same apartment has been sold several times over; the renters do not dare to leave their apartments for fear that they will never be able to return. They are, like Alfred in bed, reduced to paralysis. Their efforts are futile—once destroyed, their "perfect world" can never be reestablished.

It might be possible to view the film as a statement on postmodern society, where various social classes and ethnic groups with differing values live side by side, with no one system assuming primacy or universal validity, or, by further extension, it might be possible to read the film as a comment on the European Union and its member states. If this be true in either case, the film certainly offers a dismal view of the situation. Couched not too deeply in its bizarre and scurrilous humor, the film paints a bleak picture of what happens when economic or social factors force disruptive change on a staid society. The only two solutions offered here are death and flight. The older generation succumbs to death or morbidity since it sees no way out, and the younger generation tries to escape. Frau Haslinger runs off with the hairdresser, Frau Wanecek leaves her husband, and the Poles and Frau Gerhartl chase off to the land of their dreams, the land of ultimate exploitation, America. Still others, like Herr Freitag, Herr Wanecek and Herr Weinberger, flee into the stupor of alcohol. Any attempts to form a common front against the approaching menace also seem doomed to failure. The meeting of the tenants, where they hope to discuss their plight, ends in disarray, in spite of the intellectual attempts of the precocious Ignaz to explain the origin of the insects and the lawyer's assurances that legalistic measures have been undertaken. The individuals seem incapable of removing the barriers between themselves, and destruction comes from within. Seen in this light, the film contains a rather fatalistic and pessimistic view of the future.

If we interpret the film from a slightly different perspective, it might be possible to view all the apocalyptic destruction and disruption that is going on as a necessary first step for a new beginning to occur, as a sort of Regnarok from which a new world will emerge after the deluge. Alfred's initial words, which he repeats at the end of the film, are most telling in this regard: "We didn't know how to interpret the signs. Right from the beginning. Nobody paid any attention to the wiles of everyday reality." While these statements could be seen as a call for more vigilance, cooperation and solidarity, we would do well to recall that these were exactly the same phrases used in the Second Republic in Austria after World War II to exculpate the Austrians from any guilt for involvement with the Third Reich, thus leading to the myth of Austria as victim. Perhaps it is the guilt from the Nazi years and its subsequent coverup that lies buried at the heart of the film. This would explain all the references to the past (Frau Morgenwind reminisces about Hitler and the postwar occupation of Austria, the elderly gentleman recalls scenes from his youth, for example). This would explain the isolation and loneliness of those waiting to die (they have not been able to come to terms with or mourn for the past), this would explain the flight of the younger generation (they cannot identify with a State which refuses to accept its own identity), this would explain the fact that the apartment building is never really "renovated" but only "covered-over" (literally and figuratively) and is being mercilessly destroyed from within by the workers and the insects, this would explain why time seems to stand still for so many of the characters (they cannot face the future since they are unable to face the past), and finally, this would explain all the coffins and parody of the Last Supper—the old anachronistic ideas and mentality must die; one must accept the past, not make excuses for it, and look towards the future; one must be willing to sacrifice so that a new and more humane era can replace the old. Whether this new order can be achieved is not clearly answered in the film. The drunken ramblings at the end would seem to indicate that the present stupor of indifference and inaction is likely to continue.

Notes

1. For a detailed analysis of the characteristics of the "Volksstück" see Kegler.
2. See Horvath's essay.
3. For additional comments on these scenes in the stairwell see Lenz.
4. See *INFO*. No. 263. Wien: Filmladen, 1996.

Works Cited

Angerer, Peter. "Der heimische Film im Aufwärtstrend." *Tiroler Tageszeitung* 4 Jul. 1996.

Horvath, Alexander. "A Time to Live, a Time to Eat, a Time to Die." *INFO*. No. 263. Wien: Filmladen, 1996.

Kegler, Lydia K. "A Case of Mistaken Identity: Defining the 'Volksstück' in Its Historical Context Since the Eighteenth Century." *Modern Austrian Literature* 26.3/4 (1993): 1-15.

Lenz, Eva-Maria. "Griff ins tolle Menschenleben." *Frankfurter Allgemeine Zeitung* 31 Jan. 1996.

Rothschild, Thomas. "Spießer auf der Ameisenstraße." *Frankfurter Allgemeine Zeitung* 13 Dec. 1995.

Seibel, Alexandra. "Konstruktion und Spieltrieb." *Austrian Film News* 6 (1995): 22-23.

Abschied von Sidonie, A Farewell Twice-Visited:
Erich Hackl's Novella and Karin Brandauer's Film

Robert C. Reimer
University of North Carolina, Charlotte

Since their arrival in Europe in the middle ages, Gypsies have proved to be a cultural parodox. For centuries they have fascinated the local populace with their exotic presence, knowledge of magic, and passion for freedom. Yet, after 600 years of presence in central Europe they have failed to assimilate into the majority culture. If at times they have been celebrated, as during the heyday of Gypsy romanticism in the nineteenth century, at other times they have been persecuted. While they have been admired for their musical skills and envied for their dark beauty, they have also been scorned as thieves and beggars and slandered as child stealers.[1]

The historical narrative of Gypsy and non-Gypsy interaction in Europe as told by historians of Romani culture, makes it clear that the majority of the non-Gypsy population with which the Gypsies interact has an ambivalent relationship to them. For example, Donald Kendrick and Gratton Puxon conclude that the very tradesmen skills which made Gypsies valuable to a community—tinsmithing, tinkering, and trading—eventually gave rise to resentment as they could be seen as competitors (13-17). Gypsies have always been present and absent in the mainstream population. They may locate their enclaves on the edge of town, yet they interact with the townsfolk to earn a living. Moreover, even absent or invisible, they remain in the imagination of the general population. Placed there by hundreds of years of literary and folklorist images, Gypsies remain present as clichés: talented musicians, carefree beggars, or threatening strangers. Indeed, historian Jean-Pierre Liégeois suggests that local populations tolerate Gypsies only as fictional absence: "The only accepted and approved Gypsy is the mythical one—and he does not exist" (191). Liégeois suggests further that for most people in the mainstream, the Gypsy who does exist is feared as an outsider who endangers the culture and citizens of the majority population (198-99).

Yet, as history suggests, it is Gypsies who are in danger from the dominant culture rather than the reverse. Historian Elisabeth Klamper estimates that more than half of the 12,000 Sinti and Roma who lived in Austria before World War II died at Auschwitz (63). Other historians estimate equally high percentages for the Romani people from countries other than Austria.[2] That the Nazis were as intent on reducing the central European presence of the Romani people by carrying out a final solution against them as well as against the Jews is reflected in the establishment of anti-Gypsy offices, the creation of camps that served as places to collect Gypsies before deporting them to Auschwitz, and in statements of government officials. In 1936, for example, international authorities established the *Internationale Zentralstelle zur Bekämpfung des Zigeunerunwesens* (International Agency for Controlling the Gypsy Nuisance),[3] which they located in Vienna. After the annexation of Austria in 1938, the agency fell under the administration of the Third Reich (Sijes, 169). In February 1940, the Nazis created a camp outside Salzburg for detaining Gypsies and opened the Lackenbach internment camp for Gypsies in fall of that same year (Klamper, 60-61). Statements from government officials likewise indicate that persecution of the Romani people was ongoing and deliberate. A memorial book, *The Gypsies at Auschwitz-Birkenau*, reports that after a meeting with Propaganda Minister Josef Goebbels, Reich Minister of Justice Otto Thierack wrote: "With respect to the extermination of antisocial forms of life, Dr. Goebbels is of the opinion that the Jews and the Gypsies should be simply exterminated. The idea to exterminate by means of work is probably the best" (*Memorial Book*, preface).

Nor has the danger to the Romani disappeared, even if its intensity and deliberateness has diminished. The tendency of many in the general public today to view Gypsies as a threat to the community is disturbing. Liégeois notes that "when nothing is going right politically or economically, Gypsies are the first scapegoats, around whom a stereotyped representation permeated with every wickedness is constructed in order to justify attitudes towards them" (193). Gypsies clearly remain in public discourse as the cause of socio-economic problems. Moreover, their role as scapegoats seems to be tacitly accepted by public institutions. Herbert Heuß notes: "Whereas anti-Semitism has been banished from public discourse for the most part and anti-Semitic statements are punishable by law, racism against Sinti and Roma in the history of the Federal Republic has often been a part of official action" (156).

Two recent studies substantiate Liégeois's recognition of the Gypsies' role as scapegoat. One study examined the characterization of Sinti in the local press of Dortmund for the years 1982-1984 and concluded that the one-sided nature of newspaper reports on Gypsies created the image of a hostile and criminal-oriented minority. Furthermore, there were few attempts to depict the social and family life of the Romani, which would have balanced the negative articles on criminal behavior and intraclan warfare (Bohn, 257-72). The second study examined how German language criminological texts published after 1949 have characterized Gypsies. The author of the study demonstrates that depictions of Gypsies as drug addicts, vagabonds, mental patients, and alcoholics persisted in textbooks on crime even as late as 1988; the publication of Günther Kaiser's, *Kriminologie, Ein Lehrbuch*, was deeply upsetting to Romani groups for its many assumptions based on negative stereotyping (Berbüsse, 117-51).

Persecution and continuing discrimination has for a time persuaded some Sinti and Roma to try and assimilate into the mainstream culture.[4] The desire to assimilate is not universal, however, and may be decreasing as consciousness is raised by groups such as the *Verein zur Förderung von Zigeunern* (Union for the Advancement of Gypsies), founded in 1989. This organization fights for recognition of Gypsy rights in the Oberwart region.[5] In 1992 it won the support of politicians who recognized the Romani people as an official minority group (Jancsy, 40), and in 1993 the Austrian government recognized the Romani as the sixth official minority in Austria.[6]

The conflict for present-day Romani is that attempts at assimilation, caused by centuries of discrimination, and a renewed pride in being Gypsy, coupled with efforts at consciousness raising, have led to a crisis of identity. Hannes Skrinjar and Irina Moisejew write: "The crisis of identity has led to the formation of many small groups which 'fight' among one another: the tradition bound or strongly rooted normal citizens [fight] with those who lean toward modern reality and simply reject their past. This 'Who are we?' is reflected in songs, texts, in all of everday life. And it must be answered everyday by each group and each family" (8).

Recently, Gypsy artists have begun exploring identity in art, literature, and film. In 1990 Karl Stojka, an artist of Roma descent, had an exhibition of his paintings "Ausnahmsweis Zigeuner" at the Celeste Gallery in Vienna. In order to achieve maximum political effect among the non-Gypsy public, Stojka attached emotional texts to his works, which depict conditions of Gypsies at Auschwitz-Birkenau.[7] Not all artists look to the past, however. Mongo Stojka, for example, released an album of popular music—including swing, jazz, and rap—with lyrics in the Romani language, hoping thereby to nurture his native culture. The films of Katrin Seybold and Melanie Spitta look both forward and back. The two filmmakers have worked together on several documentaries on Sinti, among them, *Es ging Tag und Nacht, liebes Kind, Sinti in Auschwitz,* and *Das falsche Wort*, films about past persecution and the slowness of authorities to redress discrimination, and *Schimpft uns nicht Zigeuner*, a documentary on work, school, and family of Sinti in contemporary German society.[8]

Seybold and Spitta's films are of interest because of the way they use public perceptions of Gypsies to move beyond simplistic stereotypes and present the Sinti as living in a society within a society, neither wanting to assimilate nor wanting to be completely outside. Thus, Seybold and Spitta highlight a vexing paradox of the Sinti and Roma in society, indeed of any well-defined minority in the majority society: How does a group that retains a distinct identity keep that identity from deteriorating into the stereotyped perception held by many in the mainstream? And how does a minority race integrate into the mainstream without giving up its identity, that is without assimilating? Their films attempt no answers. Nor does the work of Mariella Mehr, a Swiss Gypsy, who in her literature and in her life, suggests that there perhaps is no answer to the paradox. That is, to retain identity, one must remain outside the majority culture.

Erich Hackl's novella *Abschied von Sidonie* (*Farewell Sidonia*) about a young Gypsy girl who died at Auschwitz, and the late Karin Brandauer's film *Sidonie* based on the book offer another facet to the public discourse on Gypsies within Western culture. Film and book tell the story of a ten-year-old Gypsy girl, raised by non-Gypsy Austrians, who dies at Auschwitz. Hackl and Brandauer both narrow and broaden the central conflict of the Romani culture within the European context: On the one hand, they, the film more than the book, narrow the field within which persecution operates. Emphasis on the fate of one individual, a young girl whose life seems controlled by universal rather than specific forces, leads the audience to understand Sidonie's outcome as the inevitable outcome of historical circumstances. Matthias Rub writes: "Sidonie's death in Auschwitz is as inevitable as the willingness of people to accept injustice. 'What times these are,' the policeman remarked as he saw Sidonie get into the train car with her blond doll on her arm"(34). Her fate becomes individual, unique, "a succinct and sensitive report, which does not seek our pity, of a case history 'without any claim to universality.'"(Rybarski, 80). On the other hand, the two works, in this case the book more than the film, open up the tragedy so that Sidonie comes to represent more than herself and becomes a symbol of Gypsy persecution: "The Jews have Anne Frank. The Gypsies, thanks to Erich Hackl, have Sidonia Adlersburg" (Byrne, 243). Moreover, her story bridges to the present: "Karin Brandauer recognizes in her confrontation with the old questions of the past connections to the present, which in the most recent world-political developments are becoming painful reality" (Matuscheck-Labitzke, 48).

Hackl's *Abschied von Sidonie* and Brandauer's *Sidonie* interweave private story and public history to create a cautionary tale and moral lesson for multiethnic, post-Cold War Europe. First, as the story of an individual from birth to death, they bring the reader/viewer into a seemingly familiar fairy tale world, where an abandoned child is taken in and raised by poor but loving and kind parents and finds in their care protection from the outside. Second, as official history, they present the historical forces that affect private stories of love and protection and prevent them from being fully realized. Finally, as cautionary tale, they warn of the need for courage to realize private wishes when these conflict with public policies. For the rest of this essay, I wish to look at the way in which Hackl and, to a lesser extent, Brandauer combine fictional and historical discourse to reflect the reality of Gypsies in European culture. Furthermore, I hope to show that by combining the objective tone of fairy tale and historical chronicle with the outcry of a political polemic, they lead the audience to the unexpected. That is, both writer and filmmaker intrude on the objective tone of their respective works with emotional outbursts. In this way they overcome the tendency of most fairy tales and chronicles, which often suggest through their stories that the events as described are the inevitable outcome of (mythical) historical forces.

Hackl's novella reads at times like a fairy tale and at times like a historical chronicle. This is not surprising given that both genres mix archetypal imagery, objective narration, ironic foreshadowing, and cautionary or moral intent. The author begins Sidonie's story with specific data. "On August 18, 1933, the porter of the hospital in Steyr, Austria, found a child asleep and wrapped in rags. Near the infant lay a piece of paper on which an awkward hand had written: 'My name is Sidonia Adlersburg and I was born on the road to Altheim. I need parents'" (1).[9] Within this succinct and sober reporting of fact is contained the myth of the foundling (a child asleep and wrapped in rags), the seed of a personal story (I was born on the road), and the intimations of a moral dilemma (a child with two sets of parents, the birth parents and the future foster parents). Yet as in an historical chronicle, the tale is rooted in reality: the child has a first and last name; it was born in a specific place; and it has distinct needs. This fusion of historical document with fairy-tale story continues throughout the novella. The foster parents of Sidonie, although not exactly the poor woodcutter and his wife familiar to readers from *Märchen*, are a simple working-class couple, possessed of more decency than seems possible in the real world. Yet the couple is rooted in the everyday politics of the region.

Hackl creates tension by focusing on Hans Breirathner's refusal to compromise his political allegiance to the Communist Party even though this would make his life, and that of his family, easier. "They [his friends] prodded Hans as well. Come join us, what are you doing with the reds?...He only laughed, somewhat perplexed at what to answer, and made a quick exit from the smoky bar. At home in the evenings he sat in front of the radio...and listened to Hitler's speeches on the German radio station. I don't need to hear this...with them we're heading straight for disaster. Then he would turn the dial" (47-48). This short paragraph, as others, characterize Hans and Josefa as outsiders, as members of a community who somehow have ceased to belong to that community. Characterized in this way, they are the fairy tale's superior outsider who have been called upon to perform a special task, in this case raise an outcast child. Yet, as in the opening paragraph, Hackl has located the superior outsider of the folktale in reality. Hans has a name, he has a party allegiance, and he partakes of or reacts to real historical events. The character thus functions as more than a cliché; he becomes a representative of Austrian resistance to the Nazis, symbolizing the courage and decency that communities needed if they were to resist evil and avoid being led to perdition.

Hackl most clearly combines mythical tale with historical chronicle in the person of Sidonie. The narrative continually foregrounds Sidonie's color, emphasizing thereby her position in the story as foundling and outsider. Try as the family will to make Sidonie a part of their family, she remains a Gypsy, a fact clear to everyone within the story except Sidonie: "Sidonia had no doubt that she was the legitimate daughter of her foster parents" (54). Indeed, while she grows up safely within the Breirathner home, the world threatens at any time to intrude and end her idyllic existence. From the beginning, evil or danger await the child. The doorman at the hospital warns Josefa that the child she wishes to adopt is black. In school, a classmate exposes Sidonie as an adopted Gypsy and not the real child of the Breirathners. On an excursion to a toy village, she is singled out by a little boy because of her dark color. These instances of danger are also given historical context: for example, it is newly arrived Sudeten German neighbors who ridicule and object to Sidonie's color. An adult at the toy village tells the startled boy he could not have seen a black child because Hitler had banished them all. And the meanness of the schoolmate who pointed out that Sidonie was adopted came after the story which she imagined telling Adolf Hitler. These are but a few of many examples within the novella which function within the framework of fairy tale and chronicle.

Hackl situates his story in real time and space. The tragedy takes place not in a far-off realm of fairy tales nor even in the historical terrain of a cliché-laden Third Reich. Rather, the background world in *Abschied von Sidonie* is a concretely described geographic and historical landscape. Characters live in recognizable towns. Events occur in locatable venues. Everyone and everything has a prehistory, an identifible historical cause. The story begins in 1933, in the middle of the authoritarian rule of Chancellor Engelbert Dollfuss, his proscription of opposition parties, including the Nazi Party, and the aborted *Putsch* which followed his assassination. Those events are central to the tragedy. But also central is what occurred before this time—Hans's background, his activity in WWI, his courtship of Josefa. These in turn are situated within the growing poverty of the Steyr region, in the socialist politics of Letten, referred to as red Letten from time to time. Early in the novella, for example, we read: "On August 1, 1914 Hans heard every church bell in the region pealing" (13). A few lines later Hackl writes: "Two years later ... Hans was conscripted ... he saw action at the front, Isonzo, the Tonale Pass, dying all around, for a nameless cause, hunger, death pervading their bodies, and always hunger" (13-14). Hackl describes the interwar period just as vividly and yet just as succinctly: "The munitions factory was forced to close ...The machinery equipment was moved to Steyr and used to make automobiles ... Hans had to wait for work ... Each month he wandered over to the tavern on Queng Strasse, where party meetings took place ... everyone would join in with the speaker's concluding remarks, hands off revolutionary Russia" (15). The uprising in Steyr, the annexation of Austria, the beginning of WWII, even the civil war in Spain lend the story specificity that engages readers in a historical-political discourse about Austrian complicity in the horrors of the Third Reich.

The embedded historical references in *Abschied von Sidonie* situate the story in Austria between 1933 and 1943. They also explain Hans's leftist politics and motivate his turn to Communism. Hans's experiences as a prisoner of war, as a casualty of a failed economy, and finally a victim of reemerging oppressive government action would seem to make him the perfect candidate for joining the National Socialists. But each of his successive experiences since the war has moved him closer to becoming a resistance fighter. His service during the war taught him that the government lied; his time as a prisoner-of-war showed him that barriers between people are not identical to borders between countries; the failed economy persuaded him that workers had to band together, and right wing opposition and violence convinced him that he had to resist the government. Thus, when annexation occurs, his consciousness has been raised so that there is no doubt in the reader's mind that he will join the resistance. Even granting that Hackl is adhering closely to the events as they happened and as they influenced Hans Breirathner's development as a political person, it is clear that his structuring of those events are introduced in a way to make us identify with a true hero of Austrian history and his righteous cause. Hans clearly represents those Austrian citizens who followed an individual conscience during the war and opposed National Socialism. In addition, his story, as reflected in his fight for Sidonie, reflects an alternative history that challenges official accounts of Austria's status as victim of the Nazis rather than as co-victimizer.[10]

On one level the novella's historical discourse on the tensions between red and brown political factions within Letten serves as background to the story of the foundling Gypsy. On another level, it creates the greater picture within which readers learn about the history of the Gypsies in Austria and the attitudes of the citizens toward them. At times Hackl satirizes the community's readiness to stereotype Gypsies as a sexual threat: "The younger men [Gypsies] worked hard. But unfortunately they were besieged by man-crazy women, lord knows what the girls at the market saw in them" (111). At other times he uses the stereotypes to remind readers of Sidonie's status as Gypsy as when he refers to her "mysterious, yet spirited beauty" (3) or as a "Moor's happy child" (27). Mostly, however, he focuses on Sidonie's Gypsy background to emphasize her as other, sometimes an invisible other, within the community, and also to emphasize Sidonie's own crisis of identity at being a Gypsy in a non-Gypsy world.

Sidonie is tolerated in the Letten community but remains an outsider. Indeed, there are times when she becomes invisible to the people of Letten as when after her death she is left out of a history of the community, "as if Sidonia had never existed" (123). At times it seems that Sidonie may be tolerated precisely because she does not exist for the others, for anyone outside of the Breirathner family and their small circle of friends. Her first foster mother returns the child after her husband threatens to divorce her for bringing a Gypsy into the house. The doctor at the clinic remonstrates to Josefa that the child "doesn't belong here" (26). When the authorities try to compel Hans into marrying within the church, they threaten him with removal of his natural son, not his foster child: "A Gypsy didn't count as a means of revenge" (39). The old man at the toy village which I referred to earlier refuses even to acknowledge that blacks might exist in an annexed Nazified Austria. Most important in this respect is Hackl's depiction of Gypsy absence as a natural phenomenon that comes and goes: "Years without Gypsies. Suddenly they were nowhere to be seen ... The villagers took their absence to be a law of nature ... It pleased them in the same way that the rapid decline in fires pleased them" (69).

Sidonie's disappearance from the town's collective memory reflects the greater historical picture as well. Historian Erika Thurner points out that the plight of Europe's Gypsies was mostly ignored by the postwar tribunal prosecuting Nazi atrocities in Nuremberg. "Reference to persecution against Gypsies was almost totally excluded from the trials of war criminals" (2). In spite of statistics showing the extent of Gypsy suffering, Gypsies remained absent from the postwar public discourse on Nazi victims. The postwar German government was initially reluctant to make reparations. Calling on the very researchers who had used pseudo-scientific studies on family histories to devalue the Gypsies as a people under National Socialism, the government concluded that there was no genocidal policy against the Gypsy race, that those Gypsies who were sent to concentration camps were sent there for illegal activity and not because of racial background, at least up to

1943. Only belatedly has the government granted victims of the Holocaust redress for persecution (Kendrick and Puxon, 187-209).

Sidonie's otherness affects her relationship with everyone and creates a crisis of identity within herself, echoing the identity crises today for the Romani people—whether assimilation is possible or desirable. Although she becomes an integral part of the Breirathner family and is raised as if she were their natural child, she cannot completely assimilate. Her brother Manfred worries that the black might wash off the baby as it is being bathed to which Josefa replies "It wouldn't be a catastrophe" (18), revealing perhaps some subconscious racism even while accepting the child as her own. More importantly, her response underscores that the child's physical otherness will prevent it from assimilating totally in the eyes of the community.

Sidonie sees herself as Gypsy and non-Gypsy. At school she tries to wash the color out of her skin. When the other children taunt her about being a foster child she invents reasons that she is darker than everyone around her. After her confirmation, she receives a doll with non-Gypsy features, blue eyes, blond hair. At one point the doll becomes her alter ego. When frightened at the thought of being sent away she asks Josefa and Hans to take the doll to bed with them to allay its fears. At another time the doll reminds her of her difference as when she remarks that she will return from her natural mother with a doll that would have her hair color. Finally, the doll serves as an internal symbol for the impossibility of Sidonie to have assimilated into this society as when it is trampled underfoot by a Gestapo officer. Sidonie's confusion of identity becomes resolved in the simple equation of Siegfried Schiffler, the chief inspector for the county of Steyr: "A gypsy will always be a gypsy, do what you will" (95).

For the most part, Karin Brandauer's film *Sidonie* is a faithful rendition of Hackl's story and tone. Nevertheless the film differs significantly in the way that it presents or does not present the historical discourse of socialism and Gypsies, which are as great a part of the novella as the tragedy of the title character. In part, Brandauer's reduced references to historical events can be traced to the difficulty of capturing in visual imagery the book's historical references, many told in flashback sentences of a line or two, without interrupting the linear structure she adopted for her tale. Likewise it would be difficult for the film to capture absence of the Gypsies as Hackl is able to do. Although the novelist seldom introduces the Gypsies into the narrative with actual physical presence, his references to their spirit, to the prejudices against them, and to their home on Gypsy mountain, reveal that they are on the periphery of this world. Moreover, when they are allowed physical presence, they remain outside the door, a stereotypical threat to the Breirathner family but also to the harmony of the community. In contrast, Brandauer relies mainly on the slights that Sidonie faces as a Gypsy.

Brandauer focuses her film primarily on Sidonie's story, partially changing the historical nature of the novella. She locates Gypsy presence in the main character and thereby personalizes the problem of persecution. Her interest is both the normalcy of Sidonie's upbringing in a genuinely good family, the prejudice she experienced at the hands of the narrow-minded, and ultimately the tension this produced in her as she tried, as a Gypsy, to assimilate into a non-Gypsy world. Brandauer finds her own images for this or gives prominence to some that are in Hackl's tale but embedded among other information. For example, she adds to Hackl's image of Sidonie trying to wash away her color, another image of the young girl covering herself with flour to become white. She also embellishes Manfred's violin playing to focus on Sidonie's identity crisis and on the prejudice in the neighborhood. One day the brother plays for his younger sister a haunting melody. But when he tells her that the tune is called the Black Gypsy she runs out, suddenly feeling not assimilated into the family at all. Shortly thereafter a neighbor asks Josefa to silence that awful Negro music.

Yet in spite of the focus on Sidonie's story, Brandauer manages to make the Gypsy girl's tragedy universal by enclosing her story within a frame. For her opening and closing shots, the director appropriates an image which has become linked with the tragedy of the Holocaust, people being transported away in freight cars. As the film opens, Brandauer shows an elderly Hans Breirathner looking out a train window to see a vision of Sidonie's face in the window of a passing freight car. The scene dissolves to Letten 1933, and a linear telling of Sidonie's story follows. After she is taken away in a transport, the film returns to the frame showing Hans trying to get a better look. The frame helps the film capture the essence of Hackl's novella, which also turns an individual's fate into a lesson with universal meaning: "The case of Sidonia happened hundreds of thousands of times in this or that way—in Germany, in Austria, and other places—but it should not have happened. People sit in offices, and people can decide one way or another" ("Ein bißchen Courage ...", 202).

Both Hackl's novella and Brandauer's film tell Sidonie's story in an objective, quiet tone: Hackl's prose bordering on historical transcriptions and Brandauer's visuals on non-voyeuristic image recordings. At one point, however, both artists abandon their reserve and address the tragedy that is unfolding in this otherwise seemingly normal state of affairs. When Josefa delivers Sidonie up to the social worker on the train, Hackl writes: "At this point the chronicler can no longer hide behind facts and conjecture. This is the point at which he wishes to scream in helpless rage" (103). Brandauer, while shooting this scene in the relative calm and objective tone of the rest of the movie, abandons her calm tone when Sidonie is delivered to her natural mother. Here the camera captures her and her new parents as they are put on a transport, taken to waiting freight trains and loaded into the cars. As Sidonie is shoved up to the box car, her doll falls and as the door is closed and the train pulls away, a soldier tramples on the doll's head. Both Hackl and Brandauer received some criticism for this apparent breech in objectivity. One critic writes of Hackl's personal intrusion into the narrative: "At this point Hackl no longer trusts his story to have the strength to convince through the pure power of facts. He resorts to a rhetorical excursus which weakens the narrative" (Schirrmacher). Similar criticism is voiced of Brandauer's emotional outburst: "At places where there is no confrontation, the film is overladen to the point that it loses itself in well-intentioned finger pointing: This is especially true at the end when Sidonia is herded into the freight car which is to take the Gypsies away. She lets her beloved doll fall and the boots of a Gestapo officer stand next to it in a threatening fashion. This 'commentary' was not necessary" (Illetschko, 13).

Far from destroying what came earlier, as the critic of Hackl's work claims, or of being unnecessary finger pointing, as Brandauer's critic writes, Hackl's and Brandauer's transgressions of their objective sober reporting are integral to a full realization of the works. Although Hackl's Sidonie reads like a transcription of an historical event without commentary, which many of the passages quoted above bear out, the historical form also gives the story the feeling of inevitability. History after all cannot be changed. Thus, while it may be that readers are moved by the story itself and the clear injustice that it represents, the objective style also leads them to view Sidonie's death as inescapable, as the unfolding of events which could lead to no other end.

Up to Hackl's intrusion into the story's objectivity, things merely happen. A baby is found; the first foster parents return it; the second foster parents accept it as their own; the real parents are found; it is returned to them. Moreover, up to this point, minor bureaucrat after minor bureaucrat writes out a report which is accepting of Sidonie and yet concludes that the child should be with her natural parents, a sentiment which is neither unusual, nor necessarily unjust. To be sure, these occurrences lead readers to sympathize with the child, to sense that an injustice is being committed, but Hackl wants more. He wants to correct the record.

In spite of Nazi policies of genocide directed against the Gypsies, the fate of the Romani people under National Socialism has been generally filed under other minority persecution. In part, their virtual absence until recently in accounts of the Holocaust may be attributed to the raw number of those who died. The total number of Gypsies killed, while disputed, is estimated as 250,000 (U.S Holocaust Memorial Museum) 500,000 (Erika Thurner), and one million (Ian Hancock, 1988).[11] Compared to the millions of Jews who died in the camps and also as a percentage of the eleven million who perished, the deaths seem to constitute a tragedy that history can relegate to the margins. Yet as Gypsy historian Ian Hancock points out, as a percentage of the total Romani population, even the lower estimates of the number of Gypsies who were gassed or died of illness in the camps comprises a tragedy of extinction deserving of more than a footnote in history books.

Hackl wants us to be as incensed as he was at this point in telling the story, "I had this moral urge, I was close to collapse" (Kahl, 14). Furthermore, he wants us to feel the outrage of Sidonie's father, who upon hearing of his daughter's death in Auschwitz screams "with such fury and pain that the American officer next to him started in shock" (121). Readers too should be shocked, into realizing that "The child could have been saved" ("Leben und Tod..." 39). Hackl wants readers to know that the reason Sidonie perished had less to do with historical contingencies or fate and mostly to do with the lack of civil courage shown by the specific public officials in Letten. He emphasizes that the story is a modern cautionary tale about courage and cowardice when he adds a coda about another story: "Let us imagine" (129), he begins and continues to tell a story identical to that of Sidonie, with one exception, it was about a Gypsy girl named Margit and she lived in Pölfing-Brunn, not Letten. Moreover, she did not die but was saved "for at the right moment, people thought of her" (135).

Brandauer translates Hackl's no longer being able to keep quiet into images of brutal coldness, of citizens delivering other citizens up for transport to places where they will be killed as the doll is "killed" when it falls to the ground. She interprets Hackl's transcript of history as a flashback from contempory Austria, bracketing Sidonie's story with Hans Breirathner's vision of her face in a freight train moving away from him. In this way she too brings her story to the present, universalizes it into a cautionary tale: "I am relating the fate of an individual which has universal validity. It can be transferred to other times, to other minorities, and to other persecuted people. I believe that it is only through such small stories that one can make clear how ways in which we deal with situations can lead to deadly results in a deadly era" (Matuschek-Labitzke, 48). In short, the story of Sidonie, in both its forms, becomes one more entry in a postwar mantra of warnings about repeating the mistakes of the past.

Notes

1. For a survey of Gypsy history, including the way they have been romanticized and persecuted through the ages, see: Hohmann; Kendrick and Puxon; Liégeois; and Yoors.

2. See Hancock. Quoted from an expanded draft of a paper first presented at the "Remembering for the Future: International Conference on the Holocaust," Berlin, 13-17 March, 1994.

3. *Zigeunerunwesen* is translated by different writers as "nuisance," "plague," or "terror."

4. For examples of attempts at assimilation see Jancsy, 40-41.

5. See a brief article on this organization, "Aufstand der Roma," in *Volksstimme* 25 July 1990, 3-4.

6. For more information see a brief article, "Roma wurden als sechste Volksgruppe anerkannt," in *Der Standard* 17 December 1993, 1. The other officially recognized minorities are Croatians, Slovenians, Hungarians, Czechs, and Slovakians.

7. The exhibition was reviewed in: "Verfolgt, ermordet, vergessen," *Wiener Zeitung* 5 December 1990, 4 and "Z5742 war mein Name...," *Volksstimme* 5 December 1990, 10.

8. *Schimpft uns nicht Zigeuner* (Don't Call Us Gypsies) produced by Katrin Seybold and SDF (1980); *Es ging Tag und Nacht, liebes Kind: Zigeuner [Sinti] in Auschwitz* (It Went on Day and Night, Dear Child: Gypsies in Auschwitz) produced by Katrin Seybold and SDF (1981-82); *Das falsche Wort* (Speaking Falsely), produced by Katrin Seybold and SDF (1984). For more on Seybold and Spitta's films see Reimer and Reimer, 165-66.

9. Translations come from Erich Hackl, *Farewell Sidonia*, Translated by Edna McCown.

10. For an analysis of postwar Austrian literature that challenges Austria's claim to having been a victim of Nazism see Vansant. For another view of the resistance movement see Susanne Zanke's film of resistance activist Grete Schütte Luhotzky, *Eine Minute Dunkel macht uns nicht blind* (1986). Unlike Hackl, who shows a political division within Austrians, Zanke structures her story as a dialectic between good Austrian resistance fighters and bad German Nazis. See Reimer and Reimer, 106-08.

11. These numbers come from Hancock's "Responses to the Porrajmos."

Works Cited

"Aufstand der Roma." *Volksstimme* 25 Jul. 1990.

Berbüsse, Volker. "Das Bild 'Der Zigeuner' in deutschsprachigen kriminologischen Lehrbüchern seit 1949, eine erste Bestandaufnahme." *Jahrbuch für Antisemitischenforschung* 1 (1992): 117-51.

Bohn, Irina, et.al. "Sinti und Roma in der Lokalpresse: Stigmatisierung einer ethnischen Minderheit am Beispiel der Presseberichterstattung in Dortmund 1982-1984." *Neue Praxis* 22 (1992): 252-72.

Byrne, Jack. *Review Contemporary Fiction* 11 (1991): 243.

---. "Ein bißchen Courage hätte gereicht." *Brigitte* 24 (1989): 202.

Hackl, Erich. *Farewell Sidonia*. Trans. Edna McCown. New York: Fromm, 1991.

Hancock, Ian. "Responses to the Porrajmos (The Romani Holocaust)." *Is the Holocaust Unique: Perspectives on Comparative Genocide*. Ed. Alan Rosenbaum. Boulder: Westview Press, 1996. 39-64.

Heuß, Herbert. "Das Dokumentations- und Kulturzentrum Deutscher Sinti und Roma in Heidelberg: Aufgaben und Perspektiven vor dem Hintergrund des Holocaust." *Jahrbuch für Antisemitismusforschung Nr.1*. Ed Wolfgang Benz. Frankfurt am Main: Campus, 1992. 152-159.

Hohmann, Joachim S. *Verfolgte ohne Heimat: Geschichte der Zigeuner in Deutschland*. Frankfurt am Main: Peter Lang, 1990.

Illetschko, Peter. "'Sidonie:' Symbole im Menschenlandschaftsbild." *Der Standard* 28 Nov. 1990.

Jancsy, Irene. "Schritt aus dem Abseits." *profil* 12 Oct. 1992, 40-41.

Kahl, Kurt. "Ein Autor geht auf Distanz." *Kurier* 1 Sept. 1989.

Kendrick, Donald and Gratton Puxon. *The Destiny of Europe's Gypsies*. New York: Basic Books, 1972.

Klamper, Elisabeth. "Persecution and Annihilation of Roma and Sinti in Austria, 1938-1945." *Journal of the Gypsy Lore Society, Series 5*, 3 (1993).
"Leben und Tod eines Zigeunermädchens." *Neue Züricher Zeitung* 27/28 Aug. 1989.
Liégeois, Jean-Pierre. *Tsiganes*. Paris: La Découverte, 1983.
Matuscheck-Labitzke, Birgit. "Chronik der Vernichtung." *Süddeutsche Zeitung* 27 Mar. 1991.
Memorial Book: The Gypsies at Auschwitz-Birkenau. Ed.Wydawca. Heidelberg: Documentary and Cultural Center of German Sintis and Roms, preface.
Reimer, Robert C. and Carol J. Reimer. *Nazi-retro Film: How German Narrative Cinema Remembers the Past*. New York: Twayne Publishers, 1992.
"Roma wurden als sechste Volksgruppe anerkannt." *Der Standard* 17 Dec. 1993.
Rosenbaum, Alan, ed. *Is the Holocaust Unique: Perspectives on Comparative Genocide*. Boulder: Westview Press, 1996.
Rub, Matthias. "Am Schweigen ist sie gestorben." *Frankfurter Allgemeine Zeitung* 27 Mar. 1991.
Rybarski, Ruth. "Zu Tode zitiert." *profil* 17 Jul. 1989.
Schirrmacher, Frank. "Lautlos und ohne Träne." *Frankfurter Allgemeine Zeitung* 1 Jul. 1988.
Sijes, B.A. *Vervolging van Zigeuners in Nederland: 1940-1945*. Gravenhage: Martinus Nijhoff, 1979.
Skrinjar, Hannes and Irina Moisejew. *Kurier* 7 Feb. 1995.
Stojka, Mongo. *Amari Luma*. Wien: Sing Sang Records, 1995.
Erika Thurner. *Nationalsozialismus und Zigeuner in Österreich*. Wien, Salzburg: Geyer, 1983.
Vansant, Jacqueline. "Challenging Austria's Victim Status: National Socialism and Austrian Personal Narratives." *German Quarterly* (Winter 1994): 38-57.
"Verfolgt, ermordet, vergessen." *Wiener Zeitung* 5 December 1990.
Yoors, Jan. *The Gypsies*. New York: Simon and Schuster, 1967.
"Z5742 war mein Name ..." *Volksstimme* 5 Dec. 1990.

4

The Films of Michael Haneke

Beyond Mainstream Film

An Interview with Michael Haneke

At Cannes 1997, festival director Gilles Jacob had red stickers put on the tickets for Michael Haneke's *Funny Games*, warning that the audience might find some scenes shocking. The headlines of the reviews then almost without exception referred to the "électrochoc" that had been administered to the audience, usually with comparisons to Quentin Tarantino's *Reservoir Dogs*, which in 1992 had received a similar caution about on-screen violence, and to *Man Bites Dog* (1992), the pseudo-documentary about a serial killer. *Funny Games*, however, shows no explicit violence. Haneke's films and film adaptations are disturbing because he deconstructs genre expectations, breaks taboos and questions viewing practices cultivated by the mass media.

Austria's most accomplished film director has no formal training in film, though he has a strong background in the performing arts. Following his studies at the University of Vienna, Haneke accepted a position as editor with a regional television station and also worked as a freelance stage director in some of the most highly regarded theaters in Germany and Austria. His first film adaptation, *After Liverpool* (1974), reveals the innovative style and social acumen that have become Haneke's artistic signature. His feature film, *Der siebente Kontinent* (*The Seventh Continent*, 1989), was selected as the official Austrian entry for the "Best Foreign Language Film" of the Academy Awards. As for all of his subsequent films, festival acclaim and critical recognition followed. *Benny's Video* (1992) received the Felix, the European Film Award; *71 Fragmente einer Chronologie des Zufalls* (*71 Fragments of a*

Chronology of Chance, 1994) received the Golden Hugo Award. In no small measure, the excellence of these films can be attributed to the strong support of Haneke's producer, Veit Heiduschka.

Funny Games best shows Haneke's uncompromising cinematography and provocative deconstruction of media violence. The film begins with all the conventions of a thriller. A couple and their young son arrive at their idyllic vacation home, a secluded lakeside building. Two well-mannered young men appear with a neighborly request. The atmosphere soon turns menacing, violence and psychological torture ensue and escalate. All three people are killed, the boy first. In a thriller, the ending would provide relief and restore the order of the world. With *Funny Games* the audience is left to ponder its complicity in media violence and its viewing habits.

Haneke continues to direct for television, mostly film adaptations by prominent Austrian writers: *Drei Wege zum See* (*Three Paths to the Lake*, 1976) by Ingeborg Bachmann, *Wer war Edgar Allan* (*Who Was Edgar Allan*, 1984) by Peter Rosei; *Die Rebellion* (*The Rebellion*, 1992) by Joseph Roth; and most recently Franz Kafka's *Das Schloß* (*The Castle*, 1997).

Provocative, disturbing, brilliant: this is how critics see you. What kind of audience should see your films?

My films are not really targeted for some new kind of audience, for if I had spectators who already understood what I'm trying to do in my films, then I wouldn't have to make this kind of film to begin with. One could say that my films challenge the dominant cinema, the mainstream film that promises entertainment, but actually delivers escapism and distraction. Entertainment, however, can and should be more than that. The spectators that I have in mind for my films, therefore, are the willing consumers of movies that operate with an aesthetics of distraction.

For all the action and spectacle, mainstream films tend to have reassuring endings in stable horizons. In some of your films you break the illusion of an intact world by inserting black film spacers, by fragmenting reality.

The fragment as a characteristic of modernism is found in all arts. It's just that film in general has ignored this new paradigm of representation. But, of course, every serious filmmaker has had to face this matter. It is certainly not my invention, a number of filmmakers have tried this as well, either by using black film or by some other means. What I have in mind is the realization that the world around us cannot be described as a whole and thus cannot be fully explained either. This central premise of modernism made its entry around the turn of century, a little later in the novels of James Joyce, for example, but also in music and the fine arts. Only mainstream film still pretends to be able to solve the problems of our world in ninety minutes.

Particularly your feature films are not linearly constructed, but employ iterations of similar themes, restatements and variations. Your approach is a little reminiscent of similar procedures in chaos theory, which can be taken as the current paradigm for compehending reality.

No doubt it has to do with that as well, but when one recognizes such similarities in different art forms and in science too, one should not be tempted to conclude that the artist, I use the word artist in quotation marks, since I would never call myself an artist, to continue: if an artist employs concepts and insights that accord with the current status of knowledge, he does not necessarily do so because he read an essay somewhere and adapted its contents to his work. Living at the same time, he simply has similar perceptions and draws analogous observations from his reality, and thus produces a similar sort of thing. Of course, I know about chaos theory, but I certainly did not come to use these iterations because I read some essay or book about chaos theory. I believe that every art form works with structures, and structures are produced by repetitions. Without exception the repetitions and variations in my films have their basis in music. My screenplays are always constructed according to musical criteria, and then such structures simply emerge. *71 Fragments*, for example, has such a contrapuntal form as a whole. Nor is this the first film in which I use this approach. Twenty years ago I made a film for television, *Lemmings*, and this film has a similar structure. It simply accords with my creative intuition to narrate things in this manner.

For all of your films?

I would say, yes. After all, a work of art, especially dramatic art, requires structure. Otherwise it does not work. If a screenplay is not well-structured, then I can have the greatest actors and actresses and the finest cinematographer, the film simply won't work. In theater too, of course, structure is necessary. If you look at a piece by Chekhov, for example, that is so well constructed, it is maddening. There are a thousand voices and every one of them has precisely the tone that is needed in its place.

As an audience views a film, it perhaps doesn't give much thought to larger structures.

Of course. The audience does not have to concern itself with structure. Structure is not there to be noticed. Structure is necessary so that the story that I'm narrating produces the desired effect.

In your film adaptation Who Was Edgar Allan *you have some wonderful shots, including a setup in an old studio.*

Yes, this may be of interest: the dilapidated location is the former film studio in Venice. An insider joke.

And in this sequence the camera gradually pulls back to expose the apparatus of production, thus exposing the illusion of the film.

This self-reflexive aspect can, of course, be introduced in a variety of ways. Take the murder scene in *Benny's Video*, for example. The spectator is confronted with it not directly, but on a television monitor; I would imagine that at some point the spectator then begins to understand something about his or her viewing habits. That is a less direct approach than in *71 Fragments* or in *Edgar Allan*. And my most recent film, *Funny Games*, at first sight looks like a thriller with much suspense, but at the moments of highest suspense or horror the action is interrupted again and again by having actors suddenly turn to the people viewing the film. This infringement of convention exposes their complicity, but also offers the possibility of emancipation from the action on the screen.

The viewing habits developed by watching mainstream movies set up obstacles. In the reviews of your films it is frequently observed that you work very carefully with the film material, that your technique is reductive, sparse. Do you have the same expectation of precision for your cast?

Yes, I do believe that I am exacting in my work with the cast, and I should say that I greatly enjoy working with my actors and actresses. As you know, for twenty years I directed productions for the stage. I thus learned my skills from the bottom up, and I feel very comfortable in this environment. In fact, I would say, that is the only aspect of filmmaking, that I find truly enjoyable. Every director will tell you that the most unpleasant aspect of making a film is the shooting of it. You start with certain concepts and images which you then try to express through the film. But then you encounter mostly obstacles. Indeed, the whole shooting experience seems to consist of removing and overcoming these obstacles. The work with a good cast is really the only thing that is truly enjoyable. It is fun, because the results we produce are close to what I had in mind for the film, and perhaps even more than I could have wished for, since actors and actresses are people with their own ideas. But, admittedly, I am rather insistent with my demands. Only in exceptional cases does something appear on the screen that is different from what I had intended it to be. Sometimes it is unavoidable, because the actor simply can't produce the desired result, then one has to find a compromise that the viewers won't notice. One can't be very happy about the result, but hopefully it fades into the texture of the film. But on the whole, everything is precisely fixed, the shots are closely planned in advance.

Do you have detailed discussions to prepare for the shooting sessions?

Hardly ever. Well, yes, of course, numerous discussions with my team, that is, with people responsible for costumes and production design, for example. But I have learned to do without detailed discussions with the cast. Except perhaps with children who have important scenes, I do rehearse with them, with children it is necessary to have rehearsals; but even there most of the time we rehearse only text and such things. I very much value the spontaneity of the moment. Even when I rehearse with children I only take it to a certain point and then leave it at that, so that there is still some tension left to draw on. With actors and actresses I rarely rehearse in advance, and even when I do, I never say much. My films are very unpsychological. When, in typical Stanislavsky fashion, actors come to me for explanations, I say: I don't know why. I don't know any more than there is in the screenplay. That is, the actors remain in blissful ignorance as to meaning. Actors would not put up with it, of course, but my ideal would be what Tarkovsky always did, he simply refused to give the screenplays to his actors. That is, all he ever gave them, was the text for the current scene with the instruction: learn this by tomorrow. They then did not know in which context the scene would be placed. That was superb, of course, with this approach he retained complete control. Actors always attempt to know more than their characters. Since they have read the screenplay, they already know how it all fits together. All this then needs to be unlearned, so that they only act in the given situation. Here is how I proceed. I refuse to discuss the screenplay in advance, but immediately before the take, I describe precisely, how I imagine the scene. Sometimes I act it out for them, in part. That depends very much on the people with whom I'm working. Whether they are capable of this. Ulrich Mühe, for example, played the father in *Benny's Video* and also had the lead in *The Castle;* he therefore knew what I was getting at in *Funny Games*. He is like an alter ego, I only have to tell him, do this and this, and he will give me the performance exactly as I intended. In short, I'm not a great friend of explaining action. I rather approach it in a technical manner, I say: hesitate here, say that a bit louder, in that way. No explanatory superstructure. We work very much as a craft, with children as well. To put it simply: I'm not a Stanislavsky director. In film. It is a different matter for the stage.

You have directed several film adaptations for television; what importance do they have for you?

Well, yes, it is simply that in film adaptations for television some privileged directors can afford to make films with a little more complexity. That's why in these past years my work for television consisted of film adaptations. *The Castle*, for example, was in fact made for television, even though it will now be shown in movie houses as well. In my view, film adaptations are not genuine works of art. And I don't really know of any film adaptation that really worked very well. Now take *East of Eden*, that's a beautiful film, but it doesn't even remotely do justice to the book, I would not call it a film adaptation. Perhaps an even better example would be *Solaris*, directed by Tarkovsky. Stanislaw Lem was outraged by the film, and quite rightfully so, since it is a poor film adaptation. But it is a great film. And as for me, I don't believe that I can avoid this dilemma either. It is not possible to serve two masters at the same time. Thus one has to decide. Either I use a book as a quarry for ideas for something that I want to create myself, then it is a failed project as a film adaptation. Or it is to be a film for a television program that has a commitment to cultural standards. In that case I should attempt to convey the spirit of the book; that I can do more or less skillfully, but film adaptation will never be autonomous art. I see all of my film adaptations in this category. I consider them to be an honorable enterprise that brings literature closer to an audience, not more than that.

How did you come to choose Kafka's The Castle?

I came to this book, because Kafka has always been important to me, and because, at least in German literature, he has made, let's say, the most significant contribution to the anti-psychological fragmentary novel of modernism. Furthermore, he can be regarded as the spiritual father of all of us, especially with his novels. After I had completed the adaptation of Joseph Roth's *The Rebellion*, I was asked to do yet another Roth film. That is the way it always is. After I had completed the Bachmann adaptation, I was offered another three Bachmann texts. Which of course I didn't do. And that's how it was with Roth as well. But what do you want to do? To that I said: Kafka's *The Castle*. In part because I knew that the rights to the book would become available. The last German adaptation had been done some twenty years ago by Noelte, a very unsuccessful film. Beyond that, Kafka's fragmentary ambiguous perception of reality characterizes my work as well. This project would therefore allow me to remain true to my convictions and yet do the work of someone else.

In a sense it then could be the ideal project.

Whether it is the ideal film, that I don't know. There is a particular dilemma that any film adaptation of Kafka's narratives has to face. In Kafka's narratives there is the element of the grotesque. But as soon as you transpose the grotesque into a scenic effect, it seems too theatrical. It loses its quality of realism. But Kafka is also at the same time the great realist. There is hardly anyone who can describe reality with such precision as Kafka does. Now if you become theatrical in film in order to transport the grotesque, then you lose the sense of reality. If you look at most of the Kafka films, reality withdraws from the viewer into something overdimensional and surreal. Take the adaptation by Orson Welles. His film is very impressive, but in my opinion it does a disservice to the book, to Kafka. Because of his enormous talent, it turned into a great film by Orson Welles. But he works under the standard of the book, because he abandons reality, and Kafka is nothing if not real. That means, if one decides to convey this real level of Kafka, then one has to sacrifice the grotesque. The grotesque then only appears, so to speak, in the contradictoriness between the individual components, but not in each scene itself. Everything that has been described about the grotesque is in my film, but my film has the look of a wholly naturalistic film. The grotesque appears only through what happens. In my adaptation there are none of these curiously exaggerated zombies that one frequently sees in Kafka films. All that is gone. It is an entirely realistic film and I believe that it comes closest to the spirit of Kafka's work. It is not possible to make a Kafka adaptation in a one-for-one rendering, that simply does not work. Because of this special constellation of the grotesque and the realistic, either one or the other will be compromised. In literature this can easily be done, but not in film, where everything is concrete and almost tangible. There it cannot work.

Though film is so strongly iconic, nonetheless the viewer's imagination is exercised between the images and shots.

Yes, in between, exactly. Certainly. In this film as well, I have two seconds of black film between scenes, the film is divided into segments, and one could say that the contradiction between these individual fragments produces that which goes beyond it. But it isn't really necessary to get involved in elaborate constructions, since a good deal of it is already contained in the novel.

Would you consider The Castle *a filmmaker's film, perhaps an authentic work of art after all?*

Well, I wouldn't see it that way, since it is not my reality to which I'm giving expression. I have a certain criterion for a work of art, namely that its form and content be absolutely identical. And that implies that already in the construction of the story and the screenplay the future form plays a crucial role. Already in the conception of the story, you see, while in the adaptation the story is already given. One could say that it is a process of catching up that takes place here, that is, one is forever trailing the book. I would think that a genuine work of art can not be created in this way. Even if the film should be shown in movie houses, for me it is a film for television, that's where it belongs and for that purpose it was made. That's all that it is for me. My primary objective is to motivate viewers to become readers of the book. If I succeed with that, if the film can accomplish that much, then it is a great success. More is not intended. Of course, with all adaptations I try to work as well as possible, I try to involve myself; my own signature, my own personal style is imprinted in the film. But I don't have the goal of realizing myself in such a film.

In your balancing act between Kafka's literary timbre and your own creative voice, how do you deal with dialog?

Kafka's text is very difficult to speak, that is, it sounds so very clear, but has a great complexity, the language itself. And this is where the ability of the actors becomes evident, because it is very difficult to have these texts sound like spoken speech, rather than recited literature. In this regard, I believe, the film turned out very well. In terms of acting, it is quite an exciting film in contrast to other Kafka adaptations, for example, the film by Noelte. He avoided the dilemma in his film, there is hardly any text in that film. While in our film the text is prominent. And I believe that Kafka's language is treated very well. There is one film adaptation which does appeal to me, Straub's adaptation of Kafka's fragment *America*. That film has a similar relationship to the grotesque, in that it does not represent it directly. The film is highly realistic, reality is described, nothing more. I rather like all of Straub's adaptations, it is again a matter of form, of how he deals with the text, namely by having it monotonously recited and spoken against the syntax, in order to provoke the attention of the viewer to the limits of endurance. But I rather believe that if that were done in television, people would be frightened off. For that reason I would say that the film by Straub has much more claim to being a work of art than does my adaptation. Mind you, this method of dealing with the text is not entirely his invention. I think he borrowed a little from Bresson, it is really Bresson's invention; I believe Straub was an assistant with

Bresson. But no matter, it works, he perfected it and it is just great. Only, that is a way that one can't simply imitate. You can't imitate a genius.

Formal rigor characterizes your films, but also the effective use of music, the sound track is important for your films.

Yes, one could certainly say that. However, I don't use music in the conventional way, that is, as film music to patch up a scene that is not working out. Music then provides the emotional tension that the film itself lacks. It is an absolutely dishonest means, but of course a good many films are saved by such music. Whenever I put in music into a film, it is part of the contents, it is diegetic. For example, a radio turned on. And when there is music, when music is heard, it is there for a good reason, as an allusion perhaps. For example, at the film festival in Ghent *The Seventh Continent* received an award for the most effective use of music in a film, even though I used only a few bars from a violin concerto by Alban Berg. The award was thus rather perceptive and original, since the music alluded to a Bach chorale that has a lot to do with the film action. Of course, the allusion does not have to be recognized, some spectators just hear music; but those who know its meaning, know what to do with it. For the audience it has the potential of discovery.

Austria has a small film industry, it makes it difficult to have films financed and then distributed. Nonetheless you choose to work here. Do you see yourself as an Austrian film director, is there something specifically Austrian about the films you direct?

I really don't think that I can assess that. It is a question that has been frequently put to me, not as a question, but in an attempt to categorize my work. My films irritate and provoke some people; critics then look for an explanation that will allow them to safely put the films aside. They usually come up with two reasons. First of all they could say, the *auteur* who made this film is a negative person, he is pathological, and that is why his films look this way. That is one possibility. But since my private life is not available to the public—I have never published anything about myself—they can't say what I'm like, so this reason does not apply, they can at best speculate about it. The second argument goes like this. The conditions that he describes would suggest that Austria must be an awful place, but thank God it's not that way here. These are, one could say, the standard defense mechanisms. In discussions I then always say, the films provoke you so much, whether in France, in America, or elsewhere, because you obviously know from your own experience what they are getting at. In other words, my films don't specifically target Austria, they have to do with the entire advanced industrialized world. And for that reason these films are understood in Japan just as well as in Vienna. In India or Africa these films will no doubt be regarded as irrelevant, and rightfully so. In those countries there are problems of a very different nature. My films are made for our industrialized West, for our affluent society, that's where they belong and that's where they should be seen.

71 Fragments of a Chronology of Chance: Notes to the Film

Michael Haneke

The title of the film
The title attempts to convey the conception of the film as precisely as possible. In the literature of modernism claims of holistic representation of reality have long been abandoned. Since Kafka at the latest, the fragment has unavoidably been at the basis of apprehending reality and is considered a crucial part of cognitive practice.

Only in film, the most recent and potentially most modern form of art, the manner of thinking continues on the level prevalent in the nineteenth century. Whether naively or cynically, but in any case with financial success, the comforting illusion prevails that the world can be completely described and thus explained. My film and its title take issue with this view and attempt to dismantle this attitude.

Whether "chance," "divine will," or "fate," it amounts much to the same thing. If there is a difference, it is in how things are viewed; it is therefore up to the spectator to interpret actions in a film and in life. A hundred people in front of a screen in a cinema see not one film, they see a hundred different films.

I provide a construct and nothing more—its interpretation and its integration into a value and belief system is always the work of the recipient. That is my principal concern after all: the film should not come to an end on the screen, but engage the spectators and find its place in their cognitive and emotive framework. In short, film as such does not exist, it comes to exist only in the minds of the spectators. A film's essential feature, its criterion of quality, should be its ability to become the productive center of an interactive process. The author of the film puts markers and signposts into place; the spectators' potential for fantasy and emotion then unfolds between these markers. The richer and the more open the texture of a film, and the more it captures the contradictoriness and ambivalence of reality, the greater the scope for the participatory experience of the spectator.

I attempt to provide an alternative to the totalizing productions that are typical of the entertainment cinema of American provenance. My approach provides an alternative to the hermetically sealed-off illusion which in effect pretends at an intact reality and thereby deprives the spectator of the possiblity of critical participation. In the mainstream scenario spectators are right off herded into mere consumerism.

How films are viewed

The way films are viewed needs to be changed. Things that have been seen a hundred times are no longer visually engaged. Years ago, when we first saw television reports on the war in Yugoslavia, we were shocked—today most of the people regard this coverage as unwelcome irritation. Why? Because repetition dulls our perception. But that is the case not only for the pictures of atrocity, that is true for every image and every information.

Clearly then, those who produce images and information need to find out how to make the images and information fresh and perceptible once again, how to restore to them the power that derives from their potential for critical engagement. Surely that is the challenge for the filmmaker. Spectators are used to the programming of television and the entertainment cinema, which present a world that is explainable and whose contradictions can be resolved. To have their craving for pacification gratified, they are willing to pay a great deal of money to the imperialism of illusion. By telling the story in a manner that refuses to be part of this kind of collusion, a film can be irritating and also productive. As soon as spectators find themselves alone with the questions posed by the story, without instructions for ready interpretation, they feel disturbed and begin to assemble their defenses. A productive conflict, I would think. The more radically the answers are withheld, the sooner they will have to find their own. And this process of denial, I believe, can be applied to all aspects of film as an artificial product.

Dramaturgy

I can direct a character of a story in such a way that the sum of the behavioral details do not give a sufficient explanation for the decisions that the character makes—it is for the spectator to find. For this purpose it is important, in my opinion, to strictly avoid literary psychology, that invention of the bourgeois novel of the nineteenth century which by definition "explains" and thereby re-enforces the existing conditions and right off prevents the exposing of structure.

Image

It is possible for me to scrape away the lacquer of attractiveness from the pictures, to search for precise, for "muddied" pictures instead of "nice, beautiful" and "interesting" ones. Search for "banal" images that only in their context acquire dignity and beauty! "Interesting" pictures belong in the art galleries, not in the cinema. Why are the products of the designer-directors so devoid of all mental tension? Why has the aesthetic of advertising become the goal and trade mark of the current cinema? Since all of us are inundated with artificial pictures of a "beautified" reality, one of the most difficult challenges of filmmaking requires that we maintain an unencumbered eye for the reality-value of a picture.

Editing

Contemporary film editing is most commonly determined by the practices of television-timing, by the expectation of a rapid flow of information. Apart from its visual attractiveness, a picture is to provide linear information which can be quickly consumed and checked off. Video clips and commercials have established the benchmark for timing. They offer the most persuasive guarantee for sanitized emotions, that is, for sterility.

However, emotions as well as experience have to do with time. As soon as time becomes manifest in a film, it disturbs the spectators who are used to a fast pace, especially if the pictures concern matters which they have learned to suppress. At first they react with irritation, then they are bored and finally annoyed—the classic sequence of a defensive reaction. If one has the courage to put them through this ordeal, they will in the end come to face the condition with which they are confronted in picture and sound. As a result, the contents once again will become felt, instead of being merely registered as information to be checked off.

Sound

It seems to me that the ear is fundamentally more sensitive than the eye. To put it another way, the ear provides a more direct path to the imagination and to the heart of human beings. The reception of images seems to me more filtered by the intellect. Our sensibility in the visual domain is further diminished by the flood of pictures on television, so that it is now very difficult to create pictures that leave a strong impression, let alone that evoke a reaction. In the end that leads to the situation, that the pictures in television and action movies have to escalate the degree of violence and horror in order to sustain the same effect in the spectator. The sound track gives the spectators more freedom to imagine their own picture; the image itself is rather a handicap in that it limits the scope of imagination. Since nowadays only experimental film uses this fact, it plays no role in the conventional cinema. It is therefore, I believe, not all too difficult, to jolt spectators out of their attitude of consumerism.

The trilogy

The formal language of the trilogy (*The Seventh Continent, Benny's Video, 71 Fragments of a Chronology of Chance*) is based on the aesthetic concepts that have just been considered. Out of this, of course, a commonality of subject matter results: all three films show an act of violence that lacks sufficient sociological or psychological explanation. Cases as they are sometimes reported with pretended horror in illustrated magazines or the local pages of newspapers. The real horror about them, however, is the suspicion that the supposedly irrational acts could have altogether rationally discoverable roots in our life style. This horror is dramaturgically productive. It makes it possible to have the spectators confront themselves, since they are forced to look for the answers which the film and its plot fail to give.

All three films of the trilogy describe life in the affluent world of the highly industrialized West. The first two films do so in the form of longitudinal sections through family stories, the last one presents a cross-section through the hierarchy of society. The persons in the films are not characters (that is, the sum of their behavioral details cannot be explained through a psychological interpretation), but rather projection surfaces for the fears, desires and fantasies of the spectators. Thus no social naturalism is striven for, but rather a paradigmatic model that is open on all sides. Of course, such a model only works if its constituents are concrete and exact in its details. That in the end is the measure for the quality of the work.

The climate of the three films derives from an experience that is familiar to us all, cold indifference, breakdown in communication, and the increasing violence in the immediate living space of each one of us. We don't, after all, meet the experience of the civil war only on the television news reports about Yugoslavia, Ireland, Somalia, and all the other countries that are ablaze, but at our workplace, in the subway and in the family. And I can't get the suspicion out of my mind, that it is this civil war that is close to desperation, rather than the spectacular one that is all too often seen on television, that renders people helpless, baffled, afraid and—in the true sense of the words—murderously aggressive. The sum of the so-called conventions of doing things, the little sins of omission and meannesses can without question be murderous, socially murderous—that is, what these films show. And the question that they pose, of course, concern the causes; the question is put to everybody individually and quite personally, and not to some institution. What is demanded is not ideology, but rather courage in the confrontation with the personal lie. For this reason the films are regarded as so violent, even though there is less violence shown in them than in any detective story on television. It seems to me that this definition of civil war provides an adequate basis for the trilogy.

Fragmentation and the Real: Michael Haneke's Family Trilogy

Brigitte Peucker
Yale University

Joined together in the sibling relationship of the trilogy, Michael Haneke's *The Seventh Continent* (1989), *Benny's Video* (1992), and *71 Fragments of a Chronology of Chance* (1994) constitute a body of texts concerned at the thematic level with the situation of the bourgeois family in contemporary Austria. In each film, a sociopolitical concern with the fragmentation of the family as an organic unit can be said to play itself out at the level of the plot through a series of acts of violence to the body. This thematic preoccupation is reflected at the level of cinematic style as well, where we find it in strategies used to fragment or attentuate narrative, and in the manner in which the image itself is subjected to various forms of aesthetic askesis. No doubt with Haneke's asceticism in mind, one Austrian critic, Wolfram Knorr has written concerning *71 Fragments* that its "anorexic" images seem to have been carved with the surgeon's scalpel from the "fatty images" (*Bilderfett*) of a voyeuristic cinema (116). The implication of Knorr's metaphor seems to lie as much in the suggestion that Haneke's cinematic style involves a radical act of paring down the textual body of his films, as in the obvious allusion to the task of the surgeon in Benjamin's "Work of Art in the Age of Mechanical Reproduction." As is well known, the figure of the surgeon in Benjamin's essay stands in for the cameraman, whose function it is to cut through the seamless web of reality photographically, thus obtaining the "multiple fragments" from which a new picture can then be assembled under another law (862-3). Offhand as Knorr's formulation may have been, it implies two different but related insights into Haneke's films that are worth pursuing.

The first insight suggests a notion of realism in cinema that is posited upon realism's relation to the body—whether this be to the body of the text, to the body of the fictional characters whose story is told, or to the body of a corporealized spectator whose senses the film calls into play.¹ In this latter instance, the real manifests itself in the realm of spectatorial experience, and "punishing" the body of the text finds its parallel in "punishing" the body of the spectator. This interest in the real finds expression in another strategy at work in these films, too, one which entails blurring the boundaries among a variety of images—be they photographed, filmed, videotaped, televised—and serves to provoke questions concerning the ontological status of these images. These strategies, among others, question film's relation to the real and seek to anchor it in the materiality of the body. The second insight implicit in Knorr's observation concerns a conception of film that is based upon the Benjaminian model, one whose aesthetic politics repudiates organic models for the work of art, and theorizes the filmic text with respect to acts of fragmentation rather than concepts of wholeness. My intention in this essay is to examine the intersection of these concerns in Haneke's trilogy, especially in *Benny's Video*, its second film, and to ask to what extent they reinforce or conflict with one another.

Distinguished by *Cahiers du Cinéma* critics as one of the thirteen most noteworthy films of 1993 on the one hand, nearly subjected to censorship in Switzerland, on the other, *Benny's Video* opens with the videotaped slaughter of a pig, a sequence notable for the relentlessness with which the video camera pursues its object. Rendering these images almost unendurably violent are the pig's squeals of pain. Deliberately assaulting our senses as well as offending our sensibilities, these sounds provoke a moral response in the spectator that seems inseparable from the affective one that s/he experiences: the spectator's auditory suffering is relieved when the scene of the animal's pain comes to an end. But even after its conclusion, our senses remain negatively involved with the film: the end of the video sequence is signaled by footage of video "snow" that baffles the sense of sight, while its irritating noise grates on the ear. Most obviously, the presence of snow on the screen is a palpable sign of the termination—the death—of the image chain, and it underlines the fate of the pig as well. In the first film of Haneke's trilogy, *The Seventh Continent*, its message is an even more horrifying one: "snow" signals the end of a TV broadcast now "watched" by spectators who have died during the course of the broadcast. Here the absent image on the screen is mirrored by the eyes that can no longer see, while the noise that substitutes for sound falls on deaf ears. The TV program and this bourgeois family of three—father, mother, and child—have met their end, leaving the spectator of the film to watch *its* final images.

A similar correspondence constitutes the central problem of *Benny's Video*, a film that revolves around a consciousness for which the separation of reality from representation is particularly problematic. Benny's video footage documenting the pig's death is in every way amateurish, and hence, arguably, closer to the real: it is unedited, it is steadily marked by handheld effects, and ends abruptly. If the definitive scene of graphic realism is, as Michael Fried has put it with regard to painting, the one the viewer can't bear to look at or, in this case, listen to, then this is realism *par excellence* (65). But this footage is marked in other ways as well. Images in this sequence are variously manipulated: they are subjected to slow motion, they are rewound, they are briefly frozen. This is a sequence in the process of being viewed, not only by the spectator of Haneke's film, but by a diegetic spectator as well: it is footage videotaped, manipulated, and watched by a fourteen-year-old boy, Benny. Soon he will shoot a young girl with the weapon used to slaughter the pig, the event will be recorded by the video camera that seems always to be running in his room, and he will on several subsequent occasions watch the footage of this murder. Benny will perform all of these actions seemingly without any response, affective or moral.

Haneke's film provides us with a wealth of sociological detail designed to suggest why this adolescent's life might be devoid of feeling, and how, for him, perception comes to be mediated by the technology with which he is surrounded. For Benny, visual perception takes place chiefly through a video camera, and the sounds of television and rock CDs form an aural space which envelops him. Benny is incapable of relating to anyone—even, perhaps, to himself—except through the mediation of the camera. In the delineation of his characters, Haneke eschews psychological realism; character subjectivity is almost entirely absent here. Yet social commentary lies within Haneke's purview: the film points a predictably accusing finger at Benny's parents, and the media in particular come in for a share of the blame.

Television reportage, Haneke's film suggests, has anesthetized our capacity to respond to scenes of suffering. Benny spends his time watching the choreographed violence of action movies and the restrained, "normalizing" television reporting of scenes of death in Bosnia. In these news programs, images of carnage are accompanied by voices of commentators carefully trained to exclude all emotion, thus rendering a sanitized version of the real precisely where the spectator has come to believe s/he has access to its immediacy. If the realism of film is conceptualized in spatial terms, Mary Ann Doane has argued, the realism of television lies in its relation to temporality, to its sense of "liveness" (225). But television coverage works hard to keep the shock of catastrophe at bay, and Benny reflects the commentators' calm detachment. Predictably, he cannot distinguish between simulations and the real; for Benny there is no difference between a death marked by "ketchup and plastic," as he puts it at one point, and one that produces real blood.

But he struggles to know that difference. It's interesting in this regard that, as a spectator of the slaughter sequence to which he returns compulsively and with fascination, Benny feels compelled to arrest the moving images repeatedly during the pig's death agony. Necrophilic voyeurism does not appear to be the explanation for his behavior, however, and the spectator is led to speculate about the teenager's motivation. Does Benny manipulate this footage in order to stop time, to interfere with the inevitability of the narrative? Does he arrest the image in order to examine it for stray explanatory signs provided by the optical unconscious of the camera? Or does this freezing stand in for and in some sense replay the pig's death in optical terms as the narrative life of cinema is momentarily arrested and becomes the static death of the still or photograph? In Haneke's film, the VCR becomes a tool to explore the point at which questions about death as the final reality and an exploration of the photographic medium converge.

As the film's title suggests, the boundary between the ongoing diegetic video and the so-called "reality" of the film narrative is repeatedly called into question. At various junctures, the spectator is only restrospectively made aware that footage that s/he has been watching is actually part of Benny's ongoing video. One of the most effective of such moments occurs at the end of the film when we see footage shot from the darkness of Benny's bed into the brightly lit room beyond. The spectator does not recognize the image, but the soundtrack is familiar: it is the desperately calm conversation in which his parents discuss how best to dispose of the body of the young girl Benny has killed. This sequence, out of temporal order, is momentarily confusing: although the image is unfamiliar, the spectator has heard the dialogue before. With a sense of shock we become aware that Benny had asked his parents on that occasion to leave the door of his room open because he had meant to videotape or rather, as it is dark, to record their conversation. A few seconds later, with an even greater sense of shock, the spectator becomes aware that Benny's video is once again being viewed within the diegesis of Haneke's film. This time the soundtrack consists in a voiceover conversation about the footage, a conversation that Benny holds with the policemen with whom he is viewing it. The spectator comes to realize that, deprived of a context and without the image of his parents' suffering to which s/he had initially been privy, their dialogue on tape will, in all likelihood, serve to indict Benny's parents for the murder that their son has committed. Hence the videotape functions not only as a so-called "document" of violence, but as its instrument as well: recent instances involving the manipulation of videotape evidence in the American courtroom come to mind. It is Haneke's strategy initially to obscure the context of the image—does it belong to the diegesis proper? does it belong to the videotape?—and consequently to allow *sound* to fix its meaning.

But what of the video footage that intervenes between the scene of the pig's death and this final act of "framing"? The footage of the young girl's murder is not, of course, taken directly by Benny: the videocamera is stationary, only accidentally trained on the scene, while its players move in and out of the frame, often escaping its view. Once again it is sound—the girl's screams—that makes this scene of violence so unbearable. As many critics have noticed,

Haneke has learned much about sound from the work of Robert Bresson, whose films experiment with the separation of image and soundtrack, thus consciously drawing attention to sound as a material. The realism of Bresson's films, André Bazin has written with regard to *Diary of a Country Priest*, lies in the relation between image and sound, a relation which Bazin describes as being slightly out of sync, as "something that does not match," to the effect that a "vibration" is set up between the two (140). Perhaps we can say, then, that Bazin finds in the word "vibration" a suitable term to describe a certain thickness, three-dimensionality, or even a *materiality* that arises from the interplay of image and sound in Bresson. Indeed, Eisler and Adorno have suggested a similar relation in comparing the "pictorial" flatness of the filmic image to the three-dimensionality evoked by the resonance of sound emanating from a source (67-8).

Sounds in Haneke films, like those in Bresson films, tend not to be blended, but to remain distinct, in part because the soundtrack lacks the homogenizing effects of music. Music, when it does occur in Haneke's films, is diegetic in origin, although it can sometimes function otherwise. Indeed, it is by means of the transformation of diegetic into non-diegetic music that what is in some ways the most interesting material videotaped by Benny—the footage of the trip to Egypt—is made to take on an unusual and contradictory character. The "flight into Egypt" is made by Benny and his mother while his father remains behind in order to dispose of the corpse of the murdered girl. But this sequence, despite its macabre origins, takes on some of the qualtities of a utopian space and time. While Benny and his mother choose their destination from among a number of tourist attractions represented on posters at a travel agency—from among slick, wornout, commercial images—the scenes in Egypt are characterized by a warm palette of earthtones that forms a marked contrast to the cool blues and grays of the Austrian city scenes. In the first film of Haneke's trilogy, *The Seventh Continent*, an Australian beach—the idealized destination of the family that will finally choose suicide instead—is also first visible as a commercialized image. During the course of the film, this image is subjected to motion and the sounds of the ocean are imposed upon it, suggesting the total determination of this clichéd, diminished image of desire by the media. In this earlier film, the space of this image remains forever a dystopia, a landscape of death to which the family will ultimately gain access. In *Benny's Video*, however, the presence and companionship of the mother, despite the horrifying reasons for that presence, are intended to bathe the Egyptian sequence in a positive light. Ideologically, these scenes suggest that, had the relation of mother and child been a strong one earlier, things might have worked out differently. Lurking not too far beneath the surface of this film, in fact, is the traditional belief that mothers belong at home with their children.

On the whole, Benny remains a distanced spectator of the scene, watching the landscape of Egypt from a bus as it rolls by, framed by a window, just as he might watch the moving images on his VCR. Yet certain changes do take place within this character, however, changes that are suggested by the video footage. Once again the spectator does not tend to see these images through the lens of the video camera—while they are being shot—but later, as they are viewed. One remarkable sequence, in particular, raises a number of questions about the nature and status of the images of which it is comprised. Beginning with what is clearly recognizable as footage of Benny at the beach, standing in the water and videotaping his surroundings, Haneke's camera pulls back from this videotaped image to reveal the next scene on the tape, framed now by the television set in Benny's hotel room. Briefly, the spectator sees Benny in the video, suspended in the air under a parachute, yelling, "Mama, I'm flying!" Then, in the diegetic space of the hotel room, Benny stops the video and begins to channel surf, stopping at a broadcast of a Bach concert. The image that we see on the television screen is that of an organ; the prelude that we hear is "Liebster Jesu, wir sind hier." The spectator watches as Benny moves from the bed to the window and, in one of the few point of view shots that this film features, we look out onto the nighttime harbor while the organ continues to play. Superimposed upon the organ music, then, while the image of the harbor is still in view, is the voice of Benny's mother as she enters the room: "Greetings from Papa." As Benny answers "How is he?" their conversation becomes the aural rendering of a family reconstituted. Although this "reunion" takes place within a formulaic exchange, in a voiceover, it is solemnized within the aura of religious art cast upon it by the Bach prelude.

From this point on, the movie screen is filled with a series of images that are part of the videotape sequence that the spectator saw earlier, of Benny flying through the sky like the mythological Icarus. But the visual and aural contexts of these images—the shot from Benny's point of view and the Bach prelude that we continue to hear—code them as interiorized images, as memory images projected within Benny's mind. During this sequence, the diegetic music—the broadcast of the Bach concert on television—takes on the totalizing function of nondiegetic music. As Adorno and Eisler have pointed out, music—and especially religious music, we might add—lends the image a veneer of humanity, and "seeks to breathe into pictures some of the life that photography has taken away from them."[2] But it is a veneer of humanity only, and since Haneke seems generally to prefer to strip the veneer from his images, exposing what lies beneath it, we might well wonder what is at stake here.

In fact, the Egyptian sequence of the videotape abounds with seeming contradictions. It is true that, since these images are images that, in the diegesis of the film, Benny has taped himself, this sequence suggests very graphically that for this character "interiority"—insofar as it exists at all—is mediated by the video camera. Further, this footage is more marked by subjective, handheld effects than ever, marked, that is, by the motion of the body that carries the camera. The camera lingers on the faces of small children in the marketplace who smile up at it, emphasizing its presence and Benny's as cameraman. Benny's mother walks up close to the camera and laughingly places a hat upon Benny's head, thus creating a bridge between her son and the world that he is filming. And, as is evident from the images of Benny shooting videotape, his mother herself has done some of the filming with a second camera. It is implied here that even the relation of mother and child is mediated by the video camera, and that in some sense their meeting ground is the collaborative work of the videotape itself.

But other, more somber, moments undermine the suggestion of a utopian space that this sequence seems to offer up to the spectator.

In particular, there is a shot of Benny huddled against a wall, taped by chance by his mother who urges him either to "pull himself together" or leave the picture, for the video camera must only record the "right" kind of image, one that could never be used as evidence against her son. Here, clearly, the movie camera that reveals these images is on the side of a conventionally-defined realism. But then, as the movie camera slowly pans to the right across the Egyptian landscape, the space that it reveals seems curiously idealized. The technique of the long pan and the scene that the pan reveals includes a series of hut-like structures arranged upon brownish sand and bathed in an auratic glow and, once again, the scene is unified and valorized by the Bach prelude on the soundtrack. But then the spectator catches on: both image and music constitute an allusion to Werner Herzog's *Kaspar Hauser*, upon whose dream of the Caucasus this part of Haneke's sequence draws, while the oblique reference to Benny as Icarus had recalled a figure central to the romantic imagination to mind.[3] Somewhat abruptly, these interiorizing images and the accompanying organ music come to an end. There follows a cut to the diegetic image of Benny's mother in the same landscape, walking towards the bus carrying a video camera, moving in the same direction as the pan across the landscape. Once again Haneke sets up a blurring of the boundaries between the video and the film. In this instance it is both spatial and chronological, for the scene in which the mother moves toward the bus temporally precedes the scene of Benny's remembrances in the hotel room.

Since Haneke, given his asceticism, must clearly disapprove of Herzog's brand of auratic filmmaking, with its privileging of interiority and vision, the use of this allusion within a sequence that would appear to have positive implications for the family is not immediately clear. It *is* clear, however, that Haneke initially makes use of the sense of subjectivity with which this sequence endows Benny in order to involve the spectator emotionally and ideologically in what is revealed to be a highly ironized version of the bourgeois utopia. All too soon the spectator comes to realize that the lure of subjectivity held out by this sequence is nothing more than that. The film appears to involve the spectator in this way in order to make its dénouement—the "framing" of the parents—more shocking. The final frames of *Benny's Video* represent the scene in the police station through the distancing device of multiple images shot from above on the monitors of video surveillance equipment. Doubly mediated by technology, these cold, impersonal images are on view for the benefit of an anonymous spectator representing the Law, and for us. But the final images of the scene, images that view the scene from above, are clearly cinematic images, not part of Benny's video: they are images that now frame and control the video images that they contain. The film opens with Benny's video images presented directly to the spectatorial view, and its middle section repeatedly sets up situations in which the nature of its images is at first ambiguous. But finally Haneke's film subsumes Benny's video. Its conclusion suggests that the cold formalism of Haneke's cinema has managed to contain and master these images and to present them to the spectator's now distanced critical attention. But it suggests as well that this very attitude of visual and formal control—emblematized by the surveillance cameras—must itself be subject to criticism.

No wonder, then, that closure and the kind of formal control that characterizes *Benny's Video* is the object of Haneke's formal attention in *71 Fragments of a Chronology of Chance*, a film that attempts—to some extent at least—to eliminate them. It is a film in which the claim to narrativity suggested by "chronology" is undermined by the narrative fragments presented to our view. Here Haneke does his best to undermine any latent organicism that may linger in our spectatorial practices: jump cuts and black footage separate the fragments of image sequences and bits of narratives of which the film is comprised. Yet nevertheless the film's spectator attempts to piece its fragments together patiently, examining them for their narrative content. While attenuated narratives gradually emerge from these fragments and even *merge* loosely in the act of violence in which the film culminates, the film struggles against the attempt to read it as a unified whole. A recurrent image in the film, the emblem of the puzzle pieces, is held out tantalizingly to the would-be interpreter, it is true, but surely the image of the cross that these pieces are repeatedly made to form is an interpretive red herring.

This film assaults the human sensorium with an even greater force, perhaps, than *Benny's Video*, almost as if to fragment the spectator's body in the process. The assault on the spectator is most obviously in evidence in the much-cited Ping-Pong sequence of the film, a scene in which the mechanically-emitted Ping-Pong balls of a practice device are repeatedly smashed by the player from deep space towards the screen and towards the place of the cinematic spectator. The repetitive, cacophonous sound that dominates this scene is intensified by its duration—it lasts a full three minutes—thus creating a painful sense of "real time" that heightens the spectator's awareness of herself as a corporeal, perceiving presence. Further, as the ball is repeatedly sent in the direction of the spectator, this sequence effectively plays upon our primitive fears that the image is real and will emerge from the screen to occupy our space. Repetition and duration, both engaged in this sequence to remind the spectator of her physical presence before the screen, have the obvious additional function of fragmenting the body of the classical cinematic narrative. Hence, the moment at which the spectator is most aware of her own corporeality is also the moment at which the narrative itself is most obviously ruptured. Small wonder, then, that the spectator is engaged in the recuperative desire to reconstitute the text, for to make it whole by an act of interpretation is to assert control not only over the filmic text, but over her own body as well. It is in this corporeal sense that Haneke's film is at its most "interactive," although, given the manner in which the spectator is manipulated, Haneke's claim that he is committed to an interactive model of spectatorship may seem naive at best.[4]

And, indeed, the search for wholeness is played out on the thematic level of the film as well, where it counteracts the act of violence that will end in several deaths. Once again Haneke's subject matter revolves around the bourgeois family in crisis, a crisis that indirectly promotes and is enacted in the act of violence in which the film culminates. The rift between a tired couple with a baby; the antagonistic relationship of the father and his adult daughter; the student who hides his growing despair from his mother: these are among the situations that are developed within the narrative fragments of which the film is constituted. In the context of these divided families, perhaps, another couple that wishes to adopt a child as though in an effort to make itself whole may seem misguided, but in some sense this couple is at the ideological center of Haneke's project. Adoption makes a whole out of heterogeneous parts, particularly in this instance: it is difficult not to read the couple's sponsorship of a Romanian orphan as a political statement about the integration and acceptance of immigrants into contemporary Austrian society. But what of the little Austrian girl whom they had earlier courted and promised a home? The film excludes the scenes of her suffering that it has set up, though it surely implies that integration comes at the expense of native Austrians. The wholeness of the bourgeois family as a guarantee for the wholeness of society: we are familiar with this theme from the bourgeois tragedies of Diderot and Lessing, not surprising models, considering the affective aesthetics to which Haneke so often has recourse. The latent conservatism that informs the relationship of mother and child in *Benny's Video* finds its counterpart in *71 Fragments*. Keeping in mind Haneke's insistence on the identity of form and content,[5] we can speculate that the fragmented body of the film emblematizes the rift in the contemporary Austrian family as Haneke portrays it. If this is the case, then we can say that Haneke's films are multiply-anchored in notions of organicism after all. But if adoption is the emblem that governs the body of the film, as well as that of the family unit, it is an organicism with a difference: it allows for a legislated, not only a biological wholeness, and thus makes room for a political reading, after all.

Notes

1. For a thought-provoking discussion of corporeal cinema, see Margulies, 48-64.
2. Quoted from Rosen, 171.
3. The figure of Icarus evokes that of Herzog's "Sculptor Steiner" as well.

4. Interview with Michael Haneke, *Pressemappe zu "71 Fragmente,"* 5. My thanks to Willy Riemer for providing me with this and a wealth of other Haneke material. Amos Vogel makes a similar point concerning control, 75.

5. Interview with Michael Haneke, 7. Without the identity of form and content, Haneke says in this interview, "then all that remains is journalism or kitsch with good social intentions."

Works Cited

Adorno, Theodor W. and Hanns Eisler. "Komposition für den Film." *Gesammelte Schriften*, vol. 15. Theodor W. Adorno. Frankfurt am Main: Suhrkamp, 1976.

Bazin, André. "*Le journal d'un curé de campagne* and the Stylistics of Robert Bresson." *What is Cinema?*, Vol. I. Berkeley: University of California Press, 1967.

Benjamin, Walter. "The Work of Art in the Age of Mechanical Reproduction." *Film Theory and Criticism*. 2nd ed. Ed. Gerald Mast and Marshall Cohen. New York: Oxford UP, 1979.

Doane, Mary Ann. "Information, Crisis, Catastrophe." *Logics of Television: Essays in Cultural Criticism*. ed. Patricia Mellencampe. Indianapolis: Indiana UP, 1990.

Fried, Michael. *Realism, Writing, Disfiguration: On Thomas Eakins and Stephen Crane*. Chicago: University of Chicago Press, 1987.

Haneke, Michael. Interview. *Pressemappe zu "71 Fragmente."* Wega-Film.

Knorr, Wolfram. "Trilogie der Vereisung." *Kultur* 3 Oct. 1994.

Margulies, Ivone. "Toward a Corporeal Cinema." *Nothing Happens: Chantal Ackerman's Hyperrealist Everyday*. Durham, NC: Duke UP, 1996.

Rosen, Philip. "Adorno and Film Music: Theoretical Notes on *Composing for the Films*." *Yale French Studies* 60 (1980).

Vogel, Amos. "Of Nonexisting Continents: The Cinema of Michael Haneke." *Film Comment* 3:24 (July/August 1996).

Iterative Texts: Haneke/Rosei, *Wer war Edgar Allan?*

Willy Riemer
University of Delaware

In an interview Dolly Parton was asked how it was that after all these years she still looked so well. Clean living, she said, *avoid* clean living. The embedment of a word or image, the framing of a text or shot, the perspective opened to the reader or spectator is everything: it can modify and even reverse meaning. To a considerable extent Peter Rosei's novel *Wer war Edgar Allan* (Who Was Edgar Allan, 1977) depends on just such an effect. In its complex structure, phrases and segments of text are repeated, incremented, and often grafted into changing contexts; they are subjected to binary elaboration, shifted in space and time, reattributed with a change in pronoun; and then the variants are gathered into yet larger iterative designs. Indeed, the novel can be read as a demonstration of deterministic chaos, with its iterations of intertexts, recurring strange attractors and self-similar patterns. I will consider the iterative structures of the narrative and their rendering in Michael Haneke's film adaption.

Predictably, the reviewers of Rosei's novel were baffled. The narrative has been referred to as "a detective story in the style of satanic romanticism" (*Spiegel*), as "a psychological horror story à la Poe" (Wagner); it could be taken as a *Bildungsroman* of sorts, with its journey or trip story, or as a case study of a drug addict. Certainly it is yet another Rosei "male story," with all the ingredients that Gerda Moser finds so irritating in his narratives: "Men in Peter Rosei's narratives...tend to be pedantic, they lament a lot and cultivate a certain neoromantic pathos" (244).

Wer war Edgar Allan is a twice-told story about an identity crisis. The narrator tries to make sense of events that happened to him long ago by piecing together journal entries, diverse notes and papers, as well as fragments of his literary attempts from that earlier time. As a student he had abandoned the study of medicine at various universities in Germany, but then persuaded his father to continue to finance his studies, now of the fine arts, now in Venice. He begins to drift, he drops out, turns to alcohol and to drugs. There is no explicit social dimension to Rosei's narrative; Venice, with its splendor and decay, serves merely as the objective correlative to the hallucinatory landscape of the narrator's trips. In a café he meets or imagines to have met Edgar Allan, an American, born in Boston, retired from the merchant marine. He introduces himself, "You are thinking of Poe, aren't you?!—Well, my father also thought of him" (34). And indeed, Poe's story about "Hop-Frog" (1343) provides the central intertext for the story. Edgar Allan, it turns out, has ambiguous links to a drug ring; there are mysterious murders, two aristocratic women end up dead. After numerous allusive comparisons and a vague ending, Edgar Allan simply vanishes. The result is a literary jigsaw puzzle in which most pieces are overprinted with several patterns.

First I would like to discuss two kinds of intertextuality found in the narrative: one modifies meaning by incrementing, the other by pronoun-replacement. The marker "In those days, when he was nearing his end" appears repeatedly in Rosei's novel. It sustains a depressing tone through much of the narrative, though its cause is never revealed. At the beginning of the narrative a proxy father figure makes an appearance, but Rosei does not provide ready psychological explanations. "In those days, when he was nearing his end, except for a few excursions among his fellow human beings, he lived entirely in seclusion and silence" (15). The stage is set for exploring the dynamics of the identity crisis by isolating the protagonist. This narrative has to do with a consciousness focusing on itself.

The lack of external contact is further suggested by a variant of the textual marker: "In those days, when he was nearing his end, he lived in a smallish room that was hardly furnished" (28). Not only is there little contact with others, but his physical environment too is sparse and deficient of the props and objects that express a stable identity. The next iteration provides a hybrid of perspectives. Since he shuns contact, only the narrator can know about his condition, but at the same time this condition is described as an external impression: "In those days, when he was nearing his end, his skin color could be observed to be even more pallid than usual" (40). A strange displacement is taking place.

The iterations progressively reduce the narrator's horizon from city to living quarters to personal condition. The next variant, embedded much later in the narrative, gives a suggestive glimpse of what may lie behind it all. "Nobody loves me; I no longer matter. It was in those days, when he was nearing his end" (67). Kohut's grandiose self is deprived of the structures that contribute to identity stability. Other strands of text point to the father syndrome. The narrator apparently has not lived up to the expectations of a powerful father figure in the dominant bourgeois discourse. Not a career in medicine, but questionable prospects in fine arts attract the narrator. And even this activity is a masquerade, more sham than fact. Venice becomes the narrator's escape, a place of repression, and a place where his hallucinations seamlessly merge into reality. His recourse to drugs is linked to his father, as are his attempts at writing.

In the textual weave the following iteration establishes both the narrator's affinity and a pretended identity with Edgar Allan Poe: "Poe? I write down everything that I know about him: American writer, poet, alcohol, gentleman, this voyage on a ship, when he was nearing his end, over the seas" (74). Even the realistic aspects of the narrative are thus displayed as fiction or fantasy. The external viewer notices: "In those days one could observe his skin color to be even more pallid than usual" (88). The host matrix is reestablished and elaborated in the following variant: "In those days, when he was nearing his end, he was entirely destroyed...Sometimes he wept. This did not happen out of anguish or grief, but rather out of a mixture of feelings, whose temperatures were the most refractory" (113). As in the iterations of chaos theory, an element of text is subjected to variations; the intent is not to progressively lead to a solution of a problem or to resolve a conflict. With each recurrence of the marker, the orbit of meaning sweeps around a cluster of closely related ideas that in structure resembles the strange attractors of chaos theory. In its final appearance the marker intimates this focal attraction: "It was in those days, when for him, and he knew it, the end had come, finish" (117). Just prior to this comment the reader learns of the last meeting of the narrator with the enigmatic Edgar Allan. Whose end is implied? The reader does not so much extract a singular meaning from Rosei's narrative, as participate in the intricacies of its iterative design.

Fragments of text, impressions and descriptions, are attached now to this figure, now to that, thereby generating implicit connections. This is done, for example, by pronoun replacement. A characteristic tilt of the head thus implies a relationship: "Then he [the narrator] tilted his head to the side and died" (22). Just before this text, the narrator is in a skid-row tavern, drinking, passing out and experiencing a small death. Later in the café he finds Edgar Allan, who is described in similar words: "He [Edgar Allan] had his head slightly tilted to the side" (25). As the narrative develops, the personal boundaries between these two men are sometimes blurred. The similarity of description thus links the narrator to Edgar Allan and implicitly to the writer Edgar Allan Poe. A later iteration attaches the same gesture to the Contessa, the victim of a drug crime: "When she lay with broken limbs on the street and felt death approach, she [the contessa] supposedly tilted her head to the side...Then she died" (27).

The correlations are further elaborated in the narrator's hallucinations. He often hears whispering voices. Sometimes they seem caring, at other times threatening, the same qualities that he attributes to Edgar Allan and seems to remember of his father: "The voices! Allan's voice? My father?" (75). In Tom Thornton's interpretation, the narrator's super-ego intercedes, the repressed past erupts and brings fear and guilt and schizoid behavior (268). Whenever he hears the voices, the narrator takes little pink pills or snuffs cocaine, the voices then fall silent. The narrator soon comes to realize: "There is no way past this man. I have to overcome him" (80). He decides to pursue Edgar Allan, ostensibly to reveal his role in the drug ring, the detective story, but in fact to drag out and expose his Edgar Allan super-ego.

Rosei's Edgar Allan and the narrator's search for the self are developed in a context of Freudian psychology, using a complex lattice of textual cross-references. Something that for practical reasons is not easily done in a film. Readers of a text control speed and produce images in their fantasy. They can linger and repeat as the complexity of the text requires. For a film the images appear ready-made on the screen, the pace is determined by the film director. Given the intricate fine structure of the novel, it is then not surprising that the initial collaboration of Rosei and Haneke on the screenplay soon ended; it became, as always, Haneke's film. As he explains in an interview: "We tried to transpose the text into imagery." To evoke the same shimmering ambiguity and elusive relationships, Haneke introduces iterations of images, but he also uses association and repetition as structural principles, most evidently so at the beginning of the film. Some of the associative shots are produced by changing the field of view; there is thus a great deal of camera movement, of zooming and panning, and as Ingrid Traversa has pointed out, of point-of-view shots alternating with a seemingly autonomous camera (211).

A traveling shot shows the narrator (who in the film is more of an artist) and the lawyer, who had come to tell him of his father's death, strolling along some arcades in Venice. The sun screen along the side is moved and opens the view onto the street, the camera detaches from the narrator and abruptly pans to this space to reveal Edgar Allan in the middle of the frame, as the dominant of the image. By this time, the narrator is already past, he cannot possibly see the figure; it is therefore intended for the viewer alone. The camera points and in its motion establishes the connection between the narrator and Edgar Allan. A little later the narrator buys a newspaper. At a trashbin he hesitates, with the newspaper and his father's letter in hand, then he casually discards the letter and unfolds the newspaper. He has decided to reject or suppress the past, and to take up the present with its public events. The camera zooms in to reveal the headline concerning the death of the Contessa. As the narrator walks on, he passes the model of a ship, signaling Edgar Allan and Poe.

This technique of establishing connections, though patterned after Rosei's incremented texts, is only partially successful, since it depends too much on the camera for providing the necessary links. Other examples contribute to the sombre atmosphere, but do not yield the symbolism that they have in the novel. In the novel periods of tranquillity are indicated by pigeons; when they are chased off by dogs, the reader can be sure that turmoil is to follow, or yet another drug scene. In Haneke's film dogs lope along dusky narrow alleys, as in a horror film, but it is not at all clear what we are to make of them. Nor of the flocks of pigeons.

One central image in particular has puzzled reviewers and critics alike. The spectator follows the gaze of the narrator, as his gondola moves along a narrow waterway and then enters the grand canal; in a long shot we see a barge and, straddling its deck, four large horses, or rather metallized statues of horses. Perhaps they are to suggest stage props and thus remind the spectator of the fictitiousness of the film. In a film heavy with motifs and symbols, what do these horses mean? They could point to Edgar Allan's supposed interest in betting at horse races, but it seems too elaborate and prominent a device for this. The camera tracks the barge, pans along in a point-of-view shot, and then unexpectedly the figure of the narrator appears in the frame. The effect of breaking this convention is most disorienting to the viewer, since it reveals the cinematographic apparatus that mainstream directors take such pains to conceal; it exposes film as film, film as illusion and thus questions the viewing habits developed for the mainstream cinema.

In this context, then, the horse image makes very good sense, provided that the spectator has first read Rosei's novel and remembers a short passage: in his wanderings the narrator observes a horse: "I once saw a horse, a bay horse" (101). He then goes on to describe how magnificent it looked. Only to close with: "Later I heard that the dealers had fed the horse arsenic, that in all its beauty it was ruined." The connection between the chemical that poisons the horse, and the hallucinogenic drug that destroys the narrator becomes evident.

The horses are seen a second time in the film, just as the narrator is about to pick up some cocaine. This time they are being unloaded from the boat; the horse lifted in the sling had its head removed, its center of control. The motif of the head recurs throughout the film. The narrator as an artist on three occasions attempts to draw a sculpted head attached to a wall in a narrow alley. On the first attempt the drawing features a large central eye, introducing the importance of perception. Subsequently the image is blurred and washed out as rain smudges the paper; on the final attempt towards the end of the film the location is shown, without the artist. The image can be regarded as a commentary on the narrator's condition, his absence in the final occurrence indicating a diminished preoccupation with his mind.

The artist's fascination with sculpted heads is a visual reminder of his distressing preoccupation with questions of identity. On numerous occasions he studies the effect of viewing sculpted heads under different lighting conditions; he takes the place of one of the heads and imitates its posture. He seems to conclude that appearances and reality, reality and illusion are intertwined, and that perception is unreliable.

While in the novel the father-conflict is meticulously inserted at the junctures of key text segments, it has very little play in the film. There are no voices to torment the narrator. Near the beginning of the film a black-suited lawyer appears to inform the narrator of the death of his father, to bring the fragment of a letter, and to take care of the inheritance formalities. After that, he is hardly mentioned. As the lawyer sits on a chair, one can see next to him on the wall a fanciful sketch of a horse, an image that is intercut repeatedly. The question then is not whether Edgar Allan is to be seen in a Freudian context or as an extension of a narcissistic self but rather to what extent he is the projection of a drugged mind. The viewer is systematically disoriented and challenged to keep reality and illusion apart. Sometimes markers are provided to indicate the narrator's hallucinatory realm.

In a chase sequence, for example, Haneke intercuts very short high-angle shots, barely glimpses, of the narrator cowering in the corner of a room, bare walls around him; sometimes they are close-ups showing the pinned pupils of his eyes; he is tense, pale, on a trip. The camera follows a wine bottle falling off a table without any apparent cause, then cuts to the narrator's eyes to signal his gaze, his hallucination. Edgar Allan is seen leaving the café and walking away in the arcade, but then the images reverse and he is coming back, a space and time reversal. Edgar Allan stands and looks out on a canal, gradually his face assumes the narrator's features, then reverts. In the next take he is hurrying past a movie house playing Wim Wenders' *The American Friend*. A hand-held camera tracks his steps; the narrator, now shown in pursuit, throws a rock, it does all the things that Newtonian mechanics asks of it, the film is back in a semblance of the viewer's reality.

The narrator fears that Edgar Allan is trying to drive him to madness; in the novel the narrator confronts Edgar Allan in a café with Poe's "Hop-Frog" story and tries to clarify their relative positions. In a remarkable take of the film, this matter leads to a very different result. It begins with a close-up of the narrator, apparently just beginning to tell the story. As he talks, the camera draws back, and reveals that the narrator is not in a café facing Edgar Allan, but rather in a cavernous, dilapidated film studio, with props everywhere, some of them from earlier scenes in the film: a telephone booth, a little horse statue, components of the narrator's room, and a gondola. In long shot the theatricality of the production is revealed, of the film illusion instead of the world of Hollywood pretense. The narrator is addressing not Edgar Allan, but the anonymous spectator, as if to say that film realism is what he makes of it. This comment on film practice then also gives a possible interpretation to the opening and closing sequences of the film.

The film begins with a low-angle shot of a balcony of a palace on the grand canal, two policemen appear and look down, then two elegantly attired men; a crane shot follows a gossamer white scarf, dropped by one of the men, as it floats down and into the murky waters of the canal. There are police sirens, suggesting a crime scene as can be found in films and television serials. But the shot ends with the scarf half-submerged in the murky water of the canal; men in boats stoke about in the water, presumably searching for a body. In other words, the film begins with an establishing shot, as would a mainstream film. The spectator expects an analytical narrative, with its search for evidence, motive and final resolution. The viewer takes it as pretended reality and connects it to the title sequence, that immediately follows, *Wer war Edgar Allan?* But no evidence is found, there is no resolution, the spectator's position is defined in a different way.

In the novel, Edgar Allan disppears, but leaves behind an invitation to a little get-together among friends. The relationship is not necessarily at an end. Haneke's ending is quite different. The narrator passes a police station, a poster has just been put up in a display case. The sketch, behind a wire mesh, shows a face that resembles that of Edgar Allan and the sculpted heads. But Edgar Allan is gone, he cannot be found at the café, no one seems to have seen him. When the narrator returns to the poster, he decides that it does not look like his tormentor after all, he had been mistaken, and walks away. The case is closed. And the super-ego Edgar Allan is now restrained behind the grid. The image with the police station is gradually reduced in size, a small screen within the screen; the spectator is taken out of the exposed make-believe-world, which happened to be about illusion and reality and which provided no hard answers. Neither Rosei's novel nor Haneke's film engage in the representation of a realistic world. Haneke and Rosei are both more concerned with the artistic possibilities of their medium than with the telling of a story that explains events and encounters. Using iterative fragments, they oblige the reader or spectator to participate in a creative process that involves both reason and fantasy. Haneke further provokes the spectator with long takes, unresolved shots, misleading expectations and devices that expose the illusion of the medium. As with his feature films, he confronts the spectator with his viewing habits.

Works Cited

Haneke, Michael, dir. *Wer war Edgar Allan?* Perf. Paulus Manker and Rolf Hoppe. ORF/ZDF, 1984.

Hütter, Frido. "Poetische Abenteuer im nachtländischen Venedig." *Kleine Zeitung* (Graz) 12. Sept. 1989.

Mabbott, Thomas Ollive, ed. *Collected Works of Edgar Allan Poe. Tales and Sketches 1843-1849*. Cambridge: HUP, 1978.

Moser, Gerda. "Zu Peter Roseis Männerfiguren und ihrem Verhältnis zu den Frauen. Mit einer kritischen Nachbemerkung zur Poetologie des Autors." *Peter Rosei*. Ed. Gerhard Fuchs and Günther A. Höfler. Graz: Droschl, 1994. 233-252.

Neuhauser, Thomas. "Venedig im Rausch." *Frankfurter Allgemeine Zeitung* 14. Jan. 1986.

Rosei, Peter. *Wer war Edgar Allan?* Salzburg: Residenz Verlag, 1977.

Sturz, Gerald. "Labyrinth der Wirklichkeit." *Wiener Zeitung* 48, 1989.

Thornton, Thomas. "Sucht und Suche nach der eigenen Person. Zu Peter Roseis *Wer war Edgar Allan? Literatur und Kritik* 15 (1981): 264-70.

Traversa, Ingrid. "Strategie der Fragezeichen. Multiperspektivisches Erzählen in Michael Hanekes Verfilmung von *Wer war Edgar Allan?*" *Peter Rosei*. Ed. Gerhard Fuchs and Günther A. Höfler. Graz: Droschl, 1994. 233-52.

Wagner, Renate. "Psychologische Horrorgeschichte à la Poe." *Neue Züricher Zeitung* 8 Dec. 1977.

"Poe in Venedig." *Spiegel* Nr. 53, 1977.

The Question of Cultural Identity: The Figure of the Outsider in Michael Haneke's Adaptation of Joseph Roth's *Die Rebellion*

Thomas R. Nadar
Auburn University

"They offered me two books by Roth. I decided to film this one. *The Rebellion* is the story of an invalid from the First World War, who after he returns home to Vienna, is tripped up with every step he takes. Like all the works by Roth, this story is very delicate, but very sad. It is the story of the destruction of an individual by society" (edel). Michael Haneke's account of how he came to direct this made-for-television film adaptation of Joseph Roth's 1926 novel offers some insight into the creative process and how this particular film came into being. The noted Austrian film director who has garnered international awards with such original feature films as *The Seventh Continent* (1989), *Benny's Video* (1992), and *71 Fragments of a Chronology of Chance* (1994), is known for his highly original cinematic scripts and not for his filmic adaptations of classic literary texts. Haneke began his career as a theatrical director in Berlin, Munich, and Vienna, where he directed dramatic works by Strindberg, Goethe, Bruckner and Kleist. After getting his initial break in television films in 1974, he turned to feature film making. His meteoric rise to success on both sides of the Atlantic has been unparalleled by any German-speaking director since the halcyon days of *New German Film*. Nevertheless, it must have seemed an unusual decision on the part of the Austrian Broadcasting Corporation (ORF) to approach this distinguished director to make another film in its continuing series of made-for-TV adaptations of the works of Joseph Roth. Haneke was offered his choice of two novels by the famed Viennese author, either *Hotel Savoy* (which he rejected and which was subsequently filmed by Gernot Friedel), and *The Rebellion*. Haneke's decision to film the latter work is fairly comprehensible when one considers the tragic contours of the narrative.

Joseph Roth's short novel *The Rebellion* (1926) chronicles the end of the Austro-Hungarian Empire in the wake of World War I. While Haneke, who was born in 1942, had no personal experience of either the devastating Great War or of the chaos that gripped the Austrian Republic in the 1920s, Joseph Roth knew them both firsthand. The author had welcomed the Great War with a burst of misguided patriotic fervor when he enlisted in the army despite the fact that he had been disqualified from military service for medical reasons. He spent two years at the front as a reporter where he experienced the horrors of war firsthand. He ironically referred to himself and his fellow journalists as "certified experts of the battlefield."[1] Worst of all, those horrors did not cease with the armistice.

Andreas Pum, the central character of novel and film, is an amputee and a decorated war hero (227).[2] He considers his sacrifice of a leg as a kind of necessary "red badge of courage," proof of his loyalty to the monarchy, the state. A firm believer in God and a staunch supporter of the government, Pum regards the revolution that occurs with the collapse of the Austro-Hungarian monarchy as chaotic disorder, and all those who oppose the government as "Heiden," heathens or non-believers (228). While Andreas never receives the artificial limb promised him by the authorities, he is granted a license by a military commission to become a hurdy-gurdy man and eke out a meager living. Andreas moves in with Willi, an out-of-work metal laborer, con-man and part-time pimp, and Klara, a cashier in a Viennese coffeehouse, Willi's girlfriend and "business associate." The presence of Klara stimulates Andreas' erotic imagination, and he dreams of voluptuous widows with wide hips and prominent breasts (238), convinced that he is enough of a man to satisfy even the most demanding woman. And shortly thereafter he encounters Frau Katharina Blumich, recently widowed, with her daughter Anni. Andreas - Katharina Blumich - Anni - it seems almost idyllic, but we are warned by the narrator of the existence of a potential rival for the widow's affections, a junior police inspector Vinzenz Topp described as being "seductive from head to toe" (245), living next-door to Frau Blumich in apartment building No. 37. The couple marry but their happiness is short-lived. Riding home on the streetcar Andreas overhears Herr Arnold, a well-dressed gentleman loudly complaining about the numerous blind and crippled soldiers crowding the streets of Vienna whom he regards as fakers and Bolsheviks (264). For the first time, Pum realizes that he is a cripple (263) and he begins to resent the healthy citizens with their limbs intact. When Andreas loudly shouts an insult at Herr Arnold, the conductor demands his license. Andreas refuses and is thrown off the tram where a policeman confiscates the important document. Pum's marital bliss ends when he tells his wife of the incident. In a horrifying scene Katharina screams at him, calling him a cripple and even spitting at him three times in succession (268). His wife seeks legal advice (not to mention romantic consolation) from Inspector Topp (269).

Summoned to appear in court for the incident on the streetcar, Andreas is also detained by the police (apparently for the same offense) so that he misses his scheduled appointment in court. In anger at what has happened he smashes a lamp and is locked up for twenty-four hours, and has his license revoked. In jail he begins to doubt the value of his war decoration when he is asked by the inmates why he is still wearing his meaningless medal (282). Finally discarding his combination consolation prize and band-aid (282), Andreas sees himself for the first time in the novel as no better than the other inmates, a criminal, a non-believer, an outsider (285).

Released from jail after his brief stay, Andreas is again arrested within twenty-four hours by the police and put into prison for his having failed to appear in court at the appointed time, a situation that suggests a byzantine legal system worthy of Franz Kafka. He becomes convict No. 73, an ironic inversion of the address of Inspector Topp and what comes to be Pum's unlucky number in life. Roth sketches the dreadful world of the penal institution in all its unpleasantness, the House of Justice that has the appearance of the Law set in stone (286). Pum's attention is drawn to the small window of his cell where he sees several sparrows. He requests but is denied permission by the prison warden to feed the birds, Andreas accuses the official of having a heart that is asleep, still beating but as good as dead (297)—a description which anticipates the final turn of the novel. The prison guard argues that God looks after the birds of the air (295), but we infer that Joseph Roth thinks He neither takes very good care of them nor of the little people in the world like Andreas Pum.

When Andreas is released after serving his sentence, he has turned into a pitiful old man, and Roth spares no detail in sketching the character's profound physical deterioration, suggesting that his end cannot be far off. More importantly, Andreas enters into this final phase of his life filled with bitterness and spite, an anarchist rebelling against everything he once held important or sacred: the world, the authorities, the government, and God (299).

Pum returns to his old friend Willi and together in Willi's chauffeur-driven limousine they go to pick up Andreas' belongings, which consist only of his uniform, everything else having been sold by Katharina who is now living with Inspector Topp. Willi (who has assumed a new identity and name from a dead soldier) has a new racket, providing toiletries to be sold in the fancy bathrooms of restaurants and coffeehouses. Without his license and his hurdy-gurdy, Andreas has no other option but to go to work for his friend, dressed once more in his old uniform but with five shiny newly purchased medals to heighten the effect of this pathetic war veteran. With only a pet parrot to keep him company, Andreas plans to spend his twilight years carrying out his anarchic rebellion against the world but realizes that he has grown too old for such a physically demanding undertaking (305). Receiving a second summons to appear again in court, Andreas Pum decides to admit his guilt and accept his punishment, but a stroke ends his pitiful life. When Pum realizes what has happened to him and that he is finally to receive Divine Justice (311), he protests his fate and denounces his God, a Divine Power who has abandoned all the little people like himself, a God who shows no compassion because his heart is asleep (312), as he had earlier described the prison warden. If Georg Büchner's Woyzeck imagines an afterlife as unhappy as his earthly existence, a Heaven where the poor will continue to have to work, helping to make thunder (415)—Pum's final vision of Divine Justice presents a heavenly judge who allows him a choice of a position as a guard in a museum, a park attendant, or running his own little tobacco stand on the corner (312). Andreas refuses to enter such a heaven and asks to be sent to hell instead. But Roth leaves the question unanswered for the reader whether his character is in heaven or in hell. Andreas' ultimate earthly fate—as corpse No. 73—(a mysterious coincidence Roth suggests)—is to be dissected by Viennese medical students. It is Willi who closes the novel, not mourning the loss of the man who was his friend, but thinking about the necessity of hiring another men's room attendant.

The rather detailed plot summary has been provided in order to offer a point of comparison and show how closely Michael Haneke's filmic adaptation of the Roth novel follows its literary source. At first glance, the director's faithful cinematic realization of *The Rebellion* strikes the viewer as a genuine anomaly in the history of cinema. If other directors can, without the slightest compunction, create a happy ending for the adulterous Hester Prynne, or reunite a dead Cathy and Heathcliff in a fantasy afterlife, consider this Austrian director who has filmed a literary text with only minor cuts and virtually no changes made to the characters, the story line or the literary prose of the original.

Joseph Roth's recounting of the tale of Andreas Pum is very grim indeed, and Haneke has attempted to render this atmosphere by filming most of the work in a stark black and white (an appropriate reflection of the life of the protagonist). On only a few well-chosen occasions he uses color sequences for effect. The lengthiest of these is the first visit Andreas pays to the widow Frau Blumich in her modest apartment. As the sentimental feelings of the couple are revealed for the first time, the somewhat washed-out colors seem an accurate reflection of their short-lived happiness. When Katharina excoriates her husband for losing his license, Haneke returns to his original unsentimental black and white.

Nothing underscores Haneke's close indebtedness to the literary source more than his extensive use of a dispassionate narrator who recites lengthy passages verbatim from the novel as the viewer watches the action unfold. In general, this technique creates the impression of a story being told for one's enjoyment or perhaps moral education. Clearly, the filmmaker loves the sound of Roth's original prose. On occasion, however, the narration acts in an unusual manner as a kind of estrangement from the material. In an early scene in the film, Andreas is being instructed in the use of his instrument by an employee of the Dreccoli & Co. hurdy-gurdy factory. Haneke has the narrator recite the man's dialogue just slightly ahead of the character in the film, so that the viewer is bombarded with material in rapid succession, but not in logical order: we hear it first retold by the narrator before it is spoken, and then we hear the words of the character in his conversation with Pum, a kind of odd echo of the story.

In many interviews, Haneke has made reference to his intention of deliberately creating a kind of "alienation or estrangement that keeps the viewer at a distance from the material. My film does not attempt to persuade or bombard people with images. They should maintain a healthy distance between themselves and the story."[3] If the film —and stage—director's use of the term calls to mind the theatrical theories of playwright Bert Brecht, his intent clearly mirrors the reasoning of his literary predecessor: "I don't give the viewer a way out, I don't give him the comfort of a phony explanation. That's when he'll start thinking about things."[4] Haneke explains what happens once we begin to contemplate the way things happen:

> As soon as the spectator finds himself out on his own, confronted with questions that are raised by the narrative, yet without instantly given instructions for interpretation, he feels harassed and begins to fight against it—a productive conflict in my opinion. The more radically answers are denied to him, the more likely he is to find his own.[5]

If Haneke suggests a kind of Brechtian approach to film, he also consciously rejects the slick and facilely commercial American style of filmmaking. Amos Vogel, writing in *Film Comment* states, "Michael Haneke's cinema stands at the opposite pole from Hollywood's artificial, closed universes, in which everything is ultimately explicable" (73). Haneke adds his own perspective on this:

> Other narrative strategies and formal-visual structures are pos-

sible. My films are polemical statements against the American "taking [one] by surprise before one can think" cinema and its disempowerment of the spectator. It is an appeal for a cinema of insistent questioning in place of false [answers] because [they are] too quick, for [a] clarifying distance in place of violating nearness. I want the spectator to think. My films should provide a countermodel to the typically American contemporary popular cinema, which, in its hermetically sealed illusion of an ultimately intact reality, deprives the spectator of any possibility of critical participation and interaction and condemns him from the outset to the role of a simple consumer. (73)

Haneke the filmmaker is an expert at his craft. He focuses the viewer's gaze on the players of Roth's novel with great compassion, the wounded soldiers, the blind, the maimed, and the lame. In particular, he calls our attention to the sad existence of Andreas Pum, who comes to lose everything in the wake of the Great War. On occasion throughout the film, Haneke uses partial color flashbacks to suggest the bittersweet memories of happier times. But just as snow melts in the blazing hot sun, the color sequences quickly return to sober black and white. Nowhere is this more heart-wrenching than in the scene when Pum comes to reclaim his uniform and few possessions still being held by his former wife. As Willi's chauffeur-driven limousine drives Andreas away a final time, he looks back at Katharina and stepdaughter Anni, and realizes that he has become the true outsider, no longer a part of the one place where he was made to feel he truly belonged.

In a film filled with deeply unsettling images, none is more troubling than the harrowing scene of Andreas Pum denigrated to the position of attendant selling toilet articles in the men's room of the Cafe Halali. The viewer knows that Andreas has reached the end of his earthly journey. While F.W. Murnau took pity on the old doorman demoted to men's room attendant in *Der letzte Mann* (1924), Roth and Haneke present us with a more realistic and harrowing end to Andreas' life. He receives no unexpected inheritance from an American millionaire such as the fictitious A.G. Monney. In the scene in the novel (not fully included in the film) where Andreas asks to be sent to hell, Haneke avoids what he regards as obvious and presents a series of remembered images in flashback from Pum's past.

If Haneke's cinematic technique recalls the works of other major film directors, such as Tarkovski, Bergman, Cassavetes, Iosseliani, Scorsese and Woody Allen (Haneke), his films reveal a close affinity to the works of Robert Bresson, with his tragic view of the world with no explanations offered. His filmic narrative, the dialogue, the visual images offer the viewer only clues, never answers. Haneke has commented in several articles on his affection for the French director. In *The Rebellion* the film maker seems to be paying homage to one work made by his idol in particular, *Au hasard, Balthasar* (1966). The film recounts the story of a donkey who begins life as a cherished child's pet, then is forced into hard labor, to perform difficult chores, is beaten and tormented, ends up for a time as a circus performer, is nearly worked to death grinding grain, only to be stolen by smugglers and then shot by government officials and left to die on a mountainside amid a flock of sheep. Roth's original work provides Andreas Pum with his own donkey, whose back carts the hurdy-gurdy from place to place. "Muli" fulfills a highly necessary function in the former soldier's life, but he is more than a utilitarian beast of burden. When Katharina sells the favored pet soon after her husband has lost his license, Andreas loses more than just a beast of burden; it is more like a beloved friend. Throughout the film, when Pum recalls his happier days, Muli is present at the center of the frame, and generally photographed in color rather than black and white. If the Bresson film is filled with Christian symbolism, the Haneke adaptation establishes the parallels between the Roth original novel and this film with its parallel and somewhat related tale.

Mention should also be made of Haneke's characteristic sparse use of music in his film, again very similar to the practice of Bresson. The director refrains from using background (non-diegetic) music in the film. His discreet use of a portion of the adagio movement from the Schubert C major string quintet, D.956, played as a kind of thematic motif for the main character is all that is heard. In striking contrast with the rest of the film, Haneke has created a brilliant sequence under the opening title credits which uses documentary archival footage of trench warfare and which is underscored by a surrealist instrumental medley made up of overlapping fragments of the national anthems of the countries involved in the war. No montage could convey more vividly the stark contrast between emotionally charged patriotism and the horrific reality of combat.

Michael Haneke's adaptation of Joseph Roth's *The Rebellion* represents a seldom seen side of this multifaceted filmmaker, less radical, less analytical, even overtly sensitive and highly fluid. If his other films such as *Benny's Video*, *The Seventh Continent* and *71 Fragments of Chronology of Chance* appeal to the art film crowds and have been shown and awarded prizes at the major international film festivals,[6] a film such as *The Rebellion* reveals a less rarified approach to film, more accessible to a broader audience. It is easy to concur with Amos Vogel's assessment of the work of the Austrian filmmaker, "We must welcome Haneke's attempt to broaden the scope of cinema, to confront us with new insights, to offer us wondrous intimations of the untapped potentials of this medium" (75).

Notes

1. The quote from Joseph Roth is the title of an article by Johannes Sachslehner.
2. All original quotations from the novel refer to the critical edition of Roth's collected works.
3. Quoted in Greisenegger.
4. Quoted in Kramar.
5. Quoted in Vogel.
6. *Benny's Video* was shown at the New York Film Festival in 1992. Both *The Seventh Continent* and *Fragments of A Chronology of Chance* were selected for the official program at the Cannes Film Festival. *Chronology* won the "Golden Hugo Award" for Best Film at the International Chicago Film Festival in 1995.

Works Cited

Büchner, Georg. *Sämtliche Werke und Briefe*. Vol. 1. Ed. Werner R. Lehrmann. Hamburg: Christian Wegner Verlag, 1967.

edel. "Sehr zärtlich und sehr traurig: Der heimische Regisseur Michael Haneke verfilmt Joseph Roth." *Kurier* 28 August 1992.

Greisenegger, Ingrid. "Aufbruch ans Ende." *Profil* 23 Okt. 1989.

Haneke, Michael. "Bilder vom Verlust der Welt." *Austrian Film News* Juni/Juli 1995.

Kramar, Konrad. "Ich will die Kälte nicht finden, aber sie schlägt mir ins Gesicht: Michael Haneke verfilmt *Die Rebellion* von Joseph Roth." *Kurier* 31 Okt. 1992.

Roth, Joseph. *Werke*. Vol. 1. Ed. Hermann Kesten. Berlin: Kiepenheuer & Witsch, 1975.

Sachslehner, Johannes. "... wir die beeideten Sachverständigen für Schlachtfelder ..." Joseph Roths Ansichten vom Kriege." *Coexistent Contradictions: Joseph Roth in Retrospect*. Ed. Helen Chambers. Riverside, CA: Ariadne Press, 1991. 128-147.

Vogel, Amos. "Of Nonexisting Continents: The Cinema of Michael Haneke." *Film Comment* July/August 1996.

5

Discourse of Aesthetics: Text and Intertext

Passion. Devoir. Contingency.
And No Time.

Marlene Streeruwitz

> Cinderella: Impossible! Impossible for a plain yellow pumpkin to become a golden carriage and a prince to join in marriage.

It is probably one of the more deplorable burdens of our time that we are equipped with the desires of the past century, yet compelled to live in the very different reality of our own time. Still to this day. And at the latest since the establishment of monotheism the longing for redemption has become the dominant leitmotif of our culture. The longing for the everlasting moment. The moment of fulfillment and for all time. Not to live. To die. Because for the most practical of reasons this moment as eternity can be secured only in death.

It is fitting that the theme of this longing should dominate the classical drama of modern times. From the juncture leading to the decision for this longing to its fulfillment or failure the stations of the path are traced out. Having come to rest in what it achieved. Clinging to its fulfillment, it disregards what might come next, continuance, the ritornelle of repetition, or the possibility of complete failure. Contents alone is represented through dialogue.

Following the same motif of longing, the pumpkin in Cinderella becomes a golden carriage. To the tune of a waltz. And of course the prince is included. In the operetta code fulfillment is more worldly. But the longing itself will do. And then one goes home satisfied. Harking back to the Golden Age. Here in the style of Disneyworld. Elsewhere it is Elizabethan. Or Russian. Pre-revolutionary. Of course. For in a "Real Theater" this same longing is offered in the form of a Chekhov. Or some other *classic play-wright*. That's where people are just as much and always precious. They have a longing. They say so and they wear costumes.

Male spectator at a première: Somehow. You know, it must have. Somehow like that. Like that. Must have been like that. If we had more time. For thinking things through. And for talking. They still knew how to talk. Then. It certainly could be better. Then.
Female spectator at a première: Yes. Talk. Really talk. You know. Conversations. They still had those. We've forgotten, how. Entirely. And no time. Right? We just don't have any time anymore. Just don't.

Of course, one can walk out of this première quite satisfied as well. After all, all those excuses that are so gladly believed and more or less openly fostered in cultural events are confirmed once again: One lives in the wrong time frame. In the incorrect one. Certainly. But in those times gone by! Yes! Then!

In the "Real Theater" the direction can still bring in, quote and invent any world it pleases. The authors are misused for the nostalgic reveries of the directors, and an audience that doesn't know any better falls in with a great sigh for those times gone by. And presumes it to be art.

But wrongly so. It can't be an apology about nostalgia. One didn't really have a chance. And the pressure to consume continues unquestioned with its platitudes maligning the "Wrong Theater." The justification remains intact. High culture that does not interfere with business and the paintings of intact role models.

Female spectator at a première (delicately turns her champagne glass in her right hand, searches in her Chanel bag for cigarettes with her left hand): You know. Thank you. Yes. Please. Yes. Really. You know. If one could wear such dresses. That would certainly. More feminine. You know, more exciting. I think. More exciting. As woman. Like.
Male spectator at a première (He offered her a light and lights his own cigarette. Inhaling pensively): Yes. If one so clearly knows, what the difference. I mean. I really do support equal rights. You know that. Don't you? Of course. Really. But somehow. They just plain knew. They knew what their roles

were. Yes. More clearly. Somehow everything was clearer. Right?
Female spectator at a première: Yes. Of course. And it somehow looks. Exciting. It somehow just looks exciting. Somehow. Feminine?
Male spectator at a première: And the people. I mean. Mankind. (End of intermission.)

All those who would like to turn back time by a hundred years, return to an age in which the arts, among other things, were in the service of war preparations of some imperial power or other. The outcome is well known. Education and culture prepared each generation of men in turn for this one heroic moment. For most of them it occurred in WW I. The women just were supposed to find it acceptable. Veils are to be waved to the departing cornets, nothing more.

Suspiciously often the "Real Theater" reverts by these hundred years and does this ever more frequently in operatic style. That is all the more incomprehensible, if one remembers that like all other arts in this century the theater has seized its own special freedom through form.

Of course. The contents is always about life. It can't be any other way. However, deliverance to its own liberated distinctiveness is only possible through form. Something that would not be repeatable in the theater evening after evening. The extraordinary luxury of its fleeting trace in memory.

Passion and *devoir*, of course, continue to be the reef-bound shores between which we have to navigate our life; to be dashed to pieces on them or by chance is as little difficult as it ever has been. Only, our time is different. Or at any rate we can recognize that it does not exist the way we are being made to believe. On the level of biological processes one can experience the emanation of roles and time dimensions, but certainly no biographies.

Of course in this inner turmoil the longing for biographical coherence is great. However, if a consistent whole is asserted where there are only splinters, then the conditions for kitsch are given. And most of the time that of the lie as well.

The "Real Theater" presumes a sweeping coherence of historicizing life impressions and sets out in pursuit of the essence of mankind, which more often than not turns out to be some essence of manliness. Bourgeois cravings for fulfillment and their bent on self-surrender are satisfied. Find satisfaction. Find fulfillment. If you believe Ivanov, then you can immediately go as Cinderella. The concepts of reality are not really any different.

> *Artistic director*: A Shakespeare comedy. I'll take it on myself. A royal affair. Mr. X. He has been waiting to do it for some time. Still missing in his portfolio. So he says. And a Chekhov. I'll do it myself. And for the rest, you think of something. Something new, more recent. Perhaps. One of those English playwrights. Just not such a mess. Although. I would find a Molière also quite interesting.—Just theater. You know. (emphatically) Real Theater. Oh, well. In any case, you know what I mean.
> *Woman dramaturgist*: Yes. But hadn't we said. I mean. This season. Didn't we...
> *Artistic director*: No. I think we should keep our audience in mind and put on a truly solid production. Especially now. In these times. Quality. You understand? One has to. Create a place. Another. Home base. Quite simply. And theater. "Real Theater." Well. You know, I'm sure.
> The telephone rings.

The classical drama, which concentrates on dialogue, and its successors, with their tendencies to epic dialogue, cannot adequately express the synchronicity of alienated constellations of characters. In order to constitute a contemporary reality in the theater, it is necessary to use all formal means which the theater has made its own in this century. Or none at all. But then distinctly so. And to declare the museum and thereby to avoid the trade with spurious labels attached to the arts.

Most of what can be seen in the Real Theater nowadays deals with the form-contents problem in a simple historicizing duality. The contents produces the form. The historical contents a historicizing form. Hardly ever is a dialectic process between form and contents set in motion. No imperative of form dissolves and rips out of the context into a new conception, or establishes a new understanding. Which really wouldn't be all that new. At the beginning of this century all this was already possible. And in the sixties as well. Right?

If Socratic dialogue and the Platonic novel set an end to the drama right at the beginning anyway. And if with Socrates and Plato a purely male-defined reception aesthetic came about and to this day continues in the quasi-realistic quotation of the classic to buttress precisely this male reception aesthetic, it is also logical to take a step into the time before and thereby also beyond.

Of course, in our emancipated godlessness—emancipated primarily from the father-god—it can no longer be a matter of a redemption as it is sought. If our life is to find fulfillment in itself and in the frame of that and those who surround it, then it cannot be the permafrost of the one everlasting moment which must be sought and for which all ecstasy is to be suspended. Then the concern is for the anarchic quest for happiness, as it is ever present in the fairy tale. The quest for a happiness that can repeat itself, that much we know about it. Perhaps. In the fleeting moment as we tumble towards the end. A happiness, which at least does not arrogate to itself all power to set up its dominance. We don't have a heaven to wait for. We can consider our own time.

In the theater too. But to be drama, it has to extract itself from all realism. In form at least, time must be transformed into the present. Why imitate action, when the drama itself can be the action. In the theater, which is a place of performance. The prohibition of excess and ecstasy can be suspended in this drama. The theater as the last place of emancipation. In the disco the emancipation is danced off and not converted into knowledge. The audience can once again participate in the vision. Can participate in its creation and need not remain an audience.

Spontaneous accessibility must intensify this present. The sense experiences can be realized entirely without the senses. Even at the cost of becoming entertaining. The whole broken into individual pieces and allowed to come together again in a different whole. Let pleasure yield deliverance from the scientific hold over the connections in our life. To withdraw contents from the kind of thinking that imposes order and to let chaos vanquish chaos.

> *Interviewer*: How did you get to write dramas? What is it that interests you about it? Why do you write? And what do you hope to achieve with it? And which role do you see for yourself in the theater literature? Do you think that is different for you as woman? Do you think that women will assert themselves in the theater? And why did you start to write so late? And how are you getting on, all in all?
> *M.Streeruwitz*: The subject matter of the classics was death. The subject matter of the modern drama was dying. I write about life.

The (Non)Position of Woman in Marlene Streeruwitz' Work

Sigrid Berka
Massachusetts Institute of Technology

Marlene Streeruwitz, declared the most promising new playwright of the year 1992 by the experts of *Theater heute* and in 1995 chosen as first incumbent of the distinguished lectureship in poetics at the University of Tübingen, is the shooting star on German-speaking stages (*Fachdienst* 4). She writes provocative travesties, tragic comedies in which violence breaks out suddenly and unexpectedly in very specific, yet diffuse locations, locations that could be anywhere and nowhere. These passageways or through stations beyond hope are traced on characters pieced together by quotations, clichés, and second-hand gestures. Streeruwitz' dramaturgy breaks up text and style by inserting now highly symbolic, now quite arbitrary parallel scenes that allude to the dramatic tradition of the Western world. Hardly any other author is as precise in the stage directions as Streeruwitz, who herself has experience in directing plays. The intertextual challenge (or sometimes burden) of her plays, which stands in marked contrast to the seeming simplicity of language in her first novel *Verführungen*. (1996), is an effect of Streeruwitz' conviction (adopted from French poststructuralist feminism) that woman has no language of her own ("Gesetz des Geldes"). What, then, is the position of woman in her plays? How does she solve the paradox of writing in a language that is not her own, of "creating worlds" (Streeruwitz in Fischer) despite woman's (non)position within the literary tradition? How does she develop a critique of ideologies as they relate to gender? And where can we position this critique?

In the men's restroom of *New York, New York.* (1993) the prostitute Lulu endures a vicious attack without raising her voice, while Ms. Horvath looks away from the blood-bath. This violent scene is presented in a laconic, routine-like fashion that is reminiscent of Edward Bond's plays, in one of which, *Saved*, a girl is stoned to death without interference from onlookers. In April of

1996, Streeruwitz directed Bond's absurd and highly symbolic black comedy *early morning* (1968) in the Cologne "Schauspielhaus." This play explores the cannibalistic aspects of the political machinations at the time of Queen Victoria. In *Trauer verfrüht*, Streeruwitz's choice of translation, attention is focused on Victoria's son Arthur, the one character who embodies the possibility of escape.[1] Through the process of mourning a destructive past, he, at least, succeeds in resurrecting himself from the dead and in climbing "out of a deadening historical legacy" (Hay and Roberts 75). Bond's dramaturgic technique excludes inside information; he leaves the audience as much in the dark about the direction of the action as the main protagonist. In *early morning*, Arthur's dawning understanding of his own central role in this play, his development from inactivity to action, parallels the process by which the audience is slowly enlightened about the motives behind the chaos depicted on stage. The same technique, which leaves protagonists as well as audiences (and readers) utterly confused for almost half of the play, seems to have been adapted by Streeruwitz for some of her plays. Only halfway through the play, in the thirteenth scene, does *Bagnacavallo.* (1993) give an assessment and explanation of the beginning scenes. In *Elysian Park.* (1993) the technique of slow revelation is modified in that at least the three nurses Kelly, Nelly, and Sally seem to know what they are talking about, although they suppress most of the informative content in their elliptic utterances. In scene three, for example, the women discuss the murder that Sally is going to commit, while the audience remains unenlightened until scene seven. The reason for her action will dawn on us eventually in scene fifteen. In scene three, Streeruwitz' rhetorical technique of interrupting the flow of the sentence by a sudden break forces Nelly and Sally to withhold the most important parts of their conversation (101):

> NELLY Are you going?
> SALLY Yes. Today must be the day. I think.
> NELLY And do you really think you are going to.
> SALLY In any case, that was the arrangement.
> NELLY Don't you want to. I mean. It's dangerous ....

SALLY Promises have to be kept. Or else, all is lost. And yourself as well.

Streeruwitz does not, however, go so far as to borrow Bond's insistence on individual freedom no matter what the social and political circumstances may be. It is true that the "voice of the director" in *Elysian Park.* comments at the end that the tragedy we have just witnessed is now about to dissolve into the private sphere. It is also true that the character who had been complaining about not being able to "reach herself" (99) ends her performance in this play with one last word, "I" (173). But this is not a quest for the self which has been successfully completed. The atmosphere is rather one of a living death. Very often, a scene ends in "rigid freeze" (end of 20, 22, 24) or in a staring into the distance (end of 11, 14, 25, 26, 27). *Elysian Park.* ends with two people caring for a "baby". The "baby," however, is only a puppet. Again there is nothing to suggest an escape out of a realm of delusion. The last sentences from another play, *Ocean Drive.* (1994), could stand for all of Streeruwitz' plays: "No escape. Trapped and constrained. Within and out. Right from the start" (94).

In *New York. New York.* there is no way out either, no relief from suffering for either Lulu or the hidden Prometheus, whom Ms. Horvath looks after. Only the deaf-mute homosexual, who parallels the voicelessness of the prostitute as victim, is "liberated into language" (43). Ms. Horvath comments on his regrettable state of being: "No escape. And. No release" (42). But then she plays the psychiatrist providing the deaf-mute with medication and analytic questions. This treatment eventually generates in him first a baby's babble, then right off the ultimate of languages, a chopped-up version of the second stanza of Rilke's second "Duino Elegy," and later a girl's voice before deafness breaks down over him once again. Quoting Rilke's elegiac address to the angels in a flow of stuttering, the deaf-mute distorts the closed space of serene beauty and completeness and contrasts the narcissism of his own encapsulated world with the harmony of Rilke's absolute poetry. While offering a utopian glimpse of redemption through language in a world of brutal violence, Rilke's hermetic poetry nevertheless offers a striking parallel to the closed space of the men's restroom which, in turn, mirrors the world. The chorus of the striptease girls in scene seventeen, "Disappear. Disappear," first directed at them by Ms. Horvath when they invade the male space, can be regarded as the comment of a dominantly male group whose territory is transgressed by outsiders, or as Ms. Horvath prefers to put it: "Tampons. Tampons. No. We don't have those here. Here we have condoms. Tampons! We are a gentlemen's restroom" (69). As "a formula" for the prostitutes' "elimination" (73) the chorus' song "Disappear. Disappear" involuntarily describes a poststructuralist insight into the position of woman. Within a narcissistic realm of male speculation woman cannot be grasped by specular representations or through binary oppositions. The feminine as a deconstructive moment of the philosophical and literary discourse is the paradoxical allegory of a nonrepresentable difference. In Shoshana Felman's words in "Woman and Madness," woman is "the unrepresentable as such, the eccentric residue that the specular relationship of vision cannot embrace" (39). That is why she has to disappear in Streeruwitz' *New York. New York.*, as well as in Jelinek's *Illness or Modern Women* (1987) and in Bachmann's *Malina* (1971).

In Streeruwitz' *Bagnacavallo.* (1993), Melisande, a late and much more passive descendant of Maurice Maeterlinck's foundling in *Pelléas and Mélisande* (1920), similarly wants to die rather than be loved by her kidnapper Romeo; he desires her, but nevertheless gives her a pistol as a present with which she shoots herself. The conflict between the DelSuds and the DelNords is modeled after Shakespeare's *Romeo and Juliet*. Melisande, who hardly has a voice, only expresses utterances of helplessness and hopelessness like "I can't" or "Leave me alone. Please. Leave me alone" (65). But the model "victim" does not remain unchallenged even on the level of the plot itself. Genofeva, who with the first words in this play curses her divorced husband, contradicts Melisande's self-destructive behavior: "Disappear. Just disappear. Really? Not with me." (64). Instead, she accentuates a different connotation of "disappearance" when—after Melisande's death—she takes the second woman victim by the hand and leaves the scene of destruction which the men's public and private war has brought about. "Anitra. ... Come. Let's go. ... It's not so difficult to die. One sees it every day. Come. ... *Hand in hand to the back. Disappeared behind the wall*" (87f). Streeruwitz' Anitra is a dark skinned foreigner who speaks broken German and becomes a prostitute in Romeo's service after having been abused by her former employers. But even this seemingly very realistic *Ausländerin* (foreigner), who suddenly switches from incorrect German to German epigrams from Goethe's *Faust*, thereby suggesting a literary education—"reason and science, humankind's supreme power" (38)—turns out to be, at least on the level of literary quotation, a contemporary of Melisande. She comes right out of Henrik Ibsen's *Peer Gynt,* where she is a prostitute, too, but one who outwits the Peer Gynt who tried to outwit her in the first place, and escapes with his jewelry instead of with a purified soul. So whereas the prostitute Lulu from *New York. New York.* dies at the hands of a late descendant of Jack the Ripper, Anitra returns to her home country, which, if the parallel Streeruwitz strikes up with *Peer Gynt* carries any weight, must be Turkey.[2] Both women vanish. There is no place for them, no position available but that of absence.

In *Ocean Drive.* we finally seem to have found a woman with a magnificent presence, the famous actress and multimillionaire Elizabeth Maynard, who has a place very much of her own, a private mountain she bought for herself. "Where would you still find such a place?" (11) we hear her say to the journalist whom she flew in to write her biography. But already in scene three both her presence and that of her mountain are turned irreal when Elizabeth says, "Such a place!—You can't find the like anymore. Actually. That doesn't exist anymore" (16), and later, in one of the very few passages in which she actually talks about herself, "At some point you no longer know who you are" (19).

Symbolically, a sign-post will be erected in the fourth scene, which reads "Top" but whose arrow points downwards. The lady on top of the world, on a mountain which she has had erased from all maps (39) will eventually have to go down and under, when she finds out that her private space has been invaded by tourists, researchers, by Yeti, the snowman, by social workers, convicts and, last but not least, by the drug mafia, who deprived her of her possession by buying up half of her shares. She kills the journalist and is taken away by the snowman. Presence turns into absence again. And Elizabeth's wish to dissolve into the glittering beauty around her, to walk into the sky-blue and then into nothingness (80) has turned real in a very different way. Elizabeth—as a seductive actress once a scapegoat for men's fetishizations—disappears as a projection out of a mirror or movie screen. To be, to be real seems possible only in the realm of projection. To demonstrate this model of woman and to use it as the medium for an ideological critique along the lines of feminist and cultural politics, Streeruwitz conjures up a witness with his own identity crisis, Hofmannsthal's Count Karl Bühl from *Der Schwierige* (*The Difficult Man*), here in the role of the snowman Yeti. In *Ocean Drive.* Yeti confides in Professor Severini, rambling on about his drives and about women: "Women. Women just happen to be the more complete race. They are complete with such a nonchalance. They are there and already have everything" (52). This image of woman as phallus is disqualified as fetishization. Yeti turns out to have turned into a homosexual who left his wife Helen (from *Der Schwierige*) because of his urge to cross-dress in her clothes.

An exception to the rule of women's fate seems to be Ms. Horvath in *New York. New York.*, who reigns supreme in the underworld of a pissoir. She keeps fate's threads in her knitting hands. Her name, Horvath, underscores her role as a diagnostician of a stagnant and perverted middle-class, as an agent, who in the tradition of language skepticism in Austrian literature, unmasks clichéd language, the speechlessness, and the totalitarian jargon of the characters entering her subterranean realm. She sometimes lives up to her role as, for example, in a conversation with the tour guide Sellner whose phrase, "I did not participate in the war" (53), she comments on with a sudden insight "Nobody did. It evolves by itself" (53). But while Ödön von Horváth proved to have been an advocate for women's rights by problematizing the double oppression of women in almost all of his plays, Streeruwitz' Ms. Horvath simply looks away in the face of violence and goes about her usual business. So she is part of the world, which she, as bearer of her name, promised to analyze in a most penetrating and subtle way. She is resigned about her ability to intervene. "I'm an old woman. I've seen enough" (56). As for the other protagonists, her alienation is shown as a depletion of consciousness. But she harbors a secret as the guardian of "the dear Mr. Prometheus" (23), whom she offers water and releases from water behind a closed toilet door. Prometheus, prototype of a being suffering for mankind and fighting against necessity, who was enchained by "power" and "violence," has—as the violent scenes in this "k. u. k. Bedürfnisanstalt" demonstrate forcefully—still not been released since mythical times. With her zeal for classical music Ms. Horvath seems to honor her prominent guest out of whose hands the world also received the arts (60):

> Why don't you do something beautiful, Professor? *She is moved.* Just now. Just now I was listening to my Turandot again. When the two sing. In the end. And the dead Liu. That is something. That's what you should do.

But she instrumentalizes both Prometheus and his legacy, the arts, when she uses music to escape the world of violence she is entrapped in, and when she makes money by allowing Prometheus to be photographed by a group of Japanese tourists in the last scene. She thus makes the provider of the arts an involuntary star in the culture industry. Yet by tending the bearer of civilization, Ms. Horvath seems to keep alive the hope for redemption, a word that figures prominently in this play. When she defends the toilet bowls from being destroyed by Professor Chrobath, the streetworker several times cries "redemption" (69-72). "Not here, with me around. Not here, the occident. Destroy whatever you wish. Just not here where I am" (58). Chrobath, who is awaiting the apocalypse, later succeeds in the destruction of "Western civilization" (or the toilet bowl) through an Eastern karate hit, although he pays the price of being blinded by Ms. Horvath (like Lear and Oedipus). Chrobath, who appears in several of Streeruwitz' plays and her novel, acts out his symptoms in *New York. New York.*, offering only a vague motivation ("Don't you realize? We are dissolving and disintegrating. And suddenly. Not there anymore. Nothing happened. And we are gone. Wiped out" (59f). In *Elysian Park.*, a play about three nurses tending three older men in wheelchairs underneath a freeway ramp, he serves as analyst of his New Yorkian symptoms and those of Marie, a character who surprises an interviewing social worker with a long monologue about feelings of dissolution: "The stone slabs, the graves, and I feel myself bloating and swelling..." (150). The social worker is overwhelmed—"We'll enter 'taking a walk'" (126). Prof. Chrobath, here a specialist in the area of "psychopathological textual analysis" (150) analyzes Marie's text in a way that is ironically self-referential with respect to Streeruwitz' own style of writing (151):

> The dissolution of the context of sentences, especially the identity of subject and object, points towards a deeply grounded weakening of self focus. The formal loss of grammar coincides with negative metaphors of dissolution which, in itself, can be attributed to hardly repressable anxieties of final self loss, to the annihilation of the borders between inside and out... (EP151)

The style of dissolution which Chrobath calls "typically female" (151) and which he stereotypically leads back to a missing relationship with the mother, anticipates some critics' comments. Thus Schmid-Mühlisch, for example, remarks that Streeruwitz' language corresponds to the psychotic state (5). This style of dissolution is indeed a trademark of Streeruwitz' elliptic writing. She seems to cut through her protagonists' speech with a knife, separating subjects from their actions (verbs), as in Ms. Horvath's "The smell alone. No. Please no blood. This smell, I've. Never. My god. And old Horvath" (11). In *Tolmezzo.* Stoll reminisces: "Yes. In former times. In former times. Gretl was still around then. But. You too" (11).

According to Streeruwitz, verbs keep things in check and thus are not appropriate for the present in which everything is dissolving (Schmid-Mühlisch 5). Hence she blocks the flow of speech by her notorious use of the period, which then allows only for a furor of main sentences. This is at the same time an extreme form of parataxis, a very modern heritage and a decidedly anti-metaphysical gesture. The marker of the end of a sentence interferes with linear thinking, with the promise of historical progress. Isenschmid, for example, in his review referred to the staccato style of Streeruwitz' recent novel *Verführungen.* as "the jolting and twitching stop-and-go of her shrapnel syntax." It draws the reader into the action rather than showing it, renders him or her as breathless as the main figure whose interior monologue forces the reader into close identification with her perspective, allowing no way out of this fragmented world. *Verführungen.* is framed by two calls which Helene, the novel's heroine, receives at the very beginning and the very end of her quest to come to peace with her world which is threatening to fall apart. The technical medium of the telephone in the novel's first sentence, which represents a present absence, the passive structure of the novel's last sentence, as well as Streeruwitz' cutting punctuation underscore the dominant theme in this text: Helene has lost control over her once so orderly world; she is merely driven by the people she loves or hates, and she can only take a deep breath at the end when she is being "called upon" in a more symbolic way, hopefully to come to terms with herself now. The first and last sentences read:

> The telephone rang at 3 a.m. Püppi was on the phone. Helene was to come. Immediately. Urgently. Or did she have better things to do than take care of her friend? Was she busy? Perhaps with a Swede? Helene got dressed. (7)

> So the money should be there soon. Helene leaned her head against the wall behind her. First she would do the computer course. And then it would be Christmas. And then. Next year everything would turn to the better. Helene was called up. (296)

In the world of her dramas Streeruwitz' unusual punctuation fulfills yet another function. Johanna Tomek, who directed *Sloane Square.*, comments: "The little dramas that emerge behind every single sentence are left to the spectator to think to completion" (Huber-Lang 62f).

The destruction of grammatical structures, the rhetorical device of a sudden break called aposiopesis (Wille 32f), serves at the same time to create tension and to unmask the restricted code of the speakers' missing reign over their thoughts. But it is also the grammatical consequence of Streeruwitz' dream of a theater without catharsis, in which the theatrical figures rather than resolving a conflict, just appear and disappear again, following an undramatical tempo that Streeruwitz associates with women (Detje 39-40). Fittingly, the D'Annunzio figure, who pops up out of nowhere in the twelfth scene of *Sloan Square.*, reminds the three women tourists waiting for the next subway that they are not positioned rightly in this subterranean (and at the same time theatrical) space:

> D'ANNUNZIO Ah. Indispositions. At this place. My Ladies. How can I be of help? This is a tragedy. Here. My Ladies. Allow me to accompany you to a more fitting realm. Here. My Ladies. Here is no place for you. (110)

D'Annunzio then conjures up the non-place or u-topos of an idyllic childhood, and the women follow him daydreaming about a different state of being, a Musilian "Other State," which provides them with a sudden awareness of their present feeling of alienation. Frau Marenzi, who in scene seven had declared: "Sometimes now I have the feeling that I don't. Exist at all. Never existed. Actually" (101), now speaks with Iphigenia's voice.

> Why are you full of doubt and hesitation?
> You leave your solitude's sure foothold now
> And launch into the deep, where the waves toss you,
> Where in dismay you look upon the world
> And on yourself, and fail to recognize them. (123f)

The contrast between Goethe's tragedy and Streeruwitz' play sheds light on Streeruwitz' citation technique. She collapses the enlightened humanist's voice with Frau Marenzi's sudden flashes of self-awareness which are overshadowed by feelings of self-destruction. Her utterances about the loss of self-worthiness are, in turn, annotated by the violent scenes she witnesses when a punk is killed in front of her eyes. At first she tried to stay out of this conflictive situation, "We are foreign here. That does not concern us. Leopold" (90). Nevertheless, the stage directions insist on repeating the scene three times throughout the play. It thus serves as a constant reminder of a world, and in particular Frau Marenzi's world, seemingly in order but falling apart. Hence when Frau Marenzi is asked by a fellow tourist why she, the mother of two children, does not want her daughter-in-law to have her child, she answers in a way that questions family values from antiquity to postmodernity. She thus also overshadows Goethe's humanistic conflict resolution, which has the daughter Iphigenia return back home. Frau Marenzi phrases her critique of motherhood and of her prospect of returning from a foreign island (England) to her home in Austria much less eloquently than Iphigenia, but at least with equal ambivalence regarding reintegration:

> I don't know what to say. But. Somehow. Just at the moment. When it is. When everyone sits at the dinner table. Then. It is right. But then. Afterwards. Everything gone. No reason left anymore. None. (101)

By colliding the voice of an ancient daughter with that of a modern-day mother Streeruwitz gets across her agenda (which bears similarities to Christa Wolf's antiquity projects) that the everyday life of women can, by all means, be a subject of tragedy. But there is no victorious resolution of conflict in sight, neither a ship (the antique means of uniting family members), nor a subway (112):

> FRAU FISCHER We are waiting for the subway.
> FRAU MARENZI To Victoria.
> FRAU FISCHER But none is coming.

It seems that the timing simply isn't right. That's why D'Annunzio's efforts to rescue the three women into the realm of tragedy where, in his words, "redemption has to be there for many" (115), are interrupted by a beach salesman who as importunately as symbolically tries to hawk watches. The technique of juxtaposing text material from up to five different time zones throughout one play proves effective again when the words of Marenzi's son Michael in scene three—"Mama is always afraid that she will miss something.—Even though she has never been late" (86)—are disqualified by a children's song which the three waiting women remember. It is the song about proud Lieschen who waits for a king's son but ultimately ends up with a swineherd (scene 9). The song which describes Frau Marenzi's shattered dreams of a happy marriage and proves her son's assessment of her situation wrong is moreover paralleled by the reasoning of a woman whose famous existence as an unruly queen hadn't saved her from a cruel fate either. In scene eight, the bag lady who had begun cutting up a puppet in the same scene in which Frau Maria Marenzi expresses herself against her grandchild-to-be (scene 7), is given the voice of Maria Stuart. To underscore the theme of vanity underlying the atmosphere of this play, Streeruwitz chooses the baroque Maria Stuart from Andreas Gryphius' "Trauer-Spil," *Ermordete Majestät oder König von GrossBritannien* (*Murdered Majesty or King of Great Britain*): "Damned the day when we were born of kings / who fathered kings / by kings chosen" (104).[3]

A similar juxtaposition occurs in *Waikiki-Beach.* (1993), a play about Helene, wife of the present mayor of a city who hopes to be reelected, and her lover, a journalist of a local newspaper who is a political enemy of the mayor. When the amorous couple meet in an abandoned house, because they cannot afford to be seen elsewhere in public, both the scene of their flirtations and their first dialogue bespeaks right from the start the soon-to-come break-up of their relationship: "HELENE Doesn't it work? Dear. MICHAEL Sure it does. It has to. Shit" (9). Instead of enjoying the eroticism her marriage lacks, this modern day Helena laments her existence or better non-existence "In the past I haven't been sure whether I really existed. But now. Now I surely don't exist anymore. Simply not anymore" (14). Neither Michael's suggestion that she should start working, "That serves everyone right. To have one's place" (48), nor his daydreaming about getting a divorce and marrying Helene can make her give in to his attempts at seduction. Helene's complete disillusion in scene six is the starting point of what the stage direction in scene seven calls, a "tragedy." Helene is only a ghost of herself as long as she is still alive. As we will see later on, she'll come into being in the moment of her death. Here is her dialogue with Michael in scene six (26):

> HELENE: What's there left for me to do? Without the most horrible consequences for everyone else. Nothing. I can't do anything anymore. Entangled. One day you wake up. And you are entangled. That's how it is.

Scene seven conjures up the separation scene of a more famous amorous couple, that of Antony and Cleopatra. Although Antony and Cleopatra part on good terms—"ANTONY/MICHAEL I'll leave you, lady. ... Our separation so abides and flies/ That you residing here goes with me,/ And I hence fleeting here remain with thee./ Away!" (29)—our knowledge of Cleopatra's end foreshadows that of Helene.[4]

Towards the end of the play she attempts to save a bag lady from being eliminated by some neonazis while Michael flees from the scene of violence; she herself is beaten to death. Michael and her husband Rudolf, who return too late to the scene of the crime, for political reasons agree to cover up both the murder and the love affair. The two men's initial reaction to seeing Helene's corpse, which elevates the dead body into a realm of existence, is a good example of Streeruwitz' effective rhetorical device, the ellipsis: "RUDOLF: She. She is... MICHAEL: She is." The reader may simply add a factual "is dead" here. But s/he can also fill in what still resonates from Michael's long monologue in scene nine, "is an inconvenient disturbance" (35):

> When we have sex. Perhaps for two seconds there is. An imagination of something. What do I know? Desire. Closeness. And then everybody goes and collects new strength for the next complication. ... But that seems to be your role. A disturbance. An eternal disturbance.

For Streeruwitz there is no doubt who the real murderers are. Avoiding a too simplistic model of social realism she simply chooses an ancient commentary on an ancient scene of crime to comment on the tragic outcome of Helene's love affair: Aischylos, *Agammemnon*, verses 1347-1371, as the stage direction of scene twenty-six requests. The chorus' careful pondering about how to react while the murderer escapes is seen by Streeruwitz as failure to act and providing cover for the guilty party (73). Her citation technique is thus an attempt at capturing the age-old battle between woman and man without falling into the trap of an essentialist feminism on the one hand, and a pure symbolism on the other. But even this theatrical or formal solution of fitting women's lives into a new kind of tragedy is challenged and parodied by some minor protagonists of the same play. "The Three Fat Ladies" watch the lovers' embrace as if looking at a picture in an exhibition about "realism" (22f):

> ALL TOGETHER: ... Sacrifice. Lovers. Human sacrifice.
> 2nd FAT LADY: Shall social critique be transported here?
> 3rd FAT LADY: What does social critique have to do with art? Again a man's addiction. To preach.
> 1st FAT LADY: A somewhat theatrical attempt at the couple.
> 2nd FAT LADY: It is not workable.
> 3rd FAT LADY: Here one should advise the artist.
> 1st FAT LADY: to remember a bit more radically
> 2nd FAT LADY: that if reality at all
> 3rd FAT LADY: then only the respectively completely
> 1st FAT LADY: specific reality carries a legitimation.

In her essay "Passion. Devoir. Kontingenz. Und keine Zeit." Streeruwitz explains her vision of a "theater as the last place of liberation," and emphasizes a formal solution of the problem of transforming time into presence. Whereas redemption could still be the solution of classical drama, theater today requires the cooperation of the audience in an anarchical search for happiness. Streeruwitz writes (31):

> Spontaneous accessibility has to condense this presence. The senses can also be addressed in a completely senseless way.

> Even at the cost of becoming entertaining. The whole broken into pieces and becoming a new whole. Escape the scientification of our life contexts via desire. Pull the content out of classifying thinking and cope with chaos via chaos.

Sentences disrupted by punctuation marks set an end to a strain of thought that has just begun; her plays are fragmented into often incoherent scenes. Both of these devices are part of Streeruwitz' formal solution of having to write without a voice of her own, of having to create places that are non-places, u-topoi. It is the only way in which—since the beginning of modernism—the creation of a new whole is still possible. Given the outright anti-utopianism of her plays the utopian vision of a theater as anti-world is rather striking. It is still largely indebted to what Adorno in the paralipomena of his *Ästhetische Theorie* calls "constellation." He writes (462):

> Unconsciously every work of art must ask itself if and how it can exist as utopia: always only through the constellation of its elements. The work of art transcends not by the bare and abstract difference from the unvarying, but rather by taking the unvarying into itself, taking it apart, and putting it back together again; such composition is what is usually called aesthetic creativity. Accordingly, the truth content of works of art is to be judged in terms of the extent to which they are able to reconfigure the other out of the unvarying.

This form of a formal utopia, which Adorno formulated and to which Streeruwitz still adheres, is directed against what she calls Austria's deep-rooted culture of hope.[5] The hope for a realizable utopia is hence deconstructed in a passage from *Tolmezzo. Eine symphonische Dichtung.* (*Tolmezzo. A Symphonic Poetry*, 1994) where yet another Krobath in the tradition of language scepticism philosophizes about language's potential or non-potential to express "the other" (19):

> What once was the precondition for liberation. The subjunctive.

> The possibility to imagine an other state. The possibility of possibilities. Well. It is this form now which will cost us our liberty. We are ruled by a grammar which owns the possibility of an imagination of the real in its subjunctive form, but which, due to the pauperization of its form, is expressed in the indicative mode. ... The promise of a whole that is possible in actuality—a lie by putting to rest the subjunctive in the indicative mode.

He, however, does not have the last word. His high-flying theory about the burial of language's potential is, in turn, unmasked as an explanation and compensation for his own lack of potency: "GRETL *to Manon*: He is impotent" (20). Not theory, Streeruwitz might have added, but theater is the place for (woman's) non-place.

Notes

1. Streeruwitz' translation is retranslatable as *early mourning*.
2. Compare with Ibsen 82-92.
3. Compare scene eight with lines 191-215, pp. 472-73, Second Part in Gryphius.
4. Compare with pp. 86-105, act I.3 in Shakespeare.
5. "Because of a deeply anchored culture of hope, Austria is a model for a non-enlightened world. I put my strict speech constellations against the local state of mind" (Streeruwitz, "Gespräch" 58).

Works Cited

Adorno, Theodor W. *Ästhetische Theorie (Aesthetic Theory)*. Frankfurt: Suhrkamp, 1973.
Bond, Edward. *'early morning.'* London: John Calder, 1977.
Detje, Robin. "Herrlich kalt und schön brutal." *Die Zeit* July 24 (1992).

Fachdienst Germanistik: Sprache und Literatur in der Kritik deutschsprachiger Zeitungen. 5/1996 München: iudicium Verlag.

Felman, Shoshana. "Woman and Madness: The Critical Phallacy (Balzac, 'Adieu')." *What Does a Woman Want?* Baltimore: Johns Hopkins UP, 1993.

Fischer, Werner. "Debüt einer Dramatikerin aus A in D." *Wiener Zeitung,* August 21 (1992).

Gryphius, Andreas. *Ermordete Majestät oder König von Gross-Britannien. Trauer-Spil.* Ed. Eberhard Mannack (Frankfurt: Deutscher Klassiker Verlag, 1991).

Härtl, Renate. "Marlene Streeruwitz und ihre Stücke. Porträt der Dramatikerin." *General-Anzeiger für Bonn,* August 10 (1993).

Hay, Malcom, and Philip Roberts. *Bond. A Study of his Plays.* London: Eyre Methuen, 1980.

Huber-Lang, Wolfgang. "Balanceakt ohne Netz." *Wochenpresse* February 11 (1993).

Ibsen, Henrik. Scene entitled, "Zelt bei einem Araberhäuptling, einsam in einer Oase." Act 4 of *Peer Gynt.* Stuttgart: Reclam, 1977.

Isenschmid, Andreas. "Überraschung Streeruwitz. Mal näher und mal ferner." *Die Weltwoche* May 9 (1996).

Kienzle, Siegfried. "Die Austro-Berserker." *Die Deutsche Bühne,* September (1992): 12-15.

Rilke, Rainer Maria. "Duineser Elegien," II/10-17. Vol. I of *Werke in drei Bänden.* Frankfurt: Insel, 1991.

Schmid-Mühlisch, Lothar. "Mach doch mal das Fenster auf, Mädchen! Wien als geschlossene Anstalt: Marlene Streeruwitz' erster Roman." *Welt des Buches* April 13 (1996).

Shakespeare, William. *The Tragedy of Antony and Cleopatra.* Oxford: Clarendon Press, 1994.

Streeruwitz, Marlene. *Bagnacavallo. Brahmsplatz. Zwei Stücke.* Frankfurt: Suhrkamp, 1993.

---. "Das Gesetz des Geldes. Notizen über Literatur und Marktgeschehen." *Stuttgarter Zeitung,* December 29 (1995).

---. "Gespräch mit Gisela Bartens." *Kleine Zeitung Graz,* May 13 (1995).

---. *New York. New York. Elysian Park. Zwei Stücke.* Frankfurt: Suhrkamp, 1993.

---. *Ocean Drive. Ein Stück.* Frankfurt: Suhrkamp, 1994.

---. "Passion. Devoir. Kontingenz. Und keine Zeit." *Theater heute Jahrbuch* (1992): 28-31.

---. *Tomezzo. Eine symphonische Dichtung.* Frankfurt: Suhrkamp, 1994.

---. *Verführungen. 3. Folge: Frauenjahre.* Frankfurt: Suhrkamp, 1996.

---. *Waikiki-Beach. Sloane Square. Zwei Stücke.* Frankfurt: Suhrkamp, 1992.

Wille, Franz. "Wen der Berg ruft. Gipfeltreffen: Diven, Gangster, Journalisten, Grafen, Zwergenforscher—Marlene Streeruwitz' *Ocean Drive* in Köln." *Theater heute* 2 (1994).

"Wirres vom Gletscher." *Der Spiegel*, December 12 (1993).

The *Abjectum*: Peter Waterhouse's Reappropriation of Hölderlin and the Poem-In-Progress

Erk Grimm
Barnard College

The reception of Friedrich Hölderlin's political and philosophical ideas in the 1960s drastically transformed the image of the poet as a national prophet-seer and made him either a revolutionary hero or a figure of failed utopian aspirations. In her astute critical study on these diverse images, Helen Fehervary examined and documented the history of this reception up to the discovery of a "language of feeling," by the disillusioned writers of a New Subjectivity. However, as far as the relevance of Hölderlin's poetry to writers of the last decade is concerned, there are only a few attempts to examine the poet's role in the last two decades. Similar to Fehervary's study, these examinations are primarily concerned with the position of the auratic figure in prose, poetry, and in the intellectual debates of the former East and West Germany. For instance, the more recent reappropriations of Hölderlin in the work of East German poets such as Barbara Köhler or Bert Papenfuß have only recently been investigated. Most inquiries concentrated on the literature of the former GDR, due to the more obvious political implications.[1] Consequently, the most peculiar and interesting realignment with the classical poet in Austrian literature went unnoticed and has not yet received critical attention. In his essays and poems, the Austrian writer Peter Waterhouse illuminates the significance of Hölderlin's poems, his translation of *Antigone*, and the adaption of a fragmentary play *Der Tod des Empedokles* (The Death of Empedocles) by the two French film directors Danièle Huillet and Jean-Marie Straub. In a more general context I will examine a concept of "radical" poetry,[2] the "poem-in-progress," that does not yield to a clear separation of the aesthetic and the political. Instead, the poem becomes a textual space whose "openness" appeals to the reader to rethink the utopian dimension of poetry. Waterhouse's poems are symptomatic of a shift from image to word in the age of media.[3]

This historical change is indicated by a new reading of Hölderlin's fragmentary writings. Younger poets such as Waterhouse are more interested in the visual representation of his works than in his fate as a tragic and revolutionary figure of German literature. This indicates not only the detachment from the political arena of the sixties and seventies but also the emergence of different intellectual strategies to respond to less transparent power structures of the last two decades.

Amongst the contemporary poets of the German language whose work began to appear in literary journals during the last two decades, Peter Waterhouse has only recently become more prominent. His work, including poems, plays, translations, and essayistic reflections, has been recognized by colleagues and well known critics such as Harald Hartung, Michael Braun or Gerhard Melzer (Kasper). Peter Waterhouse, born in 1956 and raised in Austria, published his first volume of poetry, entitled *Menz*, in 1983. Interestingly, he began writing poetry after travelling to the United States in 1981. During a stay at the University of California at Los Angeles, he worked on a doctoral thesis on Paul Celan.[4] This academic study triggered a strong interest in a strand of German poetry which has been called the "Hölderlin-Linie" of modernism, because of the strong impact of the Swabian poet on his modern successors.[5] It seems that Waterhouse's way of thinking and his concern for a "nomadic" and "hermetic" discourse was strongly influenced by this tradition, even though his poems are strikingly different from the style of Paul Celan's more enigmatic verses. He was able to resist the temptation of imitating the neologisms and ellipses so characteristic of Celan's poetic diction. Waterhouse could thus acknowledge the inner necessity of an idiom which questions the validity of direct and communicative language in order to express the limitations of representing Jewish suffering and despair. Alluding to Celan's seminal *Der Meridian* (The Meridian; Colin 12, 116) and the role of Büchner's *Lenz* in this speech, the title of Waterhouse's first volume of poems, *Menz*, is a wordplay on "Mensch" and "Lenz," indicating an anthropological rather than a sociological view of the subject's existential crisis. In the course of the eighties, the author achieved a peculiar, easily recognizable prosaic tone in his poetry, culminating in his celebrated volume *Passim* (1986). Significantly, his poetic project is centered upon the semantics of spoken language and is thus representative of an oral tradition of modern poetry that has been maintained in Austria but not in West or East Germany in the 1960s. In Vienna, Waterhouse had to be less concerned with distancing himself from the *parlando quotidiano* of the New Subjectivity which was widely spread in West German journals and anthologies. The fashionable idiom ruled the literary market and made it hard to articulate one's own idiom.[6] Certainly, he was exposed to the phonetic experimentalism of the Viennese neoavant-garde; a prose text published after *Menz* mixes experimental and more conventional elements in a way which Harald Hartung described as the typical post-experimental "novel-like macroform."[7] Gradually the author was getting involved in translating poems by Bob Kaufman, Carl Rakosi, the Italian hermeticists, Andreas Zanzotto, Biagio Marin, or Gerard Manley Hopkins, all of which were subject of a "translation theater" that uses the German language in an unfamiliar way.[8] Waterhouse focuses on how language is made "foreign" by rhythm, intonation, and unconventional syntax. It was more than just a linguistic experiment, when Waterhouse started to explore what is not "at home" in one's own language and represents an obstacle to the completion of a translation. As in the case of literal translation, the poet merely lends his language to open up a structure, to perform a displacement which excludes the possibility of giving expression to a true "feeling" or "meaning."

Since the middle of the 1980s, Waterhouse has contributed poems and poetic reflections of considerable length to the prestigious Styrian journal *manuskripte*. Interestingly, he became involved in a number of projects which brought him recognition beyond the Austrian border. For instance, he developed contacts to East German writers who considered themselves the "inofficial" alternative to the mass media discourse of established writers, expatriates, and dissidents.[9] Consequently, he published *Kieselsteinplan für die unsichtbare Universität* (Pebble Plan for the

Invisible University; 1990)—poetic contemplations on landscapes at the periphery of cities which might serve as a new school of aesthetic research—and contributed to the anthology *Proë* (1992), both published by an East Berlin publishing house.[10] Less known but equally important is Waterhouse's active commitment to the marginalized literary scene of South Tyrol and Oswald Egger's editorial projects.[11] More recently, he collaborated with Brigitte Oleschinski, Durs Grünbein, and the Swiss editor Urs Engeler in a polyphonic work named *Die Schweizer Korrektur* (The Swiss Proof-Reading). All these activities indicate Waterhouse's interest in a decentralized discourse and reveal his suspicious attitude toward the institutional aspects of the literary market. The poet's interpretation of a film produced by the two film directors Danièle Huillet and Jean-Marie Straub is marked by this clandestine solidarity with figures at the periphery of the cultural establishment and the concealment of his ideological position.

To Peter Waterhouse and most other poets who started their career ten to fifteen years ago, Friedrich Hölderlin was neither the "autonomous, apolitical poet" as he had been seen in the 1940s and 1950s, nor the prophet of modern dissociation or even Jacobin revolutionary as Theodor W. Adorno and Pierre Bertaux portrayed him in the following decade (Fehervary 202). The image of the poet suffering from Germany was no longer attractive to writers and readers who experienced the deflation of a national agenda and the emergence of, according to Habermas, unpredictable reactions of citizens to the political conditions, due to the "erosion" of traditional party attachments (Habermas 246-7). Whether it was this disintegration of the public sphere or the allurements of a booming art and literature market, the poets wrote for an increasingly art-oriented and non-politicized audience with a taste for "cosmopolitan" topics. It seems that the new ironic affirmation of the institutions and subversive strategies eclipsed the auratic model of resistance and resignation embodied in Hölderlin. Whereas the fame of the romantic figure reached its nadir, the interest in the intricate structure of his texts became increasingly stronger. And yet, it is not the admiration of Hölderlin's early odes and hymns that stimulated Peter Waterhouse and West German poets such as Thomas Kling,

Gerhard Falkner, or Matthias Hermann to make occasional references to the textual design. Instead it was their fascination with the planning stage of poems and the fragmentary character of Hölderlin's late work edited by Dietrich E. Sattler in 1975 (18). Sattler's historical-critical edition showed the textual constitution of a work-in-progress—emphasizing the planning stages and outlines of Hölderlin's late work—and thus relinquished the philological distinction between the final product and previous preliminary versions. What seemed to be exclusively characteristic of Mallarmé's *Un coup de dés n'abolira le hasard*, the "fragile vibration" and "enigmatic and precarious being" (Foucault 305) of the word on the page could now be detected in the classical writer Hölderlin. In Sattler's edition, the poems seem to dissolve into an energetic field of linguistic ions.[12] Moreover, the remarkable shift from the poet's biography toward the materiality of language was marked by the decreasing interest in the aura of a prophet-seer who figured so prominently in both the metaphysical and the leftist interpretations of Hölderlin's work from Wilhelm Dilthey and Ernst Bloch to Luise Rinser and Johannes Becher in early postwar poetry.[13] Regarding the position of Hölderlin as a political role model after 1945, it is worth mentioning that either parody or rejection of Hölderlin were the predominant reactions of such influential poets as Ernst Jandl in Austria or Delius, Rühmkorf, Enzensberger in the former West Germany.[14]

In tracing the reappropriation of Hölderlin up to the 1980s, it becomes evident that the production of "open" and fragmentary texts has been carried one step further with the abolition of the very agent of this production. What matters to the poets of the 1980s and Peter Waterhouse in particular, is the material of Hölderlin's drafts of poems. In contrast to Jandl, who countered the pathos of the classical poems with parody, Waterhouse makes use of the most rudimentary traces of writing. In this regard, his reception of Hölderlin shares the view of the disillusioned leftists and representatives of the New Subjectivity who shifted the focus from the auratic national figure to the private and conventional aspects of his life. Karin Struck, for instance, who explored everyday experience in her autobiographical prose and poetry during the 1970s, hailed the poet for developing a personal "Gefühlssprache" (language of feeling) in *Hyperion* and thus helping her to give expression to a sensitivity that had been constantly suppressed in the intellectual debates of the 1970s.[15]

We can see that on the one hand the Swabian poet had become demystified as a figure so that his pathos as the subjective dimension of his poetic speech became more accessible. Waterhouse is clearly indebted to this personal factor when he mentions the tenderness, "die Zärtlichkeit" in Hölderlin's poems.[16] On the other hand, it was not the emotional tone but the rudimentary form of unfinished drafts in Sattler's edition which allowed the poets of the 1980s to reach a heightened consciousness of the available techniques of writing. Fehervary acutely notes that "Hölderlin's reception has become less concerned with deciphering the ideological content or 'message' of his work than with probing the methodological processes involved in writing" (223). The Austrian poet mainly focuses on the spatiality of Hölderlin's poetry, rather than on the meaning of the undecipherable words of the manuscripts.[17] Peter Waterhouse's poignant assertion "all feelings are kitsch" illuminates his position of a sensitive but unemotional observer.[18] More generally, the turning away from questions concerning subjectivity indicates the new matter-of-factness that governs contemporary poetry. Noticeably, those poets who most vigorously explored the complexity of poetic language did not give any indication of their political attitude, they in fact obfuscated the ethical position of the lyrical subject. In order to regain a command of styles and forms after the New Subjectivity, the "authentic" and unsophisticated documentation of everyday experience had to be dismantled. Whereas politically active poets such as Enzensberger aimed at imitating and reutilizing Hölderlin's style to counter the language of mass media in monotonous reiteration, the contemporary poet Waterhouse affirms the all-encompassing discourse networks by turning its prerequisite, a communicative jargon of users, into a language without argument—or rather into a language which highlights the condition of the possibility of argument. This decontextualization and dehistorization of Hölderlin's work is inextricably linked to a political climate in which the critical intelligentsia is confronted with what they see as diffuse and impenetrable power structures. In contrast to those who interrogated German history and national politics in the previous decades, the poets of the 1980s focus on micro-structures of everyday life rather than on the master narratives.

At first glance, Waterhouse's preoccupation with the formal logistics of the poem seems to be similar to Gottfried Benn's attempt to debunk the idealistic content of Hölderlin's poetry. While pursuing a "scientific" approach, Benn had put the emphasis on technical perfection rather than the psychological dimension of poems (177). Yet, there are other, quite humanist aspects in Waterhouse's poems, namely his avowal of failure, the leitmotif of tenderness, his solidarity with tramps, hobos, Sinti, Turks, all of which indicate the resistance to succumbing to the austerity and clinical detachment of everyday routine. For Waterhouse as for Adorno, the artifact is by its very nature a form of social protest. In *Klarfeld Gedicht* (Clear Field Poem; 1988) Waterhouse characterized his position as "resistance through self-isolation," while pleading for a pluralistic stage in which there should be possible as much as possible at the same time ("möglichst vieles zugleich möglich") (99). The poem should be able to present the emptiness as a quality neglected by a society which produces quantities only. The emptiness is no utopian window which would open to an alternative reality. The Austrian poet does not portray an idealized landscape or relish the postmodern facades of Vienna.[19] Instead, the figure of his poetry mimics the daily routines of the middle-class individual in the city and reproduces the artificiality of dilapidated road ditches and embankments outside the city so that the reader is made aware of the deceptive ideal of an unreified future. In a great number of poems, the industrial zone at the fringe of the city is no longer the site of production but rather a semiotic world of colors, signs and flashing lights, all of which are juxtaposed to the colorful botany of the ditches and dumpsites. In other words, the ruined environment is an attraction itself since it is in the process of becoming a second nature.

At this point it is necessary to outline the main features of Waterhouse's poetry before discussing the relevance of Hölderlin to his concept of the poem-in-progress. Probably his greatest success was his much acclaimed *passim*, a volume of approximately eighty extremely complex but non-hermetic prose poems, which appeared in 1986. A number of poems in this volume consist of question-and-answer games which sound strangely familiar, like street conversations. And yet, the light everyday prose seems to be inadequate considering the explicit and implicit references to the philosophical works of Descartes, Leibniz, and Bloch. It is certainly not a conventional arrangement of lines which serves as an embedding of ideas concerning the constitution or orientation of a monadic subject in its cosmos. The preliminary form prevails to the degree that it reflects the incompleteness of a harmonious cosmos or utopian society to which it alludes.

Peter Waterhouse's "Gedicht im Materialstadium" (Poem in the Stage of Material; 58) from *passim* is best suited for explaining the poet's main concerns. The first part of this long prose poem offers a monological reflection about a beginning or a metamorphosis:[20]

> We are still pears, that is soft and speechless. The sky is
> still a sky, and one lives in it
> being the first butterfly. One bursts the cocoon
> and there are many words for it. One should turn on the light
> open the windows, shout some names into the nameless night.
> Even the softest idea is really treated very softly. How
> soft are we? Hard to tell...

The rhythmic pattern is defined by short sentences, a few repeated words, and some questions cutting in. The statements seem bizarre at first, but they disclose an underlying pattern. The first assertion "We are still pears, that is soft and speechless" describes a stage of prehuman existence which corresponds with other phases of biological changes such as "One bursts the cocoon" and finally "After the entire metamorphosis there walks someone who is the same." These lines indicate a possible transformation from lower organic life to rational humans; living beings might turn out to be something different, they might assume a form of existence other than their present one, characterized by softness, nakedness, vulnerability, and speechlessness. But despite their different physical appearance they remain the same: "someone in shoes as before ... a funny looking pear as pear." Modern civilization, however, does not seem to bring about any change because the speaker seems to regret the loss of silence in our technical world: "The silence is a landing of planes in its center." Paradoxically, the ear-deafening noise at the airport reminds us what real silence could mean. The speaker seems to indicate that any philosophical contemplation *in* and *on* silence is impossible in the presence of modern technology. Even though the tenor of the poem reverberates with a Heideggerian assault on technocratic society, the metaphorical identity of "silence" and "landing" underscores the view that a hermeneutical un-concealment of the origin is to no avail. Rather, the noise is the condition of the possibility of silence; what appears as a jarring opposition has to become joint in order to produce identity. This premise is most forcefully emphasized in the rather prosaic idiom itself. The stark contrast of images suggests a rejection of a technical jargon which designates its objects in abstract terms before looking at real things. And yet, the poem resists both the cliché contrast of nature versus technocracy and Heidegger's distinction of *technē* and technicity. The dreary tone of environmentalist poetry is avoided by highlighting and even ridiculing the non-perfection and clumsiness of the poet's approach. At one point, for instance, the voice intervenes after a grammatically incorrect statement by saying: "There is too much tumbling here." As in other poems, Waterhouse is acutely aware of keeping the seriousness in check by stressing the absurdity of an image. Occasionally, a quip or linguistic joke is interjected as in the following line: "Every steeple needs to go to the hairdresser once." The absurditity of such an event is even intensified by a quirky footnote to the poem, saying: "This expression goes too far, I suppose" (*passim* 50).

By mentioning the limitations of poetic language, the speaker of "Gedicht im Materialstadium" anchors his or her projection of images in everyday experience and the conventions of spoken language. Instead of remaining soft and speechless in confrontation with the brutal noise of the world, even the most conventional patterns of quotidian speech seem at least to signal a readiness of the subject to open a dialogue. It is the transitional moment of greeting which prepares the subject for a "landing" in the world. The end of the poem is aiming at this beginning of speech, the transitional and reluctant moment of opening the mouth before the conversation begins.[21] Consequently, the poem closes with a greeting that could mean a beginning or the end: "Good Day anyway."

The poem makes a clear distinction between the rules of everyday language and the eccentricity of poetic writing. But there are not only restrictions because of the conventions of *parole*; there is also a *surplus* of reality which cannot be covered by language. Due to this inadequate relation, the poem contradicts our common-sense assumptions about a subject as a site of prolific production of images. In fact, images are not available: "If only there were images for illustration." That is why the poem projects a space in which the transition from word to image can take place.[22] Waterhouse conceives of this textual space as the condition of the possibility of meaning. It is a greeting that marks this transitional space and places the reader between welcome and farewell. The salutation entails an invitation to engage in a dialogue with a poetic voice that on the one hand renounces the binding rules of poetic genres. On the other hand it opens up a field of semantic and phonetic interrelations which lets the reader participate in the process of naming an innumerable quantity (the sky, the desert, the sea) or unmeasurable quality (softness, gentleness). The very form of this poem mirrors the incongruence of science and poetry, that is the impossibility of attributing meaning to the elements of an abstract mathematical world, i.e. any given point "between zero and one." In response to the questions regarding the "objective" state of things, the voice insists three times: "Cannot be answered." To be sure, these metapoetic reflections about the limits of denoting the real do not result in a Hofmannsthalian "crisis of language." On the contrary, the material exposed to the reader is not imbued with the signs of paralysis because the poetic structure accentuates the temporal aspect of becoming form. Instead of lamenting the loss of truth at the end of the age of metaphysics, the poem affirms the sceptical question whether being is meaningful and whether meaning is existent at all (Hörisch, 10). The "objectivity" of this discrepancy between meaning and being ("Sinn" and "Sein"), to borrow a terminological tandem from Jean Luc Nancy, allows the poet to give an exuberant and jubilating account of his ineptitude to name the abstract world. Waterhouse chooses a Romantic image to render the state of being confronted with an abundance of abstract knowledge and the loss of truth; he captures the delirious "darkness" of this state in the image of the enigmatic "night" which reverberates with the end of one of Novalis' famous hymns: "But still eternal Night remained without remedy / For the somber sign of that distant power."[23]

I would argue that Waterhouse is able to embrace silence not for stressing the traumatic aspect and reminding us of the despair in Paul Celan's poems. The encounter with a language of silence is not meant to focus on mourning but rather, in a variation of Celan's premises,[24] to perceive the space of the text as a possibility of hope in spite and because of nothingness. For this reason, this is a night of joyful initiation and dance which makes one aware of what Nothingness could mean ("But Nothing is a dancehall with a thousand happy ones"). The problematic process of poetic naming becomes open to the future and insists on the ritual of welcoming the unknown. The pleasure of showing the lack of a singular meaning ("Sinn") is even expressed in the way blank spaces are used to name the unnamable as silence: "should one leave a gap / in what cannot   ?" Indeed, Waterhouse is able to affirm the moment of silence, jokingly created by the open spaces on the page, in his reappropriation of Hölderlin. More precisely, he reinterprets the religious-mythical dimension of transformative moments in Hölderlin's poetry in order to develop a spatial concept of a poem-in-progress.

Although Waterhouse has adopted the rhythm and terseness of spoken discourse, the spatial arrangement of lines in writing is the basis of his poetry. This fundamental element is reflected in his essay "Abj." which presents ideas about the retention of energy in writings by Friedrich Hölderlin, Carl Rakosi, and Andreas Zanzotto (215-238). In his reading of Hölderlin's "Der Winter" (The Winter) and "Der Vulkan" (Vulcan), Waterhouse explicates the formation of a poem as a shift from a basic tension between a few words and open spaces to the final completed arrangement of lines. The essay is occupied with the conditions of poetic speech rendered in writing, beginning with the first sketches. The abbreviation "abj." in Hölderlin's first draft of the poem "Der Winter" simply means "abjectum" (outline). According to Waterhouse, the oral performance of poetry reaches its optimal realization if it is articulated with bated breath or pent-up feelings; rather than releasing one's emotions, the optimal speech is retentive or reserved. He stresses the point that in reading the written record of its motion, speech becomes visual and spatial to the speaker so that an encounter with a landscape can take place. The Austrian poet describes the way written poetry since Mallarmé and Hölderlin—or more precisely since Sattler's edition of his poems—includes the openness of blank spaces and the materiality of letters. Hence the abbreviation "abj." which disrupts the "natural" order of letters and illustrates the arbitrariness of the "abc." The centerpiece of this essay is a comment on Hölderlin's "Der Winter," written in 1799. In its planning stage, the poem consists of a few key words dotted about on the page: "Phantasus ... Love ... North ... Yet." Something that is suppressed or retained permeates the sketch. Hölderlin made a short note "abj." in the margin to indicate to himself its preliminary character. The following drafts complete this image of an encounter and give the objection "yet" in the last line such a spin that it resulted in a complete reversal of the poem's title: "Der Winter" became "Vulkan." What had been an empty space in former drafts, was being replaced by the precise verses of the alcaic stanza, as the first lines demonstrate:

> You come now, friendly spirit of fire, and wrap
> The women's delicate minds in a veil of clouds,
> In golden dreams, and there keep safe the
> Blossoming peace of the ever-kindly.[25]

It is this crucial moment of going beyond language to reach the ineffable which characterizes Waterhouse's notion of "brightness" or Hölderlin's "spirit of fire." Eric Santner described the elusive element of Hölderlin's poetry: "the rifts of silence become the openings where the Unnamable can only be circumscribed" (84). In Waterhouse's view, the most convincing response to this "brightness" of Hölderlin's poems can be found in those media which make space visible.

The most puzzling passage of the essay "Abj." is concerned with the "translation" of Hölderlin's dramatic fragments into film. Surprisingly, Peter Waterhouse finds the most adequate translation of these difficult "Greek" verses in the radical cinema of Jean-Marie Straub and Danièle Huillet who take a Brechtian approach toward the cinematic event.[26] This team of directors, often and falsely identified by the single name Straub (Sandford 27-36), has played an outsider role in the international movie production since they refused to follow the example of Wim Wenders who gave in to high-budget commercial cinema. Their filmic style prefers extremely long shots, diagonal or tilted camera angles, often nonprofessional cast, direct recording of sound, mostly literary subjects, an overlapping of classical recitation and modern sound, and a Godardian analysis of class and character. The reactions to their films differ greatly. According to Robert Philipp Kolker, the Huillet-Straubian cinema is at the radical end of the modernist movement. He claims, for instance, that a film such as *Othon*, was "one of the most irritating films ever made" (212). Their method teaches "a lesson of restraint, an example of film as blueprint, with the spectator given the task of building the structure" and confronting himself or herself with a "composition of disorienting artificiality" (211). Huillet and Straub directed three "theatrical" films based on Hölderlin's writings, *Der Tod des Empedokles* (The Death of Empedocles, 1986), *Schwarze Sünde* (Black Sin, 1988) and *Die Antigone des Sophokles* (Sophocles' Antigone, 1992). In a Freudian slip, Waterhouse mistakenly cites the second film as *Schwarze Glut* (Black Glow), apparently thinking of the image of a volcano, and then concentrates on his main example *The Death of Empedocles*.[27] The followings aspects of this film are mentioned: the static image of the volcano, the verses being spoken in the light, the lack of camera movements, the "remarkable certainty" in which the camera faces the light, and the voice which cannot be separated from the image of Empedocles.

Waterhouse's observations illuminate some of the characteristics of *The Death of Empedocles* which might give us an answer as to what extent the specific features of Hölderlin's poetry were transferred to the visual medium. Referring to *Empedocles,* Waterhouse maintains: "The film responds to the luminous appearance of this poetry by having the poetry spoken in light ... One really does not know what language is but here it is certainly lucid" (223). Apparently, the poet tries to dismantle the notion of hermetic or "dark" poetry attributed to Hölderlin.[28] Although implicitly, he highlights the literary and photographic qualities of this cinema which opposes the mainstream of European movie production by maintaining a radical (early) Godardian style. Rather than following conventions of a narrative shot-by-shot movie, their cinema emphasizes the complexity and peculiarity of the written text and pays homage to the *genius loci*. Intuitively, Waterhouse registers a specific element of Huillet/Straub's cinema, namely the immobililty of the camera and the strategy of capturing the specificity of the locale by choosing a single position of the camera for all shots: "In these two films, one cannot expect a movement of the camera, it views straight ahead, in the remarkable certainty of the light, that is in an Empedoclesian certainty" (223). The unusual placement of the camera can even create moments in which the camera, from its optimal point of view, focuses a character before it dwells on the sky or the ground as empty and meaningless spots.[29]

The closing scene of *Der Tod des Empedokles* which shows a landscape and the sky is most probably the scene in which Waterhouse recognized the "luminous appearance of poetry." The Austrian poet must have been most impressed by the lighting techniques used in *Empedokles*. The two film directors who shot this film in Sicily employed the best lighting experts in Europe; specifically for this production, they chose to work together with Renato Berta who prefers "concentrated, 'simple' images" and "exterior shots with gentle light" instead of artifical light and harsh contrasts.[30] For the directors, the confrontation with the location, that is, showing the abuse of nature in particular, is as important as the text. The other main character, next to Empedocles, is the volcanic landscape, as Barton Byg notes (182). The closing scene offers the first panoramic view of Mount Etna accompanied by the voice-over of Empedokles: "Ha! Jupiter, liberator! Closer and closer / My hour comes and from the craggy crevice / The trusted harbinger of night is on its way, / The evening breeze, the messenger of love."[31] The shots show a harmonically composed image of deciduous trees set against the foothills of Etna. The trees are getting lighter, then darker and again lighter; momentarily, the grass is getting agitated by the wind. While sun and clouds are changing, the camera captures every nuance of luminosity until the end of Empedokles's speech. The image is reminiscent of Herzog's *Jeder für sich und Gott gegen alle* (Every Man for Himself and God Against All, 1974)—released under the English title *The Enigma of Kaspar Hauser*—of which the opening scene shows a blowing wheat field. But whereas Herzog evokes an unquestioned awe for nature, Huillet/Straub set up the landscape as a historical space of death and utopian hope. Empedocles' speech began with appealing to Jupiter, the god of weather and ended with a joyful praise of the rainbow above the waterfalls. Thereafter we watch the credit titles scrolling by while the violin of a Bach concerto fills the air. The sound of Jupiter's rolling thunder follows, indicating the death of Empedocles but also a cyclical change of nature and new beginning.

In Danièle Huillet's and Jean-Marie Straub's text-oriented cinema,[32] the landscape never serves as a mere backdrop to dramatic action. In their adaptions of Hölderlin's texts, all verses are indeed carefully scanned while the outdoors scenes are filled with the Southern light of Sicily. Empedocles, who is forced to leave society by the citizens of Agrigento, retreats to nature. Waterhouse argues that there is a parallel between the openness of Hölderlin's drafts of poems and this glaringly bright landscape in *The Death of Empedocles* (1986), *Black Sin* (1988) or *Sophocles' Antigone* (1992), filmed on location in Sicily. Playing with the political connotations of "Einigkeit" (unity, unanimity, agreement) and omitting more appropriate terms such as similarity of aesthetic features, Waterhouse contends: "I see a oneness in the white areas of Hölderlin's drafts and the films of Straub/Huillet (the whiteness, the landscape)" (224). Surprisingly, the poet focuses on the "empty" places and interprets them as indicators of the not-yet-meaningful. In *Antigone* for instance or even earlier in *Moses und Aaron* (1975), the camera explores the setting in which the characters will be engaged in dramatic dialogue/monologue. In both films, there are instances in which the camera tilts from extreme close-ups in low angle to a high angle showing the ground. The long shots of the distant background depict a landscape which is linked to the past or future of the protagonist whereas the close-ups focus on the here and there of action even if the character is not shown at a particular moment. Because it is not the character but the camera which defines the motion in such instances, the spectator has to restore a connection broken not only on the diegetic level but on the level of cinematic discourse. The action is propelled by the text rather than the image but it results in a shock, as Barton Byg explains: it is "caused by the simultaneous appearance of speaker and word" due to the fact that the directors "rely only on the text to motivate an edit, rather than a "theatrical" perception of action" (222).

Tenuousness and tension govern this film in many respects. The speakers are kept almost immobile while a spatial distance is maintained. Consequently, the vulnerability of Empedocles becomes tangible. There is less an emotional tension between the characters than a tension between the speakers and the text they have to recite. Maureen Turim has pointed out Huillet/Straub's "graphic compositions" with exaggerated angles which emphasize "bold diagonals": "Glances do not meet; they point to a space beyond the frame, suggesting that the speaking character is reciting from memory, speaking a text rather than performing a part" (240). As if language itself were holding them like puppets, the actors and actresses have to make such a physical effort to utter their lines that they are unable to act out emotions. They cannot free themselves from the rhythm of Hölderlin's long, syncopated syntax in order to express passion. Andreas von Rauch, playing Empedokles, is visibly absorbed in intonating the difficult speech so that he purses up his lips, blows the sides of his nose, and breathes hard at the end of each of sentence. His eyes are blinking, fixing the ground; there is a determined and yet almost timid expression on his face. One is reminded of Bruno Schleinstein's inwardness in Werner Herzog's

Kaspar-Hauser-adaption; indeed, both actors take pains in enunciating their script, although on vastly different levels of language proficiency.

Surprisingly, the Austrian poet does not mention the mechanical, non-expressive recital by non-native speakers and lay actors, the low-tech sound recording techniques or the readings of a voice-over text so typical of Huillet/Straub's cinema (Byg 22-23). A confrontation with the performance of Hölderlin's text does not take place, thus neglecting the lay actors' strained articulation of a speech of which the difficult rhythm suppresses passion. It is speech, however, which highlights the difficulties of giving concrete meaning to Hölderlin's stylized language. If Huillet/Straub insisted on professional acting, as Barton Byg points out, "both the text as material and the act of speaking would be erased in favor of preconceived 'meaning'" (Byg 23). In a different respect, Waterhouse addresses the issue of text-as-material. In his examination of the alcaic stanza, preceding his discussion of *Der Tod des Empedokles*, he interprets the irregularities in rhythm as "etwas anderes im selben," evidenty alluding to Hölderlin's famous "harmonisch entgegengesetzte Empfindung" (harmoniously opposed sensation).[33] The third line of the alcaic stanza includes drastic irregularities since it minimizes the iambic feeling by a prevailing rhythmic pattern of two consecutive unstressed syllables: "You come now, friendly spirit of fire, and wrap / The women's delicate minds in a veil of clouds, / In golden dreams, and there keep safe the / Blossoming peace of the ever-kindly."[34] In Water-house's opinion, this calculated unevenness of elements such as "schüze sie, die" corresponds to the previously white spaces of the page. Concluding, he maintains that the poem "receives its identity from something which is not all identity" (224). Evidently, Waterhouse is encoding a political argument by retooling its parameters into a different register. As he points out, we ought to see the characteristic feature of the alcaic stanza not in the identity of the whole but rather in the parts which are "alien" to the whole.[35] What in a different context could be read as an advocacy for a non-self-identical identity of the citizen within the "nation" is translated into a strikingly "technical," that is poetological discourse.

In another essay of his book *Die Geheimnislosigkeit* (The Unmysteriousness, 1996), Peter Waterhouse reflects on the representational aspects of Huillet/Straub's cinema. In *Antigone*, based on the Greek play translated by Hölderlin and adapted by Brecht, the directors used "the visual simplicity of the silent cinema and the staging of Sophocles' play in a Greek theater of his era" (Byg 215). Approaching his topic intuitively rather than analytically, the poet focuses on the function of empty, unnamed spaces in order to unfold his thesis concerning memory and meaning: "In Huillet/Straub's film *Antigone*, the camera turns away from the chorus at which it had looked from above and while it [the chorus] keeps on talking, [the camera] takes a shot, vertically I believe, of the clean sandy spot down in front of the feet of the chorus."[36] Robert Phillip Kolker, a film critic, maintained that it is such an "elliptical structure" which provokes "anger as much as the wish to make it yield meaning."[37] What Kolker, however, sees as a detriment to understanding the film's message and as an attack on the "viewer's comfort and solace" (208), becomes the key object of Waterhouse's observation. Based on minute details of a scene, the observer concludes that the image of a meaningless sandy spot allows us to perceive and retrieve what has always been ignored, omitted, and neglected: "The sandy spot in the film *Antigone* is a return, a remembrance, a retrieving of what has been disregarded and pushed aside" (123-24). Moreover, the "white" spot in the arena of the old Greek Theater in Sicily permits us *to remember*—precisely because the spot is not "violated" by meaning or, to put it differently, linked to a traumatic experience of the past.

In a review of the film *Antigone*, it was Peter Handke who appreciated the formal aspects: "The Straubian cinema and ancient Greek theater are virtually one in the same, of like form."[38] Nevertheless Handke severely attacked the directors' "wonderful old militancy" and "sloganistic framework of antiquated class struggle." Misinterpreting basic facts of Brecht's production of this play, Handke tried to defend Hölderlin against the Marxist playwright so that the political implications could be downplayed in favor of the aesthetic qualities (Byg 216). In contrast to Handke, Waterhouse does not comment on Straub's and Huillet's political agenda, and his considerations of form seem to suggest that the poet shares Handke's harsh criticism. However, given the fact that his discourse is loaded with references to historical trauma, memory, and the "marginalized" elements of these films, Waterhouse favors a "poetic" strategy which foregrounds aesthetic concerns in order to establish a clandestine solidarity with the filmmakers and avoid the spectacle of public controversy. Although he does not elaborate on the ideological content of Huillet's and Straub's films, he responds to its formal features as a sign of aesthetic resistance. His response is symptomatic of the disintegration of the public sphere because it is neither a tacit agreement nor an open disregard but simply the conformation as a distortion of a message. The recipient inverts the intended communication of political ideas by examining the political content of the seemingly meaningless and neglecting the meaningful form of the overtly political.

Presumably, Waterhouse identified with Huillet's and Straub's films because of a certain provisional character in both Hölderlin's late poems and the filmic adaption of his play. Image and language are confronted with each other in an experimental structure. The film critic Helmut Krebs admits, "it may appear that this is off-putting and 'clumsy,' the experience of the friction between actor and costume, gesture and language, space and figure, speaker and text. But in this friction," he adds, "dwells the anarchic power and joy of speaking and seeing."[39] By this process of translating one medium to the other, the significance of Hölderlin's poetry for Waterhouse's project becomes clear: it is a way of apprehending openness, looking at landscapes to reconfigure the self in multiple constellations.

Peter Waterhouse's reappropriation of Hölderlin is based on a curious exploration of the linguistic material and its spatial configurations. There is no affinity with the romantic or revolutionary image of the Swabian prophet-seer who appears to be, as Günter Eich once wrote in a poem, a "deposit of volatile Hölderlin." What Waterhouse finds so remarkably illuminated in the films of Huillet/Straub is the visualization of *spatial* tensions between perfection and incompletion. As the images of the film so does the written text juxtapose the meaningful and the meaningless. On the page, the words and blanks are in an absurd equilibrium since they appear to be *less* than a poem and *more* than a list of terms (220). The visual presentation of drafts and fragmentary poems in Dietrich E. Sattler's critical-historical edition has laid "a concrete foundation for realizing the theories of art as production first put forth by Brecht and Benjamin" (Fehervary 237); in its controversial form, it stimulates such an exploration and allows a fresh reading of Hölderlin's most fragmentary writings as if they were a magnetic constellation of polarized referents rather than ruins of philosophical and poetic ideas. It is perhaps a symptomatic sign of the 1980s and 1990s that contemporary poets discover the explosive effects of the materiality of language not in the academic experiments of an institutionalized neoavant-garde, the so-called "Konkrete Poesie,"[40] but in the concrete remainders of German idealism. A regained sense of the aesthetic qualities of this material, not of a perfection in form, corresponds with the "new objectivity" of the poem in which the subject can submerge or adopt different strategic roles. Regarding the reception of Hölderlin, Peter Waterhouse's work indicates that the utopian notion of historical change as well as a painful working through the traumatic past have been replaced by a concept of semantic openess in the textual space of a poem-in-progress. This openness gains its "critical mass" as it were from Hölderlin's "abjectum" and its unfolding of tenuous relations between a few words and and the abundance of empty space. Paradoxically, it is not Hölderlin's mythical narrative of redemption but the most fragmentary draft of his poetry which represents a translation of hope into the "terra incognita" of the page. Only in its imperfection, in the absence of form and the presence of material, can the poem-in-progress give an idea of the political dimension—the "openness" of Hölderlin's drafts as a space of possibilities.

Notes

1. See Sture Packalén, and Karen Leeder. The author suspects that Hölderlin's poetry serves just as material to be raided by younger poets such as Bert Papenfuß: "They understand themselves

as 'born into' that ruined postmodern landscape where the overarching structures of meaning, historical progress, and identity can now only be approached through the dismantled fragments of such structures... This access to history can either be understood as the symptom of a crisis of meaning and coherence, or as a deliberate and sometimes playful strategy for deconstructing large structures of thought" (142-43).

2. The term is borrowed from Perloff's instructive study *Radical Artifice. Writing Poetry in the Age of Media*.

3. For an account of the "central suspicion of 'imagefull' language" and the fear of "direct statement" in contemporary poetry see Perloff 57.

4. Waterhouse, "(Honig & Zoonen)"; further references to this initiatory moment of writing can be found in "Ich: Kirsche. Gedichte."

5. Dischner characterizes this affinity as part of a mystical tradition aiming at "inner vision of being" and "darkness." The author suggests a reading that does not aim at decoding the poetry but rather at finding a spiritual response. Dischner does not discuss the parallels to a tradition of German philology which rests on an emotional empathy.

6. In Austria, a few less known poets followed the trend toward the New Subjectivity or Sensitivity, i.e., Irmtraut Hilling, Helmut Doyscher, Walter J. Sauer. See Strelka, and Spiel.

7. Waterhouse, *Besitzlosigkeit Verzögerung Schweigen Anarchie*; Hartung, *Experimentelle Literatur und Konkrete Poesie* 37-38.

8. Vogel 135-137. A more critical and instructive review is offered by Schlag.

9. Arnold.

10. There are various references to the unofficial East German journals *schaden* and *verwendung* in Waterhouse's œuvre. Also, Neumann's cryptic prose text *Die Klandestinität der Kesselreiniger. Ein Versuch des Sprechens* is mentioned. This "clandestine" solidarity indicates the poet's interest in the concept of "subversion" by language as it was practiced by the anti-establishment writers of the GDR.

11. In 1989, Waterhouse was awarded the *manuskripte*-prize. On the occasion, Oswald Egger wrote his speculative interpretation "Mutmaßungen über einige verborgene Bedingungen des Gedichts 'Freiheitsgespräche entlang einer Straße' von Peter Waterhouse" (Speculations about Some Secret Preconditions of the Poem 'Conversations about Liberty along the Street').—Since 1990, Waterhouse has served as a co-editor on the editorial board of Egger's journal *Der Prokurist* which appears in Trentino-South Tyrol.

12. More recently, Sattler's editorial decision to favor variants was heavily criticized. According to Jochen Schmidt, the Frankfurt edition does not offer new results and Sattler's new arrangement of parts of texts seems to be problematic; the edition of *Empedokles* contains "far-reaching manipulations." See Schmidt 121. See also: Grätz 264-99, and Schmidt, "Welchen Text hat Hölderlin's Ode 'Natur und Kunst oder Saturn und Jupiter'?"

13. Fehervary has convincingly shown the diversity of roles of the Swabian poet in the history of postwar East German poetry, whether he was used as the apologist of GDR society by Johannes Becher or as the prototypical poet of alienation by Volker Braun and Heiner Müller. More significantly, the latter writers introduced him as a "producer" in the Benjaminian sense since he was able to relate his tragic experience to a materialist context (Fehervary 67, 155, 162).

14. Fehervary 192-98, Hamburger 400.

15. Two representatives of the New Subjectivity, Uwe Timm and Karin Struck, used the Swabian poet "as a model for a new personalized form of literary praxis" (Fehervary 229).

16. cp. Struck: "Hölderlin himself had to create his mother ...One cannot think of his ideas of blessedness and freedom without imagining a mother who is *caringly rocking* (my emphasis) her child to sleep" (134-35).—Waterhouse, however, detects "tenderness" in the language of the poem, not in its ideas. This difference indicates the shift from the ideal body in "reality" (biography) to the real body of language (imagination)—a complete reversal of focus.

17. Two counterexamples to this kind of poetic discourse are Ernst Meister's "Frag dich dereinst," and Helga Novak's "Dunkle

Seite Hölderlins." See Breuer 385-86.

18. The position of the observer in Waterhouse's poetry implies critical distance rather than naïve sympathy, that is, in an almost mathematical sense, a process of "equating" oneself with the Other: "No feelings / but equations. / All feelings are kitsch. / I believe I am totally sentimentalized. / Only in the equation I can escape kitsch." In this text which again evokes a paradoxical situation—"Surrounded by Autumnal Silence a Piece of Music Is Being Played"—, the poetic subject is a listener who remains undetached. Waterhouse, "Von herbstlicher Stille umgeben wird ein Stück gespielt" (23).

19. "… if I stand in front of the St. Stephen's Cathedral, my back facing the often mentioned, boastfully competitive Hans-Hollein-House, I am nowhere. A ruin of a washing machine and a red currant bush are more mnemonic. Red currant, washing machine, red currant—red, white, red" [=the colors of the Austrian flag, EG], Waterhouse, *Die Geheimnislosigkeit. Ein Spazier- und Lesebuch* 98.

20. The poem echoes Ernst Jandl's poem "von namen" of which the second stanza plays on the phonetic similarity of "biene" and "birne": "no I would not want to be a bee, because being busy / is not my cup of tea, but a pear/ that's what i want to be… " Ernst Jandl, *selbstporträt des schachspielers als trinkende uhr* (54). In his poem "Vergegenwärtigung in Graz" (A Recalling in Graz) Waterhouse juxtaposes the cryptic allusion to Celan ("Margarete") and to Jandl ("Man überreicht Gastgeschenke: Den 'Schachspieler als trinkende Uhr'") (One presents gifts to the host: the chess player as a drinking clock). See *Menz* 62.

21. The greeting epitomizes the poetic concept of the "abjectum" since it signals to the reader that the openess of poetic writing unfolds in time and thus entails acceptance or rejection but first of all the pre-communicative moment of acknowledging the presence of the other. In contradistinction, the phonetic poem grants instantaneous pleasure of the oral performance but it does not allow escape from the overwhelming aural experience. See Ernst Jandl's reflections on the phonetic poem in *Das Öffnen und Schließen des Mundes, Frankfurter Poetik-Vorlesungen*.

258 Erk Grimm

22. Celan: "Whenever we speak with things in this way we also dwell on the question of their where-from and where-to... a question which points towards open, empty, free spaces—we have ventured far out." Celan, "The Meridian," *Collected Prose* 50.

23. Novalis, "Hymnen an die Nacht," *Werke* 161; Novalis, *Pollen and Fragmente: Selected Poetry and Prose of Novalis* 142-43. cp. Hörisch 77.

24. In *Atemwende* (1967), the Jewish poet strove for a new idiom. As Amy Colin points out, one of the poems of this volume, "'Osterqualm'...unsettles the idea of an alleged tendency toward silence inherent in all of Celan's poetry" (141).

25. Hölderlin, *Poems and Fragments* 196-97. In comparison, Middleton's translation of this particular poem sounds less convincing since he concentrates much more on interpreting Hölderlin's phrases than on retaining a sense of awkwardness conveyed in lines such as "Blühende Ruhe der Immerguten" which he renders rather freely as "Their flowerlike peace, they are all kindness" (62-63).

26. Barton Byg has given the most precise and instructive account of their cinema. See his *Landscapes of Resistance. The German Films of Daniele Huillet and Jean-Marie Straub*. My references to Huillet/Straub are very much indebted to this excellent study.

27. Most likely, Waterhouse attended the screenings of *Der Tod des Empedokles* and *Antigone*. The film was shown October 1987 in Vienna. cp. Farocki; Hurch and Settele.

28. cp. Waterhouse: "It is a Light Song. He published it under the title of Night Songs" (221).

29. See the examples in Byg 21, 226.

30. Hüser, quoted in Byg 181-82.

31. My translation. cf. "Der Tod des Empedokles," Erste Fassung, Friedrich Hölderlin, *Hyperion. Empedokles* 340. For a discussion of the mythical reunion of earth and sun, which Empedocles experiences as the "Seele der Natur" (soul of nature) see Harrison 121-59.

32. Barton Byg notes that Sattler was a consultant to the film *Der Tod des Empedokles*. The appearance of his Frankfurt edition

must have had a strong influence on Huillet/Straub's notion of textuality, even if they used the Stuttgart edition for their script (187).

33. Hölderlin, "Über die Verfahrensweise des poetischen Gesetzes," *Sämtliche Werke und Briefe*, Bd.1. 866-89; (On the Operations of Poetic Spirit), *Essays and Letters on Theory* 62-82. For a discussion see Martin 86.

34. Hölderlin, *Poems and Fragments*. In a previous version, Hamburger translated: "Now come benevolent god of fire, and wrap / The women's tender spirit in cloudy veils, / In golden dreams, and guard their calm, the / Blossoming calm of the ever-kindly" 130-31.

35. Apparently, Waterhouse draws on ideas of German idealism, namely the interpretation of the individual as not being self-identical but as constituting itself in mutiplicity. See Jean-Luc Nancy, 202.

36. In his interpretation of the empty spot, Waterhouse sees the process of giving meaning to objects as an act of violence which destroys the innocent nature of things. But even in perceiving the material world as a place where everything seems possible and nothing is "wounded" by language, it is still surrounded by speech and meaning. The known territory cannot be turned into a terra incognita, it can only be remembered as a paradise lost. Waterhouse writes: "Suddenly, the sandy spot is innocent, perhaps even better: inviolate. Insignificant. Not violated by signification…Thus one can say: meanings are violators, furies…meaning and memory are perhaps an antithetical combination." Waterhouse, "'What he could not forget was that he had come by the road.' Zu Hopkins, Turner, Erinnern, Calais Kirchturm u.s.f." *Geheimnislosigkeit* 123-24.

37. Disapprovingly, Kolker comments on a similar moment on Straub/Huillet's "most accessible work," *The Chronicle of Anna Magdalena Bach:* "In a moment of high drama, Bach is physically removed from his place of work in the middle of a rehearsal. He is led out and down a staircase. But lest we become too involved in this excess of movement, the camera holds on the empty staircase for a very long time, forcing us to consider the events, withdraw from them, recompose ourselves, reorient ourselves back to the image…" (211).

38. Peter Handke, "Kinonacht, Kinotiernacht," *Die Zeit* (20.11.1992). Byg offers a critical analysis of Handke's review. All translations by Byg 216.
39. Quoted in Byg 207-08.
40. cp. Peter Bürger 58.

Works Cited

Arnold, Heinz Ludwig, ed. *Die andere Sprache. Neue DDR-Literatur der 80er Jahre*. Munich: text + kritik, 1990.
Breuer, Dieter. "'Wörter so voll Licht so finster' Hölderlingedichte von Günter Eich bis Rolf Haufs." *Deutsche Lyrik nach 1945*. Ed. Dieter Breuer. Frankfurt/M.: Suhrkamp, 1988.
Bürger, Peter. *Theory of the Avant-garde*. Trans. Michael Shaw. Minneapolis, MN: University of Minnesota Press, 1984.
Byg, Barton. *Landscapes of Resistance. The German Films of Daniele Huillet and Jean-Marie Straub*. Berkeley: University of California Press, 1995.
Celan, Paul. "The Meridian." *Collected Prose*. Trans. Rosmarie Waldrop. Manchester: Carcanet Press, 1986.
Colin, Amy. *Paul Celan. Holograms of Darkness*. Bloomington: Indiana UP, 1991.
Dischner, Gisela. *"bald sind wir aber Gesang." Zur Hölderlin-Linie der Moderne*. Bielefeld: Aisthesis, 1996.
Egger, Oswald. "Mutmaßungen über einige verborgene Bedingungen des Gedichts 'Freiheitsgespräche entlang einer Straße' von Peter Waterhouse." *manuskripte* 107 (1990).
Farocki, Harun. "Den Text zu Gehör bringen: Gespräch mit Andreas von Rauch." *Stadtkino Programm*. 121. Wien: October 1987.
Fehervary, Helen. *Hölderlin and the Left. The Search for a Dialectic of Art and Life*. Heidelberg: Winter, 1977.
Foucault, Michel. *The Order of Things. An Archaeology of the Human Sciences*. New York: Pantheon, 1970.

Grätz, Katharina. "Der *Empedokles*-Text der Großen Stuttgarter Ausgabe und der Frankfurter Ausgabe." *Hölderlin-Jahrbuch* 28 (1992/93): 264-299.
Habermas, Jürgen. *Die Neue Unübersichtlichkeit.* Kleine Politische Schriften V. Frankfurt/M.: Suhrkamp, 1985.
Hamburger, Michael. *Die Dialektik der modernen Lyrik. Von Baudelaire bis zu Konkreten Poesie.* München: List, 1972.
Handke, Peter. "Kinonacht, Kinotiernacht." *Die Zeit* 20 Nov. 1992.
Harrison, R. B. *Hölderlin and Greek Literature.* Oxford: Clarendon, 1975.
Hartung, Harald. *Experimentelle Literatur und Konkrete Poesie.* Göttingen: Vandenhoeck & Ruprecht, 1975.
Hölderlin, Friedrich. *Sämtliche Werke. Frankfurter Ausgabe, Einleitung.* Ed. Dietrich E. Sattler. Frankfurt: Roter Stern, 1975.
---. "Der Tod des Empedokles." Erste Fassung. *Hyperion. Empedokles.* Ed. Erich Lichtenstein. Weimar: Lichtenstein, 1922.
---. "Vulkan." *Hölderlin. His Poems Translated with a Critical Study.* Trans. Michael Hamburger. London: Harvill Press, 1952.
---. *Poems and Fragments.* Trans. Michael Hamburger. Ann Arbor: University of Michigan Press, 1968.
---. "Über die Verfahrensweise des poetischen Gesetzes." *Sämtliche Werke und Briefe.* Bd.1. Ed. Gunter Mickels. Munich: Hanser, 1970.
---. "On the Operations of Poetic Spirit." *Essays and Letters on Theory.* Trans. Thomas Pfau. Albany: State University of New York Press, 1988.
Hörisch, Jochen. *Brot und Wein. Die Poesie des Abendmahls.* Frankfurt/M.: Suhrkamp, 1992.
Hurch, Hans and Stephan Settele. "Der Schatten der Beute: Gespräch mit Danièle Huillet und Jean-Marie Straub." *Stadtkino Programm* 121. Wien: October 1987.
Jandl, Ernst. *selbstporträt des schachspielers als trinkende uhr.* Frankfurt/M.: Luchterhand, 1986.
---. *Das Öffnen und Schließen des Mundes. Frankfurter Poetik-Vorlesungen.* Darmstadt: Luchterhand, 1985.

Kasper, Elke. "Peter Waterhouse." *Kritisches Lexikon der deutschsprachigen Gegenwartsliteratur*, 38th delivery (1991). Ed. Heinz Ludwig Arnold. Munich: text + kritik, 1978.

Kolker, Robert P. *The Altering Eye. Contemporary International Cinema*. Oxford: Oxford UP, 1983.

Leeder, Karen. *Breaking Boundaries. A New Generation of Poets in the GDR*. Oxford: Clarendon Press, 1996.

Martin, Wolfgang. *Mit Schärfe und Zartheit. Zu einer Poetik der Sprache bei Hölderlin mit Rücksicht auf Herder*. Bonn: Bouvier, 1988.

Meister, Ernst. "Frag dich dereinst." *Hölderlin-Jahrbuch* 21 (1978/79).

Middleton, Christopher. Friedrich Hölderlin, Eduard Mörike. *Selected Poems*. Trans. Christopher Middleton. Chicago: University of Chicago Press, 1972.

Nancy, Jean-Luc. "La joie d'Hypérion." *L'Herne. Hölderlin*. Ed. Jean-François Courtine. Paris: Editions de l'Herne, 1989.

Neumann, Gert. *Die Klandestinität der Kesselreiniger. Ein Versuch des Sprechens*. Frankfurt/M.: Fischer, 1989.

Novak, Helga. "Dunkle Seite Hölderlin's." *Margarete mit dem Schrank* (Berlin 1978).

Novalis. "Hymnen an die Nacht." *Werke*. Ed. H.-J.Mähl and R.Samuel with H.J. Balmes. Munich 1978-1988.

---. *Pollen and Fragmente: Selected Poetry and Prose of Novalis*. Transl. Arthur Versluis. Grand Rapids: Pharus Press, 1989.

Packalén, Sture. *Zum Hölderlinbild in der Bundesrepublik und der DDR.. Anhand ausgewählter Beispiel der produktiven Hölderlinrezeption*. Stockholm: Almquist and Wiksell, 1986.

Perloff, Marjorie. *Radical Artifice. Writing Poetry in the Age of Media*. Chicago: University of Chicago Press, 1991.

Sandford, John. *The New German Cinema*. New York: Wolff, 1980.

Santner, Eric. *Friedrich Hölderlin: Narrative Vigilance and the Poetic Imagination*. New Brunswick: Rutgers UP, 1986.

Schlag, Evelyn. "Die Glocke im Ohr." *Der Standard* 3 Dec. 1994.

Schmidt, Jochen. "Welchen Text hat Hölderlin's Ode 'Natur und Kunst oder Saturn und Jupiter?'" *Zeitschrift für deutsche Philologie* 115.2 (1996): 283-288.

---. "Hölderlin im 20. Jahrhundert. Rezeption und Edition." *Hölderlin und die Moderne. Eine Bestandsaufnahme.* Ed. Gerhard Kurz, Valérie Lawitschka, and Jürgen Wertheimer. Tübingen: Attempto, 1995.
Spiel, Hilde, ed. *Die zeitgenössische Literatur Österreichs.* Zürich: Kindler, 1976.
Strelka, Joseph. "Die Entwicklung der Lyrik seit 1945 in Österreich." *Die deutsche Lyrik 1945-1975.* Ed. Klaus Weissenberger. Düsseldorf: Bagel, 1981.
Struck, Karin. "Der Dichter ist ein arbeitender Mensch. Über Hölderlin." *Literaturmagazin 2: Von Goethe lernen? Fragen der Klassikrezeption.* Ed. Hans Christoph Buch. Reinbek: Rowohlt, 1974.
Turim, Maureen. "Textuality and Theatricality in Brecht and Straub/Huillet: *History Lessons* (1972)." *German Film and Literature. Adaptions and Transformations.* Ed. Eric Rentschler. New York: Methuen, 1986.
Vogel, Juliane. "Die Exerzitien des Gerard Manley Hopkins." *manuskripte* 128 (1995) 135-137.
Waterhouse, Peter. "(Honig & Zoonen)." *Sprache im technischen Zeitalter* 107-108 (1988).
---. "Ich: Kirsche. Gedichte." *manuskripte* 85 (1984).
---. *Besitzlosigkeit Verzögerung Schweigen Anarchie.* Graz: Droschl, 1985.
---. "Was Sprache ist?" *Der Prokurist* 1 (1990).
---. "Im Lauf der Dinge." *Der Prokurist* 3 (1990).
---. "Die Akademie ist der einzige hüpfende Punkt im Staate." *Der Prokurist* 5 (1991).
---. "Von herbstlicher Stille umgeben wird ein Stück gespielt." *manuskripte* 133 (1996) 23.
---. *Das Klarfeld Gedicht.* Berlin: Literarisches Kolloquium, 1988.
---. *Die Geheimnislosigkeit. Ein Spazier- und Lesebuch.* Salzburg: Residenz, 1996.
---. "Gedicht im Materialstadium." *passim. Gedichte.* Reinbek: Rowohlt, 1986.
---. "Abj." *Die Geheimnislosigkeit. Ein Spazier- und Lesebuch.* Salzburg: Residenz, 1996.

6
Gender and (Post)Gender

Imaging (Post)Gender under Transnational Capital: Valie Export's *Perfect Pair*

Nora M. Alter
University of Florida

> The representation of reality becomes the commodity of reality.
> —Valie Export[1]

> In the postmodern, autoreferentiality can be initially detected in the way in which culture acts out its own commodification.
> —Fredric Jameson[2]

> Back to zero, then, for the issue of sex, since anyway capitalism, that was its starting point: getting rid of sex.
> —Jacques Lacan[3]

> By the late twentieth century...we are all chimeras, theorized and fabricated hybrids of machine and organism; in short, we are cyborgs. The cyborg is our ontology; it gives us our politics.
> —Donna Haraway[4]

These four epigraphs point toward the possibility of agreement and collaboration between cultural workers and theorists, even as the iron cage of commodification continually closes in relentlessly. In the postmodern world of increasingly global "cybernetic capital," stable categories of national, personal, and gender identity are becoming labile, eluding fixed definition, cyborgified.[5] Specifically, questions are raised as to what it means to be, say, Austrian, or more precisely a female Austrian cultural worker on the left—one "traditionally" concerned with questions of gender, class-politics, and social representation. How do omnipresent features of global capitalism and technocultural advance affect image production and consumption? These are some of the questions raised, I argue, by film- and videomaker, performance artist, and Feminist Actionist, Valie Export.[6]

With an eye on the theme of the conference for which this essay was originally written, "Crossing Cultural Bounds in Contemporary Austrian Literature and Film," I want to examine Export's 1986/87 video *Ein perfektes Paar oder die Unzucht wechselt ihre Haut*, her twelve-minute contribution to the international omnibus production *Seven Women Seven Sins*.[7]

The meaning of Export's title is not transparent, even after several viewings, and is not explained diegetically, that is, in the video. The English translation offered on the video distributed in North America is "A New Kind of Skin Game." In the critical literature it is translated more literally as "A Perfect Pair, or, Indecency Sheds Its Skin," but *Unzucht* commonly refers to an indecent or lewd act of an explicitly sexual nature, requiring adjectives to clarify it further. For instance, *gewerbsmäßige Unzucht* means prostitution, *außereheliche Unzucht* is adultery, and so on, and the entire video exudes an explicitly erotic, or perhaps posterotic, atmosphere in which all these "sins" may be connoted, though never denoted. *Wechseln* can mean not only "to shed" but "to exchange," including money and also in this case skins. The video seems less about uncovering something hidden under a skin, unless it is a machinic quality under the dermatological surface, than it is about the exchange of properties: man and woman as mediated by machines and commodities as a tertium quid. Similarly, the term "pair" refers not only to people but to other types of binary opposition that it is the viewer's task to specify.

Seven Women Seven Sins is a mostly tongue-in-cheek film composed of seven shorts, each based on one of the seven deadly, or capital, sins fatal to spiritual progress and salvation: Pride, Covetousness, Lust, Anger, Gluttony, Envy, and Sloth. The film was the work of seven feminist film- and videomakers: Ulrike Ottinger, Helke Sanders, Chantal Akerman, Maxi Cohen, Betty Gordon, Laurence Gavron, and Export herself, whose chosen sin was Lust. The fact that the names of the seven sins are no longer on the tip of our tongues is one index of our postmodernity; that the names of the seven filmmakers are not exactly household words, either, may speak for the oblivion of postmodernity to its would-be critics. Be this as it may, the collaborative film is a contemporary appropriation of the premodern convention of visual artists to depict the seven deadly sins. Which allowed the artist at once to condemn the sins as ordained by orthodoxy, often at the expense of women, but also a certain freedom to show the sins' considerable attractions, sometimes heterodoxically.

The depiction of the sins has accompanied film history, not least in one of the most prototypical early films, *Metropolis* (1927), in the scene where the son of the industrialist, Freder, enters a cathedral and is confronted by statues of the sins, anticipating his crucial confrontation with his Maria: the real socialist agitator and the proto-cyborg agent provocateur, the one whose revolutionary impulse must be transformed into love, the other whose threat of castration must be destroyed. The reappropriation of the trope of sin by Export and her colleagues can therefore be understood as a self-referential gesture of the filmic medium on itself, a loop back to its early history, confirming Jameson's dictum that for us postmoderns, for the "cultural logic of late capitalism," history no longer means interest in the lived experience of others in the past but rather the moment we were first introduced by the media into the media, first patched into the loop.[8] Margret Eifler has noted of Export's brand of avant-gardism that "If modernism may be compared to a handmade collage, postmodernism appears as the result of cybernetics," though "the centrifugal force of this artistic modernity was all too soon integrated, and thus neutralized, by market forces."[9] But how, then, do the ancient, if not perennial, sins manifest themselves in modern or postmodern capitalist culture, and to what extent might they still be gendered when, in Lacan's phrase, capitalism is quite prepared to "get rid of sex" if it must? And when the physical body itself has been penetrated by technological and market forces?

Export takes up the underlying theological implications by almost opening *A Perfect Pair* with a close-up of naked female breasts contained in a kind of frame. The camera pulls back to reveal the owner: a woman distributing what appears to be communion wafers in an urban public square to a more or less baffled crowd. She is dressed in a long white dress, with a long black diagonal sash (something like a Miss Universe insignia) with a reference to valentines, bordered with black hearts, and she carries a white lily. Her bare, bracketed breasts are the standard medieval iconographeme for Lust, also depicted as such in *Metropolis*. Export was trained in art history, but aficionados will also recall Export's earlier feminist-situationist Actionism which included stationing herself in Viennese streets, wearing a box around her chest, allowing men to fondle her breasts.[10] Already in these earlier performances we see one of Export's central concerns of how the human subject is itself already always commodified. However, it is less the similarities between Export's 1986/87 video segment and her earlier film works than the differences that may hold a key to the question, if not answer, to what this sequence might mean for us here.

Eifler has said of Export's earlier film *Unsichtbare Gegner* that it is interested less in "the portrayal of a particular couple" or "the particular experience of a female protagonist"; instead, Export's is an exercise in semiotic and ideological deconstruction, resulting filmically in "a painful elegy lamenting the communicative animosity between nations, societal partners, human beings, lovers, and the sexes" (245). This project continues in *A Perfect Pair*, though the modernist elegiac, nostalgic tonality of her earlier work has morphed into a more properly postmodern cynicism. In this sense Ramona Curry is right that Export's films are generally not deconstructions of male viewing pleasure (à la Laura Mulvey), indeed are not "about" individual female characters or their experiences, as is her earlier performance art, but rather are concerned with the very processes of representation, particularly of the female image. To put it another way, what is at issue in Export's work is not the "portrayal" but rather the *representation* of women.[11] Yet it seems to me that Export's more recent work is working beyond any problematic of representation, including of gender, to confront what I call *imaging gender*, even *postgender*.

Unlike Export's earlier films, which are all set in Vienna—*Unsichtbare Gegner* (Invisible Adversaries, 1976), *Menschenfrauen* (Peoplewomen, 1979), *Syntagma* (1981/83), and *Die Praxis der Liebe* (The Practice of Love, 1984)—the geographical location of *A Perfect Pair* is not specified or site specific. The urban space might be Vienna but could be many European cities as well. This comes as a surprise insofar as the architecture of a place and geography, in tandem with a human body's phenomenological interaction with site-specific spaces, had played an integral role in Export's photographs, films, videos, and staged happenings. To anticipate, this may be because cyborgs—like Capital itself—owe as little ultimate allegiance to national identity as they do to gender or sex. In Donna Haraway's phrase, "the actors are cyborg...and the geography is elsewhere."[12]

Yet, following her tradition of Body Art (which extends back to the Lettrists and Situationists near mid-century) the human body still remains a central focus of Export's new video, albeit in less obvious and traditional ways than earlier. Export explained in 1989 that "the equation material = body typifies Viennese Actionism," and nearly all her work has been informed by what she calls "historical scars, traces of ideas inscribed onto the body" (69, 73). Following Mallarmé's high-modernist theory of *écriture corporelle* (which influenced the Lettrist movement and, through it, the Situationist International),[13] Export suggests that Feminist Actionists have expanded "beyond the canvas, written it onto their own bodies, and posited their own individuality against the culture around them" (81). Yet in *A Perfect Pair* it is no longer merely the female body that has been inscribed, but the male as well. This gender conflation has serious implications, if we are interested in all types of border crossings coming from Austria. Export is pushing her rather gender-essentialist Viennese Actionism of the sixties and seventies to a more all-encompassing theory of what she terms "expanded cinema," which, she notes in 1992, "found its continuation in my medial body-material performances, into which I introduced the body as sign and code for a social and aesthetic expression."[14]

To be precise, *A Perfect Pair* does not quite open with the allusion to Export's own interventionist past, but rather with two anonymous male figures strolling in front of billboards advertising election slogans ("Für Österreich") and various products, including McDonalds, ice cream, department stores, tires ("Semperit: Der Nassgriff"), and finally lingerie. One figure is dressed like a butcher in a medieval morality play, with an outrageous calf's-head headgear; another is a shadow boxing boxer. The lingerie ad motivates cutting to the aforementioned communion scene (and also away from quasi-documentary footage to the more fictional narrative), we enter, via another extreme closeup, this time of black gloved hands, a futuristic upscale cosmopolitan bar that could be located in virtually any chic urban district on the globe, not to say universe. The camera again moves back from the close-up of the gloved hands to reveal their owner. (This technique of showing the female part before the whole parodies the metonymy that is a standard feature of male viewing formations and Hollywood cinema, in which women are often shown and viewed piecemeal.) Swirling around the black cocktail-dressed woman are computer generated written texts announcing that her body is a site of tourism: *Traumreise* (dream trip). A female bartender has the names of drinks tattooed onto her body: Bloodymary and Screwdriver, the latter being hyphenated across her body front and back: "screw" recto, "driver" verso. The beverages and advertising in the bar refer to call brands. Like the McDonalds billboard earlier, the implication is that no matter where we go, we rest assured that the same products will be universally available. Winicott might refer to these name brands as "transition objects" that make the impending new bad future less anxiety ridden than it would otherwise be, much as a child takes a familiar piece of home with it when launching out into the uncanny future.[15] For her part, Export suggests that, in an age of transnational capitalism, all regional and national differences are being effaced—symbolically if not actually—in and by seemingly endless chains of mechanically reproducible commodities. In the words of Deleuze and Guattari, "The simulacrum, the simulation of a packet of noodles, has become the true concept; and the one who packages the product, commodity, or work of art has become the philosopher, conceptual persona, or artist" (11). The driving force behind it all is transnational capital, and it remains to know its impact on the capital sins. And Export's genre, the essay film, responds as a form of "filmic philosophy."

Inside Export's bar appears one human pair in particular: the woman in black with the body as tourist site and, soon, one man especially. Yet they are simultaneously pure commodities, creations of the capitalist advertising world. No longer content merely to inscribe writing on the celluloid or video, Export images, with the use of digital manipulation, advertising labels and cards that slide in and out of the pair's physical bodies like an ATM machine. Thus she suggests how human commodification has become inseparable from its re/presentation and autoreferentiality of commodification. Everything here is for sale—every gesture, expression, action. If Baudelaire once calculated what each image in his sonnets was worth commercially, now the human body itself has been folded into the mix. Thus, in Export's video, "smelling the armpit" of the dream-trip woman in black costs $130, "stroking the thigh" another $130, and so on, from "biting the back" to "soul kisses." It makes no difference whether the interaction is heterosexual or homosexual, or is gendered in any way, so long as the money is where the mouth was. National identity, as well as sexual and gender, leaves the playing field without protest. All possible identity, including identity politics, becomes the geopolitical fetish object of an ultimately unrepresentable but omnipresent absent cause, even god.

The female half of Export's perfect pair is "Nelly," not fortuitously a gay code for a hyper-feminine male, which further complicates binary or "paired" sexuality. Nelly is stereotypically beautiful and glamorous, that is, smiles and giggles at the camera, virtually speechless. Her nameless male counterpart is an Arnold Schwarzenegger replicant (Schwarzenegger, needless to say, is Austrian and politically conservative, and a rare Austro-Hollywood megastar), an iron-pumping simulacrum of maleness. When they first meet they silently exchange deep glances: perhaps a parody of Dante's meeting with Beatrice, which inaugurates his *vita nuova*, but also a video rebus for the German *Blickwechsel*: meaning not only an exchange of glances between two people, but also a radical transposition of viewing positions. Again a computer-generated caption swirls out of his body and then around them: "One Night Stand." When the man finally speaks his voice is clearly dubbed, out of synch with his lips. As he explains, every surface and slot of his armored body has been used for advertising for architectural, engineering, interior design firms. As Export has put it in a 1992 interview, she wants to investigate "the border regions of different forms (*Formensprachen*) and connecting the space of perception

(*Wahrnehmungsraum*) with real space (*Realraum*)."[16] Her male actor informs Nelly with his post-postmodern ethics: if one is beautiful, nothing should ever be paid for, including the makeup products that render her beautiful. As he laconically adds, "the cosmetic industry uses your beauty as a weapon against age"—and so, presumably, we are enabled to live on to consume, to be consumed, and to consume yet again. Certainly production is out of the picture, except the illusion of self-production. And in a later scene we will see the male figure pumping iron to the *Schlager* "Simple Man." At one point toward the end of this scene a politician enters the bar, and asks to be photographed next to Nelly. Small surprise, she is now yet another image for his campaign of images, accompanied by computer titles: "Corruption," "The Color of Money," et cetera. But where, in this world of nearly politico-economic embodiment, is specifically Lust or any sin?

Export suddenly cuts to a scene shot in muted color, almost black and white, in distinct contrast to the high gloss color stock of the previous scene. Everyday people in a dingy bar lament the fact that they will never be in an advertisement, the highest life-form available. Their self-worth is determined by the ability to commodify and exploit their bodies. Again, the inability to commodify their bodies—described as "anti-social"—is no longer dependent on either gender or sexuality, nor their accompanying baggage of guilt, repression, and ideology. In other terms, and for better or worse, Export has opened up her early Feminist Actionism to image all possible instances of *reification*, as we might still say, but *irrespective* of sex or gender as we morph toward the twenty-first century. Yet, curiously, class distinctions linger on in the difference between the two bars, in who may become an ad.

Following two scenes (first a gambling house with international patrons around a roulette wheel, including Nelly; and then the nameless half of the pair pumping iron, with ads for various weightlifting products swirling from and around his body), we return to Nelly waking up to get dressed in a white dress, reminiscent of the scene with the communion wafers that once warded off the seven deadly sins. Onto Nelly's dress are projected a series of images of women taken from classic pinups (Marilyn Monroe) and porno-magazines. The song in the background intones "I have forgotten your name, but I remember your kisses." Looking down from Nelly's balcony, and then from ground level, we see a series of male and female figures approach a series of strange vending machines. These machines, another allusion to Export's own Activist stagings, produce various transformations of the skin: for example, a man receives a tattoo across his chest, and the word "boot" is printed on a woman's naked foot, rather like a Magritte painting.

In general, women *and* men are figured by Export less than even reified, gendered, sexual, or erotic objects than as something totally commodified. Even—or precisely—the most private fantasies are not free, predetermined, and pre-programmed. Lust, the formerly deadly or capital sin, has forfeited all possible individuation to become yet another mode of triumphant Transnational Capital.

Export's short video approaches its ends with the "perfect pair" on what appears to be a resort beach, their bodies having become commodified to the point where total commodification seems an imminent likelihood, if ultimately unrepresentable and sublime. They exchange gifts: "she" giving increasing access to her body, "he" gives wearable prosthetic devices advertising various products, of an increasingly advanced technological nature. It makes no difference when "she" coyly protests, to the effect that all this is unnecessary because "she" has paid for this ad spot herself. As the two sets of "skin" exchange themselves, and as "she" approaches orgasm, the loop of commodification, the representation of reality as the commodity of reality, becomes especially tight, cage-like. "Her" ass is used for the promotion of tires, similar to the advertised tires with which the video began so very long ago, in postmodern calculation: nearly twelve minutes. So it is that the nearly circular structure of the video, so untraditional in many other respects, reflects and/or helps to coproduce the nexus of commodity-circulation-without-production of what some of us outside the video may only hope is *late* capitalism. As always, Baudrillardian nihilism is either salutary in its frankness or just plain depressing, depending on your point of view.

What may today appear most striking about Export's video is its image of technology, not forgetting that it was made in 1986, substantially before digital manipulation and synthesis became relatively commonplace. (I'm thinking, e.g., of recent videos by Daniel Reeves, such as *Obsessive Becoming*, the title of which refers not only to the main theme, the after-effects of traumatic child abuse, but also to the morphing technology developed by Reeves to figure this theme, allowing the transformation of one face into another, et cetera.) Technology's presence in and as video sets Export's contribution apart from the other films in *Seven Women Seven Sins*, which may appear naive and old-fashioned by comparison. This tacit criticism of her colleagues may not be coincidental. As she puts it ironically in the interview of 1992, "How should a work of art look if it must confirm the commodity woman and the commodity art? The work of some women artists follows aesthetic concepts that are informed by phallic structures. More often than not, these attempts are marked by immediate success" (Mueller 214). By "phallic structures," Export appears to be referring to straight linear narrative and traditional veri-similitude—two things not to be found in *A Perfect Pair*.

By almost literally embracing technology and the media, Export pushes modernist "representation" into a relatively uncharted realm, one that, or so she hopes, transcends patriarchal vision on all sides of the camera. In response to a critic's charge that her use of technology is itself "male," she responds that "the points of departure of expression, content and representations may be gender specific but not the medium itself" (214). While this seems like technological essentialism (reminiscent, say, of the more effusive and naive moments in Walter Benjamin's famous artwork essay), this is not what Export intends. We may surmise that the "perfect pair" of her title is less a reference to Nelly and her nameless male counterpart, less to actors and themes, than a self-reference to Export's adopted technological medium and its ideology, self-critical though it may strive to be. *A Perfect Pair* can thus be viewed as the *audiovisual literalization* of certain theses of the Frankfurt School about the social and human implications of technology. Of course, this critique must be brought up to current technocultural speed, as has been done in Haraway's *Cyborg Manifesto* and, I am

Imaging (Post)Gender 277

suggesting, by Export's recent work. As Herbert Marcuse noted in 1941, "The relationships among men are increasingly mediated by the machine process. But the mechanical contrivances which facilitate intercourse among individuals also intercept and absorb their libido, thereby diverting it from the all too dangerous realm in which the individual is free of society" (144). "Critical thought," Marcuse lamented, has been transformed into "social impotence," and this due to several factors. "The foremost among them is the growth of the industrial apparatus and of its all-embracing control over all spheres of life. The technological rationality inculcated in those who attend to this apparatus has transformed numerous modes of external compulsion and authority into modes of self-discipline and self-control" (148). In Export's own words, "The nexus (*Verknüpfung*) between body, technological science, and society is a cultural expression of our times that my artistic work and my theoretical investigations attempt to define. The body as bearer of signs demonstrates a common language, which, however, can also render it exchangeable, replaceable, and determinable. Therefore it is of the essence to escape from this codification" (Mueller 217). Needless to say, whether she really does escape is unlikely, given the premises of her own argument, the upshot of which seem as pessimistic and technologically deterministic as any remark penned by the Frankfurt School, even though in *A Perfect Pair* the mood is incomparably funnier and more hedonistic (more like the later Marcuse than the earlier), the infiltration of technology into human bodies is more literal, the absorption of libido—and hence Lust—is more all-embracing. Finally, the attempt to escape from techno-culture remains significant to Export, challenging the audience as well.

But wherein lies possible escape from total codification and its concomitant, commodification? Perhaps it may be glimpsed in its very absence, between the lines, in Export's deployment of technology against itself, in its hypersimulation or overidentification, to speak with Slavoj Žižek (70-73). Alternatively, critics may not be exactly wrong to call *A Perfect Pair* Export's only "comedy" (Mueller 209). Comedies have happy endings, if for only a moment and in appearance. Clearly, Export uses the medium to combat the medium, fighting fire with fire, even if the humor may escape us. But how are we to read this homeopathically contested cinematic technology? Jameson remarks that "If everything means something else, then so does technology,"[17] and that "technology is little more than the outer emblem or symptom by which a systemic variety of concrete situations expresses itself in a specific variety of forms and form-problems."[18] When this theory is transposed onto *Seven Women Seven Sins* and onto Export's take on the problematic of sin, we must ask if the purported sin of Lust, traditionally figured as irreducibly sexual, also really means something else. This is part of what Export seems to mean by the problem of "medial anagrams," which she defines as "units of representation which are transposed into different contexts and codifications. What interests me is that even minimal shifts in context will bring out differences in signification for the same unit of representation. It is a kind of language system for image production in the technological media" (Mueller 213). In and as video, this means that sexualized and gendered sin becomes depicted, critically, as yet another screen image for another, even stronger lust, which is contemptuous of all common distinctions yet happy to use them all. For in the post-modern age, medieval Lust has been transmuted by and into a lust that grows ever greater, ever more undetectable. How to represent it? Is it technological finesse à la Horkheimer and Adorno? An invincible "invisible adversary," to recall Export's earlier film? Or can we believe the more recent Export when she imputes a potentially subversive, even utopic, power to technology even if only in its postgendered hypersimulation. She herself hesitates here, perhaps properly so. On the one hand, she is tempted to view technologies such as virtual reality (VR) as not merely replicating reality, achieving even greater pixel verisimilitude, but also as pushing humanity towards another plane of understanding and action. On the other hand, she avers that "Digital technology determines our view of the world today and in turn this technology was informed by our mathematical explanation of the universe. The question is whether this is the only representation of our world. I don't think so" (Mueller 212).

Export's precocious use of digital manipulation in *Seven*

Women Seven Sins—this was 1986/87, after all—may indeed point in an uncharted direction: to a technoculture *opposed* to transnational capitalism. Certainly, in a world where so many identities are being effaced, we see also the drive towards *other* forms of identity, but many of them are decidedly premodern in appearance and hardly progressive, as in the return of tribalistic nationalism from Algeria to Bosnia, and uncannily closer to home. By asking without answering its basic question (i.e., Is an anticapitalist postgendered politics possible, or just another capitalist production?), Export's short video pushes both within and beyond borders, so as to suggest that the "perfect pair" must be seen not only, or no longer, in terms of gender but also in the staging of a collision within and against postmodernism, within and against its most advanced visual technologies in their relentless drive to commodify everything, everybody. It should thus come as small surprise that, in the credits to her video, Export plays on her own name, her own status as a commodity. In the last sequence we see her swimming in the resort pool, wearing a sailor hat, holding a video camera, smiling. "Money-Back Guarantee" spins around her head. She swims on past a pair of legs above her, revealed to belong to our perfect pair, locked in embrace, dancing to a corny *Schlager* which plays on to the end of the video. The camera pans up to the inside roof of the pool, then cuts to the outside, before giving us our first establishing shot of the city. Superimposed across a pastiche of "1000 Schilling" bills (recalling the campaign slogan "für Österreich" at the beginning), we see Export's signature. But her full name is different, having been exchanged for another. She has renamed herself "Value Export." And so it is that not only an economy but an ethics, no matter how weak, lives on.

Notes

1. "Interview with Valie Export" (1992), Mueller 216.
2. Jameson, *The Geopolitical Aesthetic: Cinema and Space in the World System* 5.
3. Lacan 30.
4. Haraway 150.

5. See Roberts and Webster 44-75; but, for a cogent critique, also see Ross 107-34.

6. Export was born in 1940 in Linz. Based in Vienna, she has held professorships in film and video production at the University of Wisconsin, Milwaukee, The San Francisco Art Institute, San Francisco State University, and the Hochschule der Künste in Berlin. Her films are distributed in North America by Foreign Images, in Evanston, Illinois; videos are available from Facets Video, Chicago. For a bibliography of her own writing, interviews, and critical writings on her works, see Margret Eifler 241-54; for a complete filmography, see Mueller, *Valie Export*.

7. *Seven Women Seven Sins*. ZDF Produktion. 1986. 101 minutes. First broadcast in 1987, on "Das kleine Fernsehspiel."

8. See Jameson, *Postmodernism, or, The Cultural Logic of Late Capitalism* 16-25, 55-61, 217-22, and 284-86.

9. Eifler, "Valie Export's *Invisible Adversaries*," 244.

10. For her own description of this intervention, see "Interview with Valie Export" (1987), by Margret Eifler and Sandra Frieden, *Gender and German Cinema*, 1:267-78; 268-70.

11. Curry 257.

12. Haraway, "The Actors Are Cyborg, Nature is Coyote, and the Geography Is Elsewhere. Postscript to 'Cyborgs at Large,'" *Technoculture*, 21-26.

13. For a vivid account of Lettrism and Situationism, particularly in relation to punk counterculture, see Greil Marcus.

14. Mueller, "Interview with Valie Export" 219.

15. For a development and application of Winicott's theory of transitional objects to a film (*Total Recall*, starring Arnold Schwarzenegger), see Fred Glass.

16. Mueller, "Interview with Valie Export" 218.

17. Jameson, *The Geopolitical Aesthetic* 11.

18. Jameson, *The Geopolitical Aesthetic* 11.

Works Cited

Deleuze Gilles and Félix Guattari. *What Is Philosophy?* (1991). Trans. Hugh Tomlinson and Graham Burchell. New York: Columbia UP, 1994.

Curry, Ramona. "The Female Image as Critique in the Films of Valie Export." *Gender and German Cinema: Feminist Interventions.* Vol. 1:*Gender and Representation in New German Cinema.* Ed. Sandra Frieden et al. Providence: Berg, 1993. 255-66.

Eifler, Margret. "Valie Export's *Invisible Adversaries*: Film as Text." *Gender and German Cinema: Feminist Interventions.* Vol. 1: *Gender and Representation in New German Cinema.* Ed. Sandra Frieden et al. Providence: Berg, 1993. 241-51.

Export, Valie. "Aspects of Feminist Actionism." *New German Critique* 47 (1989): 69-92.

Glass, Fred. "Totally Recalling Arnold: Sex and Violence in the New Bad Future." *Film Quarterly* 44:1 (1990): 2-13.

Haraway, Donna J. "A Cyborg Manifesto: Science, Technology, and Socialist-Feminism in the Late Twentieth Century." *Simians, Cyborgs, and Women: The Reinvention of Nature.* New York: Routledge, 1991.

Jameson, Fredric. *Postmodernism, or, The Cultural Logic of Late Capitalism.* Durham: Duke UP, 1991.

---. *The Geopolitical Aesthetic: Cinema and Space in the World System.* Bloomington: Indiana UP, 1992.

Lacan, Jacques. *Television: A Challenge to the Psychoanalytic Establishment.* Ed. Joan Copjec, trans. Denis Hollier et al. New York: W. W. Norton, 1990.

Marcus, Greil. *Lipstick Traces: A Secret History of the Twentieth Century.* Cambridge, MA: Harvard UP, 1989.

Marcuse, Herbert. "Some Social Implications of Modern Technology" (1941). *The Essential Frankfurt School Reader.* Ed. Andrew Arato and Eike Gebhardt. New York: Continuum, 1982. 138-62.

Mueller, Roswitha. *Valie Export: Fragments of the Imagination.* Bloomington: Indiana UP, 1994.

Roberts, Kevin and Frank Webster. "Cybernetic Capitalism." *The Political Economy of Information*. Ed. Vincent Mosco and Janet Wasko. Madison: U of Wisconsin P, 1988.

Ross, Andrew. "Hacking Away at the Counterculture." *Technoculture*. Ed. Constance Penley and Andrew Ross. Minneapolis: U of Minnesota P, 1991.

Seven Women Seven Sins. ZDF Produktion. 1986. 101 minutes. First broadcast in 1987, on "Das kleine Fernsehspiel."

Žižek, Slavoj. *The Metastases of Enjoyment: Six Essays on Woman and Causality*. London: Verso, 1994.

The War between the Sexes:
Gender Relations in the Works of Elisabeth Reichart

Linda C. DeMeritt
Allegheny College

Elisabeth Reichart is known primarily for her portrayal of events during World War II and thus for her contribution to Austria's belated willingness to confront its Nazi past. Her best-selling debut, *February Shadows* (1989; *Februarschatten*, 1984), depicts the brutal murder of nearly 500 escaped Soviet prisoners-of-war at the hands of the local, supposedly apolitical, Austrian population, and her second novel, *Come Across the Lake* (*Komm über den See*, 1988), is set against the background of women resistance fighters. Critics heralded Reichart as one of a growing number of authors to address Austrian complicity in, as opposed to victimization by, Nazi atrocities. After years of denial, events such as Waldheim's presidential campaign in 1986 and the fiftieth anniversary of the Anschluß in 1988 prompted a reassessment of the question of national responsibility and guilt. Reichart's works were interpreted as attempts to give voice to past silence, in particular to the women whose stories had been repressed by the dominant male historical discourse.[1]

Yet from the beginning Reichart was interested in history as more than an event, as more than a recounting of silenced facts. In an interview from 1987 with Achim Roscher, Reichart elaborates upon his definition of her literature as "writing against the denial of history." She states that history concerns her as it affects the individual:

> An important starting point for my work is without doubt the reappraisal of significant events and occurrences of our most recent past. But...what interests me in particular is how history

> affects the *individual* person. How does the individual view historical processes and what effect do these processes exert on her? Her possibilities for action are limited. She can hardly be expected to achieve something fundamental on her own. However, to recognize this powerlessness, also to put it into words—this is important for me. (129)

Central to each of Reichart's works is the tension between the individual and social forces. Whether located in the family, school, state, or church, these underlying societal structures, as well as the individual's attempt—powerless as it may be—to face them, inform the author's depiction of history. Thus they contribute to our understanding of the past not only by voicing long repressed historical dates and facts, but by examining the reasons and motivation behind individual action as rooted within the societal context.

This context manifests certain constants in Reichart's works. First, it is fascist. The author understands fascism not as a specific political and economic system, but as a way of thinking and behaving that goes beyond the political to determine personal relationships. In a recent essay titled "The many I's of the Republic and I," and the title here thematizes the relationship of dependence between the subject and state, Reichart describes her childhood and schooling in Austria as a training ground for complete obedience, conformity, and subordination to authority. Curiosity, question, and independent thought are met with immediate punishment and ostracism: "Every deviation from the norm was punished...Naturally it was taboo to think independently" (114-15). A second essay reiterates these thoughts and makes more explicit the continuum between past and present reality. Prejudice and hatred are reflected in a right versus wrong conceptual system, a we versus them mentality, and the refusal to acknowledge past guilt results in a brutality today toward gypsies, foreigners, and other minority groups reminiscent of past persecution: "Once again acts of terrorism are being directed against the same people who, under National Socialism, were counted among those to be eradicated" ("Lebkuchenherz" [Gingerbread Heart] 44).

Second, violence characterizes the society portrayed by Reichart at all levels; war in the public sphere is mirrored in the private realm by war between the sexes, by violence against women. Each of Reichart's works is an example of what Elaine Martin has termed "war literature," not in the sense of portraying a specific outbreak of war, but rather defined as texts whose "underlying subtext is violence, specifically the gradations of violence that range from the bittersweet power of paternal authority to the most overt form of organized violence, war" (12). And just as Martin links "paternal authority" and war, for Reichart the potential for violence in our society is located within unequal gender relations, within the forces of patriarchy as perpetuated by social roles and institutions. The oppression and exploitation of those outside the structures of society by those ensconced within them—this is Reichart's topic, and most frequently it finds expression in the power relations between men and women.

All of Reichart's works evince the common structural origin of public and private war, of political and everyday fascism. Her first two works foreground World War II, while simultaneously showing an individual's struggle to overcome the past by challenging norms and posing uncomfortable questions.[2] In contrast, her more recent texts—specifically the collection of short stories published in 1992 and titled *La Valse*, the novel *Fotze* from 1993, and her drama of 1994 titled *Sakkorausch* (*Foreign*)—highlight the battle raging between the sexes, while situating this more private war within the public context of World War II, the war in former Yugoslavia, and World War I, respectively.

The introductory story in Reichart's *La Valse*, titled "Sonntagsbraten" (The Sunday Roast), is paradigmatic in depicting gender relations as well as in linking the familial hierarchy to fascism. In this short, but remarkably rich and powerful narrative, Reichart describes the traditional Sunday dinner in postwar Austria. The women serve the meal, receiving only the lesser pieces of the Sunday roast they have prepared, and retreat to the kitchen when it is time for the men to relive the glory of their days in uniform. War is a thing for men, and their identity is tied to the nation that at least for a time gave their lives meaning through a sense of camaraderie and adventure. For these men time has stood still. Reichart communicates the static ritualization of reality by beginning each of her paragraphs with the same words—"it began"—in spite of the fact that they are organized chronologically and progress through the forties, fifties, and sixties. Instead of forward movement, however, there can only be repetition, for the structure of power and authority characteristic of the military is duplicated on the homefront, where the father figure preserves his position of privilege and dictates rules and orders to his subordinates. No difference or alternative behavior is allowed, no questions or curiosity, all of which are immediately punished as forms of disobedience.

Reichart's story clearly links fascism with a patriarchal family unit. For Reichart, the family serves the state as a convenient vehicle through which to impose the virtues of conformity. In a recent interview, the author asks: "Why does every state promote the family? Why do we believe that everyone must live in a family? I think it is because this makes sense for the state, that we are standardized there, that values are passed on, that we are groomed and trained there" (DeMeritt, Ensberg 10). The family serves as a microcosm of a totalitarian state where the strong rule over the weak, and men prevail over women.

The connection between patriarchy and fascism is not of course unique to Reichart. The literary critic Marie-Luise Gättens discusses gender inequality and fascism as analyzed in Virginia Woolf's article from the 1930s called *Three Guineas*. There Woolf claims "that the unequal distribution of power between the genders is a key element for producing fascism" (32). Fascism, according to Woolf, depends upon a male subject who constitutes himself through power and control over others and a female subject who is controlled and overpowered (33). Klaus Theweleit, in his two-volume study of the *Freikorps* titled *Male Fantasies*, argues that gender relations, or more specifically male fear and hatred of women, were an important factor in the rise of National Socialism. More recently, Reichart's contemporary Elfriede Jelinek has stated: "Fascism originated in the family, in the relationship between man and woman, and it has retreated back into the family once again. The nucleus of fascism is the execution of power as developed and nurtured within the family" (Roscher 1991, 53). Elaine Martin in the introduction to her edited volume titled *Gender, Patriarchy, and Fascism in the Third Reich: The Response of Women Writers*, points out that the connection between patriarchy and fascism underlies many of the daughter/father autobiographies written by women in the seventies and eighties in their attempt to confront the past as well as redefine their own position within contemporary society. The essays collected there all contribute in some way to the ongoing discussion of the "interrelationship of racism, sexism, and fascism within the German patriarchal social structure" (Martin 17).

The identification of patriarchal structures within fascism does not, however, lead to a facile absolution of women from guilt in Reichart's works. Her female protagonists may be powerless, but they are not innocent, and it is their responsibility to confront the fact of their acquiescence, to work through their culpability in an attempt to understand it and shape a different present. Furthermore, Reichart's women characters are not somehow inherently or biologically less predisposed to violence than are men. Rather the difference lies in the socialization processes each gender undergoes. As Reichart states: "I do not believe that the conditioning of men is any less serious than the conditioning of women...Just different" (DeMeritt, Ensberg 15). For her, violence is a question of power, and within a patriarchal society it is men who wield that power.

The stories of *La Valse* show again and again the domination and abuse characteristic of gender relations in contemporary society. In the title story, the female narrator's every move and feeling is controlled by a father even as he lies dying in her apartment. She cannot escape her role as caretaker and makes room for her father's deathbed at the expense of her own living space. The legitimacy of violence under the Nazis has been reaffirmed in the present under the guise of the marital contract, which allows him to beat his wife and rape his two daughters (11). The title, "La Valse," is used as a metaphor for the deformation of interpersonal interaction. Instead of two people stepping together to music, the father forced his young daughter to dance alone, for his voyeuristic pleasure. Now she spins wildly to the same music until she falls from dizziness, indicating perhaps the will to escape patriarchal authority but also the futility of such an attempt. Even her sole act of rebellion, which is to appear before her father and his business cronies as a whore, is determined by her past, and the man she chooses as partner, a reincarnation of her father, rapes and humiliates her. The hope implicit in her words as her father finally dies—"So I can go now. I'm free now"—is undermined by the dubious form of escape found by her sister—suicide—and by her brothers—emulation of the father figure.

Each of the subsequent stories in Reichart's collection follows the movements of a waltz gone brutally awry. In "Verlassene Schwestern" (Abandoned Sisters) Barbara, who identifies with her mother, attempts to leave her sister Clara, the embodiment of the traditionally masculine values of societal success, abstract thought inimical to intuition and the body, and power, but she is shot in the back by her sister while leaving. In "Unter dem zuckenden Flügel der Taube" (Beneath the Fluttering Wing of the Pigeon) Reichart uses exaggeration—pointed, nasty, and above all effective—to provoke awareness and resistance to gender roles and expectations. The male protagonist so needs female subservience that he replaces his girlfriend Sonja with a more docile and wounded pigeon, Sonja the second. Then, when the pigeon asserts its independence, it is replaced by a mechanical toy. The progressive subordination and dehumanization of the female partner is made abundantly clear in the final sentence of the story: "He would have to look for Sonja the Third in the toystore tomorrow, preferably one with a built-in motor, which would hum softly, almost like a heart" (102). Reichart concludes her volume with two stories that return more explicitly to the topic of Nazism, first "Wie nah ist Mauthausen?" (How Close is Mauthausen?) and then "Wie fern ist Mauthausen?" (How Far is Mauthausen?). Thus the middle stories are framed by reference to Austria's fascist past, thereby placing the present firmly within the context of its history, gender relations within fascism, and the individual within the forces and pressures of society.

In her novel of 1993 titled *Fotze*, Reichart again extends the metaphor of war to include interpersonal relationships and, what is more, traces its roots to language.[3] Her narrator inhabits a war-torn landscape, its violence and suppression of women reflected and perpetrated above all through its language. A writer, Reichart's narrator explores the relationship between language, sexuality, and violence. She both experiences first-hand the effect of the language of domination and seeks an alternative, a language that would have the potential to empower communication.

The opening pages of the work focus on the narrator's relationship with a man she initially calls her lover with the "calloused hands." This man gives her a word—"Fotze"—for her previously unnamed sexuality, thereby allowing her to rediscover sensuality. Reichart's description of the relationship at first emphasizes the senses: smelling, seeing, touching, and hearing. This is the importance of the man's calloused hands, for they scratch the narrator's skin and emit a distinctive odor. Eventually, however, the hands of the lover become soft and odorless, thereby signalling the subordination of the senses to the proliferation of words, and the narrator relabels her lover "word addict," obsessed with "word power."

What occurs here between an individual man and woman is repeated in Reichart's novel on a societal level. The powerful in contemporary society perpetrate violence upon the powerless, and this war is reflected in and waged through language. Societal discourse has been reduced to a commercial and political language that prevents thought and cuts off communication. Thus this language guarantees efficient, but brutal, perpetuation of the dominant system. Reichart depicts the resultant society through the narrator's fifth family house, where she resides at the outset of the novel. This house, inhabited by her grandfather, father, and brothers and built in the middle of a nettle patch with materials left over from concentration camps, clearly pictures the continuing state of war in post-war Austria.

The narrator rejects the words and wars of contemporary male-dominated society and seeks an alternative. She locks her lover's words in a closet, throws away the key, and sits down at her writing table. She recalls a bunker wall from her past painted with the word "Fotze." By reliving her childhood encounter with the word, she strives to reclaim it from her lover. The narrator returns to the first family house, where she hopes to discover the language and cooperation of her grandmother, mother, and sisters. This house, in direct contrast to the fifth one, represents a type of utopian society in which various peoples can live together harmoniously, peacefully, and with their diversity preserved. The only house with a basement and nestled among other houses, it suggests a sense of permanence and community lost in contemporary reality. Headed by the narrator's grandmother, this society of women has remained embedded within the "magical nexus," where nature and (wo)man, thought and the senses, intuition and rationality still coexist.

The harmony and equality possible in the first house are reflected in the language spoken by the narrator's sisters, described as "incomplete sentences" (75) and consisting of sentences without subjects. This language, sounding helpless or defenseless at first in comparison to the smooth rhythms of societal discourse, is potentially liberating and compassionate precisely because it refuses to recognize a subject/object hierarchy. It nullifies the power of the "I" to dominate and harm the other: "And I would learn the compassionate language of my other sister. I would ban all subjects from my language, first and foremost this 'I.' All of my sentences began with 'I,' expendable, omnipotent, it brought about harm..." (78).

Reichart propounds "incomplete sentences" elsewhere in her writings, for example in the short story "Wie fern ist Mauthausen?" from *La Valse*, as a counterforce to contemporary discourse. The "ready-made sentences" of society are automatic, natural-seeming utterances which have been stated so often and flow along so fluently that we have become accustomed to them and inured to their shock value or painful truth, even in statements such as: "Boy, the gas chamber is so small." For Reichart, society's "three-word sentences" are part of the Austrian fascist legacy, for they obfuscate, oversimplify, and collapse difference, thereby silencing individual questions and alternatives ("Lebkuchenherz" 39). Thus her narrator's search in *Fotze* for a broken language must be seen as an attempt to break out of a predetermined linguistic order. However, it is also a search which ultimately fails. It proves senseless to ban the subject from language after the fact, and it proves impossible to un-think this subject. The narrator cannot escape the thought patterns and language of her society; the utopia does not exist.

Reichart's narrator is faced with the choice between cooptation by the prevailing discourse, or silence. Temporarily she assumes the language of society. Her appropriation of the linguistic, social, and sexual structures is apparent in the subjection of her sisters to the same inhumane depersonalization that she underwent earlier. By forcing them to parrot the sentences of her lover the "word addict" before acknowledging their sexuality (70), the narrator upholds the hierarchies of society, with the difference that the previously suppressed has become the suppressor. At the conclusion of the novel, however, the narrator-writer seems to accept silence as the preferable alternative after all. Silent, at least, she will not contribute further to the state of war around her.

Reichart's next work, the dramatic monologue *Sakkorausch*, reexamines many of the same themes as *Fotze*. Again an individual figure strives for self-determination within a rigid societal order, again that individual is a woman and the society described is patriarchal, and again war rages on both a broader level—World War I—and interpersonally between man and woman. The drama is based on the historical figure Helene von Druskowitz, a female "Wunderkind" who lived at the turn of the century. Born in 1856, she graduated from high school at the age of sixteen. In 1872, because the university in Vienna still refused admission to women, she moved to Zürich where she became the first Austrian woman to receive her doctorate in philosophy. She wrote prolifically, usually under a pseudonym, one of them being "Sakkorausch." By the age of thirty-five she had published at least eleven works, both critical and creative, but none of her dramas was ever performed and she was never able to establish herself as a literary critic. Instead of recognition, her efforts earned her internment in the insane asylum Mauer-Oehlig, where she remained until her death twenty-seven years later in 1918.

Reichart divides her drama into two acts, one taking place just before the outbreak of World War I and the second documenting that outbreak, and the monologue consists of Druskowitz's comments upon life both inside and outside the walls of Mauer-Oehlig. This switch in perspective between inside and outside, between prewar and war, manifests the interdependence between the personal and the political. By describing the mundane world of the asylum and its inhabitants, Druskowitz simultaneously identifies the attitudes and behaviors that ultimately lead to the destruction of other people. In the workmen, who decide to ignore a problem when confronted with their inability to fix it, we recognize lack of compassion, ignorance, and arrogance. In the guards, who terrorize the female inmates with their "grasping hands" and force them to adhere to foolish rules and regulations, we see the roots of imperialism, intolerance of difference, and blind reverence of obedience. And in the doctors, who would rather administer sedatives than reexamine their diagnosis and definition of insanity, we witness the refusal to question societal norms and expectations, in particular gender roles. These characteristics culminate in the body of unthinking, obedient soldiers described rather colorfully at the beginning of the second act as they march off—one two, one two—to war:

> There they go. Marching. A victory march! Before even entering the battlefield they're celebrating victory. As if there had ever been a victor in war. They are blind. Man is predisposed to murder. He is a born demon, the devil incarnate, the most dangerous of all living creatures. He wants war, this most brutal expression of masculine rage and lust for power.It's amazing that they are even able to count to two. After all, only the empire exists for them, only the ruler to whom they relinquish thought as they march by, mindlessly...How ugly they are, this eczema, full of narrow-mindedness and the most vile brutalization. (41)

The narrator indulges in such tirades against men with some frequency throughout the text, perhaps not surprisingly considering the last known work of the historical Druskowitz, written while she was interned in Mauer-Oehlig, is titled *Der Mann als logische und sittliche Unmoeglichkeit und als Fluch der Welt: Pessimistische Kardinalsätze* (*Man as a Logical and Moral Impossibility and as the Curse of the World: Pessimistic Premises*). Reichart has interspersed her text with original, but unmarked, quotes from this work, which starts from the premise that men are base, violent, and evil. Druskowitz advocates total separation of the sexes so as to allow women to discover their more noble nature. Their nobility, however, does not reside in biology, but rather in their distance from social structures of reality. Female superiority is not inherent, but rather depends on exclusion from society, and Reichart's narrator recognizes that women endowed with power will succumb to the same bellicose tendencies as men. Druskowitz, like the narrator in *Fotze*, realizes utopia does not exist, because a realm beyond the corruptive reach of power does not exist. Her call for the separation of the sexes is consistent with this realization, for it includes a ban on procreation and intends ultimately to guarantee the demise of a race that has caused so much strife and suffering.

Recognition of the impossibility of a utopian counterpower does not lead to surrender for Reichart's figures. Druskowitz embodies the individual struggling against the constraints of gendered norms and societal definitions of normalcy. This struggle assumes its most visible form in the fact that the historical Helene von Druskowitz continued to write even from within the walls of the insane asylum, and even though there was never an audience, either before or after internment, to receive those words. Similarly, Reichart's fictional recreation writes while simultaneously accepting the reality that no one will hear her. Druskowitz the poet comes to life in Reichart's drama in the figure of Elizabeth Barrett Browning and in the form of the bag—"die Tasche"—containing the narrator's writings. However, Elizabeth Barrett Browning is silent throughout the monologue, communicating only with the starlings she feeds, and the bag remains lost for the duration of the drama. Druskowitz mourns the silence surrounding her, mourns the necessity of her monologue, but her final words point to a time in the future when the starlings, who were driven away by the war, will return. On that day she will perform her drama for them and allow Elizabeth Barrett Browning, the poet queen, to fly:

> At some point the starlings will return. I will feed them for the sake of the queen. When they are full I will crawl into my bag and perform for them my play about bewitched Elizabeth. They

will fly into my play and bring the words to the queen. I never wanted to believe in her flying skills. My lack of belief held her here. I will hold you no longer. *Fly*! Your Highness, *Fly*!

Thus the narrator's final words do not express resignation, but the hope for a peace someday that will welcome the voice of women.

The three works discussed here, and indeed all of Reichart's works, present the reader a static picture of everyday fascism founded in patriarchy. According to Margarete Mitscherlich in her study of 1987, *Erinnerungsarbeit: Zur Psychoanalyse der Unfähigkeit zu trauern* (*The Work of Memory: Towards a Psychoanalysis of the Inability to Mourn*), confrontation with the past must deal with the structures of society in order to avoid repetition of that past: "The content of a system is not repeated, but rather the structure of a society" (14). Such an understanding of history implies a certain pessimism, or "powerlessness" to use Reichart's terminology from earlier, for the institutions of society prove resistant to change, recreating themselves in their own image throughout the decades. Reichart's texts show a present determined by the past; they reveal seemingly endless and immutable continuity. At the same time, however, individual resistance and independence depend on understanding the sources of coercion. The depiction of societal manipulation of the individual is simultaneously and perhaps paradoxically the individual's only hope to counteract that manipulation.

Reichart's female protagonists are shown to be powerless, yet the reader is not left with a sense of futility, but of struggle, and even, in particular in *Fotze* and *Sakkorausch*, of hope. It is certainly no accident that the narrators of these two works are writers; for Reichart, literature represents a hope for change. In her "Viennese Lectures on Poetics" she states: "And literature—it is our most foolish hope, and this is exactly what makes it so precious. Every day it becomes more important in its impotence" (141). Through her portrayal of counterexamples, figures who strive, though unsuccessfully, for self-determination and tolerance, and through a poetic language that counteracts the reduction of thought, Reichart reveals the fascist underpinnings of contemporary patriarchy and hopes—however foolishly—to awaken in her reader at least the longing—she has termed it "a longing founded in knowledge" (Roscher 129)—for change.

Notes

1. The titles of recent articles on Reichart manifest the direction of critical reception, for example: "Breaking the Silence: Elisabeth Reichart's Protest against the Denial of the Nazi Past in Austria" (Michaels) or "'Vergangenheitsbewältigung' in Austria: The Personal and the Political in Erika Mitterer's *Alle unsere Spiele* and Elisabeth Reichart's *Februarschatten*" (Wigmore).

2. Hilde in *Februarschatten* must fight the legacy imprinted upon her by her authoritarian and antidemocratic family background, and Ruth Berger from *Komm über den See* attempts to stand up to the pressures of her school to conform. For an excellent discussion of the structures of society in these two earlier works, see Kecht.

3. For a more detailed discussion of *Fotze*, in particular of the language used by Reichart, see my article titled "The Possibilities and Limitations of Language: Elisabeth Reichart's *Fotze*," *Out From the Shadows*.

Works Cited

DeMeritt, Linda and Peter Ensberg. "'Für mich ist die Sprache eigentlich ein Schatz': Interview mit Elisabeth Reichart." *Modern Austrian Literature* 29.1 (1996): 1-22.

DeMeritt, Linda. "The Possibilities and Limitations of Language: Elisabeth Reichart's *Fotze*." *Out From the Shadows*. Ed. Margarete Lamb-Faffelberger. Riverside, CA: Ariadne Press, 1998. 136-50.

Gättens, Marie-Luise. "Language, Gender, and Fascism: Reconstructing Histories in *Three Guineas, Der Mann auf der Kanzel*, and *Kindheitsmuster*." *Gender, Patriarchy, and Fascism in the Third Reich: The Response of Women Writers*. Ed. Elaine Martin. Detroit: Wayne State University Press, 1993. 32-64.

Kecht, Maria-Regina. "Resisting Silence: Brigitte Schwaiger and Elisabeth Reichart Attempt to Confront the Past." *Gender, Patriarchy, and Fascism in the Third Reich: The Response of Women Writers.* Ed. Elaine Martin. Detroit: Wayne State University Press, 1993. 244-73.

Martin, Elaine. "Women Right/(Re)Write the Nazi Past: An Introduction." *Gender, Patriarchy, and Fascism in the Third Reich: The Response of Women Writers.* Ed. Elaine Martin. Detroit: Wayne State University Press, 1993. 11-31.

Michaels, Jennifer E. "Breaking the Silence: Elisabeth Reichart's Protest Against the Denial of the Nazi Past in Austria." *German Studies Review* 19.1 (February 1996): 9-27.

Mitscherlich, Margarete. *Erinnerungsarbeit: Zur Psychoanalyse der Unfähigkeit zu trauern.* Frankfurt a/M.: Fischer Verlag, 1987.

Reichart, Elisabeth. *Februarschatten.* Vienna: Österreichische Staatsdruckerei, 1984. *February Shadows.* Translated and with an Afterword by Donna Hoffmeister. Riverside, CA: Ariadne Press, 1989.

---. *Fotze: Erzählung.* Salzburg/Vienna: Otto Müller Verlag, 1993.

---. "Die Grenzen meiner Welt sind die Grenzen meiner Sprache." Viennese Lectures on Poetics. *Wespennest* 82 (1991): 114-42.

---. *Komm über den See.* Berlin/Weimar: Aufbau Verlag, 1988.

---. *La Valse: Erzählungen.* Salzburg/Vienna: Otto Müller Verlag, 1992. *La Valse: Short Stories.* Translated with an Introduction by Linda DeMeritt. Albany, NY: State University of New York Press, forthcoming.

---. "Das Lebkuchenherz auf der Brust". *Reden über Österreich.* Ed. Manfred Jochum. Salzburg/Vienna: Residenz Verlag, 1995. 31-44.

---. *Sakkorausch: Ein Monolog.* Salzburg/Vienna: Otto Müller Verlag, 1994. *Foreign: A Monologue.* Translated and with an Introduction by Linda DeMeritt. Albany, NY: State University of New York Press, forthcoming.

---. "Die vielen Ichs der Republik und ich." *"Was wird das Ausland dazu sagen?": Literatur und Republik in Österreich nach 1945.* Ed. Gerald Leitner. Vienna: Picus Verlag, 1995. 114-126.

Roscher, Achim. "Elisabeth Reichart im Gespräch." *Neue deutsche Literatur* 35 (1987): 129-132.
---. "Gespräch mit Elfriede Jelinek." *Neue deutsche Literatur* 39 (1991): 41-56.
Theweleit, Klaus. *Male Fantasies.* Vol. I and II. Minneapolis: University of Minnesota Press, 1987. Trans. by Stephen Conway. *Männerphantasien.* Vol. I and II. 1977.
Wigmore, Juliet. "'Vergangenheitsbewältigung' in Austria: The Personal and the Political in Erika Mitterer's *Alle unsere Spiele* and Elisabeth Reichart's *Februarschatten.*" *German Life and Letters* 44.5 (October 1991): 477-87.

The Female Poet as Persecuted Jew: Gender (Mis)representation in the Works of Ingeborg Bachmann and Sylvia Plath

Kirsten A. Krick-Aigner
Wofford College

The following study raises questions concerning the representation and *mis*representation of gender in the prose and poetry of the Austrian author Ingeborg Bachmann (1926-1973) and the American writer Sylvia Plath (1932-1963) and will explore how the history of the Third Reich and the Holocaust informed their writings. Both Bachmann and Plath attempted to come to terms with the events of National Socialism in their fiction and were among the first (non-Jewish) authors to deal with the Holocaust so early on during the post-World War II era. By staging their father figures as fascist throughout their works, Bachmann and Plath's female characters take on the role of the Jewish Holocaust victim, emotionally and pyschologically tortured and "murdered" by the father. Although neither author was Jewish, nor experienced the Holocaust firsthand, Bachmann and Plath's female characters identify with Jews persecuted and murdered in the Holocaust.

A scene from the 1992 Hollywood screen adaptation of Pat Conroy's novel, *The Prince of Tides* (1989) directed by Barbara Streisand, emphasizes a complex and troubling issue that is raised in Bachmann and Plath's fictional writings. In this film, the character Tom Wingo must come to terms with his past in order to help his suicidal twin sister Savannah, a poet, remember the repressed events of her childhood. The sister's psychiatrist, Dr. Susan Loewenstein, helps Wingo remember his abusive father and the traumatic evening when he and his siblings were raped by escaped convicts. In the course of their sessions, the psychiatrist reveals to Wingo that his sister, who is not Jewish, has published fiction under the Jewish pseudonym, Renata Halpern, and had initially come to her seeking psychiatric treatment as the daughter of Holocaust survivors. Dr. Loewenstein wonders: "She couldn't fool me about being Jewish, but what fascinated me was why she chose to be the child of Holocaust *survivors*? What was she trying to survive? What *is* she trying to survive?" Throughout the film it becomes evident that Savannah uses events of the Holocaust as a trope for society, patriarchal power and violence in which gender and victimization are bound up in the poet's identity.

Conroy's fictional character Savannah, who believes herself to be the child of Holocaust survivors, is portrayed as a poet writing about victimization, thirty years after Bachmann and Plath associated their own fictional female writers with victims of the Holocaust. Bachmann and Plath's strategy of transforming gender into ethnicity is however a dubious one. If they equate women with Jews in their fiction, then can the extermination of over six million victims be compared to a destructive personal relationship? Does this comparison not negate the significance of the human tragedy of the Holocaust?

By historicizing Bachmann and Plath's work within postwar women's fiction, I will show how their writing is informed by both their reaction to the events of the Third Reich, as well as by the Austrian psychoanalytic tradition with which both were familiar and in which women have been associated with Jews. Although it is problematic that these authors use the Holocaust as a metaphor for the father figure and society, I will show how the social history of these writers is reflected in their work and how it is possible to appreciate *how* both authors deal with the Holocaust in their fiction.

Bachmann and Plath both explore themes of the destructive father figure, the obstacles of being a woman author in the 1950s and 1960s, and the authors' relationship to the German language and the Third Reich. Plath, born in 1932, and Bachmann, born in 1926, share a number of striking similarities: both women were gifted scholars and writers who felt isolated from their peers and society by their desire and need to write. While Bachmann received her doctorate in philosophy from the University of Vienna, Plath received her bachelor's degree from Smith College and completed two years at Cambridge University on a Fulbright scholarship. Both authors went on to win numerous prestigious awards for their fiction. They each suffered from depression throughout their lives, experiences which would be reflected in their portrayal of women writers in their novels, such as Plath's *Bell Jar* and Bachmann's *Malina.* Plath attempted suicide at the age of twenty-one and took her life in 1963 at the age of thirty-one, ten years prior to Bachmann's own tragic death at the age of forty-seven from the complications of accidental burns.

Bachmann's experiences during the Third Reich and in postwar Austria are reflected in her depictions of women throughout her fictional work, especially in her novel *Malina,* the novel-fragments *Der Fall Franza (Franza's Case)* and *Requiem für Fanny Goldmann (Requiem for Fanny Goldmann),* under the collective title of *Todesarten (Death Styles),* written between 1963 and 1973. Bachmann perceived herself to be restricted both as an individual and as an independent author by a male-oriented society, a perspective reflected in the character of the female narrator, who is also a writer, in the novel *Malina.*

Bachmann's role as an independent author can be better understood when viewed in the context of her social history. Jacqueline Vansant's work *Against the Horizon. Feminism and Postwar Austrian Women Writers* explores some issues facing women in Austria during the Third Reich and the postwar years. After the National Socialist motto "Women return to the home" of the 1930s, women were pushed into agriculture, as well as the war industry (19). After Austria's annexation in 1938, only ten percent of the women were allowed to attend the university and all were obliged to partake in a "Pflichtjahr," a year-in-service, at either a home or a farm. After Austria declared itself a neutral country in 1955, the period of postwar reconstruction remained nonetheless conservative with respect to women's roles as mothers and wives. One can imagine that a woman such as Bachmann, who had received a doctoral degree and who scorned marriage, did not find much support in her desire to become a financially independent writer.[1] Vansant observes that Bachmann's fictional women are also isolated within society and are confronted with male projections and definitions of womanhood (50). In Bachmann's *Der Fall Franza,* for instance, Franza's brother, husband and male doctors define her as insane throughout the novel, ultimately causing her mental unraveling and death.

Plath's own isolation, depression and suicide can also be traced to her experiences as a woman writer in the United States during the 1950s, as Paula Bennett describes in her essay collection about women writers *My Life: A Loaded Gun: Female Creativity and Female Poetics*: "Until the last year of her life (Plath) seems to have been sincerely convinced that no matter how hazardous a marriage and a family might be to her as a poet, to her as a woman, they offered the only possible path to success " (99). She goes on to say that "both Plath and her mother identified success as a woman with a successful marriage, because like virtually every woman living in the United States, in the mid-twentieth century, this is what they had been told" (101). Plath's letters home indicate that she was severely depressed about not being able to fulfill her goals as a writer once a wife and mother. On June 20, 1959 she wrote to her mother: "I have turned from being an intellectual, a career woman: all that is ash to me. And what do I meet in myself? Ash. Ash and more ash."[2] Like Bachmann, Plath felt that she could only be herself through writing.

In spite of being from cultures with very different historical, political and societal backgrounds, their similar experiences as women authors during the postwar years produce parallels in Bachmann's and Plath's works. Both discuss themes of the fascist father figure and of the woman as the victimized Jew, as well as the woman writer suffering from mental illness. While Plath wrote "Dying/Is an Art" in her poem "Lady Lazarus," Bachmann named her novel cycle *Todesarten*, "ways of dying," or "death styles."[3] *Todesarten* is a collection of narratives about women "murdered" by the father figure who represents a destructive society in which women are forced into roles that obliterate their sense of self, as well as their creativity. Bennett's description of Plath's *Bell Jar* is very similar to how one might describe *Todesarten*:

> Plath's *Bell Jar* is about women. More specifically, it is a book about growing up as a woman in a culture that is fundamentally unfair and hypocritical in its inequality. ... (Plath's) goal is to find a means to be both feminine and equal, that is, to be socially acceptable as a woman while still retaining her power

as an autonomous individual and a potential professional. (125)

In their literary work, both authors criticize society's domestic roles for women which prevent them from achieving independence and success as writers and intellectuals.

In considering their kinship as authors, it is of note that Bachmann owned both the 1968 German translation of *The Bell Jar* and an English edition of *Ariel* from 1961.[4] Although Bachmann had already written much of *Der Fall Franza* and *Malina* by the time the translation of *The Bell Jar* (*Die Glasglocke*) was published, the similarities are remarkable, yet not unusual for the situation of postwar women authors with an awareness of recent European history.

In 1968, five years after she had begun working on *Der Fall Franza* and *Malina*, Bachmann wrote an essay on her reactions to *Die Glasglocke*. She described Plath's portrayal of mental illness and depression as "shocking" and "devastating,"[5] without, however, mentioning Plath's discussion of the father figure which she herself was working on at the time. Bachmann, like Plath, associates the father figure with National Socialism throughout her later prose. Describing the marching of Hitler's troops into her hometown Klagenfurt as the first traumatic experience of her childhood, and more importantly as the "origin of her memory," Bachmann writes:

> There was a specific moment that shattered my childhood. The march of Hitler's troops into Klagenfurt. It was something so horrifying, that my memory begins on this day: through a premature pain, with a strength that I would perhaps never experience again. ... But this monstrous brutality that was noticeable, this screaming, singing and marching—that rising up of my first deathly fear.[6]

Whereas her memory would "begin" with the "brutality" of Hitler's troops, one of Bachmann's last experiences before her death was her visit to the death camps of Auschwitz and Birkenau. In interviews given in 1973 while visiting the camps, she spoke of her interest in the Holocaust, especially the extermination of Jews in Poland, as

Female Poet as Persecuted Jew 303

well as her large collection of materials concerning these events.[7] Bachmann's prose reflects her lifelong preoccupation with the events of National Socialism. She discusses the Holocaust primarily in her unfinished novel cycle *Todesarten*, but also touches upon questions of victimization during the Third Reich in her short stories "Drei Wege zum See" (Three Paths to the Lake) from 1972 and "Unter Mördern und Irren" (Among Murderers and the Insane) from 1961. In *Malina*, the father figure takes on the role of a Nazi, murdering the female narrator in a gas chamber, as the female narrator recounts:

> My father calmly takes a first hose down from the wall, I see a round hole, which he is blowing into, and I duck; my father walks on, takes down one hose after the other, and before I can scream, I am breathing in the gas, more and more gas. I am in the gas chamber, that's it, the largest gas chamber of the world, and I am in it alone.[8]

This passage makes clear that the gas chamber not only becomes a metaphor for the murder of the daughter-writer by the father figure, but also for the female narrator's feelings of isolation and madness within a male-oriented society. In *Der Fall Franza* Franza has a similar dream in which her husband Jordan, who is referred to as a sadistic fascist, murders her in a gas chamber, as she describes: "... Tonight I dreamt I am in a gas chamber, all alone, all the doors are locked, no window, and Jordan is attaching the hoses and letting the gas stream in, how can I dream such things...."[9] Bachmann once again applies the image of the gas chamber to illustrate Franza's isolation and terror of being trapped in her destructive marriage to Jordan.

Throughout *Todesarten*, Bachmann portrays male-female relationships as a reflection of the power-structure and violence of society as a whole and, more specifically, of the Holocaust.[10] In *Der Fall Franza*, the character Franza pays a visit to a doctor, Doktor Körner, whom she recognizes as one of the Nazis who had experimented on women prisoners while working on the euthanasia projects of the Third Reich. Here again, Franza stages herself as the

Jewish victim by begging him to kill her with a lethal shot with which he had murdered Holocaust victims in the past. In the novel fragment *Requiem für Fanny Goldmann*, the Holocaust becomes an issue for Fanny's ex-husband, Harry Goldmann, who is described as a man who in later years deals with his Jewish background by traveling to Israel and studying Jewish history (494). Politically active throughout her literary career, Bachmann incorporated many of the political discussions of her time concerning the Holocaust in her works and attempted to deal with these historical events by transforming her reactions to these events into fiction.

Like Plath's character Esther, Bachmann herself struggled with the fact that the language in which she wrote against fascism belonged to the same Germany she saw intimately connected with Hitler.[11] For Bachmann, however, the difference between Austria and Germany was not so much a question of physical borders, but rather a question of different cultural languages which carry with them a marked set of socio-cultural codes.[12] In writing, she felt herself to be in a double bind because she could not escape from the German language that belonged to her purported enemies, as she stated in a 1965 interview: "For a long time I have come to realize for myself the difficulty in that I write in German, that I relate to Germany only through this language, but am dependent on a realm of experiences and a realm of perceptions of another region."[13] Eight years later, Bachmann would make the highly problematic statement that the destruction of Poland would never have come to the minds of Austrians: "However, how the end came about, I believe no Austrian would have thought of that, have had such thoughts as the Germans did...."[14] Interviews with Bachmann in the 1970s repeatedly point out her naive and idealistic view of Austria's innocence during the Third Reich, despite her critical portrayal of the country's role in the events of the Holocaust in *Malina* and much of *Der Fall Franza*.

Like Bachmann, Plath also uses the Jewish Holocaust victim as a metaphor for women as victims of patriarchal society. Steven Axelrod's 1990 Plath biography discusses the author's ambivalent daughter-writer relationship with her father as reflected in the character Esther Greenwood in *The Bell Jar*. The passage concerning the fictional author's father reveals an uncanny parallel to Plath's own father. After referring to the German heritage of her parents, her father's early death, as well as her brother's proficiency in German, Plath's character Esther continues: "What I didn't say was that each time I picked up a German dictionary or a German book, the very sight of those dense, black, barbed-wire letters made my mind shut like a clam."[15] In *The Bell Jar* the German language reflects the violence and murder associated with German history and the Holocaust, issues which would plague Plath about her own German heritage throughout her life.

Living in the postwar era, Plath was also faced with the problematic history of her own German heritage and discussed her ambiguous relationship to the German language in her fiction. For Plath, women were victims of society in much the same way that Jews had been victims of the Third Reich. Bennett supports this view by stating that the female characters in Plath's work are portrayed as "always playing and wanting to play the role of the Jew to their husband's/father's Nazi" (154). In Plath's poem "Daddy," for instance, written during the four months before her suicide in 1963, she writes: "Every woman adores a Fascist"[16] and further, about her father: "I never could talk to you./The tongue stuck in my jaw.//It stuck in a barb wire snare./Ich, ich, ich, ich,/I could hardly speak./I thought every German was you./And the language obscene//An engine, an engine/Chuffing me off like a Jew./A Jew to Dachau, Auschwitz, Belsen./I began to talk like a Jew./I think I may be a Jew."[17] In Plath's poem "Lady Lazarus," also written during this time, the narrator again identifies herself as a Jew: "A sort of walking miracle, my skin/Bright as a Nazi lampshade,/My right foot//A paperweight,/My face a featureless, fine/Jew linen.//"[18] The female narrator of the poem becomes the Jew who has been murdered and turned into objects of beauty, however, at the same time takes on the position of the Nazi who sees the beauty of these "objects."

In their prose, Bachmann and Plath draw disturbing conclusions concerning the desire to be relegated to the realm of victimhood. They equate women with Jews in their position as victims within society, and hence place the responsibility of victimhood on the victim and not on the aggressor. The association of Jews with women has, however, been made much earlier by Austrian-Jewish psychoanalysts such as Otto Weininger, Otto Rank and Bruno Bettelheim, in whose works both Bachmann and Plath were well studied. Bachmann's psychology studies in Vienna from 1946 to 1950 and her internship at the well-known mental institution Steinhof outside of Vienna provided the author with a formal knowledge of psychoanalytic theory and history grounded in the Viennese tradition beginning with Freud, one which would inform her ideas about a woman's role in society. Axelrod's biography makes evident that Plath was also familiar with Rank's work while writing her novel *The Bell Jar*.

Although Walther Rathenau had stressed the feminine nature of the Jew in his 1897 essay "Höre, Israel!" (Hear me, Israel!),[19] Otto Weininger's *Geschlecht und Charakter (Gender and Character)*, published in Vienna in 1903, was the first psychoanalytic work to associate women with Jews as victims of society. Weininger's views of women are almost legendary, as the following statement illustrates: "... the highest ranking woman stands endlessly below the lowest ranking man" (404). He summarized the similarities between Jews and women by stating, for instance, that they lacked personality, held together in groups, were unable to distinguish good from bad and had no self-esteem (411-12, 414, 417, 431). Jewish women in particular, he attested, captured the essence ("die Idee") of the woman, and further, Jews and women related to one another as a "type" (429). Weininger spoke perhaps of his own fears when he claimed that hate represented the fear that a person feared in himself or herself: "Hatred, like love, is a phenomenon of projection: mankind only hates those through that which he hates in himself" (407). In his later work *Taschenbuch (Pocketbook)* from 1919, Weininger continued this tack: "Hatred against woman is the unresolved hatred of one's own sexuality" (626). He further portrayed women as lusty and Jews as lascivious (417). Weininger clearly illustrates the phenomenon of Jewish self-hatred in his work, a sentiment originating in the hatred of "others" within the dominant and non-Jewish society. Bachmann's writing was perhaps also influenced by Weininger's discussion about this "fear of the other."

For instance, while Jordan demonstrates hatred for his wife in *Der Fall Franza*, Franza comes to realize that it is precisely her "otherness" that he desires to extinguish, as she goes on to say: "Why was I so hated? No, not I, the other in me...."[20] Sander Gilman's work *Jewish Self-Hatred* portrays such self-hatred as the result of accepting the values, social structures, and attitudes of the determining group. He therefore does not consider Weininger's association of women and Jews unusual, since, as he points out, both Jews and women were becoming more visible on the horizon of European consciousness in the late nineteenth century through their articulated demands for legal and cultural emancipation (244).

Otto Rank's work *Beyond Psychology* from 1941, which both Bachmann and Plath owned, was influenced by Weininger's writings and also compares women to Jews; however, his work stresses "the overwhelming importance of the father" in the Judaic tradition (275). Rank claimed that women "suffered from the very beginning a fate similar to that of the Jew, namely, suppression, slavery, confinement and subsequent persecution" and showed how women were therefore depicted as "enslaved, inferior, (and) castrated" (287-88). Both Bachmann and Plath use the metaphor of the Holocaust in their fictional work to illustrate their own feelings of suppression and confinement within patriarchal society.

What makes Bachmann and Plath's association of the victimized woman with the persecuted Jew so disturbing to present-day readers, is that this metaphor, informed largely by pre-Holocaust psychoanalytic writings, is carried over to the postwar, transformed by the events of the Holocaust. Bachmann and Plath were, however, not the only authors to represent female gender with the figure of the persecuted Jew in the Holocaust. Christa Wolf's *Kindheitsmuster* (*Patterns of Childhood*, 1976) and Klaus Theweleit's *Männerphantasien* (*Men's Phantasies*, 1977) represent two further examples.

Despite the controversial use of the Holocaust as a trope for interpersonal relationships and society, such associations can be read in a socio-historical context. James Young, for instance, shows how the Holocaust affected and informed writers such as Plath and how it transformed the perceptions of their world and society. In this sense, Young's discussion of the representation of the Holocaust in Plath's work applies equally well to Bachmann's fiction, as he writes: "... rather than disputing the authenticity of (Plath's) figures, we might look at her poetry for the ways the Holocaust has entered public consciousness as a trope, and how it informs both the poet's view of the world and her representation of it in verse" (132). Bachmann and Plath's fiction might therefore be read within the socio-historical context in which their portrayal of women as Jews reflects their own perception of women's roles during the postwar.

Dr. Loewenstein in *The Prince of Tides* questions Wingo about his sister's role as a female poet by asking: "What is she trying to survive?" Bachmann and Plath's work seems to offer one possible response. The poet Savannah, like the writer Esther Greenwood in Plath's *Bell Jar* and the female author in Bachmann's *Malina*, attempts to survive what Bachmann calls the "Mordschauplatz" (the crime scene) of society by actively writing poetry and prose.[21] Like Dr. Loewenstein, who raises the question why Savannah would choose to be the child of Holocaust *survivors*, it remains both fascinating and troubling that Bachmann and Plath chose to associate their female characters with Jews murdered in the Holocaust.

Notes

1. Bachmann stated in an interview that she was "against marriage and any legal relationship." Bachmann, *Wir müssen wahre Sätze finden: Gespräche und Interviews* 144.
2. Plath, *The Journals of Sylvia Plath* 312.
3. Plath, "Lady Lazarus," *The Collected Poems* 245.
4. Pichl, "Katalog der Privatbibliothek Ingeborg Bachmanns," *Ungedrucktes Manuskript*.
5. Bachmann, "Das Tremendum—Sylvia Plath: *Die Glasglocke*. Entwurf." 359-40.
6. Bachmann, *Wir müssen wahre Sätze finden*, 111. Gerhard Botz points out that Hitler's troops were not the ones screaming and displaying brutality in the streets of Klagenfurt, but in fact the thousands of Kärntner Nazis who greeted the tide of German troops

201. Peter Beicken also cites the *Klagenfurter Zeitung* of March 15, 1938, which called this "marching in" "Austria's return home to the motherland" 29.

7. Bachmann wrote: "I have read documentaries...and I have had dreams of terror and nightmares every day here, where I am in Poland for the first time. Because it is something else when one reads a documentary about Auschwitz or Birkenau .... I have a large library of documentaries, also about Warsaw." Bachmann, *Wir müssen wahre Sätze finden* 142.

8. Bachmann, *Malina, Ingeborg Bachmann. Werke III* 175.

9. Bachmann, *Der Fall Franza, Ingeborg Bachmann. Werke III* 407.

10. In 1973 she stated in an interview that male-female relationships were always fascist in nature and that society was always at war. Bachmann, *Wir müssen wahre Sätze finden* 144.

11. Rudolf Hess shouted "Germany is Hitler and Hitler is Germany" into the crowds at the 1934 Nuremberg Rally (Kaes 13). The belief that Austria was a victim of Hitler's plan of attack has more recently been called a lie about history (Geschichtslüge) by historians. See Bartsch and Goltschnigg 195.

12. Of Austria, with its "political and cultural peculiarity," Bachmann wrote in 1955: "The Austrians have participated in so many cultures and have developed a different feeling about the world than the Germans." Bachmann, *Wir müssen wahre Sätze finden* 11-12.

13. Bachmann, *Wir müssen wahre Sätze finden* 63-64.

14. Bachmann, *Wir müssen wahre Sätze finden* 132.

15. Plath, *The Bell Jar* 40.

16. Plath, "Daddy," *The Collected Poems* 223.

17. Plath, "Daddy," *The Collected Poems* 223.

18. Plath, "Lady Lazarus," *The Collected Poems* 244.

19. Gilman 243.

20. Bachmann, *Der Fall Franza, Ingeborg Bachmann. Werke III* 400.

21. Bachmann, *Malina* 276.

Works Cited

Bachmann, Ingeborg. *Malina. Ingeborg Bachmann. Werke III.* München: Piper, 1993.

---. "Das Tremendum—Sylvia Plath: *Die Glasglocke.* Entwurf." *Ingeborg Bachmann. Werke IV (1978).* München: Piper, 1993.

---. *Wir müssen wahre Sätze finden: Gespräche und Interviews.* Ed. Christine Koschel and Inge von Weidenbaum. München: Piper.

---. *Der Fall Franza. Ingeborg Bachmann. Werke III.* München: Piper, 1993.

---. *Requiem für Fanny Goldmann. Ingeborg Bachmann. Werke III.* München: Piper, 1993.

Bartsch, Kurt and Dietmar Goltschnigg. "Österreichische Nachkriegsliteratur. Sozialgeschichtliche Voraussetzungen und Literaturbetrieb." *Modern Austrian Literature* 17.3-4 (1984).

Beicken, Peter. *Ingeborg Bachmann.* München: C.H. Beck, 1988.

Bennett, Paula. *My Life A Loaded Gun: Female Creativity and Feminist Poetics.* Boston: Beacon Press, 1986.

Botz, Gerhard. "Historische Brüche und Kontinuitäten als Herausforderungen. Ingeborg Bachmann und post-katastrophische Geschichtsmentalitäten in Österreich." *Ingeborg Bachmann— Neue Beiträge zu ihrem Werk. Internationales Symposium Münster, 1991.* Ed. Dirk Göttsche and Hubert Ohl. Würzburg: Königshausen & Neumann, 1993.

Gilman, Sander. *Jewish Self-Hatred: Anti-Semitism and the Hidden Language of the Jews.* Baltimore: Johns Hopkins UP, 1986.

Kaes, Anton. *Hitler to Heimat: The Return of History as Film.* Cambridge, Mass.: Harvard UP, 1989.

Pichl, Robert. "Katalog der Privatbibliothek Ingeborg Bachmanns." Unpublished manuscript.

Plath, Sylvia. *The Journals of Sylvia Plath.* Ed. Frances McCullough and Ted Hughes. New York: Dial Press, 1982.

---. "Lady Lazarus." *The Collected Poems.* Ed. Ted Hughes. New York: Harper & Row, 1981.

---. "Daddy," *The Collected Poems.* Ed. Ted Hughes. New York: Harper & Row, 1981.

---. *The Bell Jar.* New York: Harper & Row, 1971.

Rank, Otto. *Beyond Psychology*. New York: Dover, 1958.
Vansant, Jacqueline. *Against the Horizon. Feminism and Postwar Austrian Women Writers*. Westport, CT.: Greenwood Press, 1988.
Weininger, Otto. *Geschlecht und Charakter*. München: Matthes & Seitz, 1980.
Young, James E. *Writing and Rewriting the Holocaust: Narrative and the Consequences of Interpretation*. Bloomington: Indiana UP, 1988.

7

Borders and Boundaries

Transcultural Profiles in Contemporary Austrian Jewish Literature

Matthias Konzett
Yale University

In their introduction to an anthology of essays on the recent revival of Jewish culture in Germany, editors Sander L. Gilman and Karen Remmler speak of the "demand by many Jews that they be heard on their own terms" and the present "possibility of a vital Jewish culture in Germany" (11). While admitting that no consensus can be reached on the nature, course and success of this recent cultural development, Gilman's and Remmler's anthology marks a major advance in German literary and cultural studies by foregrounding "the reciprocal instability of Jewish and German identity" (2). Tireless self-analysis of German guilt by German authors has thus become refracted through and replaced by another unacknowledged Germany, asserting its distinct German-Jewish perspective concerning the interpretation of German history. Excessive focus on a vanished Jewish culture, as Jack Zipes correctly remarks, allowed Germans to install themselves as experts on Jewish culture: "It seemed that the deader the Jews, the more Germans could exhibit their interest in Jewish culture" (18). The recent emergence of a distinct Jewish discourse, it appears, paves the way for a corrective of this self-revolving national discourse in German culture. Thus, a monolithic aspect of Germany's postwar culture is finally more openly challenged and negated as a myth.

Gilman and Remmler show, however, that this act of Jewish self-inauguration is still marked by a problematic internalization of difference experienced from within German culture. Therefore it labors under the burden of having to negate and transform an ascribed or imagined difference (physical and cultural pathology, memorialization of Jews as dead and invisible) into a positive identity resisting reification. For example, Gilman's analysis of Jewish male discourse focuses on the construction and questioning of identity markers such as circumcision that are visibly inscribed onto the body. Remmler's analysis, conversely, focuses on the metaphorical transformation of the female Jewish body into a symbolic site of traumatic memory and mourning. Present Jewish literary discourse, Gilman and Remmler similarly conclude, is marked by a negative symbiosis that paradoxically achieves its desired recognition only by recourse to those cultural forces (stereotypes of race and gender, monolithic images of German culture) that negate its existence. Seen critically, its discourse remains caught up in the struggle between national or official and ethnic or unofficial representations of German and German Jewish identity.

In this essay, focusing on the limited example of Austrian Jewish literature, I would like to explore other possibilities of recognition beyond those of positively or negatively asserted identities and beyond the polarity of national or ethnic contention. To be sure, I am not proposing Austrian Jewish literature as an alternative to its German counterpart. Nor do I wish to invalidate the importance of Gilman and Remmler's sobered understanding of identity claims and their inevitably ensuing cultural typifications. Instead, I am concerned with a complementary interpretive model which remains faithful to the immediate geographic and cultural topography of the writer which situates her or his body in the surrounding field of socialization (cultural heritage, discursive traditions, political and cultural public spheres, concrete social interactions).[1] By way of an analysis of the contemporary Jewish writers Elfriede Jelinek, Robert Schindel and Doron Rabinovici, I wish to show how these writers are ill at ease with national or ethnic categorizations and instead attempt to enlarge these definitions toward a metropolitan, transnational and transcultural identity as the result of their specific acculturation in the city of Vienna. With its unique urban culture, Vienna, much like New York, Paris or Berlin, has in many ways defied the national boundaries that are said to contain its identity. My argument here is to show that Jelinek, Schindel and Rabinovici reflect this cosmopolitan heritage in their writing and critically recuperate cultural positions prevalent in turn-of-the-century Vienna.

In this respect, Jelinek, Schindel, and Rabinovici resemble other contemporary Austrian writers like Bernhard or Handke who have little use for a national definition of their artistic endeavors. Handke, for instance, has produced a remarkable diasporic literature built on a self-chosen imaginative and, more recently, geographic exile from Austria. Bernhard, although he never left Austria for any length of time, strongly ridiculed Austria's so-called indigenous culture (Konzett). The persona of the critical *Nestbeschmutzer*, the writer exposing the narrow provincial and nationalistic profile of his own country in the manner of a Heinrich Heine or Karl Kraus, became Bernhard's lifelong vocation. Other writers like Peter Rosei or Christoph Ransmayr have settled their imaginations in abstract or concrete spaces beyond the Austrian territory such as the peripheral regions of the former Habsburg empire (Turkey, Romania, Franz-Joseph-Land). Indeed, the uncertainty of national affiliation displayed in all these writers recalls the instability of cultural identity during Austria's imperial decline as reflected in Robert Musil, Joseph Roth or Hugo von Hofmannsthal. These writers, while flirting with an imperial Austrian identity, have ultimately shunned any sharp nationalistic contours and preferred instead to represent its inhabitants as men without qualities, exiles, or evasive eccentrics (*Schwierige*).

In this essay, then, I will explore transcultural profiles of identity that resurface in Jelinek, Schindel, and Rabinovici's examination of Jewish identity in present Austria. In my use of the term identity, I am referring to meaningful affirmations of social and cultural practices that are profoundly influenced by, though not exclusively limited to, affiliations of gender, race, and nationhood with their inevitable genetic and essentialist resonances. A transcultural identity would thus be characterized by the ability to function and interact in a variety of socio-cultural contexts, and particularly in those that are not immediate to one's background and experiences. This identity encompasses cross-cultural influence yet does not entirely eradicate difference. In the case of our three writers, as I will attempt to show, this transcultural identity is expressed through complex subject positions informed by multiple and overlapping discourses. And, unlike in the case of other contemporary Austrian writers adopting a similar perspective (Handke,

Bernhard, Roth), I will stress that the three writers also share a different legacy (Viennese Jewish culture, the Shoah) that makes an important difference in their negotiation of cultural boundaries. This difference, to be sure, is not merely part of an inherited tradition but grows out of active reappropriation, interpretation and assertion.

My essay will explore Jewish identity in present Austrian writing in two parts. First, in a brief review, I would like to point to the cultural instability of Jewish and Austrian identity as defined in various contexts of Austrian history (turn-of-the-century Vienna, inter-war and Nazi era, post-World War II and reconstruction era, Waldheim and present era). Such contexts will help us understand the complex patterns of recuperation that inform present Jewish identity in Austria. Secondly, an analysis of the three writers focusing on rhetorical and plot strategies will demonstrate both their confrontational and evasive staging of Jewish identity. These strategies will allow them to demand recognition from within a disturbingly revisionist and "normalizing" cultural climate, on the one hand, while also stemming against equally dubious manifestations of ethnic fetishization and philo-Semitism. The writers thus present an intriguing model of cultural diversity, aiming beyond any multiculturalism that does not take overlapping and shared zones of social definition into account.

While the emphasis on a transnational tradition in Austrian literature would seem to account for Jelinek, Schindel and Rabinovici's cosmopolitan stance growing out of this tradition, this emphasis at the same time obscures the roots of this transnationalism, suggesting that it is essentially Austrian. The national labeling of a transnational identity conceals its cross- and multi-cultural origin. As Steven Beller has suggested, the origin of Austria's transnational culture must be located in the late Habsburg era and its encounter with a diasporic Jewish culture that was already cosmopolitan in outlook: "While there are other traditions and backgrounds which added to Vienna 1900, it was the Jewish experience which was the most prevalent among its central figures and its audience, even when that experience is defined in social and not even ethnic terms" (70). Thus, contrary to the myth of an exclusive Jewish assimilation to Austrian culture, Beller makes a compelling case for a similar reverse assimilation of Austrian culture to that of its Jewish residents. Within this multicontextual space of cultural encounter and hybridity, nationalism did not have a chance to solidify in Vienna as it did in the various and more homogeneously structured territories of the empire.

Historians generally agree that the multinational and dynastic character of the Habsburg empire did not allow for a strong, or at least clearly defined, sense of national identity as witnessed, for example, in late imperial Germany.[2] This uncertainty about the ultimate identity of Austria's supra-national monarchy also extended to its definition of Jewish ethnicity in a Vienna with its variety of Jewish communities ranging from ultra-orthodox to liberal, from Hungarian, Galician, Czech, Polish to Austro-German Jews. As Marsha L Rozenblit correctly points out, Jewish cultural assimilation in Vienna, unlike Germany, did not imply the acculturation to a single national identity: "One could easily be an Austrian—an essentially supra-national identity not attached to a particular ethnic group—and also remain a Jew" (11). Ruth Beckermann notes a similar cultural diversity among Jews even in their traditional Viennese district and former ghetto, the Leopoldstadt, where a majority of Viennese Jews resided:

> In the Leopoldstadt diversity was the principle. One could be a Jewish socialist or communist, a chassidic Jew...or a member of a small sephardic community or a Zionist. One could be a Zionist and at the same time active as a Social-democrat, one could be an assimilated Viennese Jew and distance oneself from Eastern Jews, one could abandon one's Jewishness, or one had already forgotten that one was Jewish. In the 1920s, the Jews had already grown to a multi-layered community. For many their belonging to a class, a professional or a political group was more obliging than their being Jewish. (13)[3]

Thus, Beller, Rozenblit and Beckermann's assessment of Viennese culture implies that, while it was in many respects co-synonymous with Jewish culture, it was never reducible to a single definition of

Jewish culture or tradition. For a brief period, the notion of a homogeneous national identity, already prevalent in other European countries (Germany, France, Italy, England) and developing at the various peripheries of the empire (Hungary, Serbia, Bohemia), was negated in Vienna with its multicultural diversity.

Nevertheless, Austria's post-imperial history produced its own peculiar nationalism (pan-Germanic) that made it an eventual ally of Germany's militant nationalism, leading to the expatriation and extermination of Austria's Jewish community which had helped to build and shape so decisively its cultural heritage. Once faced with economic pressure, the multicultural experiment of Austria quickly came to a halt and gave way to ethnic polarizations that had increasingly solidified in the shadow of Vienna's liberal bourgeois culture. In this climate of rising German nationalism, Jewish culture in Vienna was forcefully subjected to a conceptual collectivization that eventually allowed for its systematic extermination (Botz 185-207). Along with it, the multicultural and cosmopolitan world of fin-de-siècle Vienna indebted to Jewish culture disappeared from the cultural landscape of Austria.

The reconstruction of a separate national identity in Austria's post World War II society, after this interlude of German nationalism, appears at first as a contradictory enterprise. With regard to the supra-national heritage of the empire, one could only nostalgically retrieve a world in which peaceful co-existence of diverse cultures had been possible but which now were no longer co-present to the degree that they had been. With regard to Austria's post-imperial history, one had to confront equally a problematic landscape of intense political polarization that had led Austria into civil strife and the subsequent dictatorship of its corporate state. The attempt to revive Austria's national identity in the postwar era, one can thus safely say, was a revival *ex nihilo* based on no applicable prior model in Austrian history.

As critics have pointed out, the revival of a national identity was largely inspired by the pragmatic reason of emphasizing Austria's difference from and non-complicity with Nazi Germany. Austria could thereby regain its sovereignty as a state without having to account fully for its role in the Jewish genocide. Barbara Kaindl-

Widhalm discerns in Austria's postwar history no endemic process of democratization but one that is merely administered from above: "The foreign military defeat set the conditions for internal political changes" (3). Austria's national identity thus appeared to younger writers and intellectuals as an insidious ideological device covering up its problematic past rather than a positive set of national and constitutional tenets presumably shared by its citizens. The young Handke, for instance, already expressed his doubts and reservations at the very beginning of Austria's postwar republic:

> It had been announced that by means of a state treaty with the Allied powers, we would finally become FREE. However, as nothing changed, with the exception of a national holiday that was introduced, but one still heard that we were now FREE, I began to view gradually the words "free" and "unfree" as word games. (14)

During the Grand Party Coalition era of the 1960s and the subsequent Kreisky era of the 1970s, this atmosphere of pragmatic nationalism was perfected into what is known as Austria's consensus society with its efficient and smoothly coordinated economy and its extensive welfare apparatus guaranteeing social stability.[4] Consensus society, however, as a recent study by Daniel Jonah Goldhagen has shown, played a more insidious and powerful role during the Nazi era in providing the hostile national cognitive models of Jews and its accompanying exclusivist and eliminationist ideology. Goldhagen's contribution to our understanding of the Shoah lies in his sociological analysis of epistemic paradigms that had framed a diverse cultural group such as the Jews into a homogeneously perceived enemy of the German nation, and, indeed, provided the negatively defined consensus identity of this nation.[5] The model of consensus society in postwar Austria, while in many ways founded on a progressive attempt to avoid labor confrontation, still recalls a regressive side that harks back to the Nazi era and its engineered and steered social consensus.

In the context of furthering democratic practices from within such an instituted consensus society, the socialist chancellor Bruno

Kreisky figured as a political innovator who left an indelible mark on Austria's history by inaugurating an unprecedented era of liberalism, social reform and cosmopolitan outlook. However, even the highly popular Kreisky ultimately did not touch upon the deeper problem of an unchallenged collective consensus upon which Austria's postwar society was rebuilt. The chancellor, being also of Jewish descent, ultimately chose not to dwell on this heritage in an Austria that wished to forget its history. Instead, Kreisky promoted an international politics that, for instance, intervened in an unorthodox manner for the Palestinian right to self-determination. While avoiding the confrontation of his own ethnic heritage in Austria's public sphere, Kreisky, much to Israel's chagrin, responded sensitively to the plight of an ethnic minority on an international level. This critical and self-effacing stance towards his own Jewish heritage, as Robert S. Wistrich points out, was entirely coherent from within Kreisky's world view:

> At most one could define the Jews as a *Schicksalsgemeinschaft* (a community of fate)…based on a common history of suffering. But they were emphatically not a world-wide people as many Zionists claim…Indeed, the entire concept of Jewish peoplehood as it was interpreted by Zionism implied for Kreisky the inadmissible adoption of the Nazi fiction of a Jewish race. (237)

Kreisky's complex understanding of his Jewish heritage, clearly indebted to Vienna's turn-of-the-century cosmopolitanism, escaped, however, not only Israel which expected more solidarity for its newly founded and embattled nation state but also the majority of Austrians who were content in not having to deal with this "problematic" background of their beloved chancellor. Indeed, Kreisky's liberal principles of socialism that looked beyond ethnicity facilitated a persistent mood of historical amnesia during this period of Austrian reconstruction and emerging affluence.

While writers like Ilse Aichinger, Paul Celan and Ingeborg Bachmann had early on confronted Austria with its problematic past, this examination never reached the wider political public sphere in a climate of instituted silence and amnesia until Waldheim became president in 1986.[6] With Waldheim, finally, Austria's silenced past became an open public theme and allowed writers to articulate their concerns with more national and international attention than ever before. Bernhard's drama *Heldenplatz* (1988), for example, triggered a national controversy over how Austria's heritage ought to be remembered. Since the main protagonists in Bernhard's play were Jewish, this controversy also had to acknowledge the continued presence of living witnesses to Austria's dubious history. Indeed, Bernhard's play was only the beginning of an ethnic examination of Austria's identity that followed in the wake of Waldheim but was also as a result of the collapse of the Eastern bloc and its repression of conflicting ethnic interests as well as Germany's reunification and its problematic stance on citizenship and asylum.[7] Thus, in the early 1990s, a more explicit preoccupation with Austria's Jewish history and its community of survivors and their descendants commanded the attention of media and public sphere. Be it on the concrete municipal level with its restoration of Jewish cultural sites in Vienna or on the level of the cultural public sphere and its critical examination of Austria's fascist and post-fascist history (Bernhard, Jelinek, Schindel, Kerschbaumer, Reichart, Roth), Jewish themes and concerns now received more resonance in Austria.

And yet, while this ethnic focus has allowed one to transcend the monolithic myth of Austria's national identity, its collectivization of Jewish interests still remains problematic. Demographically, for example, Austria's present Jewish community "is largely made up of survivors of concentration camps, displaced persons or refugees who only arrived in Austria to begin a new life after 1945, 1956 (Hungary) or 1968 (Czechoslovakia)."[8] Austria's former Jewish community who went into exile has, for the most part, not returned to Austria. This rupture in the continuity of Austria's Jewish community, complicated by the varying subject positions of its present community with their diverse linguistic, cultural and political heritages, recapitulates the diversity of Vienna's Jewish community at the turn of the century. Thus, to speak of a contemporary Austrian Jewish literature appears almost impossible.

As our brief historical review has shown, both Jewish ethnic and Austrian national identity never achieved stable coordinates in recent Austrian history and were subject to constant transformation.

In the following discussion of Jelinek, Schindel and Rabinovici, I will therefore explore the problematic category of an ethnically defined literature against this background of ongoing cultural transformations. How can one speak of Jewish writing without leveling diverse historical heritages or resorting to ethnic stereotyping? And, how do Austrian Jewish writers assert their cultural difference in a meaningful manner while avoiding similar pitfalls? We will examine here Jelinek, Schindel and Rabinovici's literary strategies to convey a sense of a complex and transnational identity within which ethnic difference is neither entirely dissolved nor absolutely asserted.

What unites the present Jewish communities beyond their apparent diversity is a common history marked particularly by traumatic persecution but by practices of resistance and solidarity as well. Kreisky's notion of a community of fate (*Schicksalsgemeinschaft*) is indeed an example of this limited universal that cuts across cultural difference. In a concrete sense, Kreisky's loss of 21 family members, Jelinek's of 51 members, or Schindel's of his father and members of extended family unites their otherwise different biographies.[9] Peter Sichrovsky's work on the traumatic history shared by survivors and their descendants can be seen similarly as a unifying expression of otherwise diverse Jewish cultural identities. This identity of a common fate of persecution also does more justice to assimilated Jewish populations and their secular and hybridized lifestyles as well as to those who were labeled and grouped as Jewish by the enforcement of racial laws. In addition, this shared traumatic history separates writers like Jelinek, Schindel and Rabinovici from non-Jewish writers who are sympathetic to their position such as Handke, Bernhard, Reichart or Roth. While the latter may have suffered a cultural loss resulting from the persecution and marginalization of Jewish culture in Austria, they do not have the direct experience of ethnic victimization and persecution.

Jean Améry's critical remark on Hannah Arendt that Nazi

violence can never be banal for those who have suffered it physically clarifies this difference also from within Jewish intellectual discourse that on occasion took on the detached position of sociological comment more commonly found among non-Jewish analyses of the Holocaust (25). Améry's remark would further suggest a cross-cultural solidarity of Jewish suffering with other collectively victimized groups such as the Gypsies, Native American Indians or African Americans. It would appear as if the definition of a Jewish community bound by fate would quickly dissolve due to its overly universal tendencies in which all victims become Jews (Bernard Malamud). What does it mean, then, when a person claims to be a Jew apart from traditional cultural and religious affiliations? How does a legacy of persecution (*Schicksalsgemeinschaft*) spell out an identity that is still different from other persecuted groups or individuals? "The social articulation of difference, from the minority experience," writes Homi Bhabha, "is a complex, on-going negotiation that seeks to authorize cultural hybridities that emerge in moments of historical transformation" (2). Bhabha, addressing minority identities in general, questions their demarcation through absolute boundaries of tradition or collectivization. Instead, a complex process of negotiation and recognition defines the tenuous boundaries of minority identities. In this context, being a Jew, as our examples will demonstrate, means to address a specific history and heritage that cannot be taken for granted as an already "authenticated cultural tradition" (Bhabha 3), but that defines itself in active communal negotiation and contention concerning its cultural and ethical significance. Jewish identity construed as such a cultural identity includes both its ongoing clarification and the resistance with which it is met by other competing social interests from within and without.

Concerning our three writers, this emphasis on cultural negotiation being at the origin of any identity is displayed concretely through the use of performative figurations on the level of interwoven texts and discourses (Jelinek), multi-plot configurations (Schindel) and a conflicting semantics of identity (Rabinovici). All three writers, in fact, write against the grain and consensus that usually surrounds traditional identity politics with its already established semantic fields of inclusion and exclusion. Their performative language ruptures such a binary model that defines belonging and not belonging in a culture as well as minority and majority status. Cultural understanding, as their works suggest, is the direct outcome of interaction and negotiated boundaries. Demarcations of group identities are therefore strategic rather than final, dramatic rather than epistemic. Our examples will further point to this process of negotiation as part of a conflicting discourse landscape that we share (Jelinek), as the negotiation of Jewish and non-Jewish encounters in everyday situations (Schindel), and as intra-Jewish differences on the significance of Jewish identity (Rabinovici).

Elfriede Jelinek's play *Totenauberg* (1991) stages her access to a Jewish identity relentlessly in the performative terms of socio-cultural negotiation. The central drama of her play evolves around a fictive encounter and belated dialogue between Arendt, the "rootless" Jewish refugee and political philosopher, and Martin Heidegger, the "natively grounded" thinker of the history of Western ontology. Arendt's Jewish identity, as the play shows, cannot be taken for granted but has to be recast and renegotiated in the present cultural landscape in which the epistemic notions of belonging (Heidegger's *Zugehörigkeit*) and displacement (Arendt's uprootedness) once again clash as competing definitions of culture. As Gitta Honegger notes, characters in this play "turn almost literally into 'figures of speech'" (15). It is thus the conflict of discourses on essentialist and non-essentialist interpretations of culture that provide the dramatic action in the play. This linguistic scenario of competing discourses takes place against the background of an equally disharmonious visual scenario of a thoroughly commodified tourist landscape littered with corpses of mountain climbers that have fallen to their death. Moreover, this visual landscape evokes even more disturbing associations of mass death through cinematic interludes depicting the deportation of Jews. Jelinek's visual and verbal scenarios offer thus a sobered perspective on the cultural death that overshadows Austria's economic reconstruction, one built on a persistent historical amnesia.

This amnesia, as the play suggests, has grown even stronger

after the fall of communism as the last visible alternative to a pervasive Western capitalism where cultural identities have now become marketable commodities and the primary privilege of the affluent. Austria's post-industrial leisure society marketing its *Heimat* and *Wintersport* arena as a tourist commodity while guarding its territorial boundaries against economic refugees of Eastern Europe has not only forgotten its past but has managed to resurrect it in a more sanitized and socially acceptable manner. Asylum laws, ecological awareness and physical health and fitness routines replace the former visible aspects of fascist ideology stressing dubious constructions of biological native right and organic wholeness of culture. Under such revisionist circumstances, as Jelinek shows, Jewish identity remains one of wholesale expulsion and invisibility that can only indirectly point to the artificiality and pathology of Austria's cultural landscape. In the play, Arendt's voice can barely differentiate itself from and stem against the overwhelming power of other discourses (sport, *Heimat*, genetics and motherhood) that have equally usurped Heidegger's notions of reflective *Dasein* (being) and *Zugehörigkeit* (belonging). Indeed, much of the play parodies Heideggerian rhetoric by undermining its essentialist assumptions through polysemic contamination via other discourses. Serious Heideggerian reflections thus take on an aspect of comical banality, while at the same time unmasking a deeper and persistent cultural narcissism: "By means of sport we become the ornament of our being...Sport has now become our true interpretation (*Auslegung*), our work" (Jelinek 72).

With its polysemic ironies, Jelinek's *Totenauberg* is far from reinstating and reinserting a defined type of identity, much less Jewish ethnicity, into Austria's hegemonic culture. Jelinek's acknowledged debt to Karl Kraus' linguistic scrutiny of cultural icons and identity lends her writing a cosmopolitan irony that belies any facile accommodation of a national or ethnic identity.[10] Following in the tradition of Austria's assimilated Jewish writers, Jelinek articulates ethnic concerns from within a multicontextual perspective that subordinates ethnic concerns to a more complex and hybrid model of cultural identity. Even though her play specifically refers to the traumatic experience of the Holocaust as a potential unifying focus for Jewish identity, it remains thoroughly multilayered and relocates the past always through its present reconfigurations of cultural ideologies such as the marketable discourse on *Heimat*, the asylum debate and the notions of ecology and organic health. Likewise, Jelinek's characters possess no sharp boundaries and their discourses are for the most part inter-changeable. The author's severe cultural critique of commodified discourse thus constitutes at the same time a constructive refusal to entertain a sentimental Jewish identity in an era of philo-Semitism with its abundant fetishism of exemplary Jewish victims and its fascination with "dead and half-dead Jews" (Henryk Broder).

Even Arendt, often seen as the exemplary Jewish philosopher of this century, is more soberly described by Jelinek as "a good essayist in practical thinking" who never had the luxury of exploring pure ontologies in Heideggerian fashion but had to settle for a hybrid set of reflections that arose from her cultural displacement and adjustment.[11] Jelinek's linguistic scenario of competing and overlapping discourses that resonate in Austria's cultural landscape ultimately restores Arendt's displacement as a cultural position indigenous to Germany or Austria rather than making her exile appear as an exceptional anomaly from within a presumably grounded *Heimat*. To quote Bhabha once again, one could say the following of Jelinek's play: "In restaging the past it introduces other, incommensurable cultural temporalities into the invention of tradition. This process estranges any immediate access to an originary identity or "received" tradition" (2). Locating displacement at the center of Austria's cultural discourses in which notions of belonging mask discontinuity, rupture, and difference, the author highlights the complex subject positions and ideologies that compete with one another in any construction of culture. In so doing, she recovers the diasporic element that had shaped Vienna's cultural identity at the turn of the century and which had subsequently been demonized in Austria as being exclusively Jewish rather than the unique result of cross-cultural encounters.

Robert Schindel's novel *Gebürtig* (1992) at first similarly takes a critical view of Austria's dubious normalization, belying a climate of enforced harmonized consensus: "Your fathers have pushed our people into the ovens, your mothers have prayed the rosary and the sons generously want to incorporate us, disregard the past, and, untarnished, want to be the victims themselves" (15). Nevertheless, Schindel still believes in the possibility of cultural rebirth to the extent that it involves a genuine engagement with history affecting the present and its sphere of intercultural encounter. With a sympathetic perspective, Schindel's multi-plot novel shows most of his characters struggling for more viable forms of cultural identity in which difference and commonality can co-exist and in which the past is acknowledged but not necessarily the single determining avenue to Jewish identity: "Is it permissible for our Jews to remain occasionally dead or must their bones and ashes always remain sharpened?" (16). Schindel's heterogeneously structured novel succeeds in presenting us with a credible intersubjective world interposing itself between the various negotiations of cultural identity ripe with contradictions and inconsistencies.

The appropriate vehicle for this tentative, diverse and flexible reconstruction of culture is the multi-plot narration with which Schindel highlights both progressive and regressive attempts in which public and private boundaries are negotiated between Jewish and non-Jewish characters. The centrality of social and cultural co-dependence is emphasized by the twin characters Sascha Graffito and Danny Demant who are symbiotically connected to one another as passive observer-narrator and acting character respectively, thus producing together a narratively enframed life or story. This symbiotic model subsequently plays itself out in a series of other paired characters whose lives intersect with Danny and Sascha's. At the outset, the novel depicts patterns of interaction typical of Austria's amnesiac society: "He emphasized his Jewish heritage; she said that she could do little with that, she wasn't interested in politics" (35). The work further highlights generational conflicts between survivors and their descendants such as Emmanuel Katz who becomes the indirect victim of his mother's traumatic memory or Susanne Ressel who questions her father's fond memories of communist activism and comradeship during the Spanish civil war (20, 92). Eventually, however, the novel presents more positive transformations such as the public outing of a repressed Jewish identity (Katz, Adel) or a hidden Nazi past (Konrad Sachs), the commitment to confront once again a traumatic past as a witness in a Nazi trial (Gebirtig) and the approximation of the Shoah experience, albeit highly ironized, as stand-ins in a Holocaust movie set.

Thus, in Schindel's novel, the predominance of the characters' positive transformations along with the flippant, though ultimately benign, humor would appear to promote a false harmonization at the novel's end. Its intent of exposing the historical amnesia of Austria's consensus society is undermined by what some critics may identify as sentimentality or ethnic *Kitsch*. However, the novel's tone, admittedly not without its own problems, resists a sanctimonious quality that has become of late a cliché in the treatment of the Holocaust, turning critical reflection into iconic reverence for events claimed to be beyond human comprehension. Like his German colleague Maxim Biller, Schindel attempts to break this spell of unquestioning awe and reticence by means of irreverent satire so as to allow for a continued inquiry into Jewish history and identity. Compared to Jelinek's *Totenauberg*, Schindel's novel evokes a similar heteroglossia of commodified discourses surrounding cultural identities. However, Schindel's more conciliatory work highlights the assimilative potential that Vienna harbored beneath its diasporic identity which allowed, apart from cultural tension, for hybridities and mutually enriched cultural contexts.

This transregional and cosmopolitan confidence is reflected in the novel's constant shifting of scenery between Vienna, Venice, Hamburg, Munich, Frankfurt and New York, all distinctive cities with distinctive traditions. Schindel's more easy-going cosmopolitan perspective, critically grounded in distinct regional settings, does not attempt to globalize or universalize its thematic of various cultural encounters between Jews and non-Jews. Indeed, each of the novel's encounters produces a unique negotiation of Jewish identity from within uniquely interpreted cultural settings. The novel's depiction of attempts at self-comprehension and identity is in this respect often linked to the reflective act of writing that creates a necessary distance to an immediate set of historical or personal circumstances. Emmanuel Katz, tyrannized by his mother's

Auschwitz past, offers such an instance of an attempt to give birth to a new identity other than through the memory of victimization. After the death of his father, and a series of forced attempts to assert his Jewish identity (growing a beard and accusing other Jews of denying their identity), Katz quits his banking profession and settles for writing a book on Holocaust survivors and their inability to escape their past, an insight that is tragically borne out by his mother who eventually dies of a "belated Auschwitz-death" (199). On the other hand, this attempt at emancipation is also more contingently linked to the matrix of desire that somehow subverts predictable boundaries of cultural identity and difference. Katz's emancipatory effort from an overwhelming heritage through the distance of writing is thus tainted by his private "weakness for slim, tall women…, the more German, the better" (27), revealing an ongoing tacit admiration for German culture.

In Schindel's *Gebürtig*, seemingly stable cultural boundaries are qualified by various peripheral and centrifugal topographical movements away from and towards Vienna as the novel's main locale as well as by linguistic and regional differences. Schindel's novel thus foregrounds a multi-contextual (rather than multicultural) negotiation of identity that occurs on many discourse levels and not merely on the level of bipolar oppositions between typified ethnic, national or regional identities. Renewing the significance of Jewish identity and its public visibility, Schindel ultimately manages to avoid a facile pluralism and a dogmatic politics of identity obliging every Jew to be Jewish in the same manner. Since Jewishness, as Schindel realizes, overlaps with other private and public identities, it recedes or presses into the foreground in accordance with changing subject positions influenced by age, gender, generation, community, region and language. Its visibility, while desirable in Austria's all too homogeneous cultural landscape, cannot be reduced to any single strategy or form of public disclosure.

Doron Rabinovici's prose collection *Papirnik: Stories* (1994) resists Schindel's sympathetic ironization of the recently emerging politics of identity. Instead, from within an ambience of a seemingly secure banality, the author stages a return of violence, anxiety and repressed historical content. "Papirnik," for example, the framing story of the cycle, depicts a character made of books and scrolls and ends abruptly in the character's self-immolation and an evocation of Nazi book burning. Like Jelinek, Rabinovici displays serious doubts about the visibility of a Jewish identity that is nowhere acknowledged nor sought after in a culture seemingly at home with itself. Rabinovici stems against this invisibility by refusing likewise the legitimation of the dominant culture. Through his narrative style where the semantics of single words and names often receives heightened attention, the author subtly lays bare their implicit cultural and political connotations. In the story "Noémi," for example, the city of Vienna is mentioned only cryptically as "W" and thereby belittled in its significance and identity. A café location, so central in Schindel's work as a terrain of intersecting biographies, is in the same diminutive manner more critically defined by its proximity to the monument of Vienna's anti-Semitic mayor (Lueger) that has without any challenge survived into the present. By means of these minimal rhetorical strategies, Vienna turns into a site of negativity and absence, reflecting a loss rather than a presence of culture.

In "Noémi," a story about two adolescents attempting to come to terms with their cultural and ethnic heritage, a single name similarly is at the center of its unfolding action. The story's vehicle, the name "Noémi" with its readily presumed Jewish origin, triggers a comedy of errors revolving around competing models of ethnic authenticity. As part of an intra-Jewish critique, Rabinovici critically explores in the story the phenomenon of an ethnic revival of identity and its own peculiar forms of betrayal. In the story, the separate and exiled identity of Jews in Austria is initially represented by the Zionist *Jugendbewegung* (youth movement) in which its two protagonists Amos and Georg find a temporary yet ambivalent shelter: "Like a stretched barbed wire, events took their course between them and the rest of the city" (36). This seemingly clearly demarcated exiled identity, however, is complicated by the Jewish community's own inner differences over what constitutes Jewish identity (historical heritage, geographical location, matrilinear bloodline) as well as by the protagonists' mimetic rivalry for the same woman who, with her seemingly Jewish name "Noémi," embodies both the promise and the betrayal of their tenuous identity. Thus, challenging Austria's nationalism with their transnational Zionist beliefs, Amos and Georg nevertheless succumb to an obsession with their own origin projected onto the presumably Jewish Noémi: "He asked for her name. 'Noémi.' Thereafter he had incorporated her and made every attempt to meet her again" (34). And as is recalled later in the story: "Georg saw how his friend looked at her and a yet nameless desire arose within him for the first time" (50).

This erotic obsession with a legitimate origin, especially on the part of the half-Jewish Georg whose mother is not a Jew, ultimately undermines the construction of a common identity and solidarity. As in Schindel's work, a less stable matrix of desire subverts the seemingly more stable cultural identities. Both Amos' and Georg's initial Zionist aspirations are undone by a triangular desire in which Jewish identity is displaced onto a fetishized object and thus the focus of mimetic rivalry. The story's ending, in which the two adults now look back on this youthful episode, places the flirtation with Zionism into a similar adolescent and naive context. Both protagonists have in the meantime abandoned their desire to live in Israel and resigned themselves to a more settled secular identity.

However, apart from this sobering ending, the protagonists ultimately learn that identities cannot be innocently acquired nor revived. During their stay in Israel, they find out that they are after all Viennese Jews with a particular tradition that does not fully coincide with the tradition of Israel. Their urbane humor and sketchlike parody of anti-Semitism, for instance, is not appreciated during a community event in the kibbutz where the pressure of such an ideology is viewed differently. As both Amos and Georg come to realize: "Anti-Semitism: Here they let [this ideology] die in ignorance. [Amos and Georg], however, wanted to mirror its unreflected content and wanted to expose it in its contradictory nature. They were at once accused of Jewish self-hatred" (40-41). Internal dismantling of cultural stereotypes in the manner of a Karl Kraus, Amos and Georg must realize, is a restricted and not commonly shared Jewish practice. Thus, the acquisition of identity entails a necessary shattering of idols, reminding the protagonists of their specific geographic and cultural position in what appeared to be a seamless and unproblematic world of pan-Jewish solidarity.

While opening up Jewish cultural definition from within itself to a cosmopolitan perspective, Rabinovici, like Jelinek and Schindel, does not settle for a fashionable multicultural model that would be welcomed by more liberal elements in Austria. His major reservation is once again a semantic one, struggling with a tacit consensus underlying the notion of cultural pluralism. The desired harmonization of diverse cultural claims, as Rabinovici's stories demonstrate, does not necessarily guarantee recognition but demands assimilation to a norm, even if such a norm is now more heterogeneously articulated. Reflecting on the semantics of public debate, Rabinovici exposes this strategic elimination of difference and dissent in one of his stories which foregrounds the overruling force of consensus in which difference is only preserved in the form of tokenism:

> They will tolerate what I have to say only in so far that they can incorporate me into one of their solutions of consent. My position is not supposed to reach the public, but my presence here is meant to lend your harmony its suitable counterpoint. (93-94)

Like Jelinek or Schindel, Rabinovici is acutely aware of the commodification of cultural identities which subjects them to commercial, national and ideological interests and rituals of democratic decision making. The assertion of Jewish identity in Austria is therefore further complicated by the horizon of cultural expectation that surrounds it. Is it always productive, for example, to represent a living Jewish community in a society that wants to forget its annihilationist politics of the past and now take pride in its present political freedom? Visibility of difference, as Rabinovici's stories indirectly suggest, can also be exploited for token democratic expressions of freedom and recognition. Rabinovici's analysis thus highlights the problematic semantic manipulation of cultural identities in which any positive assertion can possibly be turned into its opposite.

As this illustration of Jelinek, Schindel and Rabinovici has attempted to show, the politics of recognition in contemporary Austrian discourse does not rest entirely on an increased visibility in a culture nor on any clearly marked ethnic collectivity, even if such a community is construed as a force of resistance. Instead, Jelinek, Schindel and Rabinovici attempt to foreground the complex work that underlies any negotiation of identity. To be Jewish, for these writers, means foremost to challenge one's own secure sense of identity defined by traditional affiliations and to enter the multi-contextual spheres of private and public cultures with their uneasy compromises and balances. Thus, they alert us to the increasingly post-ideological landscape of a new public sphere in which there is no longer any privileged point of perspective seemingly more innocent than others. At the same time, they remind us that any position is ideologically suspect unless it enters the challenge of cultural diversification and hybridization which makes cultural recognition, and therefore identity, possible.

Notes

1. Remmler, in her discussion, initially acknowledges "different geographical, political and cultural contexts" (186) as decisive factors in determining the author's specific Jewish identity; however, in her discussion, this consideration is overridden by a collective treatment of female Jewish identity, paralleling Gilman's discussion of male Jewish identity. Moreover, this identity is demarcated entirely collectively, ignoring the possibility of an individual's unique appropriation or revision of it. For example, Remmler claims: "For German Jewish women writing in German, the attachment, however ambiguous and painful, to German culture through memory, family, or language positions them in spaces not shared with non-German women of Turkish, African or Eastern European origin" (186). German Jewish women, in Remmler's view, have turned into a distinct sociological group, presumably preventing them in their absolute difference from sharing their own or assimilating any experiences from other minorities in Germany.

2. Anderson notes that "German's nineteenth-century elevation by the Habsburg court, German as one might think it, had nothing whatever to do with German nationalism" (78). Johnston finds this absence of a strongly defined national identity once again in Austria's postwar republic which he terms a "nation without qualities" (177).

3. Translation of all German cited material is mine unless otherwise indicated.

4. See, for example, Menasse's study *Die sozialpartnerschaftliche Ästhetik*, where the author extends the economic concept of cooperative consensus to the entire cultural landscape of Austria. The concept of social partnership, according to Menasse, lies at the root of Austria's political infrastructure. Its principle agency rests with an instituted parity commission which controls and settles wage and price negotiations in order to avoid open labor conflict. Social partnership, as Menasse concludes, aims for a total harmonization of social relations without, however, removing the original reasons for conflict (91). The social landscape, including Austria's democratic institutions, are thus said to be strongly marked by pre-arranged consensus, lack of critique and pseudo-democratic procedures. Incidentally, Menasse belongs to the same generation of Austrian Jewish writers that are discussed in this essay.

5. Goldhagen's work, which can arguably be challenged, is invoked here mostly with regard to its model of social consensus and not for its ultimate adequacy as an explanation of the Holocaust.

6. See, for example, Zeyringer's study *Innerlichkeit und Öffentlichkeit: Österreichische Literatur der achtziger Jahre*, which locates the turning point of Austria's consensus society at the end of the liberal Kreisky era (1985). Political corruption or *Verfilzung*, neo-conservatism and the election of Waldheim, according to Zeyringer, contributed to a more outspoken engagement by writers and the redefinition of their task in terms of openly expressed cultural resistance.

7. See Huyssen 67-84.

8. *Jewish Life in Austria* 5.

9. See Wistrich, "The Kreisky Phenomenon" 236; Jelinek, "Wir leben auf einem Berg von Leichen und Schmerz" 8; and Schindel's autobiographical poem "Erinnerungen an Prometheus" 11-16; and the review "Die unterste Falte der Seele" (88-89), providing biographical information on the author.

10. In an interview Jelinek states: "That is precisely the culture I come from—the Eastern-Jewish world, the tradition of language critique, Karl Kraus…Coming from an urban cultured middle class, [I] have the desire to smash language, to strip it to its bone, to tear the last bits of truth out of it, to rip open its chest" ("This German Language…" in *Theater* 25 (Spring/Summer 1994): 21). In the same manner, Jelinek conceives evasively of her national identity when asked what Austria means to her as a *Heimat*: "Yes it is, but only in its great ethnic and cultural diversity. Especially Eastern Austria. I'd say Vienna is home, this Eastern Slavic-Jewish culture I come from, my family comes from. With authors who come from the western states, it's a different tradition. That skepticism towards language, also that burlesque playing with language practiced in Jewish cabaret" (22).

11. Jelinek, "Wir leben auf einem Berg von Leichen und Schmerz" 7.

Works Cited

Améry, Jean. *At the Mind's Limit*. New York: Schocken Books, 1986.

Anderson, Benedict. *Imagined Communities*. London: Verso, 1991.

Austrian Federal Press Service, ed. *Jewish Life in Austria*. Graz: Styria, 1992.

Beckermann, Ruth. *Die Mazzeinsel: Juden in der Wiener Leopoldstadt 1918-1938*. Wien: Löcker Verlag, 1984.

Beller, Steven. *Vienna and the Jews 1867-1938: A Cultural History*. Cambridge: Cambridge UP, 1990.

Bhabha, Homi K. *The Location of Culture*. London: Routledge, 1994.

Botz, Gerhard. "The Jews of Vienna from the *Anschluss* to the Holocaust." *Jews, Antisemitism, and Culture in Vienna*. Ed. Gerhard Botz, Ivar Oxaal, and Michael Pollak. London: Routledge, 1987.
"Die unterste Falte der Seele." *Profil* 18 (April, 1992): 88-89.
Gilman, Sander L. and Karen Remmler, eds. *Reemerging Jewish Culture in Germany: Life and Literature Since 1989*. New York: NYU Press, 1994.
Goldhagen, Daniel Jonah. *Hitler's Willing Executioners: Ordinary Germans and the Holocaust*. New York: Knopf, 1996.
Handke, Peter. "1957." *Ich bin ein Bewohner des Elfenbeinturms*. Frankfurt: Suhrkamp, 1972.
Honegger, Gitta. "This German Language ... : An Interview with Elfriede Jelinek." *Theater* 25.1 (Spring/Summer 1994): 14-22.
Huyssen, Andreas. "Nation, Race, and Immigration: German Identities after Unification." *Twilight Memories: Marking Time in a Culture of Amnesia*. London: Routledge, 1995.
Jelinek, Elfriede. *Totenauberg*. Hamburg: Rowohlt, 1991.
---. "Wir leben auf einem Berg von Leichen und Schmerz." *Theater Heute* 9 (1992):1-9.
Johnston, William M. "A Nation Without Qualities: Austria and Its Quest for a National Identity." *Concepts of National Identity: An Interdisciplinary Dialogue*. Ed. Dieter Boerner (Baden-Baden: Nomos, 1986).
Kaindl-Widhalm, Barbara. *Demokratie wider Willen: Autoritäre Tendenzen und Anti-semitismus in der 2. Republik*. Wien: Verlag für Gesellschaftskritik, 1990.
Konzett, Matthias. "*Publikumsbeschimpfung*: Thomas Bernhard's Provocations of the Austrian Public Sphere." *The German Quarterly* 68.3 (1995): 251-70.
Menasse, Robert. *Die sozialpartnerschaftliche Ästhetik*. Wien: Sonderzahl, 1990.
Rabinovici, Doron. *Papirnik: Stories*. Frankfurt: Suhrkamp, 1994.
Rozenblit, Marsha L. "The Jews of Germany and Austria: A Comparative Perspective." *Austrians and Jews in the Twentieth Century*. Ed. Robert S. Wistrich. New York: St. Martin's Press, 1992.

Schindel, Robert. "Erinnerungen an Prometheus." *Im Herzen die Krätze: Gedichte.* Frankfurt: Suhrkamp, 1988.

---. *Gebürtig.* Frankfurt: Suhrkamp, 1992.

Sichrovsky, Peter. *Wir wissen nicht was morgen wird, wir wissen wohl was gestern war: Junge Juden in Deutschland und Österreich.* Köln: Kiepenheuer & Witsch, 1985.

Wistrich, Robert S. "The Kreisky Phenomenon: A Reassessment." *Austrians and Jews in the Twentieth Century.* Ed. Robert S. Wistrich. New York: St. Martin's Press, 1992.

Zeyringer, Klaus. *Innerlichkeit und Öffentlichkeit: Österreichische Literatur der achtziger Jahre.* Tübingen: A. Francke, 1992.

Zipes, Jack. "The Contemporary German Fascination for Things Jewish." *Reemerging Jewish Culture in Germany: Life and Literature Since 1989.* Ed. Sander L. Gilman and Karen Remmler. New York: NYU Press, 1994.

Modeling a Dialectic: Peter Handke's
A Journey to the Rivers or Justice for Serbia

Scott Abbott
Brigham Young University

> [The altered philosophy] can in principle always err; and only thus is it in a position to achieve something... In opposition to the total mastery of method, philosophy contains, as corrective, the moment of play.
> Theodor Adorno, *Negative Dialectic*

The foreword to the American, Spanish, French, and Italian translations of Peter Handke's *Eine winterliche Reise zu den Flüssen Donau, Save, Morawa und Drina oder Gerechtigkeit für Serbien* (*Journey to the Rivers*) [1] provides a glimpse into the short but colorful history of the essay's reception:

> Dear foreign reader: this text, appearing on two weekends at the onset of 1996 in the *Süddeutsche Zeitung*, caused some commotion in the European press. Immediately after publication of the first part, I was designated a terrorist in the Corriere della Sera, and Libération revealed that I was, first of all, amused that there were so few victims in the Slovenian war of 1991, and that I was exhibiting, second, "doubtful taste" in discussing the various ways of presenting this or that victim of the Yugoslavian wars in the western media. In *Le Monde* I was then called a "pro-Serbian advocate," and in the Journal du Dimanche there was talk of "pro-Serbian agitation." And so it continued until *El País* even read into my text a sanction of the Srebrenica massacre.—Dear French, Spanish, Italian, American reader: Now the text is translated, and I trust that you will read it as it is; I need not defend or take back a single word. I wrote about my journey through the country of Serbia exactly as I have always written my books, my literature: a slow, inquiring narration; every paragraph dealing with and narrating a

problem, of representation, of form, of grammar—of aesthetic veracity; that has always been the case in what I have written, from the beginning to the final period. Dear reader: that, and that alone, I offer here for your perusal.
Peter Handke, April 1996

Less than four months after Handke's essay first appeared in the *Süddeutsche Zeitung*, Tilman Zülch's *Die Angst des Dichters vor der Wirklichkeit: 16 Antworten auf Peter Handkes Winterreise nach Serbien*[2] appeared, a collection of vitriolic pieces that include statements like the following:

> The author...in the end, feels he is totally misunderstood and from the back pocket that replaces his brain draws the alibi that he has written an essay on peace. (Günter Kunert, 62)

Or,

> [Peter Handke] has now finally conquered the province of profound trash. He has become a deluded voice for war and *Blut und Boden*, a voice that unsettles because it is methodical. (Gustav Seibt, 71)

At issue, both in Peter Handke's essay and in the responses to it, are the effects of rhetoric: of his own, of the journalists he attacks, and of his critics. Handke claims his work is a self-reflexive, "slow, inquiring narration" in the service of peace. He accuses specific journalists and newspapers of demagogy. His critics argue that his self-deluded rhetoric promotes nationalism and war. In what follows I will trace a pattern in Handke's essay that makes it, on my reading, a model of dialectical rhetoric, of narrative, non-systematic philosophy.

The essay, whose double title—*A Journey to the Rivers or Justice for Serbia*—indicates that this will be a travel narrative *and* a political essay, is divided into four parts with the simple titles: Before the Trip, Part One of the Trip, Part Two of the Trip, and Epilogue. "Before the Trip" and "Epilogue" contain most of the controversial accusations about the European press and its "coverage" of the wars in Yugoslavia, while parts one and two of the trip contain most of the actual travel narrative.

In "Before the Trip," written, like the rest of the essay, after the trip, Handke describes his preparations. He contacted the two Serbs who would accompany him. He saw, just before leaving, Emir Kusturica's new film "Underground," and found it an engaging combination of dreaming and actual history. He was surprised, then, to see the film reviewed by Alain Finkielkraut in *Le Mond* as pro-Serbian and terroristic. From this and similarly incomprehensible "misreadings" (which, by the way, foreshadow how Handke's essay will be "read"), he turns to press reports of the wars in Yugoslavia. He cites European and especially German/Austrian complicity in the disintegration of Yugoslavia: a favoring of, acceptance of, and support of the breakaway republics of Slovenia and Croatia that, in his estimation, led to the war, or better said, made it likely. The political actions, Handke argues, have their basis in a bias against Serbia that European culture has promulgated for decades (he mentions, for example, the post-empire Austrian rhyme "Serbien muss sterbien"—Serbia must die) and that newspapers like *Le Monde* and the *Frankfurter Allgemeine Zeitung* have played up. After questioning the "facts" as reported, he ends the opening section by asking: "Who will someday write this history differently, and even if only the nuances—which could do much to liberate the peoples from their mutual inflexible images?"

The essay's second section begins with the trip to Belgrade. Žarko Radaković, a journalist, novelist, and Handke's translator into Serbo-Croatian and Zlatko Bocokić, a friend from Salzburg, meet Handke there. There is a walk through the city, a visit to a market in Zemun, a trip to see Bocokić's parents, a drive to a monastery with the writer Milorad Pavić and a meeting that night with the writer Dragan Velikić.

The travel narrative continues in the third section with a description of gasoline vending as the three men leave Belgrade to drive to the town of Bajina Bašta on the Drina River to visit Radaković's ex-wife and daughter. There they hear about the war, they are snowed in, they cross a bridge briefly to the other side, they

Modeling a Dialectic 343

listen to heroic tales sung by a guslar, and they finally leave Serbia by way of Novi Sad. Before the section ends, Handke remembers a trip to Slovenia just a month earlier which confirmed his fears that the new state had lost the multicultural openness it once had as part of Yugoslavia.

In the epilog, Handke recounts a morning in Bajina Bašta when he walked alone to the bus station and then to the Drina River. While standing on the shore he asked questions about what really happened at Srebrenica and returned to his attack on the media in general and on the *Frankfurter Allgemeine Zeitung* specifically:

> And, in the meantime, it even interests me how in the central-European Serb-swallowing rag, the *Frankfurter Allgemeine Zeitung*, whose primary hate-mongerer, their tap root of hate, an editorialist writing almost daily against everything Yugoslavian and Serbian in the style (?) of an executioner ("to be eradicated," "to be cut off," "to be removed"), a Reißwolf & Geifermüller (slashing wolf/shredder and vicious-tongued miller, a play on the last name of Johann Georg Reißmüller, an editor of the *FAZ*)—it interests me how this journalist might have arrived, from his German throne, at his word-slinging tenacity .

The epilog ends with a suicide note left by an ex-partisan who shot himself in despair as his country began to destroy itself in civil war.

Although this summary is generally accurate, it is simply inadequate. Like the readings by Handke's critics, it leaves out the multiple and conflicting voices the essay manages to incorporate. For a more careful reader, Handke's essay asserts in the context of self-doubt, recognizes its own contingency in the face of justice, finds justice in contingency and multiplicity, and models honesty in complexity of style while attacking the dishonesty of simplistic journalism.

Peter Handke has long been interested in the possibilities of dialectical thinking. In his interview with Herbert Gamper, for example, he returned several times to the subject of Nietzsche and the dialectic: "I see [Nietzsche] not as a negator, but as a dramatic custodian of something that was always there, and yet naturally also as a very fruitful destroyer of that which did not deserve to be conserved. This dialectical relationship, these two things, make Nietzsche who he is" (171); "One can see in [Nietzsche] a model human existence: one who does not in any sense want to establish systems, who does not want to interpret the world according to a system. The fragmentary, halting style of writing and the few wonderfully painful poems...allow the reading of his works to be a joyful slow studying" (172).[3] These statements about the purposely paradoxical philosopher who argued for contingency *and* a will-to-power make explicit Handke's sense for dialectic as an interplay between despair and hope, conservation and destruction, and as furthered by an anti-systematic, fragmentary, positive creation of meaning through language: "The law of art: glorification, but dialectical glorification (it is not the Golden Age, but rather the Dialectical Age)"; "Didactic, argumentative philosophy will always be foreign to me, as opposed to narrative philosophy."[4]

As I think about Handke's dialectical practice and attempt to test my reading of Handke as dialectician on *A Journey to the Rivers or Justice for Serbia*, a recent attempt by an American philosopher to read Nietzsche as thinking after, even if still in the language of metaphysics, provides a helpful context. In *The Question of Ethics: Nietzsche, Foucault, Heidegger*, Charles Scott looks at what he calls Nietzsche's self-overcoming, an open process occasioned by questions about the values that structure his own discourse as well as the discourses of traditional morals: "In the discussion of the play of will to power and eternal return in Nietzsche's writing—a play of metaphysical assertion, antimetaphysical assertion, and nonmetaphysical recoil in the process—we discern not only the conflictual directions that are methodically maintained, but also a middle-voiced recoiling function."[5] The middle voice, thinkable neither in the active nor the passive voices, is where, in Scott's reading of Nietzsche, self-overcoming in metaphysics takes place: "It is the voice of differing, moving of itself, without the thought of transcendence" (32). Scott's argument is complicated and fascinating and deserves further explication; but I sketch the gesture of his thought here as an example of what I think Handke means when he speaks of dialectical thinking. It is thought within polarities (like the metaphysical / antimetaphysical assertions Scott mentions) that nevertheless recoils at its own dualistic structure. It is a momentary break in the structure that allows difference and motion and play to reveal metaphysical thought's repression of the always present play of conflictual forces. It is self-overcoming thought, as Scott writes, that calls into question the presumptive authority of its organizing ideas to make room not for its own truth but for other truths (30).

In recent years Handke has published essays on tiredness, on the jukebox, and on the achieved day, practicing a literary form with a long history, a form whose peculiarities have been well described by Theodor Adorno in "The Essay as Form." Consider the following thoughts pertinent to Handke's work that appear in the context of Adorno's ongoing attack on the dogmatic identity thinking of post-Enlightenment scientific thought: "[The essay, as a form] rebels against the doctrine, deeply rooted since Plato, that what is transient and ephemeral is unworthy of philosophy..." (10); "The customary objection that the essay is fragmentary and contingent itself postulates that totality is given, and with it the identity of subject and object, and acts as though one were in possession of the whole....[The essay's] weakness bears witness to the very nonidentity it had to express...In the emphatic essay thought divests itself of the traditional idea of truth" (11); "Thought does not progress in a single direction; instead, the moments are interwoven as in a carpet. The fruitfulness of the thoughts depends on the density of the texture" (13); "This kind of learning remains vulnerable to error, as does the essay as form; it has to pay for its affinity with open intellectual experience with a lack of security that the norm of established thought fears like death" (13); "...the essay is more dialectical than the dialectic is when the latter discourses on itself...The daring, anticipatory, and not fully redeemed aspect of every essayistic detail attracts other such details as its negation; the untruth in which the essay knowingly entangles itself is the element in which its truth resides" (19).

These fragments of Adorno's essay read like descriptions of the formal experiments of Handke's essays. We don't, however, have to rely exclusively on Adorno or Scott for theory, for Handke's essays are themselves self-reflexive essays on the essay. In the "Essay on the Successful Day," for example, the narrator's confident but botched description of Van Morrison's "Coney Island" immediately follows an impatient request by the narrator's interlocutor for a direct, certain description of an achieved day (in contrast to the indirect and halting nature of the essay up to that point):

> But with all your digressions, complications, and tergiversations, your way of breaking off every time you gain a bit of momentum, what becomes of your Line of Beauty and Grace, which, as you've hinted, stands for a successful day and, as you went on to assure us, would introduce your essay on the subject. When will you abandon your irresolute peripheral zigzags, your timorous attempt to define a concept that seems to be growing emptier than ever, and at last, with the help of coherent sentences, make the light, sharp incision that will carry us through the present muddle in medias res, in the hope that this obscure "successful day" of yours may take on clarity and universal form.[6]

In response, the narrator suggests a double form that includes the form the interlocutor has rejected: "Isn't it typical of people like us that this sort of song keeps breaking off, lapsing into stuttering, babbling, and silence, starting up again, going off on a sidetrack—yet in the end, as throughout, aiming at unity and wholeness?" (127).

It is exactly this double form, this ongoing dialectic that aims at wholeness through fragments, that Handke's detractors, along with most of his defenders, have missed—a form that my summary failed to mention as well.

Although I stated that the essay ends with a suicide note, I left out the first part of that final paragraph. During the trip through Serbia, Handke writes, he noted only two things in his notebook: "'Jebi ga!' *Fuck him,* common curse"—and the section of the suicide's farewell letter. These are the poles between which the entire essay moves: obscene aggression and fatal resignation. There are moments of both along the way, especially in the first and last sections of the essay; but for the most part, especially in the travel narrative, Handke describes what he calls, citing Hermann Lenz and Edmund Husserl, "third things," things colored by the bi-polar aggressions and despairs of war, but also somehow independent from them, third things not unrelated to the "middle-voiced recoiling functions" Scott sees in Nietzsche's thought.[7]

Because he is worried that his writing may approach the simplistic rhetoric of bad journalism, and because he fears that he will be misread by simplistic readers, Handke questions both writing and reading: "And whoever is now thinking: 'Aha, pro-Serbian!' or 'Aha, Yugophile'...need read no farther" (13). "And whoever thinks this is indifference instead of choking, need read no farther" (36). The reader is asked to read the complicated argument with care, or not read at all. And Handke requires similar discipline of himself in his writing.

Early in the essay, for example, a critical voice breaks in to ask: "What, are you trying to help minimize the Serbian crimes in Bosnia, in the Krajina, in Slavonia, by means of a media-critique that sidesteps the basic facts?" Handke answers: "Steady. Patience. Justice. The problem—only mine?—is more complicated, complicated by several levels or stages of reality: and I am aiming, in my desire to clarify it, at something thoroughly real through which something like a meaningful whole can be surmised in all the mixed-up kinds of reality" (29-30). And near the essay's end, Handke's wife asks: "You aren't going to question the massacre at Srebrenica too, are you?" to which he answers: "No,...But I want to ask how such a massacre is to be explained, carried out, it seems, under the eyes of a worldwide public" (121). "Note well:" he writes, "this is absolutely not a case of 'I accuse.' I feel compelled only to justice. Or perhaps even only to questioning, to raising doubts" (124).

In the face of this self-critique, what does it mean when critics claim that Handke is denying the massacre at Srebrenica?[8] It means, I think, that they are reading unfairly, taking statements out of their dialectic context. Or, perhaps, while recognizing the double nature of Handke's text, they mistrust his complicated sense for justice, they suppose his questions and denials are simply camouflage for an unbridled polemic, they feel that while claiming the opposite, Handke's images are as inflexible as the critics' own, that his history is as rigid as theirs.

It is possible, of course, that they are right. But when compared with the one-sided rhetoric of his critics, Handke's text feels to me like a model of dialectic reasoning. Of the many examples I could give, one will have to suffice. Note the almost excruciating care Handke takes here to demonstrate not only his command of both sides of the issue, but his moral commitment to a justice that embraces both:

> Later, from the spring of 1992 on, when the first photographs, soon photo sequences or serial photos, were shown from the Bosnian war, there was a part of myself (repeatedly standing for "my whole"), which felt that the armed Bosnian Serbs, whether the army or individual killers, especially those on the hills and mountains around Sarajevo, were "enemies of humanity," to slightly vary Hans Magnus Enzensberger's phrase in reference to the Iraqi dictator Saddam Hussein...
>
> And in spite of that, almost coincidentally with the impotent impulses to violence of someone visually involved from afar, another part of me (that in fact never stood for my whole), did not want to trust this war and this war reporting. Didn't want to? No, couldn't. Because, namely, the roles of attacker and attacked, of the pure victims and the naked scoundrels, were all-too-rapidly determined and set down for the so-called world public.

Of the two parts of himself, only the one shocked at Serb aggressions stands for all of him. There is no question, then, of absolving the Serbs of responsibility for their violence. But justice, in this situation, is broader than that, and requires that other questions be asked as well.

What could be more reasonable? And what could be more conducive to peace? Why can't journalists covering the wars in Yugoslavia, Handke asks, read and tell a more complicated story?

"And with this kind of maturity, I thought, the son of a German, pull out of this history that repeats every century, out of this disastrous chain, pull out into another story." Let others write the factual story of these wars, Handke writes: "Nothing against those—more than uncovering—*dis*covering reporters on the scene (or better yet: involved in the scene and with the people there), praise for these other researchers in the field!" (122); "To record the evil facts, that's good" (133). He, however, the son of a German and thus heir to a propensity for Wagnerian totality, wants to write another story, an additional story.

The "and" that connects the paragraphs on the two parts of himself cited above and the proliferation of initial "ands" in sentences and paragraphs as the essay comes to a close, work formally to create multiplicity, initiating the continuing motion of a productive dialectic. While this is not a new device for Handke (he employs it with similar intent in *Mein Jahr in der Niemandsbucht*, and *Repetition* ends with the admonition to the storyteller: "...take a deep breath, and start all over again with your all-appeasing 'And then...'"⁹), it is a crucial move in this essay that risks the untruths of obscene defiance and suicidal despair, that asserts that the "transient and ephemeral" are worthy of description during a war, and that relies on density of texture in place of infallible argument for its truths. "The untruth[s] in which the essay knowingly entangles itself," turning on the multiple axes of the coordinating conjunction, are more truthful finally than the non-dialectical assertions of Handke's illiterate critics.

I'll end my obviously biased account of *A Journey to the Rivers or Justice for Serbia* with the essay's final questions and assertions. Judge for yourselves whether this is the writing of a benighted advocate of *Blut und Boden*, or of an essayist whose courageous play of ideas lays him open to error, and thus to truth as well:

> But isn't it, finally, irresponsible, I thought there at the Drina and continue to think it here, to offer the small sufferings in Serbia, the bit of freezing there, the bit of loneliness, the trivialities like snow flakes, caps, cream cheese, while over the border a great suffering prevails, that of Sarajevo, of Tuzla, of

Srebrenica, of Bihać, compared to which the Serbian boo-boos are nothing? Yes, with each sentence I too have asked myself whether such a writing isn't obscene, ought even to be tabooed, forbidden—which made the writing journey adventurous in a different way, dangerous, often very depressing (believe me), and I learned what "between Scylla and Charybdis" means. Didn't the one who described the small deprivations (gaps between teeth) help to water down, to suppress, to conceal the great ones?

Finally, to be sure, I thought each time: but that's not the point. My work is of a different sort. To record the evil facts, that's good. But something else is needed for a peace, something not less important than the facts.

So, now it's time for the poetic? Yes, if it is understood as exactly the opposite of the nebulous. Or say, rather than "the poetic": that which binds, that encompasses—the impulse to a common remembering, as the possibility for reconciliation of individuals, for the second, the common childhood.

How then? What I have written here was meant for various German-speaking readers, and just as much for various readers in Slovenia, Croatia, and Serbia, for experience tells me that that common recalling, that second, common childhood will arise exactly through the detour of recording certain trivialities, at least far more lastingly than by hammering in the main facts. "At one place on the bridge there was, for years, a loose board."—"Yes, did you notice that too?" "At one place under the church choir the steps began to echo."—"Yes, did you notice that too?" Or simply to divert from the shared, shared by us all, captivity in the rhetoric of history and topicality into a much more productive present: "Look, now it is snowing. Look, children are playing there" (the art of diversion; art as the essential diversion). And thus I felt, there on the Drina, the need to dance a rock across the water toward the Bosnian shore (but then couldn't find one).

Notes

1. Translations of this text and others cited here are mine, unless otherwise noted.
2. Göttingen: Steidl, 1996.
3. See the most recent study of Nietzsche and Handke, Vollmer's *Das gerechte Spiel: Sprache und Individualität bei Friedrich Nietzsche und Peter Handke*.
4. Handke, *Die Geschichte des Bleistifts* 344, 294.
5. Scott 32.
6. *The Jukebox and Other Essays on Storytelling* 126.
7. Cf. the following from Handke's play *Das Spiel vom Fragen* 143-44:

Spielverderber: Wird aus dem morgendlich heiteren Spiel vom Fragen, wie es mir vorschwebte...am Ende doch wider meinen Willen ein Drama? Gibt es denn keinen dritten Weg? Ist mir nicht öfter schon eine Flucht nur gelungen, weil ich sie erst versuchte in dem Bewußtsein, es sei ohnehin hoffnungslos? Aber ist der Dritte Weg in den Märchen nicht jener des Todes?...Wird es von uns, anders als einst von dem heroischen Zug der Cheyenne zurück in ihr Heimatland, einmal heißen, wir hätten mit unserer Reise zum Sonoren Land eine der sinnlosesten Wanderungen der Geschichte unternommen?...Welch Glaube—an das Sinnlose, die sinnlosen Unternehmungen.

8. See, for example, Tilman Zülch's foreword to *Die Angst des Dichters vor der Wirklichkeit*, which ends by identifying Handke with the "long tradition of denial of genocide in the Europe of the twentieth century" (22).
9. Tr. Manheim. New York: Collier, 1989. 246.

Works Cited

Adorno, Theodor. "The Essay as Form." *Notes to Literature: Volume One*. Trans. Shierry Weber Nicholsen. New York: Columbia UP, 1991. 3-23.

Gamper, Herbert. *Aber ich lebe nur von den Zwischenräumen.* Zürich: Amman, 1987.

Handke, Peter. *Eine winterliche Reise zu den Flüssen Donau, Save, Morawa und Drina oder Gerechtigkeit für Serbien.* Frankfurt am Main: Suhrkamp, 1996.

---. *Die Geschichte des Bleistifts.* Frankfurt am Main: Suhrkamp, 1985.

---. *Das Spiel vom Fragen.* Frankfurt am Main: Suhrkamp, 1989.

---. *Mein Jahr in der Niemandsbucht.* Frankfurt am Main: Suhrkamp, 1994.

---. *The Jukebox and Other Essays on Storytelling.* Trans. Ralph Manheim and Krishna Winston. New York: Farrar, Straus and Giroux, 1994.

Scott, Charles. *The Question of Ethics: Nietzsche, Foucault, Heidegger.* Bloomington: Indiana University Press, 1990.

Vollmer, Michael. *Das gerechte Spiel: Sprache und Individualität bei Friedrich Nietzsche und Peter Handke.* Würzburg: Königshausen & Neumann, 1995.

Theorizing the Internet:
Scholarly Collaboration, Authorial Identity,
and the Bounds of Listserver Culture

Angelica Fenner
University of Minnesota

Many of us would probably concur that the acquisition of a modem, internet software and an e-mail account has irreversibly transformed our understanding of the boundaries of scholarly communication, collaboration, and research. Four years ago, when I innocently ceded to a friend's urgings to install the requisite paraphernalia on my laptop, I hardly anticipated gradually succumbing to a compulsion to spend hours every night browsing the messages posted on several electronic listservers (also known as computer bulletin boards), drawn into the vortex of riveting discussions on literary topics and current events and benefiting from pragmatic exchanges of bibliographical information, course syllabi and reading lists. And yet, like so many technological innovations of this century which have defied the borders of space and time, there have been ramifications beyond that of convenience or accessibility; to borrow the words of Walter Ong: "technologies are not mere exterior aids but also interior transformations of consciousness" (82). The internet has, in fact, reconfigured both how I understand and experience the notion of community and how I project my own identity into virtual encounters with other e-mail users. I was afforded a concrete forum within which to further reflect upon these processes when I participated in a collective literary analysis of Austrian author Robert Schneider's recently published novel, *Schlafes Bruder*; this internet experiment took place within the parameters of a private listserver with the intention of presenting critical results at a symposium on contemporary Austrian literature and film held at the University of Delaware in 1996.

The listserver was launched when Barbara Laman, who also hosts the Austrian Studies listserver at the University of North Dakota, collected and circulated information on the five participating scholars' institutional affiliation and research interests. While some participants had a previous history of acquaintanceship upon which to ground their interactions, others could only deduce their positioning within an electronic space disarmingly barren of social inscription. My own initial impulse to try to establish an intersubjective rapport through the customary structure of mutual question and answer felt thwarted by the plural nature of address within this type of collective discussion. Behaving like genteel visitors at an intimate tea party, we all seemed to struggle to find a happy medium between taking either too direct an interest in the comments of any one individual and waiting in helpless silence for someone else to steer the conversation. It also became evident that when comments are at once posted to everyone and no one in particular, the sense of personal accountability in sustaining the momentum of discussion can easily dissipate and, in fact, did at one point arbitrarily lapse into four weeks of complete silence. If one considers the broader temporal framework of the project, it is perhaps also true that following the project's commencement in January, many of us were lulled into complacency by the seemingly remote September date at which the culminating results were to be presented. For it has usually been my experience that the preparation for any kind of a conference presentation takes place in a solitary flurry of activity in the months just prior to the targeted event. What ultimately awakened my sense of accountability to the project was an encounter within real rather than virtual space; after chatting with Willy Riemer at the NEMLA conference later that Spring, I finalized my commitment both to the group and to the symposium and mailed my registration check.

Thus began a new phase for me, one in which I became more active in contributing to the pace of discussion while at the same time experiencing renewed hesitations that revealed much to me about my own assumptions of how scholarship should be produced. Essentially, I would say that my participation was characterized by proffering one or two insights per posting, yet always with an attendant reluctance to pursue these thoughts beyond their initial outline; this, despite the fact that I was virtually percolating with ideas after reading *Schlafes Bruder* and had immediately drawn up for myself an ambitious and varied list of possible discussion points. I do not believe this reticence stemmed from a sense of insecurity about the validity of my ideas, for the other participants seemed consistently receptive and encouraging of whatever ideas happened to be circulating. Rather, I was afraid that all my inspirations, my hunches, my brainstorming—all these things that I have, in essence, tended to perceive as an extension of my own psyche—would disperse along the various conduits to the other group members, undergo appropriation, transformation, degradation—in essence, death by textual dismemberment. While this is a self-perception I have only achieved through hindsight and reflection, I suspect many people would similarly recognize themselves to be the product of this type of scholastic training and socialization, in which intellectual rumination is understood as a deeply personal and singular enterprise. This cognitive and perceptual stance finds its most overt expression in the marketing of hermeneutical premises as copyrighted commodities that circulate in journals, are published as monographs by university presses and are furthermore critically gaged as measures of professional achievement during departmental hiring and promotion.

Even as the academy harbors a longstanding investment in cultivating among its faculty and students what Fredric Jameson would refer to as a specifically "modernist" sense of a unitary intellectual self, it is also a site struggling to accomodate the growing momentum of postmodern sensibilities. In his 1984 essay, "Postmodernism and Consumer Society," Jameson describes this so-called "cultural dominant" in terms of the emergence of a decentered and dispersed subjectivity, a shift from the experience of depth to surface phenomenon within the space-time continuum, and the relinquishment of a belief system anchored in the existence of the so-called "real" for a world of simulation. In effect, what I was experiencing within the medium of electronic communication was a hypostatization of precisely so much of the poststructuralist theory (I am thinking specifically of Bahktin, Barthes, Derrida, Foucault and, to an extent, Baudrillard) which I had processed cognitively but apparently was unprepared to integrate at a sentient level. This anxiety about the possible dissolution of my authorial identity—a mild crisis of authorship, as it were—calls to mind the loss of innocence described in Roland Barthes' 1968 manifesto, "The death of the author." He proposes a theory and practice of textuality wherein the author gives way to a writing which "substitutes language itself for the person who until then had been supposed to be its owner" (reprinted in 1977, 143). Indeed, the format of group discussion on the internet tends to erode at any sense of origins or originators, or even of a detectable genealogy of ideas. Once a particular argument is posted to the group, it is guaranteed to either be ignored entirely or to assume a life of its own. Its evolutionary course in the aleatory sequence of responses becomes impossible to retrace as participants may alternately transmit with virtual simultaneity or with an extensive time lag if they have not logged on for several days. When systematic linear pursuit of any particular argument becomes a practical impossibility, the channels of reasoning, in turn, disperse and are perforce impossible to attribute to any single contributor. How similar this phenomenon seems to Barthes' summation of writing as "that neutral, composite, oblique space where our subject slips away, the negative where all identity is lost, starting with the very identity of the body writing" (142). Within such a scenario it apparently matters not *who* writes, nor even, who *reads*, for even as the shift from the text's orginator to its receptor would seem to privilege the role of reader, in effect, Barthes goes on to describe the reader as "without history, biography, psychology" (148). Similarly, on the internet, the more tangible concrete aspects of our identities remain hidden from other users. Whether actively participating in internet discussion or silently lurking, we appear to function as an enabling space and a process permitting text and meaning to develop anonymously.

I would thus propose that the very structure of electronic communication maps out, indeed, literalizes the topography pertaining to the individual embedded in language, of subjectivity born through the Symbolic. The electronic medium denatures or renders invisible the immediate social context of individual users, thereby necessitating a more differentiated sensibility by means of which to navigate the strands of meaning which nevertheless inhere. Navigation as such can serve as a powerful spatial metaphor with which to assess the variegated courses charted in internet discussion. In his research on the hypertext medium George Landow has already suggested that such descriptors as "nonlinear" and "nonsequential," which are based upon merely negating more traditional narrative forms and media, are inadequate to the task of formulating new theoretical paradigms (1992, 4). He introduces the terms multilinear and multisequential, which I think more accurately describe the persistent struggle in listserver discussions to sustain certain strains of argumentation, even when one cannot anticipate the sequence in which postings will be submitted or with which previously articulated comments these postings will take issue. The email user becomes a flâneur of virtual space, browsing through his/her accumulated messages and making arbitrary spur of the moment choices about which postings to respond to and thereby participating in the common charting of a course that can never be fully retraced in an identical format. Narrative in listserver discussion is thus not a predefined route or electronic space; it is only created as we collectively move forward, mapping a new "geometry of space" (Rosello) in which the distinction between readers and writers collapses and we all become "screeners," to borrow a neologism from Mireille Rosello's essay on hypertext, "The Screener's Maps."[1] Of course, the notion of "screeners," which I introduce here primarily for polemical purposes, is problematical since some discussion participants tend more towards writing (i.e., contributing ideas) and others more towards reading (also cynically referred to as lurking). Within the listserver domain, Rosello's term undermines the important role of authorship in sustaining the momentum of discussion, as well as possibly lending more agency to lurkers than is really justified. It is nevertheless a provocative concept drawing into question the rigid distinction between readers and writers and reiterating the post-structuralist premise that every individual's speech and writing inevitably draws upon another's fragments of grammar, vocabulary, syntax and discourse.

Psychoanalytic discourse potentially offers a particularly fruitful lens through which to assess the impact of computer technology upon lived human subjectivity, because psychoanalysis, like the posited human psyche it attempts to diagnose, is a discourse that has survived numerous transmogrifications, beginning with Freud's modernist view of human motives as grounded in drives and in the internalized dictates of the centralized and controlling superego.[2] The later postmodern Lacanian model, on the other hand, posits an inherently dispersed subject whose unconscious is structured like a language so that the illusion of coherence emerges from a chain of associations. I would argue that the forfeiture of natural authority/ authorship which characterizes scholarly collaboration on the internet recalls precisely this latter dramaturgy of subjectivity. Intellectual thought can herein be understood as yet another of Lacan's *petit objects a* —that is, something we illusorily experience as part and parcel of ourselves; to be confronted with its separation is to experience a loss which in many contexts is framed as contiguous with castration, or—to use a less territorialized term —amputation. The ruptures and displacements in narrative flow occuring in electronic communication overtly restage the implacable logic of division and dispersal of subjectivity, a recurring cycle of enunciative moments fleetingly experienced as unitary and singular only to be dispersed by the collective momentum of further discussion—a phenomenon also subsumed by Lacan under the appellate of *aphanisis*.[3] This "fading of the subject," he has reasoned in *The Four Fundamental Concepts of Psychoanalysis*, occurs when the subject assumes a position in the Symbolic order marked by the signifier that takes his/her place; paradoxically, the subject's disappearance at the level of the real makes possible its position in the chain of signification:

> The signifier, producing itself in the field of the Other, makes manifest the subject of its signification. But it functions as a signifier only to reduce the subject in question to being no more than a signifier, to petrify the subject in the same movement in which it calls the subject to function, to speak, as subject (207-08)...The subject appears first in the Other, in so far as the first signifier, the unitary signifier, emerges in the field of the Other and represents the subject for another signifier, which other signifier has as its effect the *aphanisis* of the subject. Hence the division of the subject—when the subject appears somewhere

as meaning, he is manifested elsewhere as "fading," as disappearance. (218)

As disembodied writers on the internet, we similarly lose our anchor in the real for the other readers who receive our postings and for whom we are reduced to a reified speech act. Which active listserver participant has not, by now, had the experience of fetching his/her messages, hastily scrolling through them and then stumbling across one inducing a sense of peculiar familiarity, only to be jolted by the recognition of reading one's own posting as distributed to the entire group! What balder confrontation with the "self as other" than that of reading one's own script as that of a total stranger and reliving the primordial terror of non-self-identicality, of insurmountable disjuncture across the chasm of the Symbolic. I think each contributor to the listserver ultimately acts out his/her own private drama of suture, struggling for a manner in which to bind together this collective corpus and sustain the illusion of narrative flow and integrated subjectivity.

Within the past decade, a number of social scientists have heralded the utopian possibilities which this emerging culture of simulation on the internet offers both for exploring and expanding the parameters of intersubjective encounters and for creating seemingly democratic, negotiational and nonhierarchical ways for users to participate, think and interact.[4] As Charles Ess points out in his essay, "The Political Computer," this type of optimism with regard to communications networks yields some isomorphic similiarities with the Habermasian theory of communicative action as discussed in *Theorie des kommunikativen Handelns* (1981). For Habermas tries to forge a middle ground between the critique launched by the Frankfurt School against the perceivedly alienating and potentially oppressive nature of modern technology, while also embracing the progressive agenda of the Enlightenment, i.e., commitment to rational improvement of the human condition over time. Crudely summarized, his theory of communicative action is based upon the reasonable interactions that can be discerned in quotidian experiences between people, in which conflict is resolved through dialogue rather than by force. Consensus is achieved when persons in dialogue present their opinions from their individual point of view and are able to establish some sort of agreement that represents a synthesis of individual local concerns and universal assumptions or norms. Electronic communication potentially literalizes these human relations by so to speak equalizing the playing field among participants; everyone has an equal opportunity to contribute and thus participates on seemingly consensual terms, while speaking from a position that is geographically dispersed and discursively localized. Furthermore, the lack of nonverbal clues about physical appearance, socio-economic status, sexual orientation, and age may well facilitate a neutral realm relatively free of bias or judgment.

While Ess's expatiation of the parallels between electronic communication networks and Habermasian theory is by no means simplistic or reductive, I think his reasoning needs to take into account the reality that information technology as we know it fundamentally consists in denaturing context, i.e., in isolating information from its source and, perforce, from its enunciator; and that this form of dislocation may not always be experienced as emancipatory. During the electronic discussion of Robert Schneider's novel, I was struck by the consistent, although seemingly unconscious compensatory drive among participants to overcome this disjunction between the message and its immediate context by contributing morsels of "small talk" relating to their quotidian reality: commenting on the regional weather, other academic obligations competing for their attention, what they did on the weekend, etc. Social scientists conducting research on the prevalence of precisely this type of so-called "socio-emotional content" in computer mediated communication networks (such as computer bulletin boards) have determined that such exchanges on average constitute approximately 30% of network communication, even when the interactions are goal and topic-oriented.[5] Socioemotional content, which they (Love & Rice) define as "interactions that show solidarity, tension relief, agreement, antagonism, tension and agreement," is to be distinguished from so-called "task-dimensional content," which consists in "interactions that ask for or give information or opinion" (95). The distinction between these two categories, construed within the empirical agenda of social science research, strikes me as ambiguous and vulnerable to deconstruction. Important for my line of argumentation is foremost the fact that interlocutors confronting a virtual realm suspended from any material space or social context do employ speech strategies that betray their unconscious yearning to uphold a sense of origin(ality) in the face of a medium that lends every electronic contribution the aura of the simulacrum. Sharing mundane information about one's daily realities serves, among other purposes, to secure the individual asymptotically along the space-time axis.[6]

If discussion groups on the internet are essentially developing new narrative forms, and if we concur with Lyotard's assertion that "narration is the quintessential form of customary knowledge" (18), then we are now embarked upon a significant epistemological shift whose full significance we have barely even begun to grasp. Within an electronic medium that renders authorial and textual identity increasingly malleable and indeterminate, and in which we work with surface data often reaching us without a specific history and without a delimited source (i.e., without origins), how can we both dwell in multiplicity and also function as coherent entities? Perhaps the electronic medium by necessity beckons its users to engage the same discursive strategies for demarcated situated knowledges which have already been in place within feminist scholarship since at least the 1970s.[7] For just as feminist discourse grew out of a need to reinscribe material and social aspects of women's identity into public discourse, so also the internet user may struggle alternately against the erasure of identity within a decontextualizing medium and consciously seek mechanisms with which to occasion her/his discursive reintegration. I am also reminded of Donna Haraway's concept of the cyborg (cybernetic organism), which she defines as "a hybrid creature, composed of organism and machine... appropriate to the late twentieth century" (65). As a scholar of the history of science, Haraway's research is anchored precisely in such a revaluation of the various implications of communications and data systems for the definition of subjectivity. Her utopian vision seeks a new "geometry for considering the relations of difference other than hierarchical domination, incorporation of 'parts' into 'wholes,' or antagonistic opposition" (67).

Ultimately, I would maintain that the ebullience expressed by many theorists with regard to the internet needs to be soberly assessed with an eye towards exigencies specific to the academic enterprise. While electronic publishing and the new medium of hypertext have expanded the definitions of textuality and of scholarship and made inroads upon the inflated Romantic myth of unsullied originality in authorship, it is also still the case that most scholars continue to survive and function within institutional frameworks placing pressure upon them to generate precisely such products of perceivedly autonomous labor,[8] what Genette terms "the fetishism of the work—conceived of as closed, complete, absolute object" (147). Furthermore, none of us are disinterested participants in any communication, even the seemingly abstract exercise of interpreting Robert Schneider's novel. Regardless of how virtual or simulated the internet encounter might seem, all of us speak within the electronic discussion from a place of situated knowledge inflected by such vectors of identity as ethnicity, class, gender, age, national origin and—for that matter—our ranking within the hierarchies of the academy.

The challenge of reconciling these issues became most compelling when the internet panel was confronted with the logistics of presenting concrete results at the symposium. We could have pursued essentially two different paths that I can ascertain: either to co-create a single paper written in a more or less synchronous fashion on an agreed upon topic, or to elect topical areas to be covered by discrete writers. Already reduced from five participants to three through the attrition symptomatic of overcommitted academic schedules, we had also lost some common momentum during the discontinuities in communication during summer travel. My own strong interest in theorizing subjectivity and authorship on the internet led me to focus exclusively on this topic, while Barb Laman and Gerry Reaves focused on respective issues pertaining directly to Schneider's novel. The conclusions that I have drawn are therefore highly subjective, reflecting both my experience of this particular collaborative experience as well as my broader participation in other moderated academic listservers. As such, my

Theorizing the Internet 363

comments are by no means empirical assessments, nor can they aspire to speak for the experience of other users; at best, I hope to have outlined areas for further reflection and discussion.

Notes

1. Landow has also coined the term "reader-authors" in his discussion of hypertext. Within electronic media, listserver discussions constitute a different genre than hypertext; however, the same problematic adheres regarding blurred boundaries between authors and readers.

2. Sociologist Sherry Turkle (1995) has already outlined lucid parallels between the history of psychoanalytical discourse and the evolving perceptions of computer intelligence during the latter half of this century. Early characterizations of computers as machines that submit to the hacker's programmings have since given way to the contemporary theories in emergent AI (artificial intelligence) of a human subject that has relinquished its claim to a fixed stable identity and occupies instead an excentric space in relation to technology (see especially 125-48).

3. I am indebted to Durand's application of the concept of aphanisis to narrative theory (1983).

4. See Haraway, Nelson, Bolter, Landow, Turkle.

5. In their joint article, Love and Rice remark on their research: "Nearly 30% of the total message content was socio-emotional. This is a generous amount in light of suggestions that CMC systems are low in 'social presence' or could be seen as 'information poor' media, especially considering the professional orientation of the conference members, and is in line with prior studies of SE content of CMC" (97).

6. The attempt to create a common context within an essentially denatured medium can be readily recognized in the genre of the television talk show. Such events generally try to contrive context by means of a stage simulating the ambience of a living room, within which the guests/speakers are then arranged as if to form an intimate circle. Interestingly, the actual panel presentation of the

internet collaboration results at the symposium was similarly staged, using a couch and armchair arranged to face the audience obliquely. The effect was distinctly simulacral.

7. Within page-bound scholarship, the necessity of acknowledging one's positionality as a scholar, writer and critic was most effectively brought to light by a number of feminist theorists of the 1970s and 1980s. The essays of the following have become virtually canonical with respect to this issue: Mohanty, Pratt, Reagon, and Rich.

8. Landow offers the example of two scholars in British Columbia, Lisa Ede and Andrea Lunsford, who embarked upon a book about collaborative writing and its institutional and literary significance; Lundsford's colleagues refused to include any of her coauthored works in her review for promotion (1992, 92).

Works Cited

Barthes, Roland. "The Death of the Author." *Image/Text/Music*. trans. Stephen Heath. New York: Hill and Wang, 1977.

Bolter, J. David. *Writing Space: The Computer, Hypertext, and the History of Writing*. Hillsdale, N.J.: Lawrence Erlbaum, 1991.

Delany, Paul, and George P. Landow. *Hypermedia and Literary Studies*. Cambridge, MA: MIT Press, 1991.

Durand, Régis. "On *Aphanisis*: A Note on the Dramaturgy of the Subject in Narrative Analysis." *Lacan and Narration: The Psychoanalytic Difference in Narrative Theory*. Ed. Robert Con Davis. Baltimore: John Hopkins University Press, 1983: 860-70.

Ess, Charles. "The Political Computer: Hypertext, Democracy, and Habermas." *Hyper/Text/Theory*. Ed. George P. Landow. Baltimore: Johns Hopkins Univeristy Press, 1994. 225-67.

Genette, Gérard. *Figures of Literary Discourse*. trans. Alan Sheridan. New York: Columbia University Press, 1982.

Habermas, Jürgen. *Theorie des kommunikativen Handelns*. 2 vols. Frankfurt: Suhrkamp, 1981.

Haraway, Donna. "A Manifesto for Cyborgs: Science, Technology, and Socialist Feminism." *Socialist Review* 80 (March-April 1985): 65-107.

Jameson, Fredric. "Postmodernism and Consumer Society." *The Anti-Aesthetic: Essays on Postmodern Culture*. Ed. Hal Foster. Seattle: Bay Press, 1983: 111-25

Lacan, Jacques. *The Four Fundamental Concepts of Psycho-analysis*. Ed. Jacques-Alain Miller, trans. Alan Sheridan. New York: W.W.Norton, 1978.

Landow, George P. *Hypertext: The Convergence of Contemporary Critical Theory and Technology*. Baltimore: Johns Hopkins University Press, 1992.

---. Ed. *Hyper/Text/Theory*. Baltimore: Johns Hopkins University Press, 1994.

Levi-Strauss, Claude. *The Savage Mind*. Chicago: University of Chicago Press, 1968.

Love, Gail, and Ronald E. Rice."Electronic Emotion: Socioemotional Content in a Computer-Mediated Communication Network." *Communication Research*, 14.1 (February 1987): 85-108.

Lyotard, Jean-François. *The Postmodern Condition: A Report on Knowledge*. Trans. Geoff Bennington and Brian Massumi. Minneapolis: University of Minnesota Press, 1984.

Mohanty, Chandra Talpade. "Under Western Eyes: Feminist Scholarship and Colonial Discourse." *Boundary* 2 3.12/13 (1984): 333-58.

---. "Feminist Encounters: Locating the Politics of Experience." *Copyright* 1 (1988):30-44.

Nelson, Theodor H. *Dream Machines: New Freedoms through Computer Screens—A Minority Report. Computer-Lib: You Can and Must Understand Computers Now*. Chicago: Hugo's Book Service, 1974. Rev. ed., Redmond, Wash.: Microsoft Press, 1987.

Pratt, Minnie Bruce. "Identity: Skin Blood Heart." *Yours in Struggle: Three Feminist Perspectives on Anti-Semitism*. Ed. Elly Bulkin, Minnie Bruce Pratt, and Barbara Smith. New York: Long Haul Press, 1984: 11-63.

Ong, Walter. *Orality and Literacy: The Technologizing of the Word*. London: Methuen, 1982.

Reagon, Bernice Johnson. "Coalition Politics: Turning the Century." in Smith, Barbara, Ed. *Home Girls: A Black Feminist Anthology*. New York: Kitchen Table, Women of Color Press, 1983: 356-68.

Rich, Adrienne. "Notes Towards a Politics of Location." *Blood, Bread, and Poetry: Selected Prose 1979-1985*. New York: Norton, 1986:210-31.

Rosello, Michelle. "The Screener's Maps: Michel de Certeau's 'Wandersmänner' and Paul Auster's Hypertextual Detective." Hypertext/Text/Theory. 121-58.

Schneider, Robert. *Schlafes Bruder*. Leipzig: Reclam, 1994.

Turkle, Sherry. *The Second Self: Computers and the Human Spirit*. New York: Simon & Schuster 1984.

---, *Life on the Screen: Identity in the Age of the Internet*. New York: Simon & Schuster, 1995.

Index

Abbott, Scott 13
Acker, Robert 12
Adorno, Theodor W. 181, 183, 188, 231, 232, 238, 241, 278, 340, 345, 351
Aichinger, Ilse 322
Akerman, Chantal 268
Allahyari, Houchang 12, 70, 89-96, 98, 99, 103-05
Allen, Woody 206
Alter, Nora M. 14
Alter, Robert 23
Amann, Klaus 47
Améry, Jean 324, 325, 337
Anderson, Benedict 336, 337
Angerer, Peter 128, 137
Arendt, Hannah 324
Arnold, Heinz Ludwig 260
Avedon, Richard 40

Bach, Johann Sebastian 169, 182, 183, 184, 249, 259
Bachmann, Ingeborg 13, 45, 46, 160, 166, 220, 298-311, 322
Bakhtin, Mikhail 355
Barthes, Roland 355, 356, 364
Bartsch, Kurt 309, 310
Barylli, Gabriel 108
Baudelaire, Charles-Pierre 273
Baudrillard, Jean 19, 20, 28, 355

Baum, Thomas 85
Bazin, André 181, 188
Becher, Johannes 239, 256
Beckermann, Ruth 319, 337
Behler, Ernst 30
Beicken, Peter 309, 310
Beller, Steven 318, 337
Benhabib, Seyla 31
Benjamin, Walter 176, 188, 276
Benn, Gottfried 241
Bennett, Paula 301, 308, 310
Berbüsse, Volker 140, 154
Berg, Alban 169
Bergman, Ingmar 206
Berka, Sigrid 12
Bernhard, Thomas 106, 317, 318, 323, 324
Berta, Renato 248
Bertaux, Pierre 238
Bettelheim, Bruno 306
Beuys, Joseph 37
Bhabha, Homi 325, 328, 337
Biller, Maxim 330
Bloch, Ernst 239
Bloch, Judy 110, 117
Bocokić, Zlatko 342
Bohn, Irina 140, 154
Böll, Heinrich 51
Bolter, David J. 363, 364
Bond, Edward 217, 218, 219, 232
Botz, Gerhard 309, 311,

320, 338
Brandauer, Karin 12, 138, 142, 148, 149, 150, 151
Braun, Michael 236
Braun, Volker 256
Bresson, Robert 168, 181, 206
Breuer, Dieter 257, 260
Broder, Henryk 328
Brown, Patricia Leigh 31
Browning, Elizabeth Barrett 293
Büchner, Georg 236
Buñuel, Luis 127
Bürger, Christa 31
Burger, Hermann 47
Bürger, Peter 18, 260
Byg, Barton 249, 250, 251, 252, 258, 260
Byrne, Jack 142, 154

Calinescu, Matei 27, 32
Camartin, Iso 47
Cassavetes, John 206
Celan, Paul 236, 245, 257, 258, 260, 322
Chaplin, Charlie 82
Chekhov, Anton Pavlovich 162, 211, 214
Cohen, Maxi 268
Coleridge, Samuel Taylor 21
Colin, Amy 236, 258, 260
Conroy, Pat 298
Corti, Axel 12, 59, 80, 106-26
Courtade, Francis 110, 111, 125
Cronenberg, David 127
Curry, Ramona 270, 280, 281

D'Annunzio, Gabriele 226, 227
Delany, Paul 363
Deleuze, Gilles 272, 281
DeMeritt, Linda C. 13, 286, 287, 295
Demetz, Peter 10
Derrida, Jacques 355
Descartes, René 20
Detje, Robin 232
Dilthey, Wilhelm 239
Dischner, Gisela 255
Doane, Mary Ann 179, 188
Dollfuss, Engelbert 145
Dorfer, Alfred 94, 105
Doyscher, Helmut 255
Drawert, Kurt 50
Drews, Jörg 47
Druskowitz, Helene von 291-93
Duchamp, Marcel 37
Durand, Régis 364

Egger, Oswald 238, 256, 260
Eich, Günter 253
Eifler, Margret 269, 270, 280, 281
Eisler, Hanns 181, 183, 188
Elsaesser, Thomas 117, 118, 119, 121, 122, 123, 125
Engeler, Urs 238

Ensberg, Peter 286, 287, 295
Enzensberger, Hans M. 239, 348
Erdrich, Louise 23
Ess, Charles 359, 360, 364
Export, Valie 9, 14, 36, 37, 38, 267-82

Falkner, Gerhard 239
Farocki, Harun 258, 260
Farokhzad, Fery 104
Fehervary, Helen 235, 238, 240, 254, 256, 260
Fekete, John 25, 30, 32
Felman, Shoshana 220, 233
Fenner, Angelika 14
Fiedler, Leslie 17, 23, 32
Fine, Marshall 115, 125
Fink, Humbert 46
Finkielkraut, Alain 342
Fischer, Werner 233
Fliedl, Konstanze 47
Foster, Hal 9
Foucault, Michel 239, 260, 355
Franz, Veronika 105
Fried, Michael 178, 188
Friedel, Gernot 199
Frieden, Sandra 280
Froehlich, Hans J. 47
Fuchs, Ernst 36

Gamper, Herbert 343, 352
Gättens, Marie-Luise 286, 295
Gavron, Laurence 268

Gehry, Frank 36
Genette, Gérard 362, 364
Gilliam, Terry 127
Gilman, Sander 310, 311, 315, 335, 338
Glass, Fred 280, 181
Goldhagen, Daniel Jonah 321, 336, 338
Goltschnigg, Dietmar 309, 310
Gordon, Betty 268
Grätz, Katharina 256, 261
Greenaway, Peter 127
Greverus, Ina-Maria 125
Giovannini, Joseph 43
Glawogger, Michael 12, 127-37
Gökberg, Ülker 104, 105
Graff, Gerald 30, 32
Graves, Michael 21
Greisenegger, Ingrid 207, 208
Grimm, Erk 12
Groth, Michael 125
Grünbein, Durs 238
Gryphius, Andreas 228, 232, 233
Gstrein, Norbert 49
Guattari, Félix 272, 281

Habermas, Jürgen 20, 32, 238, 261, 359, 360, 364
Hackl, Erich 12, 138, 142, 143, 148, 149, 150, 151, 154
Hader, Josef 94, 105
Haider, Jörg 95

Hamburger, Michael 261
Hancock, Ian 151, 153, 154
Handke, Peter 14, 40, 41, 252, 260, 261, 317, 321, 324, 338, 340-52
Haneke, Michael 12, 57-59, 62-63, 65, 85, 159-75, 176-88, 193-208
Harather, Paul 12, 60, 94, 95, 105
Haraway, Donna 267, 271, 276, 279, 280, 281, 361, 365
Harms, Ingeborg 49
Harrison, R.B. 261
Härtl, Renate 233
Härtling, Peter 47
Hartung, Harald 236, 261
Hassan, Ihab 24, 32
Hay, Malcom 218, 233
Heidegger, Martin 19, 243, 326, 327
Heiduschka, Veit 11, 62-67, 160
Heine, Heinrich 317
Heinrich, Ludwig 105
Hermann, Matthias 239
Herzmanovsky-Orlando, Fritz 106
Herzog, Werner 184, 187, 249, 250
Hettche, Thomas 49
Heuß, Herbert 140, 154
Hilbig, Wolfgang 50
Hilling, Irmtraut 255
Hodjak, Franz 50
Hoesterey, Ingeborg 30, 32, 43
Hofmannsthal, Hugo von 222, 317
Hohmann, Joachim S. 153, 154
Hölderlin, Friedrich 235-263
Hollein, Hans 34
Honegger, Gitta 326, 338
Hopkins, Gerard Manley 237
Hoppe, Rolf 197
Hörbiger, Paul 69
Hörisch, Jochen 245, 258, 261
Horkheimer 278
Horvath, Alexander 127, 128, 137
Horváth, Ödön von 59, 222
Hotschnig, Alois 49
Huber-Lang, Wolfgang 225, 233
Huillet, Danièle 235, 238, 247, 248, 249, 250, 251, 252, 253, 258, 259
Humer, Egon 56
Hurch, Hans 258, 260
Husserl, Edmund 347
Hütter, Frido 197
Huyssen, Andreas 30, 32, 336, 338

Ibsen, Henrik 221, 232, 233
Illetschko, Peter 151, 154
Ioseliani, Otar 206
Isenschmid, Andreas 233

Jacob, Gilles 159
Jameson, Fredric 21, 22, 27, 267, 269, 278, 279, 280, 281, 355, 365
Jancsy, Irene 140, 153, 154
Jandl, Ernst 239, 257, 261
Jelinek, Elfriede 220, 286, 316-39
Jencks, Charles 9, 32, 35, 43
Johnston, William M. 336, 338
Jonke, Gerd 46
Joyce, James 22

Kaes, Anton 119, 125, 311
Kafka, Franz 58, 65, 85, 115, 160, 166, 167, 171, 201
Kahl, Kurt 151, 154
Kaindl-Widhalm, Barbara 320, 321, 338
Kaiser, Günther 140
Kaiser, Joachim 47
Karasek, Helmut 47, 48
Kasper, Elke 236, 262
Kaufman, Bob 237
Kecht, Maria-Regina 295, 296
Kegler, Lydia K. 137
Kendrick, Donald 138, 148, 153, 154
Kienzle, Siegfried 233
Klamper, Elisabeth 139, 154
Klier, Walter 52
Kling, Thomas 238
Knorr, Wolfram 176, 188
Köhler, Barbara 235

Kolker, Robert Philipp 247, 252, 259, 262
Konzett, Matthias 13, 317, 338
Kramar, Konrad 207, 208
Kraus, Angela 50, 51
Kraus, Karl 82, 317, 333
Krebs, Helmut 253
Kreisky, Bruno 321, 322, 324, 336
Krenn, Fritz 48
Krick-Aigner, Kirsten A. 12
Kroker 31
Kunert, Günter 341
Kusturica, Emir 342
Kuzniar, Alice 42

Lacan, Jacques 41, 267, 269, 279, 281, 358, 365
Laman, Barbara 353, 362
Landa, Jutta 12
Landow, George 357, 363, 364, 365
Langhoff, Anna 50
Lanzmann, Claude 117
Lauretis, Teresa de 30, 32, 38, 43
Leeder, Karen 254, 262
Lehner, Fritz 59
Lem, Stanislaw 165
Lenz, Eva-Maria 137
Lenz, Hermann 347
Levi-Strauss, Claude 365
Libeskind, Daniel 36
Liebmann, Irene 50
Liégeois, Jean-Pierre 138, 153

List, Niki 11, 62, 73-79
Löschnak, Franz 96
Love, Gail 360, 363, 365
Luhotzky, Grete Schütte 153
Lynch, David 127
Lyotard, Jean-François 19, 26, 28, 33, 361, 365

Maeterlinck, Maurice 220
Malamud, Bernard 325
Mallarmé, Stéphane 239, 246, 271
Manker, Paulus 197
Mann, Thomas 22
Marcus, Greil 280, 281
Marcuse, Herbert 277, 281
Margulies, Ivone 187, 188
Marin, Biagio 237
Marischka, Ernst 105
Martin, Elaine 285, 287, 295
Martin, Wolfgang 259, 262
Matt, Peter von 47
Matuscheck-Labitzke, Birgit 142, 152, 155
McCown, Edna 153, 154
McLuhan, Marshall 27
Mehr, Mariella 141
Meister, Ernst 256, 262
Mell, Marisa 98
Melzer, Gerhard 236
Menasse, Robert 336, 338
Menzinger, Stefanie 49
Meyer, Robert 129
Michaels, Jennifer E. 295
Middleton, Christopher 262
Mischkulnig, Lydia 52

Mitscherlich, Margarete 294, 296
Moisejew, Irina 140, 155
Mohanty, Chandra Talpade 364, 365
Monroe, Marilyn 274
Moore, Charles 21
Moser, Gerda 189, 197
Moser, Hans 69
Mueller, Roswitha 38, 43, 276, 277, 278, 279, 280
Mueller-Stahl, Armin 107
Mühe, Ulrich 164
Mühl, Otto 37
Mukherjee, Bharati 23
Müller, Heiner 256
Mulvey, Laura 270
Murnau, F.W. 205
Musil, Robert 317

Nadar, Thomas R. 12
Nadolny, Sten 47
Nancy, Jean Luc 245, 259, 262
Nelson, Theodor H. 365
Netenjakob, Egon 106, 109, 125
Neuhauser, Thomas 198
Neumann, Gert 255, 262
Newman, Charles 33
Nietzsche, Friedrich 19, 343, 344
Nitsch, Hermann 37
Novak, Helga 256, 262
Novalis 245, 258, 262

Obermüller, Klara 47

Oleschinski, Brigitte 238
Ong, Walter 353, 366
Ortheil, Hanns-Josef 30, 32
Ottinger, Ulrike 268
Özdamar, Emine Sevgi 50

Packalén, Sture 254, 262
Paik, Nam June 37
Palm, Michael 105
Papenfuß, Bert 235, 254
Parton, Dolly 189
Pavić, Milorad 342
Peck, Jeffrey M. 105
Pedretti, Erica 47
Pefanis, Julian 30, 33
Perloff, Marjorie 255, 262
Peschke, Anton 12, 94, 95, 99, 104-05
Petritsch, Barbara 107
Peucker, Brigitte 13
Pichl, Robert 308, 311
Plath, Sylvia 13, 298-311
Plenzdorf, Ulrich 47
Pochlatko, Dieter 11, 68-72
Poe, Edgar Allan 190, 191, 192, 196
Polgar, Alfred 114
Portzamparc, Christian de 21
Pöschl, Hanno 97
Pratt, Minnie Bruce 364, 365
Prix, Wolf D. 36
Puxon, Gratton 138, 148, 153, 154

Rabinovici, Doron 316-39
Radaković, Žarko 342
Rakosi, Carl 237, 245
Rank, Otto 306, 307, 310, 311
Ransmayr, Christoph 317
Rathenau, Walther 306
Rauch, Andreas von 250
Reagon, Bernice Johnson 364, 366
Reaves, Gerry 362
Rebhandl, Bert 109, 125, 126
Reed, Carol 122
Reeves, Daniel 276
Reich-Ranicki, Marcel 46
Reichart, Elisabeth 13, 283-97, 323, 324
Reimer, Carol J. 155
Reimer, Robert C. 12, 155
Reitz, Edgar 114, 116
Remmler, Karen 315, 335, 338
Rice, Ronald E. 360, 363, 365
Rich, Adrienne 364, 366
Riemann, Katja 77
Rilke, Rainer Maria 219, 233
Rinser, Luise 239
Roberts, Kevin 280, 282
Roberts, Philip 218, 233
Roll, Gernot 114, 119
Rorty, Richard 20, 29, 33
Roscher, Achim 283, 295, 297
Rosei, Peter 160, 189-198,

317
Rosello, Mireille 357
Rosen, Philip 187, 188
Rosenbaum, Alan 155
Ross, Andrew 280, 282
Roth, Friederike 47
Roth, Gerhard 39, 43, 80, 85, 318, 323, 324
Roth, Joseph 12, 59, 107, 160, 166, 199-208
Roth, Thomas 85
Rothschild, Thomas 128, 137
Rozenblit, Marsha L. 319, 338
Rub, Matthias 142, 155
Rühmkorf, Peter 239
Ruttmann, Walter 38
Ryan, Judith 30, 33
Rybarski, Ruth 97, 105, 142, 155

Sachslehner, Johannes 207, 208
Saeger, Uwe 50
Sander, Otto 99
Sanders, Helke 268
Sandford, John 247, 262
Santner, Eric 246, 262
Sattler, Dietrich E. 239, 240, 254, 256
Sauer, Walter J. 255
Saussure, Ferdinand de 19
Sauvaget, Daniel 124, 126
Scherpe, Klaus R. 31
Schiller, Friedrich 21
Schindel, Robert 316-39

Schirrmacher, Frank 150, 155
Schlant, Ernestine 9, 17
Schleinstein, Bruno 250
Schmid-Mühlisch, Lothar 224, 233
Schmidinger, Dolores 105
Schmidt, Jochen 256, 262
Schneeman, Carol 37
Schneider, Robert 353, 362, 366
Schottenberg, Michael 9, 39
Schubert, Franz 122, 206
Schwarzenegger, Arnold 273, 280
Schweiger, Til 77
Schweighofer, Martin 11, 55-61
Scorsese, Martin 206
Scott, Charles 344, 351, 352
Seibel, Alexandra 127, 137
Seibt, Gustav 341
Seidl, Ulrich 56, 127, 128
Settele, Stephan 258, 260
Seybold, Katrin 141, 153
Shakespeare, William 220, 233
Sicheritz, Harald 69
Sichrovsky, Peter 324, 339
Silberschneider, Johannes 107
Skrinjar, Hannes 140, 155
Sobchack, Vivian 125
Sontag, Susan 17, 19, 33
Spiel, Hilde 47, 255, 263
Spitta, Melanie 141
Steiner, Ulrike 105

Steinwachs, Ginka 47
Stojka, Karl 141
Stojka, Mongo 141, 155
Straub, Jean-Marie 168, 235, 238, 247-53, 258, 259
Streeruwitz, Marlene 12, 211-34
Streisand, Barbara 298
Strelka, Joseph 255, 263
Struck, Karin 239, 256, 263
Sturz, Gerald 198
Swiczinsky, Helmut 36
Swossil, Werner 11, 80-85

Tarantino, Quentin 159
Tarkovsky, Andrei 164, 165, 206
Theweleit, Klaus 286, 297, 307
Thierack, Otto 139
Thieringer, Thomas 123, 126
Thornton, Thomas 192, 198
Thurner, Erika 147, 151, 155
Timm, Uwe 256
Tomek, Johanna 225
Torberg, Friedrich 47
Traversa, Ingrid 193, 198
Trojanow, Ilja 50
Troller, Georg Stefan 107, 115, 117, 122, 126
Turim, Maureen 250, 263
Turkle, Sherry 363, 366

Vansant, Jacqueline 153, 155, 300, 308, 311
Velikić, Dragan 342
Venturi, Robert 33
Vogel, Amos 188, 204, 207, 208
Vogel, Juliane 255, 262
Vollmer, Michael 351, 352

Wagenhofer, Philipp 104-05
Wagner, Renate 105, 189
Waterhouse, Peter 12, 235-63
Webster, Frank 280, 282
Weibel, Peter 37
Weininger, Otto 306, 307, 310, 311
Weinzierl, Ulrich 47
Welles, Orson 166
Wenders, Wim 41, 196, 247
Werfel, Franz 107, 111
Wickham, Christopher J. 12
Wideman, John 23
Wigmore, Juliet 295, 297
Wilder, Thornton 121
Wille, Franz 225, 234
Wilson, Robert 41
Winicott 272, 280
Wistrich, Robert S. 322, 337, 339
Wolf, Christa 227, 307
Wolfgruber, Gernot 107
Woolf, Virginia 286

Yoors 153
Young, James 307, 310, 311

Zanke, Susanne 153

Zanzotto, Andreas 237, 245
Zeyringer, Klaus 336, 339
Zipes, Jack 315, 339

Žižek, Slavoj 277, 282
Zülch, Tilman 341, 351
Zweig, Stefan 108